Making an Antislavery Nation

Making an Antislavery Nation

Lincoln, Douglas, and the Battle over Freedom

GRAHAM A. PECK

UNIVERSITY OF ILLINOIS PRESS
Urbana, Chicago, and Springfield

Library of Congress Cataloging-in-Publication Data
Names: Peck, Graham A., 1969– author.
Title: Making an antislavery nation: Lincoln, Douglas,
    and the battle over freedom / Graham A. Peck.
Description: Urbana: University of Illinois Press, 2017. |
    Includes bibliographical references and index. |
Identifiers: LCCN 2017016680 (print) | LCCN 2017017687
    (ebook) | ISBN 9780252099960 (ebook) | ISBN
    9780252041365 (cloth: alk. paper)
Subjects: LCSH: Slavery—Political aspects—United
    States—History—19th century. | Lincoln, Abraham,
    1809–1865. | Douglas, Stephen A. (Stephen Arnold),
    1813–1861. | Antislavery movements—United States—
    History—19th century. | United States—Politics and
    government—1783–1865.
Classification: LCC E449 (ebook) | LCC E449 .P39 2017
    (print) | DDC 306.3/62097309034—dc23
LC record available at https://lccn.loc.gov/2017016680

to Rosemary,
with love, gratitude, and affection

Contents

Maps

Map Sources

Howard W. Allen and Vincent A. Lacey, eds. *Illinois Elections, 1818–1990: Candidates and County Returns for President, Governor, Senate, and House of Representatives.* Carbondale: Southern Illinois University Press, 1992. (Maps 4–8)

Charles N. Zucker. "The Free Negro Question: Race Relations in Ante-bellum Illinois, 1801–1860." PhD diss., Northwestern University, 1972. Table II, 155. (Map 2)

George Ryan, Secretary of State. *Origin and Evolution of Illinois Counties.* State of Illinois, 1994. (Maps 2–8)

G. Woolworth Colton's Railroad Map of Illinois. New York, 1861. Library of Congress Geography and Map Division. Permalink: https://lccn.loc.gov/98688465. (Map 1)

Making an Antislavery Nation

Introduction

ON MARCH 4, 1861, the first Republican Party president, Abraham Lincoln, delivered his inaugural address on the East Front of the U.S. Capitol. It was a portentous moment. In the four months since his election to the presidency on a platform opposing slavery's extension, the seven Deep South states had seceded. Determined to preserve slavery from the threat posed by the Republican Party, they had founded the Confederate States of America, whose constitution, in the words of its leading exponent, Alexander Stephens, was based on the "great truth that the negro is not equal to the white man; that slavery—subordination to the superior race—is his natural and normal condition."[1] Seeking to avert a civil war over slavery, Lincoln assured the nation that the Southerners' fears were unfounded. Southerners apprehended that a "Republican Administration" would endanger "their property, and their peace, and personal security," he acknowledged, but neither he nor his party had a "purpose" to "interfere with the institution of slavery in the States." Consequently, he urged Southerners not to "hazard so desperate a step" as secession and war without first determining whether "the ills you fly from, have no real existence."[2]

Lincoln's appeals proved futile. Southern support for slavery, and hence Southerners' resistance to Lincoln's well-publicized commitment to slavery's "ultimate extinction"—evident in his instructions to Republican congressmen during the secession crisis to hold "as with a chain of steel" to the party's anti-slavery extension creed—torpedoed all compromise efforts and precipitated a remorseless four-year Civil War.[3] To most Southerners, the possibility of emancipation produced more alarm than the prospect of war.

Yet the Republicans' unwillingness to cede ground reflected Northerners' equally profound apprehensions over slavery. Their obduracy begs explanation. After all, despite harboring considerable antislavery sentiment, Northerners had only organized a political party against slavery reluctantly, having since the Philadelphia Constitutional Convention in 1787 subordinated their antislavery impulses as the price of union. By the antebellum decades, paeans to the Union were a staple of political discourse. Whig and Democratic Party politicians regularly denounced abolitionists as disunionists; and, to a very considerable degree, northern Democrats' political power shielded Southerners from northern antislavery sentiment. Hence the emergence of the Republican Party in the 1850s, which castigated slavery, adopted key ideas from political abolitionists, and promised to rededicate the nation to freedom, marked a transformation in northern public attitudes. Lincoln's election in 1860, following an almost unbroken chain of Republican victories in the free states, correspondingly registered a seismic shift in northern politics—one that had momentous national consequences given Southerners' ironclad commitment to slavery. At stake was the fate of freedom in America. Slavery's advocates wielded great power and refused to yield the practice of human bondage, so the triumph of an antislavery political party by 1860 is perhaps the single-most vital story about freedom's preservation in America. Explaining how and why it happened is the object of this book.

᠊᠊᠊᠊᠊ᢒ

The short explanation is that profound and persistent conflict between slavery and freedom convinced a majority of Northerners by the 1850s that the nation's commitment to the ideals and practice of freedom was imperiled. Hence they created a party that promoted a powerful antislavery nationalism, seeking, as Lincoln put it, to "re-adopt the Declaration of Independence, and with it, the practices, and policy, which harmonize with it."[4] Through the auspices of the Republican Party, those practices and policies would preserve freedom in America.[5]

The conflict between slavery and freedom, however, had roots that long predated the 1850s. Its origins lay initially in the contrast between the American Revolutionaries' claims for universal freedom and the reality of widespread slavery in the states. If the idea of universal freedom was to be honored, then slavery, somehow, needed to be eradicated. Addressing this problem, however, became more difficult in 1789 when the United States Constitution created a federal structure that brought the states together without clearly determining whether a slave or free policy would predominate in the national government. This was no trivial matter. After all, southern delegates in Philadelphia's Constitution Hall had negotiated for constitutional clauses on taxation, representation, the slave trade, and fugitives from labor that benefited slaveholders, who in the future could be expected to continue protecting their economic and political interests.[6] The politics of slavery quickly became thornier when Americans confronted the question of whether a slave or free policy would apply to national territories. It was an issue of immense significance because the land's cultivation produced most of the country's wealth, while the land's settlement largely would determine the relative economic and political power of slavery and freedom in the future. By 1800, therefore, Americans already faced interrelated moral, political, and economic problems over slavery that defied solution unless Southerners endorsed emancipation or Northerners renounced universal freedom. Yet, over the next few decades, northern states emancipated their slaves, while southern states passed laws against manumission in order to prevent the growth of a free black population that might foment slave uprisings. These simultaneous developments deepened Northerners' and Southerners' powerful existing stakes in freedom and slavery while creating two relatively integrated political blocs on any question involving slavery. With good reason, Thomas Jefferson feared a geographical line dividing the country into sections. As Kenneth Stampp argued long ago, the uneasy coexistence between slavery and freedom in America by the middle of the nineteenth century virtually assured political conflict. Americans could and did extol their society as the ark of human freedom while busily enslaving millions of human beings, but not without generating some impassioned protest and a great deal of painful self-reflection about national ideals. Whether the country could manage the strain indefinitely was the only question.[7]

Mitigating factors made conciliation possible. Recognition that the country had inherited slavery, and could not easily slough it off, encouraged antislavery Southerners and Northerners in the post-revolutionary years to await its demise patiently. Indeed, because the federal government had no power over slavery in the states, gradual emancipation by state action was the country's only realistic path to abolition. Yet for many Southerners, even gradual emancipation raised the alarming specter of either a biracial society or social disintegration spearheaded by free blacks bent on vengeance. Consequently, only northern states embraced emancipation in the republic's early years. Rather than browbeating southern slaveholders to follow this example, most antislavery Americans chose the path of prudence, respecting slaveholders' property rights while seeking to rear the patriotic and political edifice of the Union, whose first principle was conciliation of the country's many competing interests. This approach had much to recommend it: Americans opposed to slavery could contribute to the country's political and economic integration in order to promote prosperity and foster cross-regional ties of interest and sympathy, with the hope that slavery would be swept away by the powerful tides of time and progress. Countless Unionist appeals by northern and southern politicians in the decades that followed showed the fruits of this nationalist approach, although cross-regional ties ultimately concentrated near the border of slavery and freedom, such as on the Ohio River, where the familial and commercial mingling of Northerners and Southerners kept Unionist ideals alive for the longest time.[8]

The decades of peace bought by conciliation, however, produced a momentous shift in American politics. Southerners' growing devotion to slavery challenged both the idea of universal freedom and the corresponding assumption that Southerners bore primary responsibility for resolving the country's core conflict. If Southerners repudiated the prospect of emancipation, then peaceful resolution of the conflict required Northerners to renounce universal freedom. Slowly but surely, Northerners awoke to this unwelcome realization during the antebellum decades. Although they were never likely to concede freedom, one particular mitigating factor made it conceivable: Northerners could embrace white freedom and black slavery, as did most Southerners, by judging blacks unfit for liberty. Considering the deeply racist character of northern society, this was not impossible.[9] But it would require a signal change of perspective in a region increasingly committed to the universal ideal of freedom.

Hence some conceptual clarification is required in order to understand what the words *freedom* and *slavery* meant to most Northerners from 1787 to 1860. In addition to indicating an individual's legal standing as person or property, the terms also captured a complex of ideas and relationships that in practice constituted *freedoms*. Broadly conceived, freedom conjoined personal independence—most notably economic opportunity, religious liberty, political equality, and individual rights—to a national mission promoting the social, spiritual, and material progress that flowed from free institutions. By that logic, slavery represented freedom's antithesis: despotism for the enslaved and stultification for society. Consequently, the Republicans' antislavery nationalism, like virtually all powerful ideologies, also served a tangible material end. It not only represented most Northerners' ideals, but also protected their livelihoods and ways of life, and promised to extend the freedoms they enjoyed to all future Americans and potentially countless others throughout the globe. It was utterly antithetical to slavery.

Southerners' understanding of the same words set the North and the South on a collision course. To most Southerners, slavery enhanced whites' personal independence, economic opportunity, and political equality, while reflecting and bolstering America's progressive institutions wherever slavery spread. Black slavery, in short, promoted white freedoms. This idea deeply shaped American history before the Civil War. Indeed, the defining difference between antislavery and proslavery Americans, and in large measure the critical difference between antebellum Northerners and Southerners, was competing understandings of what constituted freedom.[10] After all, Northerners who adopted the southern idea essentially endorsed slavery, and likely opposed antislavery politics, even if they were not as militantly proslavery as most Southerners. Similarly, some antislavery Southerners, especially in the Upper South, battled for years to eradicate slavery. But most Northerners and Southerners adopted their region's central view. Hence the nation's persistent political struggles over slavery from the Constitutional Convention to the Civil War flowed from a fundamental difference in perspective about the meaning of freedom. At stake by the 1850s was nothing less than control of the country's past, present, and future.[11]

The long explanation will take a narrative form, reaching back to the years of the early republic in order to trace how the conflict between slavery and freedom eventually led Northerners to embrace antislavery politics. Lincoln's election was hardly preordained, and explaining his path to the White House requires attention both to long-term, deeply rooted antagonisms between slavery and freedom, and to short-term contingent decisions by individuals whose actions spurred conflict over slavery at specific times with unpredictable consequences.[12] The story will include the history of not only antislavery reformers but also slavery's defenders and the many Northerners who opposed slavery in the abstract but resisted politicizing it; the paths of all of them are important to the story's outcome in 1860. Finally, it will pay considerable attention to the underlying social and economic history that informed antislavery politics. Most antebellum Northerners achieved personal independence and economic security through the acquisition and cultivation of land, a fact that shaped not only how they experienced freedom, but also how they imagined it. And Northerners' ideas about slavery were never divorced from their understanding of freedom.

The story will focus on Illinois, a state whose history is especially important to understanding the rise and triumph of antislavery politics. In many respects Illinois's history was similar to that of other western states settled in the antebellum era. It boasted a seemingly endless supply of cheap and highly fertile land, which attracted repeated waves of eastern migrants and foreign immigrants who wanted to make a better life for themselves. As in other free states, Illinois's settlers preferred freedom to slavery; if they had not, they would have settled on the southern frontier. Moreover, like other western settlers, Illinoisans generally urged continued western expansion. Hence, Illinois's history well reflects the key economic antagonism between freedom and slavery in America: the relentless westward march of a farming population whose economic mobility was largely predicated on the availability of land that had to be organized as either slave or free. This book will tell the northern half of that history.

Yet the book will also leverage atypical aspects of Illinois's past in order to illuminate important ideas and turning points in the history of antislavery politics. For starters, Illinois's history offers a unique window into the intractability of the conflict between slavery and freedom. In the early 1820s, proslavery Illinoisans urged slavery's legalization. Illinoisans defeated the proslavery movement at the polls, but the conflict illustrated four things that would continue to shape northern politics in subsequent decades: first, that northern voters considered the slavery issue immensely significant; second, that they distinctly preferred freedom to slavery; third, that most of them did not wish to live in close proximity to a free black population; and fourth, that slavery's northern apologists wielded considerable power and influence. These interrelated factors suggested that Northerners would respond diversely to subsequent conflicts between slavery and freedom. They were not likely as a whole to endorse proslavery politics, but whether they would rally together in an antislavery movement was a different question. Having little regard for blacks, and much attachment to the Union, most Northerners likely would tolerate slavery as long as it was somewhere else. They certainly perceived no immediate need to insist on freedom's primacy in the nation.

Conflicts between slavery and freedom sharpened the issue in Illinois over the next several decades. Most notably, the 1837 murder of abolitionist Elijah Lovejoy by a proslavery mob in Alton—and the consequent growth of both abolitionism and anti-abolitionist violence—compelled Illinoisans to ask whether southern slavery imperiled northern civil rights. Meanwhile, the kidnapping of free blacks, the transit of slaves through Illinois, and the escapades of fugitive slaves all raised legal questions about freedom's primacy in the state. The answer to these questions came fitfully from the interrelated forums of public opinion and the Illinois judiciary, but by the late 1840s most Illinoisans had adopted the doctrine that freedom reigned supreme in the state, and correspondingly they expressed a growing desire for free soil national expansion. But these attitudes did not readily translate into antislavery politics. In 1848, Illinois's newfound Free Soil Party, which proclaimed freedom's primacy in the nation and promised to prohibit slavery in national territories, received only 12.6 percent of the state vote, a result roughly in keeping with its showing throughout the North. Although the sharpening national conflict between slavery and freedom had produced stridently proslavery southern partisans, whether Northerners would ever embrace a crusade against slavery was anybody's guess.

In fact, Illinois's politics underscores that creating an antislavery party in the North was no simple matter. The Democratic Party, which was the chief obstacle to antislavery reformers in every free state, ruled Illinois with an iron rod. Between 1836 and 1856, Illinois's Democrats rolled up impressive majorities in elections at the expense of the state's Whigs and boasted the remarkable leadership of U.S. senator Stephen A. Douglas, who organized the party in the 1830s and used it as a base for his rapid ascent to the summit of national politics by the 1850s. Both Douglas and the Illinois Democratic Party would prove resolutely hostile to antislavery politics. The state's Democratic congressmen repeatedly supported slavery on key roll calls throughout the antebellum decades, and its Democratic newspaper editors generally kept up a drumroll of opposition to antislavery reform. These patterns held firm in the 1850s, when Douglas battled tenaciously against Lincoln and the Republicans. Illinois was the bastion of the Democratic Party in the North, and the Democrats' enduring strength made Illinois a swing state in the 1860 election. In no other free state was the Democratic Party more likely to survive conflicts over slavery. That fact shaped the nation's history.

Secure in his citadel, and hence concerned mostly with the fortunes of the national party and the Union, Stephen A. Douglas transformed the national struggle over slavery in the 1850s. He sought to resolve sectional tensions over slavery's expansion by authorizing territorial legislatures to determine slavery's legality, a policy that became known as "popular sovereignty." This approach seemed to have merit. After all, during the late 1840s, stark divisions between northern and southern congressmen over whether to permit slavery in the southwestern territories acquired from Mexico had put the Union at risk. From Douglas's perspective, taking the issue out of Congress's hands made a great deal of sense. He therefore incorporated popular sovereignty into a territorial bill he drafted in 1850 to organize New Mexico and Utah Territories. Its passage—part of the broader Compromise of 1850—allayed sectional strife and calmed the political whirlwinds. But his subsequent, and far riskier, decision to reinforce the principle and the policy of popular sovereignty backfired badly. In 1854, in an effort to organize Nebraska Territory with popular sovereignty, Douglas proposed a bill that, when passed as the Kansas-Nebraska Act, met the demands of southern congressmen and repealed prohibitions on slavery established by the Missouri Compromise in 1820. The repeal mattered deeply. Instead of superintending a permanent solution to the problem of slavery's expansion, which Douglas intended, the act precipitated a sustained firestorm of opposition from outraged Northerners, whom Douglas was only too willing to fight. Among his reasons for sponsoring the bill was the belief that the Democratic Party would emerge purified from a conflict over slavery. Contemptuous of antislavery reformers who jeopardized the Union, and sympathetic to slaveholders, he believed that the party would be stronger and better able to sustain the Union if shorn of its antislavery element, so he used his bill to put antislavery Democrats to the test. Rarely has a politician dispensed with allies so cavalierly, but Douglas was powerful, capable, confident, and visionary—and thoroughly determined to resolve the country's most intractable political problem. It is doubtful whether any American politician has ever made a more fateful choice on a legislative matter.

Douglas's decision unleashed antislavery politics in Illinois and throughout the nation. For the first time, northern opponents of slavery could contend persuasively that slavery threatened the heritage and practice of freedom in America. This was essentially the same argument propounded by antislavery Illinoisans in the 1820s, who had argued for the preservation of freedom in the state, but only after Douglas warred on the Missouri Compromise was it a credible argument for the country at large. Among the northern opponents of slavery roused by Douglas's bill was a resurgent Abraham Lincoln, who reentered politics to grapple with slavery and who repeatedly made the case for an antislavery nation. Lincoln insisted on freedom's primacy in a nation whose founders proclaimed the rights of all men to "life, liberty and the pursuit of happiness." As Lincoln put it, the Declaration of Independence defined "a standard maxim for free society" that should be "constantly looked to, constantly labored for, and even though never perfectly attained, constantly approximated," which, if accomplished, would augment "the happiness and value of life to all people, of all colors, everywhere." This was a stirring defense of freedom in America—and, prospectively, the world. Lincoln's ideas and leadership made antislavery nationalism the linchpin of Republican Party politics and made him the most electable Republican in the nation.[13]

⌒

This book reinterprets the rise of antislavery politics, a subject that has been intensively studied by many distinguished historians. It draws heavily—and justifiably—on their work, but it also seeks to recast the history of antislavery politics. Five ideas that contribute to the recasting deserve mention. The first is that antislavery politics cannot properly be understood without comprehending that the politics of slavery dates at least to 1787.[14] The Northwest Ordinance and the Constitution profoundly shaped the future of slavery in America. This insight is certainly not new, but it is not well reflected in Civil War historiography.[15] Indeed, over the past fifty years, leading Civil War historians have argued that the emergence of the Republicans after 1854 was only made possible by the prior collapse of competition between Whigs and Democrats, which enabled Northerners to organize a party around antislavery reform. Those historians have therefore emphasized the significance of a wide variety of contingent political events between 1844 and 1856 that weakened the Whig and Democratic Parties. While it is true that the successful emergence of the Republican Party required voters to change their partisan affiliations, the history of Illinois shows that the politics of slavery, and hence antislavery politics, not only long predated the Whig and Democratic Parties but also deeply influenced partisan debate once those parties were formed.[16]

A second, related, idea is the significance of northern Democrats to the disruption of national politics in the 1850s. Rivers of print have been spilled for decades on abolitionists, Republicans, secessionists, and southern Democrats, whose historiographical primacy rests on the seemingly bedrock presumption that antebellum politics is a tale of the extremes crushing the center. In this telling, northern Democrats and southern Whigs—the political centrists—were ultimately pushed aside and rendered impotent, leaving historians to explain the compelling story of ascendant radicalism.[17] This portrait is not so much wrong as it is overdrawn. The politics of slavery reached a tipping point in 1854 with the Kansas-Nebraska Act, a law forged at the epicenter—not the margins—of American politics. Abolitionists and fire-eaters did not have the power to drive the act through Congress. Rather, Stephen A. Douglas and Democrats loyal to him provided the critical initiative and votes that altered irrevocably the trajectory of American politics. Douglas's actions were neither inexplicable nor unjustifiable. He was trying to resolve the long-festering and extremely volatile conflict between freedom and slavery through the auspices of the Democratic Party, which he considered the ark of Union. Acknowledging the role of centrists in the coming of the Civil War does not depreciate the significance of radicals or reactionaries; in fact, it better delineates the radicals' political influence and thus more persuasively explains the rise of antislavery politics.

A third, corresponding, point is the salience of the Democratic Party's turn to proslavery politics. Important exceptions aside, historians have not generally portrayed northern Democrats as proslavery.[18] This is partly because the party changed over the years, and partly because even in its later years northern Democrats were not as proslavery as most Southerners. Nevertheless, northern Democrats' increasing need to conciliate the South on slavery, especially after 1854, changed the party's tenor, policies, and composition. Douglas's determination to make popular sovereignty the party creed intensified this shift. In addition to making the Kansas-Nebraska Act a test of party loyalty, which initiated a war against antislavery Democrats, Douglas rejected the idea of universal human rights, justified white enslavement of blacks, urged the acquisition of additional slave territories in the Caribbean, particularly Cuba, and maintained that America could forever persist as a slaveholding nation. All of this put him closer to the southern understanding of freedom than to the northern one, and helps to explain why the Republican Party rose so rapidly. The central difference between Douglas and the South was that Douglas would not endorse slavery in localities where whites opposed it, but his unflinching support for slavery where whites supported it put him at loggerheads with the Republicans. The battle between slavery and freedom was not only between the North and South; it was also a battle, as it long had been, in the North itself.

A fourth, coupled, insight is that Northerners' embrace of an antislavery nationalism made possible the triumph of antislavery politics. Historians have long debated the connections between abolitionism and the Republican Party. Recently, James Oakes has resuscitated an interpretation that emphasizes the abolitionists' importance, arguing that the abolitionist doctrine of "Freedom National" provided the constitutional rationale for antislavery politics.[19] But important as that was, the Republicans needed more than a constitutional justification in order to recruit most Northerners to their standard. The twin northern bulwarks of slavery were racism and unionism: the first deflected concern about slavery's morality, and the second justified tolerating slavery, regardless of its morality, to preserve the national compact. Lincoln and the Republicans used antislavery nationalism to combat each argument. If the nation was committed to the principle of freedom, Lincoln argued, then Americans could not condemn an entire race to servitude forever. This national precept resonated with all Northerners who considered slavery morally wrong. Equally important, however, is that antislavery nationalism reached out to the many Northerners who valued their own freedoms more highly than those of slaves. Lincoln told them that a refusal to combat slavery endangered "the white man's charter of freedom" by "discarding the earliest practice, and first precept of our ancient faith." According to Lincoln, only the Republican Party, which cleaved to freedom, could be trusted to implement policies promoting it. The concept of an antislavery nation thus played the critical role in transforming Northerners' perception of antislavery politics. In the 1830s and 1840s most Northerners considered antislavery politics an abominable abolitionist crusade, but by 1860 they endorsed it as a conservative defense of freedom against a proslavery betrayal of the national creed.[20]

Yet the fifth, and most consequential point of reinterpretation, is that the rise of antislavery politics reflected a fundamental conflict between freedom and slavery in America. The crisis over slavery cannot be boiled down to one issue, such as national expansion, or to one ideological framework, such as northern hostility to the Slave Power, or to one chronological period, such as the secession crisis, or to any particular group, such as abolitionists, or to one locality, such as Illinois, or to any specific moment of contingency, of which there were a very large number in the country's first seventy years. Rather, the slavery crisis was rooted so deeply in the nation's past, and so intertwined with slaveholders' social, economic, and political power, that it kept springing back to life despite a never-ending series of compromises or other initiatives designed to end the strife.[21] Indeed, the Civil War did not begin in 1861 so much because compromisers failed during the secession winter, but because all the prior compromisers had failed before them. Perhaps the best gauge of slavery's abiding influence is that compromises over it repeatedly had unintended consequences: in 1787, when concessions made to slaveholders in order to create a union ultimately encouraged a subsequent generation of slaveholders to destroy it; in 1820, when a congressional law to limit slavery's growth in western territories set the stage for a bloody and embittering conflict over slavery in those territories more than thirty years later; and in 1850, when compromise measures that both major political parties pledged to uphold in order to stamp out slavery agitation provided a key rationale for the Kansas-Nebraska Act of 1854, which did exactly the reverse. Those prior failures, along with innumerable smaller conflicts between slavery and freedom that influenced life in both sections of the country for decades, escalated tensions to such a level by 1860 that Northerners elected a president on a platform hostile to slavery and Southerners elected to dissolve the Union in order to preserve freedom as they understood it. Illinois's history, like that of every other state, reflected this broader national story and, to a considerably greater degree than most, also shaped it.

⸍

As the foregoing analysis suggests, slavery profoundly influenced American politics. From the country's inception, the proper relation between slavery and freedom in the United States was never obvious. Sorting it out was the task of time and future generations. It was a thankless task, however. Because the country's fundamental laws regarding slavery remained ambiguous in key respects, there was no clear way for men of starkly differing opinions to come to a resolution. Hence, the triumph of the Republican Party in 1860 resulted from a protracted political struggle by advocates of one version of American freedom against advocates of distinctly different versions. The outcome was always in doubt, even as the stakes increased dramatically. Such circumstances intensified bitterness between Northerners and Southerners in the country at large, and correspondingly precipitated severe struggle in the northern states between the champions of freedom and Union. The former feared the prospect of a slaveholding oligarchy hijacking the nation's principles, institutions, and destiny, and the latter feared a fratricidal war that would wash the land in blood. Over time, Abraham Lincoln and Stephen A. Douglas would come to personify the northern struggle over slavery. More than any other northern politicians, they would shape its outcome. But our story does not begin with them. It begins at the turn of the century, in Illinois Territory, which in the halcyon days of 1787 seemingly had been promised to freedom by the founding generation.

Prelude

An Inheritance of Slavery

FROM THE START, ILLINOIS's history reflected the country's struggle between slavery and freedom. Like the nation, Illinois inherited slavery. Slave labor was introduced to the Illinois Country of New France in the early eighteenth century by French colonists who wanted domestic help and agricultural laborers. By 1752, black and Indian slaves constituted roughly 45 percent of the population in the French villages. At the conclusion of the Seven Years' War in 1763, the British acquired the Illinois Country from the French but possessed it only briefly, being driven from it in 1779 by Virginia militia commander George Rogers Clark, and ceding it to the United States in 1783 in the Treaty of Paris. The Americans did not emancipate the French slaves, thus effectively deferring to future Illinoisans the question of whether the law of freedom or slavery ultimately would prevail.[1]

In 1787, the Confederation Congress's Northwest Ordinance seemingly prohibited slavery and involuntary servitude north of the Ohio River, but in fact the ordinance reflected the country's indecision about slavery in the wake of the American Revolution. The ordinance provided no mandate or means for enforcement, and its language was ambiguous and contradictory. In particular, the sixth article, which outlawed slavery, conflicted with prior articles, creating legal uncertainties that subsequently enabled territorial officials to permit indentures of slaves. Technically the indentures were consensual, and thus legal, but in practice the slaves did not volunteer for servitude. Nevertheless, protected by law, and eager to exploit slave labor, slaveholders brought hundreds of bondsmen across the Ohio River from 1800 to 1820. Slaves aged fifteen years or older could be legally bound for life, while male and female slaves below age fifteen could be indentured only until the respective ages of thirty-five and thirty-two. Despite this, slaveholders frequently indentured young slaves for much longer terms, which deepened the political and economic influence of involuntary servitude and increased the likelihood that slavery might eventually prevail in at least some part of the Northwest Territory. Established before the American Revolution, slavery in Illinois, like slavery in the nation, would prove difficult to eradicate.[2]

Indeed, during the territorial period, slaveholders repeatedly sought to legalize slavery. In 1788, 1796, 1799, 1800, 1802, 1805, 1806, and 1807, slaveholders lobbied or petitioned Congress to modify or repeal the antislavery provisions of the Northwest Ordinance. However, unwilling to sanction slavery in the northwestern territories, Congress rejected or ignored their pleas. In response, proslavery politicians in Indiana Territory, of which Illinois was a part, created an indenture system in 1803 in order to coax southern slaveholders north. But antislavery settlers began to resist proslavery politics in 1808, virtually guaranteeing that freedom would predominate in Indiana. Unbowed, and skillfully opportunistic, Illinois's slaveholders joined with Indiana's antislavery faction to elect a territorial delegate to Congress, Jesse Thomas, who politicked for a separate Illinois Territory, which Congress established in 1809. Sheared of the proslavery Illinoisans, Indiana outlawed slavery in 1816. But in Illinois, slaveholders now ruled.[3]

Illinois's politicians moved quickly to strengthen involuntary servitude. In 1810, the territorial governor, Ninian Edwards, and two territorial judges, Jesse Thomas and Alexander Stuart, who collectively exercised plenary power over the territory, struck down a provision of the indenture laws that emancipated slaves whose masters failed to indenture them within thirty days after bringing them to Illinois. In 1813, after Congress had authorized the establishment of a territorial legislature, its members promptly enacted a severe black code that prohibited the migration of free blacks into Illinois and required all existing black residents to prove their free status. In 1814, the legislature legalized one-year indentures that protected "the right of property in the master, in and to the services of such slave or slaves," drawing an exceedingly fine line between slavery and indentured servitude. By strengthening slaveholders' property rights and repressing the growth of a free black population whose existence and actions undermined black servitude, these laws encouraged slaveholders to settle in Illinois.[4]

However, the slaveholders' domination of Illinois was soon challenged. The peace treaty signed at Ghent in 1814, which ended the War of 1812, unleashed a flood of westward migration that brought a phalanx of influential antislavery figures to Illinois. They included the future congressman Daniel Cook, a young Kentuckian who in 1817 had boldly advocated a national program of gradual emancipation in a public letter to President James Monroe, and a future state legislator, George Churchill, who in 1818 published a series of powerful essays against slavery under the pseudonym "Agis." The arrival of such men, along with many settlers who supported them, eroded the slaveholders' power. Consequently, only a small majority of the delegates elected to Illinois's 1818 constitutional convention appear to have favored slavery. Indeed, antislavery Illinoisans may have been underrepresented at the convention given Churchill's contention that "some *slaveholders* were *smuggled* into the Convention by making great profession of their opposition to slavery." Nevertheless, the proslavery delegates apparently did not attempt to legalize slavery, quite possibly because they lacked the votes, but almost certainly because they feared Congress's power to block Illinois's admission to the Union.[5]

But they did protect it handsomely. In a notable departure from the precedents set in Ohio and Indiana, which had also been a part of the Northwest Territory, the Illinois constitution guaranteed existing slavery and contracts of indenture. Moreover, while declaring that slavery and involuntary servitude could not "hereafter" be introduced into the state, the constitution permitted one-year indentures until 1825 at the saltworks near Shawneetown, involuntary indentures for minors, and multiyear indentures for "cases of apprenticeship." All of these clauses created loopholes for slaveholders. Lastly, in a dramatic departure from Ohio and Indiana precedents, the constitution did not prohibit subsequent amendments legalizing slavery. When the constitution came before Congress, Representative James Tallmadge of New York claimed that these provisions violated the Northwest Ordinance. He opposed Illinois's admission to the Union because its constitution recognized "existing slavery." Unpersuaded, the House of Representatives resolved to admit Illinois by a vote of 117 to 34. Illinois's inheritance had left its mark. The state's constitution, like the nation's, proclaimed freedom but harbored slavery. Like their fellow Americans, Illinoisans would have to sort out the complications that followed from such a beginning. The first and by far the most important complication was adjudicating between Illinoisans who thought slavery promoted freedom and Illinoisans who thought the reverse.[6]

MAP 1. Illinois Place Names

1. The Nation's Conflict over Slavery in Miniature

Illinois, 1818–1824

BETWEEN 1818, WHEN IT entered the Union as a free state, and 1824, when its residents defeated a proslavery movement, Illinois reproduced the nation's problem with slavery in miniature. The state was dedicated to freedom, but the state's constitution protected existing slavery and indentured servitude. Consequently, the meaning of freedom in Illinois was not yet clear. Many Illinoisans carried antislavery sentiment to their new home, migrating to the state with the hope of owning their own land and enjoying greater political liberty. Such migrants utterly opposed legalizing slavery. Yet proslavery arguments were beginning to take root in Illinois, as in the South, and the prospect of economic benefit enticed other Illinoisans to consider supporting slavery's legalization. Hence, when Illinois's economy faltered in the early 1820s, crippled by a nationwide depression, slaveholders pushed for a constitutional convention to legalize slavery. They contended that slavery was the key to unlocking the state's prosperity, and they hoped that Illinois's population, most of which hailed from the South, would endorse the idea. But the convention movement was soundly defeated at the polls. To a greater degree than previous historians have recognized, this result reflected a surge of antislavery migrants into the state during the eighteen months of political campaigning, but more generally it reflected Illinoisans' conviction that slavery's legalization would undermine rather than enhance freedom. So, in 1824, after several decades of uncertainty, Illinoisans decided conclusively to oppose slavery in the state, considering it antithetical to freedom. Whether they would make the same judgment about slavery in the nation remained an open issue.

The lure of land and liberty brought settlers to Illinois. Whether traveling from Europe or the southern backcountry, immigrants often shared the same basic impulses. England's William Hall objected to social stratification, political oppression, and rampant poverty in his native land, where he struggled to support a "numerous family." Once in Illinois, he celebrated "the feeling that we are at last on our own Estate *Free, & Independent*, secure in the enjoyment of the Fruits of our Industry." Migrants from the upland South shared these sentiments. Descendants of peripatetic eighteenth-century small farmers who over the course of three generations had migrated from Pennsylvania, Virginia, and the Carolinas into Tennessee, Kentucky, Ohio, and Indiana, upland Southerners typically had little money and less education, and each generation sought cheap, uninhabited land on which to raise a family. The vanguard of white settlement in the Upper South and Lower North, they drove out Indians and hewed farms from timber land. By the early nineteenth century, they began filing into southern Illinois, and by 1818 they constituted about 70 percent of the population in the newly created state. Englishman George Flower rendered a vivid depiction of these uprooted southern poor folk, describing a barefoot, emaciated family walking alongside a "little rickety wagon" pulled by "a horse as lean as a greyhound." Such families hailed from "Alaba*ma* or Caro*line*," he said, and "a more perfect picture of destitution can not be seen."[1]

Some of these Southerners sought a home free from slavery. Peter Cartwright had a small farm in Kentucky, but rising land prices precluded any chance that his children could acquire land near him. In 1823 he decided to move to Illinois, abandoning his "comfortable little home" in order to "get entirely clear of the evil of slavery," improve his "temporal circumstances," and raise children "where work was not thought a degradation." Cartwright's reasons for emigrating were hardly unique. Slaveholders routinely pushed out subsistence farmers by bidding up the price of land on which commercial crops could best be grown. But in Illinois, Cartwright and others like him sought a promising home pledged to freedom.[2]

Some settlers' love of liberty stimulated strong antislavery sentiments. Englishmen Morris Birkbeck and George Flower founded a settlement in Edwards County in 1817 and encouraged English immigration to it. In promotional letters published in England, Birkbeck wrote that America "is indeed a land of liberty and hope, and I rejoice unfeignedly that I am in it." He extolled the religious liberty of Americans and their commitment to democratic government, although his admiration of freedom intensified his loathing of slavery, which he called "a foul blotch" of "leprosy" on the

United States. Despite their considerable wealth and their roots in a society that privileged rank, respect for the egalitarian ideal ran deep in both men. Flower confessed to his mother that "the most perfect equality" of citizens in America unnerved him. He disliked being "accosted with familiarity by a parcel of ignorant upstart slovenly fellows." But he forthrightly defended the political system resting on that equality. "[T]he Advantages of republicanism are too striking to be hidden," he wrote, "and far outweigh any of its own Inconveniences."[3]

Future governor Edward Coles exemplified the settler spurred by the ideal of liberty. Although a slaveholding Virginia aristocrat, Coles immigrated to Illinois on an antislavery mission. Deeply moved by the doctrines in the Declaration of Independence, and profoundly admiring its author, in 1814 he urged Thomas Jefferson to promote emancipation publicly. Jefferson refused, but Coles resolved to free his slaves because they "could not be property" according to his "understanding of the rights and duties of man." En route to Illinois in 1819, he freed his slaves on the Ohio River, cherishing bold antislavery ambitions. He sought to prove that the "descendants of Africa were competent to take care of and govern themselves." To that end, he gave three of his adult ex-slaves one hundred and sixty acres of unimproved land and urged them "to hire themselves out" until they earned enough money to farm independently. He presumed that their capacity for economic improvement would determine their readiness for political liberty, and he dreamed that their success would promote emancipation throughout the South.[4]

To be sure, most Illinoisans opposed the idea of permitting blacks to enjoy the benefits of liberty or economic opportunity. The 1820 federal census recorded only 457 free blacks in Illinois, and more than one hundred of those lived in white households, probably as dependents. They faced severe discrimination. The state's 1818 constitution prohibited them from voting and serving in the militia, and in 1819 the General Assembly prohibited them from living in Illinois without a properly registered certificate of freedom and from testifying against whites in court. Challenging popular sentiment sanctioning these laws, free blacks petitioned the Illinois House of Representatives for voting rights in 1822. They reported that white men "without the least color of claim" plundered their property and kidnapped their children, and they hoped that suffrage rights would enable them "to obtain that protection to our persons and property" enjoyed by whites. Having been "rocked in the cradle of liberty and equal rights, taking our ideas of liberty from you," they "zealously" wished to "participate in that blessing." Legislators referred the petition to a select committee already charged with considering measures to abolish slavery in Illinois and to prevent the kidnapping of free blacks. The majority and the minority reports of the committee, despite presenting radically different views on slavery's abolition, both skirted the subject of black suffrage, for which there was little public support.[5]

But Illinois's political leaders did laud the liberty and equality of whites. Their constituents gave them little choice. English traveler John Woods memorably described such backwoods settlers as "a most determined set of republicans, well versed in politics," among whom a man "without shoes and stockings, is as independent as the first man in the States." Yet the territorial governor of these barefoot republicans from 1809 until 1818 was slaveholding grandee Ninian Edwards, a wealthy, well-connected Kentuckian who dressed elegantly, lived lavishly, traveled stylishly, and owed his appointment to President Madison. Nevertheless, Edwards described himself as a representative of the people, whose "duty" was to protect "the equal rights of his fellow-citizens." Furthermore, he expressed devotion to the principles of "liberty and equality, those fundamental rights of man," and assured Illinoisans that "as a citizen" he felt "no superiority to any other honest, well-behaved man, however humble his station in life may be." Indeed, Edwards promised to discharge his duties for "the public good," and to "appeal" always "to the people," trusting that he could "always confide" in "the candor, the good sense and justice of the people." Whatever they may have said privately, Edwards and other Illinois politicians deferred to the common man in public. In keeping with this principle, they also supported policies the frontier electorate desired.[6]

⌇

The acquisition and exploitation of land made possible the personal independence and economic opportunity that Illinois's settlers associated with freedom. Hence, like their western counterparts, Illinois politicians sought above all to liberalize federal land laws. Prior to statehood, Illinois Territory's congressional delegate Nathaniel Pope strongly protested President Monroe's proposal to raise the price of public lands. After statehood, Senators Ninian Edwards and Jesse Thomas, along with congressman Daniel Cook, favored the sale of government land on credit, the reduction of the price of public land, and the passage of bills to enable squatters more easily to purchase land they had improved. In 1821, with the economy in a tailspin, Edwards, Thomas, and Cook supported a debtor relief measure that delayed the date of forfeiture for unpaid lands, permitted debtors to revert land back to the government without financial penalty, or reduced the price for debtors who paid their balance within eighteen months. A political opponent's charge that Cook had not supported a reduction in the price of public lands, an allegation the congressman sharply rebuked, demonstrated the importance of public land law to the prospects of frontiersmen, whether dirt poor or well capitalized. Access to land influenced where they lived, when they could buy, how much they could buy, and how long they had to wait before reselling the land to future settlers at a profit.[7]

Illinois's politicians also sought to foster settlement and trade by constructing the Illinois-Michigan Canal. In 1818 the state barely had enough settlers to build a canal, much less use it. Only the southern third of the state was settled, and Indian titles from the northern half of the state had yet to be extinguished. Nevertheless, Governor Shadrach Bond strongly recommended the construction of a canal in his first message to the legislature in 1818. At considerable cost the legislature funded an engineering study of the canal in 1821. Most politicians supported the canal, some opposition in southern Illinois notwithstanding. Its advocates argued that it would provide market access to the East and promote immigration to Illinois, thus increasing real estate values, tax yields, and local capital. In 1822, Governor Coles also urged canal construction, stating that it would spur "industry & enterprise, defusing wealth and happiness." Subsequent governors and congressmen strongly supported the canal, and in 1827 the state secured a federal land grant to fund its construction. Yet the canal was not built until 1848, partly due to mismanagement, but largely due to the state's limited resources. The precociousness of canal politics in the early statehood period illustrates politicians' desire to facilitate markets in order to promote the state's settlement, improve living conditions, and hasten economic development.[8]

The state's poor southern migrants stood to gain appreciably from the state's economic development. To be sure, their poverty prevented intensive participation in market agriculture. They had neither the tools nor the oxen to break up prairie land, so they settled in easily plowed but less fertile timber land. The accessibility of wood and water also encouraged them to settle on forested land, as did the limited market for grain. Such newly settled land was unlikely to have easy market access, but poor farmers had few other options. Speculators owning better land demanded compensation for tenancy, usually a set amount of the crop or specific improvements to the property, and those obligations required extensive labor that undermined the tenants' ability to produce marketable surpluses. Therefore most poor settlers, who likely constituted at least two-thirds of the population, simply squatted on unused land. As one eastern migrant indignantly observed, squatters accumulated capital by clearing the land and selling their "improvements" to the "rale owner" when he appeared. Squatters who saved enough money to purchase a plot from the government could significantly better their economic fortunes. Gershom Flagg reported in 1819 that land "bought two or three years ago for two dollars an acre is now selling at 10 and 12." Admittedly, this appreciation occurred during a land boom, and poor settlers rarely owned the land that was likely to appreciate the most. Nevertheless, land ownership enabled settlers to support themselves, promised a respectable return on capital if they chose to move farther west, and, if they had market access, enabled them to produce surpluses to the extent they desired. The opportunity to occupy or own such land had not existed to the same extent in the southern backcountry.[9]

By contrast, the capital that eastern migrants and European immigrants brought to Illinois made market production potentially lucrative. The purchase of land, animals, and farming implements upon arrival enabled them to produce surpluses. But they needed robust markets to absorb their agricultural production and multiply the value of their real estate. For this reason they pressed for internal improvements to facilitate commodity transport. The founding of the English Settlement in Edwards County by Birkbeck and Flower symbolized this commercial inclination, even though their wealth and ambitions made the settlement unique. Birkbeck argued that densely populated settlements nourished economic specialization, capital accumulation, transportation corridors, and trade networks. "I wish to see capital and population concentrated," he wrote, "with no bond of cohesion, but common interest arising out of vicinity." Consequently, he and Flower recruited laborers to the English Settlement by selling cheap land. They expected their estates to reap the benefit of rising land values and growing trade outlets. In this way a market society benefiting labor and capital would emerge from the wild frontier.[10]

However, markets for produce and livestock were insufficiently developed in early Illinois. Horatio Newhall learned this lesson in 1823. Needing a coat, he paid 120 bushels of corn for two yards of cloth. He indignantly wrote back to his family in the East that an Illinois farmer "can get enough to eat, and that is all." Newhall's surplus production that year had almost no value. The same problem hindered the English Settlement. George Flower recalled that farmers in his colony produced surpluses of corn, pork, and beef by 1821. But to sell it, he wrote, they had "to quit their farms and open the channels of commerce, and convey their produce along until they found a market." Farmers gladly abandoned this practice once merchants paid cash for produce, but that change was a long time in coming. In the meantime, farmers attempting to sell surpluses met repeated roadblocks.[11]

By contrast, land speculation, or the market in land, seemingly offered the easiest and best return on capital, and thus most early settlers were in hock for land. As Gershom Flagg wrote in 1821, "Most of the People are in debt for Land and many otherwise more than they can posably pay." The ubiquity of debt followed from the availability of credit. From 1804 until 1820, the government encouraged credit sales for land by requiring an $80 down payment for $320 of land. To make their initial payment, most settlers used paper money circulated by banks. The extent of speculation flowed from misguided optimism rather than from economic necessity. As future governor Thomas Ford remembered, albeit somewhat hyperbolically, settlers purchased "a quarter section of land" for "nearly every sum of eighty dollars" in Illinois. They assumed that immigrants to the state would continue to stimulate property values, which made a decision not to invest seem timid and foolhardy. But because the engorged land market rested ultimately on the market in trade, land speculating offered grave risks as well as great rewards.[12]

The risks became evident in the early 1820s, when a sharp decline in trade bankrupted innumerable Illinois farmers and eastern speculators. A nationwide economic contraction simultaneously diminished demand for farm products in major markets like New Orleans while curtailing the immigrant flow to Illinois. Farmers who had purchased land on credit could not fulfill their obligations without selling agricultural surpluses for cash. Meanwhile, neither farmers nor speculators had much hope of selling land to immigrants. Property taxes therefore loomed as a great threat because the state sold the land of delinquent taxpayers for the price of unpaid taxes and interest. As Gershom Flagg reported in 1825, "I purchased last June about 15 hundred acres of valuable land for the taxes which amounted to $103." At 6.9¢ per acre, he benefited handsomely from the bursting of the speculative bubble. But the uncounted thousands of bankrupt speculators did not. They demanded relief.[13]

State legislators attempted to ride to the rescue. In 1821 they created the State Bank of Illinois in Vandalia and directed it to issue $300,000 in bank notes, mostly to be distributed in loans of $100 or less to individuals who could not offer real estate as collateral. The legislature compounded the consequences of this ill-judged measure by refusing to back the notes with specie. Instead, the relief bill stipulated that 10 percent of the notes would be redeemed annually over the next ten years at 2 percent annual interest. This essentially transformed the notes into state bonds and radically depreciated their value. After all, notes that could not be immediately redeemed, and might never be redeemable, could hardly be exchanged at par. Foreseeing this outcome, the legislature mandated that debtors had three additional years to discharge their debt if creditors refused to accept the state's notes at face value. As a stopgap measure, the legislation prevented widespread bankruptcies, but because the value of the notes dropped to 62.5 percent of par within two months, and to 30 percent of par within two years, the measure further inhibited trade by deranging the currency. The unwillingness of capitalists to extend credit under such circumstances restrained economic activity. Almost everyone had to tighten their belts, and many settlers chafed at the unexpected hardship.[14]

Illinoisans' economic distress created an opportunity for proslavery partisans to promote slavery's legalization. Their motivation was clear enough: there was money to be made. And because a large majority of Illinois's political leaders—some of them slaveholders—heralded from slave states, political support seemed assured. Such men generally tolerated, even if they did not necessarily advocate, slavery's expansion. Frustrated by wagonloads of wealthy slaveholders passing daily through Illinois on the way to Missouri in the early 1820s, Illinois's proslavery advocates sought to change the law. The settlement of such slaveholders in Illinois meant big crops, expanded trade, and rising land values.[15]

༄

Proslavery Illinoisans' attempt to legalize bondage unleashed a severe conflict in the state between slavery and freedom. The proslavery movement likely was stimulated by slaveholding politicians in Kentucky, Missouri, and Washington, D.C., who wanted to strengthen slavery's political power and sought to retaliate against northern opposition to Missouri's admission as a slave state, which had convulsed Congress from 1819 to 1821. But its strength flowed from the longstanding desire of Illinois's slaveholders to foster their economic self-interest. In July 1820, the antislavery editor of the *Edwardsville Spectator*, Hooper Warren, who claimed to have gained knowledge of a plan to legalize slavery, publicly charged that "slavemongers" sought both to gain control of most of the state's newspapers and to replace representative Daniel Cook with a proslavery politician. Warren's warning came on the heels of the proslavery *Illinois Gazette*'s proposal to revise the constitutional provision prohibiting indentures at the saltworks after 1825. The first efforts to alter the laws were taking shape.[16]

One year later, proslavery partisans put forward Illinois's chief justice, Joseph B. Phillips, for governor. Although he did not initially advocate slavery's legalization, within a few months one of his supporters publicly encouraged "those favorable to the toleration of slavery to rally round Judge

Phillips, as a man through whom their objects can be accomplished." Decrying "abstract philosophy, in excluding what would be beneficial," the author urged voters to "act like freemen—be no longer dictated to by priests, or bound down by those who oppose your interest." This appeal was unusually blunt and powerful, and it expressed what would come to be the core proslavery arguments in Illinois. However, slavery's influence on the election is difficult to assess precisely because three other candidates declared for the office, including Edward Coles, who opposed slavery. Factional allegiances, regional ties, and personal relations, not just slavery, shaped the voting. In the end, Phillips and Supreme Court Justice Thomas Browne split the populous southern region, where many voters favored slavery, while Coles won every county in recently settled central Illinois, whose inhabitants generally opposed slavery. Their votes gave him a narrow victory and demonstrated the dangers immigrants posed to the proslavery movement. Changes to the constitution took time, requiring both a two-thirds vote of the state's legislators to approve a referendum to determine whether to hold a constitutional convention, and a majority vote in favor of the convention at the referendum. The incoming tide of antislavery immigrants showed that proslavery legislators had little time to waste.[17]

Slavery's supporters passed the convention resolution in the next legislative session. Their ability to do so very likely flowed from careful and quiet management of critical state legislative contests the preceding year, when the *Illinois Gazette* had acknowledged that "[g]reat exertions will, in all probability, be used to procure a call for a Convention to re-consider the important provision, in our constitution, against slavery." Horatio Newhall similarly had reported that "a large party" favored "calling a convention," whose "*real*" although not "avowed object" is the "introduction of slaves into the State." The results of the election left the convention advocates barely shy of a two-thirds majority in each house. Several months of maneuvering followed, but on February 10, 1823, the resolution passed the Senate, 12 votes to 6. The next day, confident of success, the convention's advocates put the measure to a vote in the House of Representatives. Much to their mortification, however, the vote of one turncoat turned victory into defeat. But the convention's supporters refused to concede. The next day, under highly questionable proceedings, they removed the turncoat from the assembly and awarded his seat to a politician whose vote passed the convention measure. For the next eighteen months, until the referendum, slavery dominated Illinois politics.[18]

The issue impassioned Illinoisans. In 1824 Newhall wrote that partisan feeling "destroys, in a great degree, all social intercourse between persons of different parties," with both the slave and free party "equally sanguine" of success. William Brown, for a time editor of the *Illinois Intelligencer*, later recalled that old "friendships were sundered, families divided, and neighborhoods arrayed in opposition to each other," with "[p]istols and dirks" forming "a part of the personal habiliments of all those conspicuous for their opposition to the Convention measure." Thomas Ford remembered that handbills and pamphlets on the slavery question "flew everywhere," and that the "rank and file of the people were no less excited than their political leaders." John Reynolds recollected "aged and crippled" men being "carried to the polls," and apolitical men bestirring themselves to vote. Indeed, the Scottish Covenanters, a radical religious sect, voted en masse against the convention despite generally refusing to participate in what they considered an ungodly government. Slavery's future in Illinois was an issue of immense importance to its residents, who considered not only the freedom of black slaves but also their own to be at stake.[19]

The convention party immediately contended for the people's right to amend the constitution. In an address read to a public meeting in the state capital on February 17, convention party leaders maintained "that the great and fundamental principle upon which all republican governments rest, (the will of the majority)," ought to prevail. On this basis, they encouraged the support of those who "consider it desirable that industry shall be encouraged, emigration promoted, and wealth introduced into our state, whereby the difficulties and embarrassments, under which we now labor, will be removed." This shrewd advocacy of what antebellum Americans later would call "popular sovereignty" enabled them to avoid advocating for slavery per se. They defined the moral issue as the people's power to do as they pleased, and then simply urged the people to consult their interest when shaping state law. As the *Republican Advocate* observed, "It is undeniably true that the people are the best judges of their own interests," and therefore "THEY should decide." Correspondingly, the conventionists contended that the convention's foes sought to silence or subvert the people. "A Kaskaskian" denounced antislavery state legislator Thomas Mather as an "aristocrat" who had ignored his constituents' wishes by voting against the convention, while "OE" charged that wealthy antislavery leaders warped open debate and frustrated the people's will by distributing free copies of the *Edwardsville Spectator*. In thus using popular sovereignty to justify slavery's legalization and to discredit their opponents, the conventionists followed the novel and portentous proslavery argument advanced by Missourians and their southern defenders during the Missouri crisis: that white men had a constitutional right to enslave blacks, pending only the sanction of state law.[20]

Conventionists also appealed to Illinoisans' interest by arguing that slavery would invigorate the economy. The *Illinois Gazette* maintained that the salines required slave labor to be profitable and warned that without the salines southern Illinoisans would have reduced access to markets. The *Gazette* also grumbled that rich slaveholders were pouring into Missouri because Illinois excluded slavery. The recruitment of such settlers to Illinois would "soon people our woods and prairies, and transform them from uncultivated though fertile waste, to delightful farms." The *Republican Advocate*'s editor, William Orr, urged slave cultivation of the American Bottom's "500 square miles" of rich alluvial soil, which stretched south of Cahokia on the Mississippi River. Orr believed that slave labor would produce abundant crops of tobacco, cotton, and hemp, benefiting cash-strapped Illinoisans by commanding "the specie of other countries." And "Ames" observed that slaveholders would rent out slave laborers when necessary, as in the South, thus assisting their neighbors. These economic arguments reflected the core motives of the convention party. An Ohioan who spoke privately with Illinois's proslavery senator Jesse Thomas reported that the "object which they avow is the increase of value, to their real estate, and their commercial interests." This object had widespread appeal. Land agent David Robson wrote to his employers in 1823 that land would "sell much better" should Illinois legalize slavery, while Thomas Lippincott, a leading anticonventionist, recollected later that appeals to "the pocket" proved seductive because slavery's immediate economic benefits were "undeniable" and "palpable."[21]

Yet conventionists also justified slavery's expansion into Illinois on humanitarian grounds. State legislator Conrad Will, one of the earliest and boldest public advocates of a constitutional convention to legalize slavery, contended that Illinoisans could render "an essential service" to "humanity and justice" by instituting a system of limited slavery with a provision for later emancipation. Some subsequent convention advocates reiterated this argument, while others simply claimed that slaves would benefit by removal to Illinois's rich lands. "It is not our object to ravish from the bleeding bosom of Africa, those unfortunate beings," wrote "Veritas," but "to render more pleasant the burden already imposed upon them by the hand of destiny." This humanitarian argument softened the conventionists' naked appeals to economic interest. They generally did not claim that slavery benefited blacks, a contention that few Americans advanced in the early 1820s, but they did desire to clothe their proposal in reputable garb. Such appeals targeted the sensibilities of Illinoisans who desired the gradual emancipation and colonization of America's slaves, ideas which attracted the support of many eminent Americans in the 1820s and surely made some converts in Illinois. An Indiana correspondent of an influential Illinois politician illustrated the appeal of gradual emancipation by wishing "the slave party in your State a partial success." While not an advocate of "unconditional Slavery," he thought "mitigated slavery" would "be beneficial to all new States and would be the most likely to eventuate in the final emancipation of the coloured race." He proposed a specific policy to emancipate slaves brought to Illinois, and stated that if "you introduce this kind of slavery you may expect to see me a citizen in 24 hours after I hear of the decision."[22] Americans' difficulty in sorting out the meaning and practice of freedom in the early 1820s could hardly have been more sincerely expressed. Correspondingly, the fate of freedom in Illinois was entirely uncertain.

⌒

Yet convincing Illinoisans to support slavery was no easy matter given the implacable resistance put up by the convention's opponents. Immediately following passage of the convention referendum, antislavery legislators secretly met with other antislavery leaders at the capitol. They discussed how best to defeat the measure, pledged financial support for the antislavery *Edwardsville Spectator*, and wrote an appeal to the people of Illinois in which they castigated the legislature's "extraordinary" proceedings, warned that Illinoisans could not abrogate the Northwest Ordinance without endangering "the union of these states," and remonstrated the "great national sin" of slavery. In following months, with the assistance of Protestant ministers, anticonventionists established antislavery societies in counties throughout the state. Meanwhile, Governor Coles contributed his $1,000 annual salary to the cause, recruited an abolitionist Philadelphia Quaker to produce antislavery tracts, and along with many other antislavery leaders peppered the press with antislavery missives. Their vigor spread antislavery ideas and mobilized Illinoisans to oppose the convention.[23]

Antislavery writers challenged the conventionists' understanding of popular sovereignty by emphasizing the country's antislavery heritage. "Aristides" lambasted the idea that "*republicans have an undoubted right to enslave a portion of their fellowmen*," instead contending that "*all men are by nature free and equal, that personal liberty is inherent and indefeasible.*" Morris Birkbeck likewise maintained that "[f]reedom is the basis of our social compact." While a popular "majority can regulate the institutions founded on this basis," he insisted that the "basis itself is impregnable," and concluded that no legislature or convention had the "power to give one man a title to the liberty of another, any more than to his life." Consequently, he censured the conventionists for rendering themselves "unworthy" of "the blessings of this free constitution." Similarly, "Martus" argued that black bondage contravened the "self-evident" proposition that all men were born equally free and independent, while "An Old Resident of Illinois" judged that advocacy of slavery requires "a change in our political institutions" that shall merit the "execrations" of posterity. Repeatedly, anticonventionists emphasized the incompatibility of slavery and American nationalism. This argument, which loomed large in Illinois's convention struggle, would exercise a profound influence in the subsequent history of antislavery politics.[24]

The anticonventionists also insisted that slavery's economic benefits would be fleeting. They contended that freemen motivated by self-interest outproduced slaves driven by the lash, claimed that slavery's degradation of labor inhibited the work ethic of white people in slave states, and observed that slaveholders' self-sufficiency suffocated economic development. Not only engorging "large tracts" of land, charged "Aristides," slaveowners also had "little interest" in improving the country through "roads, bridges, canals, and literary institutions." Meanwhile, he continued, slavery hindered local markets by restricting the flow of capital, which circulated more actively in free states because laborers earned and expended wages. To anticonventionists, these factors explained why the population and land values of free states outpaced those of contiguous slave states. Many Illinoisans agreed with these judgments; land agent Alfred Cowles, for example, observed that Missouri had not made "greater progress in population, wealth, increased value of Lands, or improvement than Illinois, and I presume not so great," and concluded that slavery's introduction would preclude "advances in improvement which the free States exhibit." Such convictions operated strongly against slavery's introduction.[25]

Antislavery leaders also dismissed their opponents' humanitarian claims. Writing as "One of Many," Coles contended that introducing slavery to "a new and fertile region" would "greatly" increase the market for slaves and correspondingly inhibit emancipation elsewhere. Moreover, he maintained Illinois's adoption of slavery would give it "a new and imposing sanction," thus prolonging its "duration in other places." Coles also denied that proslavery politicians would promote gradual emancipation, indignantly noting that the same men who had passed legislation in 1819 to exclude free blacks from Illinois would never fill "our state with free negroes" by emancipating slaves. Morris Birkbeck also turned the logic of the humanitarian argument on its head, contending that the introduction of slavery into Illinois would augment America's slave population because population diffusion created "a more favorable proportion between the means of subsistence and the number of inhabitants." As evidence, he asserted that slave populations in the original slaveholding states had grown despite an outflow of slaves to western states. Slavery's legalization in Illinois would expand and perpetuate, not ameliorate, slavery's evils.[26]

Antislavery writers also exploited racial prejudice. "Spartacus" argued that the combination of "limited slavery" and "gradual emancipation" would "tend greatly to increase the number of free negroes" in Illinois, a prospect "Brutus" considered "truly alarming." Concurring, "Q" sardonically observed that the bringing of Africans to Illinois "is a very benevolent and philanthrophic wish, as it regards the blacks; but I believe the white population, in general, *would rather be excused.*" Most antislavery leaders, including Coles, Birkbeck, Churchill, and Lippincott, explicitly disavowed such sentiment, resting their strongest arguments on the equality of man, but the convention movement doubtless gained support from the many voters who considered blacks a pestilence.[27]

The anticonventionists also warned Illinoisans against bringing slave revolts to their door. If freedom was, as Birkbeck maintained, "the right to do every thing but injury, and the enjoyment of protection from being injured," the enslavement of blacks endangered whites. For this reason, "A friend to Freedom" opposed introducing "into our houses a class of persons who have no inducement to be virtuous, but every incitement to do ill—who would be ready, at the first opportunity, to cut our throats, poison our families, and burn our dwellings." John Warnock, a candidate for the Illinois Senate, likewise declared that nothing was more dangerous "to the peace and safety of the community" than to create an oppressed and vengeful caste, while "G. H." more pointedly asked Illinoisans whether they were ready for "the Africans to free themselves?" To prevent just such a bloodbath, Birkbeck noted that Southerners prohibited the education of blacks, barricaded their houses, stored arms, and patrolled nightly. Southerners' fears reflected the palpable tensions in what Coles called "an unnatural and miserable community." The violence, rage, paranoia, and periodic alarms of slave societies destroyed the blessings of liberty that Americans so proudly vaunted.[28]

The various appeals highlighted much that was to come in future years. Most notably, antebellum Northerners' major arguments for and against slavery—popular sovereignty and antislavery nationalism—appeared in embryo form. Both ideas harked back to the country's revolutionary heritage, which meant that the nation's conflict over slavery was also inescapably a contest over the meaning of freedom, and particularly whether a free people could rightfully enslave others. Yet for Illinoisans, as for Americans more generally, the debate over slavery was never purely about national values. Their economic interests, racial attitudes, religious convictions, and political commitments also deeply shaped their perspectives on slavery. In Illinois, those factors did not clearly align in favor of freedom, and therefore slavery's fate remained uncertain until the end of the convention debate.

On August 2, 1824, the electorate turned out in droves to decide the question. The 11,612 voters massively exceeded the 4,516 who turned out several months later for the 1824 presidential contest, and also outstripped the 8,606 who had voted during the 1822 gubernatorial election. The percentage of participating eligible voters was about 65 percent in 1822, but it was at least 75 percent in 1824, and probably nearer 80 percent.[29]

The antislavery party won a convincing 57 percent of the vote, 6,640 votes to 4,972, compiling a 1,668 vote margin. Partly this reflected their effective organizing and persuasive rhetoric, which convinced some Illinoisans that slavery's introduction would destroy liberty's blessings. As Horatio Newhall realized a few months before the election, "a pretty considerable change" had occurred "in public sentiment." But the continuing population growth in the state's northern counties from 1823 to 1824 played an equally critical role. The *Illinois Intelligencer* wrote near the end of 1823 that Illinois "this year received a considerable accession of strength to the north-west and north-east of this State, by emigration; and the government having just brought the Sangamon lands into market, we may reasonably expect a further augmentation of our numbers, from the same cause." Although the exact rate and distribution of population growth during the eighteen months before August 2, 1824, cannot be determined, the *Intelligencer* was unquestionably correct.[30]

A comparison of the 1822 gubernatorial vote with the 1824 convention vote strikingly demonstrates the newest settlers' key role. Voters from the eight counties that most strongly opposed the convention cast 2,828 ballots and gave a 1,868 vote majority against the convention, which was more than the anticonventionists' overall margin of victory. Three of these counties had been carved from other northern counties since 1822, and seven of the eight were located in the state's northwestern and northeastern regions. Voters from the five preexisting anticonvention counties cast 1,506 ballots in 1822, but in 1824 voters from the eight counties cast 1,322 more votes, an 87.8 percent increase. Meanwhile, voters from the eight strongest proconvention counties cast 2,164 ballots in 1822, a number that ticked up to 2,509 by 1824, a 15.9 percent increase. These counties yielded only a 1,003 vote margin in favor of

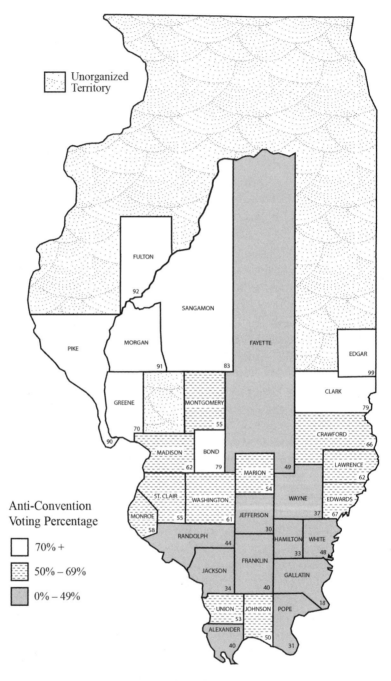

MAP 2. Vote against Convention Referendum, 1824

Note: Numbers reflect Anti-Convention percentage of the vote (rounded).

the convention.[31] Clearly, Illinois's admission into the Union in 1818 as a free state had changed the tide of settlement by discouraging slaveholders, and the subsequent arrival of antislavery immigrants in the northern portion of the state played a key role in permanently excluding slavery from the state.[32]

↩

Nevertheless, freedom's triumph in Illinois did not presage its triumph throughout the nation. On the contrary, the severity of the convention struggle portended future conflicts over slavery. The constitutional referendum reflected American slaveholders' increasing conviction that they had both a moral and a legal right to pursue the economic opportunities afforded by property in man, whether in existing states or new territories. But their conviction contradicted powerful national ideals about the meaning of freedom, and therefore their efforts to put their ideas into practice precipitated polarizing struggles, evident in both the debates over Missouri's admission and Illinois's convention battle. Antislavery Illinoisans certainly fought desperately to preserve freedom, and they succeeded partly because legalizing slavery in a free state was so difficult, akin to abolishing it in a slave state. In both cases, constitutional protections, existing social and economic interests, and contempt for blacks predominantly favored those defending the status quo. Yet those same factors meant that ending slavery in the states where it already existed would be extremely challenging, and if slavery did not end in those states, future national conflicts over slavery were exceedingly likely. After all, whenever the federal government needed to establish a single slavery policy, on whatever issue, a clash between the partisans of freedom and slavery likely would ensue. But this disturbing possibility did not trouble Illinoisans in 1824. They had fashioned a free state. Now it was time to reap freedom's blessings.

2. Democrats, Whigs, and Party Conflict, 1825–1842

THE EMERGENCE OF THE Democratic and Whig Parties in the 1820s and 1830s turned Illinois politics toward the issues of democratization and economic development. Historians have traditionally interpreted the rise of party conflict between Democrats and Whigs, which occurred across the country, as evidence of slavery's political subsidence. Certainly both parties preferred to keep slavery out of politics. Yet debate over democratization and economic development encouraged Illinoisans to define freedom in ways that would later produce significant clashes with the South. Initially, democratization caused Illinois's Democratic and Whig politicians to pass legislation that promoted economic opportunity for the state's predominantly farming population. Legislators incorporated banks to spur investment and commerce, and supported internal improvements measures, such as road, canal, and railroad construction, to facilitate transportation. However, the disastrous failure of Illinois's banks and internal improvements by the late 1830s spurred sharp partisan debate over government-subsidized economic development. Democrats lambasted banks, which they believed created a privileged class of citizens who wielded illegitimate political and economic power, while Whigs remained committed to government-sponsored efforts to promote social progress. These visions diverged significantly, but both presumed continued agricultural settlement and the market exchange of agricultural goods. Consequently, both reflected Illinoisans' desire to make best use of their freedom and incubated a latent antislavery logic in Northern politics. Partisan debate, in short, promoted ideas that would later be used against slavery at the same time that demographic changes silently but inexorably pushed the nation west. Party imperatives thus set the stage for an expansionist Democratic Party to reignite national conflict over slavery and freedom in the 1840s.

༄

Andrew Jackson personified an emerging democratic political culture in the 1820s. His victory over the British at New Orleans revived the nation's sagging morale during the War of 1812 and endowed him with tremendous popularity. In 1816 the government appointed him to head a commission to conclude treaties with the Indian tribes in the South, whom he quickly forced to cede enormous tracts of land to the United States. In 1818, the administration authorized him to pursue fleeing Seminole Indians into the Spanish province of Florida, and while doing so he brazenly conquered the province itself. To many Americans, Jackson's military exploits and Indian removal policies suggested a manly character that contrasted with the cabals and schemes of national politicians. Jackson assiduously cultivated such perceptions in campaign propaganda, and in other respects he proved an astute and cagey politician. Listening to the advice of his political confidants, he shrouded policy issues in the billowing folds of his martial fame and anti-aristocratic appeal. This strategy was calculated to draw in men who admired the general and all he seemed to symbolize, especially his capacity to reinvigorate the country's political virtue. Such logic repelled elites who perceived Jackson as an unlearned and violent warrior unsuited for the presidency. Nevertheless, Jackson's public image successfully united the republican ideal of virtuous and independent office-holding with populist democracy.[1]

Although uncertain of Jackson's politics, Illinois's leaders hoped to capitalize on his popularity. Jackson's managers had concealed his policies so successfully that no one really knew what he supported, even after his election in 1828. Believing that he would slight "agricultural & manufacturing interests," one Illinoisan declared that the latter "interests are awake, and Jackson & the South cannot put them down." Yet others dismissed the idea that Jackson would resist "great national measures" such as "internal improvement & Domestick manufactures." Despite his opaque politics, Jackson's popularity attracted ambitious politicians. In 1827 a correspondent of soon-to-be-Democrat Sidney Breese advised him not "to be lashed to the mast" of President Adams's "sinking ship." Jackson's election to the presidency drove this point home and freed Adams men to jump to Jackson, and the result was a scramble for patronage among state politicians.[2]

The administration attempted to establish order by superimposing a national party on factional alliances. Customarily, national leaders provided patronage to regional strong men in exchange for votes. These alliances shifted frequently because regional leaders possessed considerable autonomy. By contrast, Jackson attempted to impose regularity by requiring state politicians to coordinate their actions with the national party. In this endeavor, he heeded the suggestions of his Secretary of State, Martin Van Buren, who had already built a cohesive and disciplined party in New York. But building a national party proved difficult. As Treasury Secretary Samuel Ingham complained, the "communications" he received from Illinoisans "all refer to the parties *in the state* as a predominating object." He reproved the tendency of Illinois Jacksonians to ensure election by allying with "Adams & Clay men," warning that the administration intended to "maintain its character for consistincy" and would not tolerate indiscretions. As Ingham knew, alliances with the Adams and Clay men weakened party discipline by elevating unreliable politicians into office and by sustaining the strength of the opposition in state politics. The administration wanted to build a national party, which required that Jacksonians remain distinct from their opposition in state as well as national elections. Prior to Jackson's candidacy, antipartisan sentiment and the apathy of Americans in national elections precluded attempts to connect state and national politics. Even with Van Buren's shrewd use of Jackson's popularity, the process proved difficult and protracted.[3]

The Bank War began to distinguish the real Jackson men. Jackson had distrusted banks since his own near bankruptcy in 1797. Moreover, he had never believed that Congress possessed the power to create a national bank, and he had desired to reform or even eradicate the Second Bank of the United States from the inception of his presidency. Although Jackson decided not to address bank reform in his first term, bank President Nicholas Biddle precipitated a confrontation. Biddle successfully prodded Congress to recharter the bank in 1832, which forced Jackson either to acquiesce or to veto the bill in an election year. Characteristically, Jackson attacked. His stirring veto message assaulted the antirepublican character of the bank, and in the following election he swept to triumph despite the bank's general popularity. He then carried the war to the bank. In September 1833 he removed federal government deposits from the bank and vested the deposits in state banks, typically ones sympathetic to his administration. Enraged, Biddle responded by contracting the nation's currency, which helped to precipitate a financial panic and succeeded for a time in swinging public support against Jackson. But Jackson rallied Congress by working with congressional leaders, lobbying congressmen, and encouraging antibank mass meetings at the state level. By April 1834, with popular favor turning against the bank, the House upheld Jackson's policies. The bank was never rechartered.[4]

The Bank War primed the emerging Democratic Party to implement and defend partisan practices. Young politicians like Illinois's Stephen A. Douglas had no allegiance to the old factional system. To create a cohesive organization, they sought to nominate party candidates for office and to compel orthodoxy on policy, and for this purpose they introduced the convention system. Gatherings of local Democrats at the ward or county level appointed delegates to district or state conventions, which subsequently established a party platform and nominated party candidates for office. The need for Democratic Party conventions was made especially evident in 1834 by events in Jacksonville, where Douglas had inaugurated partisan organization. After electing three ostensibly antibank state legislators, Jacksonville's Democrats quickly learned that two of them had "secretly pledged themselves to the Opposition." The statewide returns consoled the indignant Douglas, who took revenge once the legislature convened. Having gained control of the statehouse, the young Jacksonians promptly passed measures in line with their majoritarian sentiments, vesting the legislature with the power to elect state's attorneys, authorizing the people to elect county recorders and surveyors, and appointing a set of circuit-court judges whose sympathies lay with the Democratic Party. This determination to enforce party discipline, including by purging dissenters, soon became characteristic of both national Democratic Party politics and Douglas's leadership style, and would later play a profound role in intraparty battles over slavery.[5]

In addition to spurring party organizing, the bank and convention issues crystallized Democratic Party ideology. Most fundamentally, Democrats insisted that the people's representatives must implement the people's will. This was a radical departure from the widespread eighteenth-century conviction that democracy incubated mobocracy through demagogues who incited people's passions. In contrast, Democrats feared aristocrats, believing that they would hijack democracy by thwarting the people's will and extracting special privileges from the government. To counter these aristocratic threats, Democrats promoted equal rights and majoritarian democracy.[6]

Illinois Democrats advanced these egalitarian doctrines in the wake of the Bank War. The *Illinois Republican* excoriated the bank and "all other chartered monopolies and exclusive privileges," sought to "*punish*" representatives who disregarded "the will of their constituents," and advocated the "right of the People" to select nominees for office through conventions. After the election, Stephen Douglas exulted that "the cause of *Democracy* is triu[m]phant, and that the *People* are disposed to retain the advantage they have gained over the aristocracy." He marveled that "equality and equal rights" prevailed in Illinois, and he celebrated that Illinoisans were democrats "in principle and in Practice." Officially articulating this creed in 1835, the Illinois Democratic Party's state convention address, which Douglas co-authored, promoted partisan organization, contending that conventions "embody and give effect to the popular will." Skillfully, the authors of the address seized the word "democracy" as the party's talismanic name, urging "the democracy" to "rally around" those "distinguished individuals selected by a majority of their friends as the most competent and best calculated to support and sustain it in all its pristine force and efficacy." Unifying the Democracy was essential. The address denounced officers of the Bank of the United States for attempting to "mould and direct public opinion" in the recent election, and charged that this "instrument" of the aristocracy had threatened the "liberties of the people." In this context, the financial panic Biddle had precipitated by contracting credit graphically illustrated the "illegitimate influence" wielded by monopolies.[7]

This critique reflected the Democrats' opposition to economic or political privileges, such as bank monopolies, that undermined economic or political liberty. The national bank was hardly alone in enjoying special rights from a legislative charter. Illinois's legislature, like those in other states, routinely granted monopolies and other privileges to individuals or corporations. In one notorious case, the Wiggins Ferry Company acquired a state charter in 1819 that granted the company exclusive ferrying use of the Illinois River bank opposite St. Louis. To reinforce its monopoly, the company also secured proprietary use of French Cahokian land that Congress had preempted from sale. Over time, farmers, merchants, and teamsters, angered by the company's "extortionate" charges, demanded an alternative. In 1835, Democratic state legislator Adam Snyder introduced resolutions that urged Congress to alienate the land, and in 1839 the legislature authorized the county to operate a competing ferry. The company's lawyers contended that the state legislature could not violate the 1819 charter, but Democratic Judge Sidney Breese struck down their suit, maintaining that "free competition" replaced "exclusive privileges" and restored equal rights.[8]

Yet the Democrats' commitment to equal rights and democratic practice also contained the seeds for a rebellion against slavery. Indeed, by the mid-1840s, some northern Democrats would begin expressing hostility to a slaveholding aristocracy, warning that its constitutional privileges and expansionist impulses threatened the twin bastions of freedom: democracy and free labor. This hostility to slavery was not surprising. Slaveholders, to a far greater degree than bankers, possessed special political powers in the federal government, and slaveholders used their power to spread slavery, bringing them into direct conflict with the interests of northern farmers, whom the

Democratic Party assiduously served. But those antislavery seeds would take time to sprout. In the 1830s, Democrats faced a different foe: the Whig Party.[9]

Like the national Whig Party, Illinois's Whig Party organization emerged in fits and starts between 1828 and 1836. Primarily, it was patched together by men who opposed the Democrats. Some Illinois Whigs opposed Jackson's economic policy or use of executive power; others distrusted Martin Van Buren or detested his demand for party regularity, which they considered antidemocratic. Similarly, variations among the anti-Jackson forces nationwide led the Whigs to run three presidential candidates in 1836: Massachusetts senator Daniel Webster, who headed Whig ballots in his home state; William Henry Harrison, the Virginia-born former Indiana territorial governor and Ohio senator, who ran in the other Northern states, Virginia, and the border states; and Tennessee senator Hugh Lawson White, the party candidate in most slaveholding states. Although Van Buren beat back these challengers, the Whigs emerged as a credible party throughout the nation, winning almost 50 percent of the vote and cultivating a substantial following in virtually every state. Illinois's Whigs split their loyalties in the 1836 presidential election between Harrison and White, who together polled a respectable 45.3 percent of the vote. It seemed a promising beginning, but the party needed to develop more cohesive principles and policies in order to establish an organization with wide-ranging appeal.[10]

Hints of the Whig Party's future course—and the antislavery implications of its ideas—were evident by 1836. In Springfield, the Whig presidential ticket received 65.7 percent of the vote, marking an early beginning to Whig dominance in Sangamo County and much of central Illinois. Equally evident was the Whigs' strong desire for federal- and state-sponsored internal improvements to promote commerce, and state-funded common schools for society's moral advancement. Abraham Lincoln, who soon would be a prominent Illinois Whig legislator, declared in an 1832 campaign address that the Sangamo River should be improved to facilitate both the export of "surplus products" and the import of "articles from abroad." Meanwhile, Lincoln judged education to be the pillar of civic virtue, "morality, sobriety, enterprise and industry," and hence termed it the "most important subject we as a people can be engaged in." Lincoln aptly captured the Whigs' desire to use democracy's collective means to promote the common good. However, this commitment to social progress implicitly pitted northern Whigs against slavery, which was characterized not by education and individual uplift but by the permanent subjection of a despised caste.[11]

These Whig antislavery attitudes were quickly evident in the North at large. In 1836, when northern Democrats led by Van Buren supported a

Southern-sponsored gag rule designed to prevent discussion of antislavery petitions in the House of Representatives, Northern Whigs opposed it. Indeed, some of them repeatedly sought to introduce antislavery petitions from their constituents. But party differences on slavery, so significant in the 1840s and 1850s, rarely propelled debate between Democrats and Whigs in the 1830s. The Bank War had been the primary fuse igniting partisan combat, and economic issues would continue to dominate politics through 1844. In this regard, the debates between Democrats and Whigs accurately reflected voters' central interest: the quest to make money from the land. This was as true in Illinois as in the rest of the nation.[12]

⟿

Men on the make preponderated in Illinois during the 1820s and 1830s. As illustrated by the lives of the young Lincoln and his contemporary Daniel Brush, such men worked a variety of jobs to improve their social and economic standing. Lincoln settled in central Illinois after living in Kentucky and Indiana, while Brush hailed from Vermont and settled in southern Illinois. As children, both lost a parent and grew up poor with little formal education. As youth, both farmed for their family's subsistence and worked as hired hands for neighbors. As young men, both clerked and owned stores, and both piloted boats down the Mississippi. Both men made their way into law and politics, and both eventually became distinguished citizens. Their careers were unusual only in the degree of success they enjoyed. Most male settlers migrated to the frontier intending to better their situation, and young single men in particular tried their hands at whatever paid, and frequently changed employment. Not all men successfully accumulated wealth, but their desire to do so ensured that geographic and social mobility characterized frontier life.[13]

In pursuit of a better life, immigrants poured into the state in the decade following the slavery controversy. Between 1825 and 1835, the state's population increased from 72,817 to 270,179. Southern Illinois's population grew from 51,728 to 104,156, but most of the new migrants settled in central Illinois, where the population rocketed from 21,089 to 142,409. Seventy-four percent of the latter increase concentrated in western Illinois counties that bordered either the Illinois River or Mississippi River and boasted access to transportation and markets. Southern and central Illinois's new migrants overwhelmingly hailed from the Southern states. However, beginning in 1833, following the conclusion of the Black Hawk War, which precipitated the expulsion of Indians from Illinois, Northerners also began arriving in large numbers. They were assisted by New York's completion of the Erie Canal

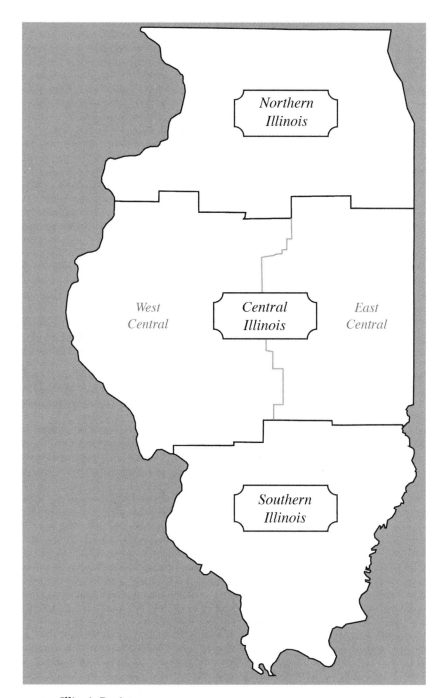

MAP 3. Illinois Regions
Note: This map is based on 1860 county boundaries. All calculations presented in the book about Illinois's regions comport closely with the tripartite division illustrated here, even though county boundaries changed from 1818 to 1860.

in 1825, which enabled convenient boat passage from Buffalo to Detroit or Chicago. By 1835, 23,614 predominantly Yankee settlers lived in the top third of the state, and Chicago had begun its commercial career.[14]

The influx of almost two hundred thousand new settlers into Illinois generated widespread optimism by spurring urban growth, stimulating trade, and sparking a land boom. Stephen A. Douglas, recently arrived from Vermont, wrote from Jacksonville that land speculation and animal husbandry yielded great profit with little labor. He insisted that his brother-in-law's *"future prospects"* required emigration from New York to Illinois. Similarly, Swiss émigré Kaspar Koepfli described the insatiable demand for wheat, the "inexhaustible soil," and the "effortless, inexpensive, and profitable" raising of livestock. He urged Swiss farmers to emigrate and promised that "there is no danger here of completely lean years such as have been experienced in Switzerland."[15]

The northern-born immigrants gave an especial push to market development. Their arrival and spread throughout northern and central Illinois from 1830 until 1860 resulted in a tripartite division of the state and had enduring economic consequences. Southern-born migrants dominated southern Illinois, northern natives populated the northern counties, and a mixed population occupied central Illinois. Unlike many Southerners, Northerners usually arrived with farming implements, furniture, and livestock, purchased the improved land of earlier settlers, and commenced market production. They also inclined more strongly to opening stores and shops, and hence spurred trade. Possessing greater capitalization and market acculturation than southern-born settlers, emigrants from the North expanded Illinois's agricultural and livestock surplus and stimulated economic exchange.[16]

Merchants' influence escalated during the economic expansion. The leading merchants were located on the Mississippi River and channeled trade through hinterland towns. Chief among them were St. Louis's merchants, who used New Orleans as their hub to the East and who also traded with cities on the Ohio River. St. Louis merchants generally had a price advantage over western competitors when buying and selling produce and merchandise, and consequently farmers within "an area of thirty to forty-five miles" of the city enjoyed a "ready market" for grain and meat. In addition, the city's merchants began to develop a wholesale trade by extending credit to hinterland merchants, who reached many more consumers. Chicago's merchants also developed an important economic role in the 1830s. The Great Lakes and the Erie Canal connected Chicago directly to New York, poising Chicago to become the nation's premier western city. Savvy speculators began bidding up Chicago property in 1833, and mass migration to the city in 1834 and

1835 quickly created a substantive local market. By 1836, Chicago merchants regularly forwarded New York trade to St. Louis, Galena, and smaller towns in northern Illinois and northwestern Indiana. Other cities also spurred trade, such as Alton, which dominated the upper Mississippi River Valley hog trade in the 1830s. Meanwhile, merchants abounded in burgeoning towns like Springfield. Increasingly accessible, markets enabled farmers who produced surpluses to enjoy significantly improved living standards.[17]

However, shortages of merchant capital still inhibited trade markets. Men with capital generally preferred to loan money or speculate on land. Money at interest brought in at least 15 percent per year, and usually 20 percent to 25 percent, and loan sharks who extended credit prior to federal government land sales charged 35 percent to 60 percent. Moreover, the long hours and high risks of the mercantile business compared unfavorably to speculation and money lending. In particular, the scarcity of specie and banknotes frequently forced merchants to barter with local farmers for produce that was difficult to sell in distant markets such as New Orleans, which augmented the challenge of repaying eastern wholesalers for store goods acquired on credit. For these reasons, merchants remained relatively scarce and undercapitalized in the 1830s.[18]

Distinctive trade markets in Illinois resulted from merchants' uneven distribution throughout the state. Islands of trade formed where merchants operated, benefiting nearby farmers but barely influencing others. For example, Jackson County had only one store in 1829, and only several more in 1839, and large portions of adjacent counties had no stores at all. Peter Cartwright's experiences as a Methodist circuit preacher in 1825 highlights farmers' uneven access to markets. Some church members traveled sixty miles merely to grind their wheat, but some lived close enough to markets that Cartwright admonished them to raise their standard of living by purchasing bedsteads, chairs, silverware, and clothing. The heterogeneity of markets prevented Illinois farmers from participating in the market on similar terms. The price of manufactured goods varied according to the location, capitalization, and sales volume of frontier merchants and peddlers. Produce values depended on a merchant's location, capitalization, partnerships, and contracts to fill federal government orders. Although frustrating for farmers, price variation characterized frontier trade markets.[19]

Rearing livestock gave farmers the best chance to turn land into cash. Raising cattle and hogs required little effort or capital, and grown livestock proved highly marketable. Farmer Joseph Suppiger accurately described cattle raising as "the most profitable utilization" of land. Yearling cattle cost about three dollars and sold four years later for six or seven times that amount. In the interim, the cattle grazed on unoccupied prairie, required supervision only during severe winters, and reproduced rapidly enough "to develop into a large herd in a few years." Sows cost about three dollars and produced ten to eighteen offspring per year. The pigs ate acorns and nuts in timbered land and needed little winter care. Butchered twenty months after birth, the pigs sold for six dollars each. Moreover, livestock were as easy to sell as to raise. Huge cattle drovers like Isaac Funk and Jacob Strawn purchased livestock for resale, and on a local level farmers like Suppiger built their herd by buying cattle from poorer neighbors. In other cases, farmers simply drove their animals to market. Squatters, farm owners, and cattle kings all invested in cattle and hogs.[20]

Nevertheless, the market in land remained the primary investment of most Illinoisans. The federal land offices sold 45,801 acres in 1825, 176,448 acres in 1830, and 2,096,623 acres in 1835, and although eastern capitalists purchased much of Illinois's land, they constituted a small minority of speculators. New Salem farmer Charles Clarke wrote to his mother that many "a rich farmer lives in a house not half so good as your old hogs pen and not any larger." Farmers cared less for "fine buildings," Clarke believed, than they did for "adding land to land." Indeed, the growth of claim clubs reflected the desire of squatters and small farmers to monopolize land for resale. Settlers frequently settled on land before the government sold it at auction. To protect these holdings, they banded together in claim clubs, agreeing to chase off claim-jumpers and to threaten deep-pocketed competitors who might outbid them at auction. But their virtuous façade could not mask their own speculative behavior. Club bylaws invariably permitted members to claim far more land than they needed. They farmed only a half or a quarter of their land and forced later immigrants to pay a premium for the rest. In this regard they were no different than individual farmers who resold land, nonresident speculators, or town speculators who advertised lots in the eastern press. Speculation was the fastest route to wealth in the West.[21]

Given their market orientation, Illinoisans wanted to spur economic development. Additional settlement and improved trade promised cheaper goods, rising land prices, and a steady market. Therefore a large and growing number of Illinoisans wanted to build a canal between Lake Michigan and the Illinois River in order to connect farmers and merchants to eastern markets, and almost all Illinoisans supported internal improvement projects in their local regions. As the *Illinois Intelligencer* wrote in 1826, "it is not the richness of the soil, or its capacity to produce bountifuly, but its location, that renders it valuable." Hence the *Intelligencer* strongly supported the proposed canal, observing that "this land, in its present state, is valueless, and will only become valuable by the improvement contemplated." Illinoisans debated how best to develop the state's economy, but a consensus held firm. Settlers valued markets and sought to enhance them. For this reason, partisan politics initially provided a powerful spur to state-subsidized economic development. Democratization would go hand in hand with increased market production.[22]

$\backsim$

Illinoisans had idealized economic opportunity from the start. In the early 1820s, when Indians still controlled northern Illinois, the General Assembly urged the state's congressional delegation to secure a federal land grant for construction of the Illinois-Michigan Canal. The delegation succeeded in 1827, and for the next decade the canal remained the preeminent internal improvement issue in state politics. During the 1830 gubernatorial campaign, John Reynolds won over voters in northern Illinois by advocating construction of the canal, and soothed regional rivalries by promising to improve river navigation in southern and eastern Illinois. Despite his election, financing difficulties and the intervening Black Hawk War delayed authorization for canal construction until 1835. By that time, with Chicago emerging from the mud, central and southern Illinoisans' demand for improved market access received reinforcement from northern Illinoisans' increasingly urgent appeal for access to eastern markets.[23]

Spurred by this enthusiasm, legislators proposed a variety of railroad projects in the 1830s, culminating in Democrat Sidney Breese's bold 1835 plan to build a central railroad running vertically through the middle of the state. He maintained that the road would encourage the settlement of southern and central Illinois, promote access to both northeastern and southern markets, and raise land values. The state legislature responded to railroad enthusiasm in 1836 by incorporating sixteen railroad companies, including one to build Breese's road. Political support for internal improvements in Illinois, as in the rest of the West, reflected widespread frustration with transportation difficulties that inhibited trade and settlement.[24]

Indeed, encouraged by popular outcry, the legislature enacted a mammoth system of improvements in 1837. Stephen A. Douglas introduced resolutions that authorized money for various projects: a central railroad running from the canal mouth to southern Illinois; a railroad crossing the state; the improvement of two rivers; and continued canal construction. This ambitious plan likely would have bankrupted the state, but other legislators thought it timid. A later version of Douglas's bill removed the canal, which received funding in a separate act, but added six more railroads and provided for improvements to a mail route and three more rivers. The bill passed 61–25 in the House and 25–15 in the Senate. Southern Illinois Democrats championed the bill with particular fervor, although majorities from both regions and both parties supported it. Opponents to the measure generally hailed from areas that already had adequate market access, such as western Illinois, although some southern Illinois Democrats judged that their constituents opposed the measure, and voted accordingly. Nevertheless, public celebrations followed passage of the measure, and politicians from both parties eagerly claimed credit for it.[25]

But public attitudes eventually soured when the state failed to complete any of the railroads or the canal before money ran out. Recklessly, the legislature had authorized simultaneous construction of all the railroads, rather than building them sequentially and using the completed roads to generate revenue. The state's difficulty in selling bonds to pay for the improvements compounded this initial error. Its bond fund commissioners arrived in New York just as the Panic of 1837 deranged money markets. The panic, which originated with the Bank of England's decision to curtail American credit, caused banks throughout the nation to suspend specie payments, and the result was widespread deflation. Derailed by this development, the commissioners returned to Illinois after receiving no bids for their bonds. They disposed of several million dollars of bonds after the panic eased, but thereafter they had little luck. Meanwhile, cost overruns wasted much of the money spent by the state. Although the legislature learned in December 1838 that the per-mile cost of railroad construction was 50 percent higher than had been estimated, legislators did not reallocate the state's resources in response to this grim news, and a year later the state ran out of funds. Only twenty-four miles of one railroad had been completed, and its operation proved unprofitable. The canal fared little better. Its construction fund ran dry by the end of 1838, and although the legislature subsequently authorized the sale of $4 million in canal bonds, the state's agents struggled to sell them because financial markets were saturated with state securities selling under par. By 1842, the state had exhausted every funding possibility, and construction stopped with the canal unfinished. After six spendthrift years, the state had nothing to show for $10.5 million of debt, for which the annual interest was eight times as large as the state's tax revenue.[26]

But Illinoisans had equal reason to rue the state's banking policy. Illinois's two banks dated to Jackson's removal of federal deposits from the Bank of the United States in 1833, a decision that virtually all Whigs and many Illinois Democrats opposed. In a Whig-like philippic, Sidney Breese called the president's removal of deposits from the Bank of the United States "ill advised, uncalled for, and contrary to the true intent and meaning of the law."

More diplomatically, Democratic Party congressman Zadoc Casey deemed it his duty "to oppose the recharter of the present Bank of the U. States," but promised to give "all the aid" in his power "to the establishment of an institution that shall give a sound & uniform currency to every part of the country," provided it was "debarred" from "participating in the general politics of the nation." John Reynolds also treaded carefully. He usually endorsed Jackson, a national bank, and a national currency, provided the bank did not "injure the people in their rights or liberties" or "interfere with the purity of elections." However, when "playing for all the pockets," as one critic complained, he presented himself also as "Ultra-Jackson and Anti-Bank." Casey's and Reynolds's ambivalence reflected Democrats' deep animosity toward bank president Nicholas Biddle's conduct and their widespread desire for a stable currency. Many Democratic politicians shared their sentiments. About 30 percent of the party's legislators in the 1834–35 General Assembly supported a national bank, whereas about 60 percent of them supported some kind of state banking. By contrast, 97 percent of Whig legislators supported a national bank, and 55 percent supported state banking. The Democrats' distrust of a national bank whose concentrated power could threaten democracy and equal rights thus sharply distinguished the parties, but banking in principle did not divide them nearly as profoundly. State banking was ultimately the compromise position. Bereft of national bank notes, Illinoisans required a replacement.[27]

Eager for an improved currency and seduced by the idea of bank profits, the Illinois General Assembly chartered two state banks that winter. The legislature extended the charter of the Bank of Illinois at Shawneetown while also establishing the State Bank of Illinois. The charter of the new bank authorized it to raise capital by selling shares in the amount of $1,500,000. Both charters passed with substantial support from each party in each legislative branch, indicating the widespread interest in establishing a circulating medium and promoting economic development. As the *Illinois Advocate and State Register* proclaimed in 1835, "the people of Illinois" must "plunge at once into the stream of business, and seize upon fortune as it flies."[28]

But involvement with the internal improvements program proved fatal for the banks. Needing to meet the interest obligations on the state's bonds, state legislators in 1837 invested $3 million in the state's two banks, primarily by purchasing bank stock with state bonds. Of those legislators who cast a vote, about 50 percent of the Democrats and 85 percent of the Whigs supported the bill, with the Democrats' greater reservations reflecting their fear of concentrated banking power, fears intensified by Whig domination of both banks' boards. Supporters of the law hoped to use bank dividends to pay the interest on the state's bonds, while the banks intended to increase profits by issuing more loans and notes. But the infusion of $3 million of state capital dramatically altered the banks' investment strategy. The banks' directors previously had been fairly conservative, but the demand for conservative credit instruments, such as bills of exchange to facilitate interregional trade, was largely fixed. Bank credit invested in bills of exchange could not substantially exceed the dollar value of western commodity exports. Realistically, increased trade flows could not possibly absorb the banks' new capital. Almost inevitably, bank directors gravitated to riskier investments.[29]

The banks dramatically expanded note circulation. The State Bank expanded it from $1,430,000 in January 1837 to $3,060,000 in July 1839, while the Bank of Illinois expanded it from $65,000 in August 1837 to $712,000 in December 1838. Together, the banks increased note circulation by $2,277,000, generating a great deal of speculative investments that led to banking losses. Meanwhile, personal and commercial debt rose to astronomical levels. Lawyer David Davis estimated in July 1837 that Illinoisans owed the State Bank a sum greater than "the present circulating medium of the State." In the next five years the debt sinkhole deepened. As Thomas Ford later recalled, by 1842 the "whole people were indebted to the merchants; nearly all of whom were indebted to the banks, or to foreign merchants; and the banks owed everybody; and none was able to pay."[30]

Worse yet, the banks added rampant corruption to reckless inflation. One problem was the bank's influence on the state legislature. Legislators often requested money to facilitate land speculation, and the banks complied in order to cultivate friends in the General Assembly. A more pressing problem was that the banks' charters did not prevent bank officers from loaning money to themselves or to stockholders. Although some officers expressed concern about the dangers posed by "very honest but ambitious" bank directors, most of them did not begrudge themselves funds. A prosaic example involved Henry Eddy, a director of the Bank of Illinois, whose partner in land speculation sought to woo a millowner to their townsite by offering bank loans. More portentously, State Bank directors loaned very large sums to stockholders while also funneling almost $500,000 to themselves and their firms. Given that the bank approved only about $700,000 for all loans up to $500,[31] the abuse stood out sharply. Worse yet, the bank loaned the staggering sum of $800,000 to the directors of the branch bank in Alton, who violated the State Bank's charter by attempting to corner the Galena lead ore trade. That catastrophic transaction alone almost bankrupted the bank. In January 1840 the legislature mandated that the bank could loan no individual more than $35,000, but the damage had already been done.[32]

The banks' recklessness created enormous hardship for Illinoisans. Low specie reserves eventually forced the banks to suspend specie payment and pressure debtors for repayment. The consequences were harsh. Debtors had incurred obligations during an inflationary spiral but paid for their debt after the monetary contraction cut prices sharply. Indeed, the State Bank's circulation dropped from $3,105,000 in November 1840 to $1,454,000 in December 1842, and the circulation of the Bank of Illinois dropped from $1,262,000 to $757,000 during the same period. Deflation produced a flood of bankruptcies, especially among farmers and merchants. In 1840 Adam Snyder lamented the "dimunition of the price of Labour, produce, and real estate." Real estate worth more than $500,000 had been "sold under execution" in Madison and St. Clair Counties, he wrote, because men "are in debt and can get no money to pay." That same year, Bloomington's David Davis observed that ever since 1837 "the medium of the Courts have been in requisition for the purposes of liquidation." Few people escaped unscathed from the drastic economic contraction.[33]

These conditions in Illinois, and similar problems in other states, precipitated the rise of antibanking Democrats. In county and state conventions from 1839 to 1842, Illinois party members denounced banking. Delegates at the 1839 Democratic state convention resolved that illegal bank speculation had checked "the true channels of commerce." Lee County Democrats complained that the bank practice of offering "discounts to a few" distributed capital inefficiently and unequally. Union County Democrats observed that state funding enabled banks to issue a dangerous excess of paper money. And Governor Carlin warned in 1840 that bank corruption created a form of "political slavery" for the people. These criticisms expressed a core Democratic Party idea: elites' manipulation of special privileges from the government distorted economic competition and imperiled democracy. To end the abuses, Democrats in the General Assembly attempted in 1840 and 1841 to kill the State Bank but failed because about 25 percent of the Democratic legislators voted with Whigs to save the bank. Pro-bank legislators likely feared liquidating a bank that owned almost $2 million of marketable state debt. In 1842, Whigs and Democrats forged a compromise whereby the banks exchanged state bonds and auditor's warrants for bank stock. By this method the state retired almost $3 million of debt, and under those conditions legislators finally closed both banks and an ugly chapter in the state's history. Yet, despite the economic carnage, Illinoisans' fundamental orientation did not change. They still wanted to make money off the land.[34]

ᔧ

Antibanking Democrats remained dedicated to creating economic opportunities for the common man. Like other Democrats, they urged unbridled national expansion and the use of federal land sales to transform communal Indian land into private property, and this desire to commodify the land and its products also inspired their eager land speculation and support of internal improvements. They had internalized the Anglo-American commitment to individual private property accumulation, and hence their antibanking diatribes denounced banks for distorting what they considered the natural patterns of commodification and accumulation. For example, Governor Thomas Carlin objected in 1839 to an "unnatural increase of paper currency" because it imparted "a fictitious value to property" and precipitated "a wild and extravagant spirit of speculation." His successor, Thomas Ford, more happily reported in 1844 that the removal of the banks' "artificial and mischievous system of currency" had restored "the natural laws of trade" and secured "the value of property and labor." These men were leading antibanking Democrats, but they opposed banks, as Ford put it, only because they were "better without them than with them."[35]

Adam Snyder exemplified the Democrats' antibanking mentality. Born impoverished, his sustained participation in the market economy made him prosperous. Then he speculated avidly to grow his capital. Yet after the Panic of 1837, in true Jacksonian fashion, he revolted against banking laws that created a privileged class of citizens, denouncing the "degrading" idea of squandering public money to bolster "a monied encorporation of private individuals." He insisted that the State Bank had dramatically expanded its note issue since receiving state monies, and he believed that "its situation is alarming *panic, or no panic.*" He relented somewhat a few months later. He then wished to establish a "healthy" circulation of paper money by gradually contracting credit, thus avoiding rapid deflation and enabling the states subsequently to undertake a "reform of banking monopolies and abuses." The economic aspect of Snyder's critique was singularly conservative. He presumed that markets operated more efficiently and fairly without excessive currency fluctuation. He wanted to abolish banks that recklessly inflated the economy, and he expected that doing so would result in a more productive market society. Although he did not fully realize it, better banking technology and effective regulation would have tempered his objections. In this respect, he differed little from most others in his party.[36]

Many Democrats recognized that sound banking promoted economic opportunity. Congressman John Reynolds insisted that Democrats supported "legitimate" banks that aided "the operations of commerce." Likewise, the Address of the Democratic Party in 1839 urged "no war upon the proper uses, but upon the abuses of banks." The address claimed that bank suspensions defrauded the public to the "*extent of depreciation*" upon bank notes. It also reprobated public financing of banks, which enabled bank stockholders to invest the capital of others. And it levied a stinging attack on the economic convulsions consequent on excessive note issue. Yet despite this, Democrats could not shake the fact that moderate issues of paper money aided the economy. Williamson County Democrats disparaged existing banks but admitted that banking could prove "useful" if corrected. Lee County Democrats wanted the State Bank replaced with a "more equal and efficient system of banking." La Salle County Democrats feared bank corruption but thought banks promoted "public convenience and prosperity." The ambivalence of Democrats did not prevent them from destroying banks that failed to mend their abusive ways. However, it predisposed them to explore future banking technologies. At root, the Democrats' commercial instincts contradicted radical antibanking policy.[37]

Chicago's growth also eventually undermined the Democrats' hostility to banking. In the early 1840s the city's need for banking was fairly moderate. However, Chicago's population grew sevenfold in the 1840s, and the city became a leading grain processor, with its exports of flour and grain sprouting from ten thousand bushels in 1840 to one million bushels in 1845 and three million bushels in 1848. The storage and shipment of grain consumed most of the city's capital. Consequent currency shortages attracted financiers to Chicago despite the state's prohibition on banking. For instance, George Smith's insurance company discounted notes, accepted deposits, and dealt in bills of exchange. Smith circulated notes worth $100,000 in 1843, $250,000 in 1845, and almost $1,500,000 in 1851. His currency spread throughout the region because he unfailingly redeemed his money in specie on demand. As Smith's success indicated, Chicago's market rendered antibanking sentiment obsolescent. Eventually, northern Democrats would ally with Whigs to relegalize banking.[38]

Nevertheless, the party's war on banks did differentiate Whigs and Democrats. It was probably the most significant factor in elevating the Democrats to unquestioned hegemony in state politics by 1842. Andrew Jackson had racked up almost 70 percent of Illinois's vote in 1828 and 1832, but the emergence of the Whig Party cut deeply into the support of his Democratic successor, Martin Van Buren, who won only 55 percent of Illinois's vote in 1836. The competition between the parties intensified over the next four years, partly because some voters blamed the Democrats for the nation's economic problems, partly because a surge of migrants into Illinois's northern counties strengthened the Whigs, and partly because the Whigs embraced democratic campaign tactics such as rallies, conventions, and voter canvassing. Hence, when running for reelection in 1840, Van Buren won only 50.9 percent of the vote in Illinois. But this was as close as the Whigs would ever get to toppling Illinois's Democratic Party. They had antagonized immigrant voters in 1839 with an attempt to disenfranchise aliens, and their uncompromising

support of the state banks after 1835, whose boards of directors they dominated, eventually exacted a fierce toll on their party. Enmity toward banks
took on epic proportions as the depression deepened, bankruptcies mounted,
and a legislative investigation exposed the bank managers' venality, greed, and
recklessness. In the 1842 elections, the Democratic gubernatorial candidate
won almost 54 percent of the vote, and Democratic candidates won more
than two-thirds of the General Assembly seats. During the rest of the decade,
the Whigs exercised negligible influence in the General Assembly, elected
congressmen only from central Illinois, and ceded southern Illinois to the
Democratic Party. For more than a decade, the Democrats would call the
shots in Illinois. They would prove incredibly eager to acquire more land.[39]

⁓

The politics of slavery largely went into remission from 1825 until the
1840s, in Illinois as in other states. This did not reflect any moderation of
attitudes toward slavery in either the South or North. To the contrary, slavery's
rapid expansion into the southwestern United States intensified Southerners'
commitment to slavery while encouraging the rise of an abolitionist movement. Nevertheless, the many Americans who feared disunion combated
such attitudes, especially in the North. They were able to do so because the
country acquired no territory that changed the balance of slave and free
states until Texas's annexation in 1845. Meanwhile, the entry of Arkansas
and Michigan into the Union in 1836 and 1837 caused relatively little furor
because slavery's status in those territories had not been in dispute. For these
reasons, most Americans focused instead on democratization and economic
development. Illinois's early history showed that these issues were bitterly
divisive when mixed with slavery, but even on their own terms they generated
heated antagonism. After all, democratization reallocated political power,
and government-subsidized economic development reallocated wealth. It is
hardly surprising, therefore, that political debate over these issues spurred the
creation of the Democratic and Whig Parties. By fostering partisan ties that
crossed sectional boundaries and promoted Unionism, the parties contributed to slavery's political subsidence. However, antislavery politics had gone
into remission only because most American voters wanted to address other
issues, most politicians desired to promote party harmony and sectional con-
cord, and neither group had to confront the thorny issue of slavery's expansion. These circumstances were not likely to persist indefinitely. After all,
slavery defined the South, profoundly shaping its economy, social relations,
and political organization, and disproportionately benefiting slaveholders,
who wielded tremendous political power and strove for slavery's expansion.[40]

Yet, in the North, partisan debate over democracy and economic development largely reinforced antislavery sentiment. At root, the debate was about how best to promote political liberty and economic opportunity in a society of free men. Northern Whigs urged collective action to promote individual and social progress, as Lincoln's 1832 campaign circular illustrated, and this ideology fostered antislavery attitudes among most northern Whigs, who considered slavery an obstacle to progress. Meanwhile, northern Democrats celebrated and sought to protect the rights of the people, and presumed that progress would work itself out as long as the people remained free to pursue their own interests, unmolested by political or economic elites. Democratic ideology thus also carried antislavery attributes, and some northern Democrats would later condemn slaveholders as they once had bankers: as grasping aristocrats who cared nothing for the rights or interests of ordinary people. To be sure, to the extent that Democrats were willing to extend rights only to whites, Democratic ideology also afforded powerful protections for slavery, and most northern Democrats over the next twenty years, following Douglas's leadership, would make the creed of racial difference the North's central bulwark against antislavery politics. But the northern Democrats' eventual division on slavery was not readily discernible in the 1830s. What was discernible was a beckoning frontier that promised economic opportunity for a new generation of American farmers. Both southern and northern Democrats equated the acquisition of that land with freedom itself and pursued it relentlessly. In so doing, they would drive a wedge that splintered Democratic Party unity—and force Americans to adjudicate slavery's future in the nation.

3. Manifest Destiny, Slavery, and the Rupture of the Democratic Party, 1843–1847

IN THE MID-1840S, Illinois Democratic Party politicians' ardent advocacy of national expansion helped rekindle the nation's battle over freedom. The state party's leaders intended no such outcome. Instead, they reflected the wishes of their constituents, who coveted new land and seconded what John O'Sullivan of the *Democratic Review* called the nation's "manifest destiny" to inhabit the continent. Indeed, flag in hand, and inspired by a spread-eagle nationalism, Illinois Democrats led the charge for new territory, confident that expansion would promote both party unity and economic opportunity on the frontier. But Americans had never really decided whether slavery traveled with the flag, and therefore national expansion reignited debate over the meaning of freedom. No national territory could be both free and slave, and thus the acquisition of new land from Mexico forced Americans once again to debate slavery's relationship to freedom. As had been the case in Illinois in the 1820s, the result was profoundly divisive. By bringing nationalism to the forefront of American politics and forcing Americans to adjudicate slavery's national standing, Manifest Destiny soon poisoned Illinois Democrats, the Democratic Party, and the country at large.

Illinoisans could hardly be blamed for looking outward, because the state's economy remained moribund during the early to mid-1840s. Money remained scarce and commodity prices low. In 1842, for instance, corn in McLean County commanded only about one-third of its 1833 price, and hogs brought little better. Low prices made trade unprofitable for many farmers and merchants, which reduced commerce and increased local bartering. But barter did not provide the cash that farmers and merchants needed to pay their bills. Widespread bankruptcies therefore remained a serious problem until the middle of the decade. A young Springfield lawyer observed that "an immense amount" of property was on the market in 1844. Five hundred dollars would purchase a "comfortable home," he wrote his parents, and "as much land as you want." Illinoisans' once halcyon dreams of economic abundance, spurred by railroad and canal, increasingly seemed a mirage.[1]

Chicago's economy was the notable exception. Blessed by easy lake access to the New York market, and strong backing from New York financiers, Chicago's merchants sold eastern goods at the region's lowest prices, while paying the highest prices for western produce. Farmers consequently flocked to Chicago to sell wheat and buy goods in the early 1840s. Meanwhile, Chicago's merchants also bought other grains, along with wool, pork, and beef, and established a large wholesale trade with hinterland merchants. The pork and beef trade stimulated the city's meatpacking industry, and the continuing influx of migrants into northern Illinois created a market for lumber that Chicago's merchants controlled.[2] Indeed, influenced by lake access and Chicago's market, the state's northern region attracted a swarm of settlers between 1835 and 1845, growing 596 percent, from 23,614 to 164,267 inhabitants. By contrast, southern Illinois's population grew 87 percent, from 104,156 to 194,468, while central Illinois's population increased 113 percent, from 142,409 to 303,264. The balance of political power still lay south of Chicago, but migration patterns and the city's burgeoning economy underscored Northerners' rising influence. However, the state's changing demographics did not obscure a central commonality in the early 1840s. The overwhelming predominance of agricultural interests in Illinois encouraged politicians to promote farming by enhancing settlement and trade. To achieve this end, the state's congressmen turned to Washington, D.C., for assistance.[3]

The politicians' primary objective was improving transport. The failure of the state's internal improvement measures meant that travel remained difficult. Poorly marked and frequently impassable roads delayed land transport, river obstructions crippled and sank boats, and inadequate harbor facilities impeded commercial exchange in Chicago. A typical jeremiad railed against the state's "[m]iserable roads, deep slough, execrable bridges, [and] swollen streams." These conditions inspired political action. In 1844, Chicago's Democratic congressman, John Wentworth, requested a land grant to complete the Illinois-Michigan Canal. He also urged port-of-entry status for Chicago and introduced the first of four annual rivers and harbors bills. He was particularly interested in improving the Illinois River and the Chicago harbor, but his ambitious rivers and harbors bills logrolled support from a wide array of western congressmen. Among Illinois's Democratic congressmen, Stephen A. Douglas, John McClernand, and Orlando Ficklin also advocated improvements for rivers in their districts, and every Illinois congressman advocated the extension of the national road through Illinois. These measures had firm public support. The unanimously adopted address of a major meeting in Bond County vowed to sustain "the right of the West to liberal appropriations for the benefit of her commerce," which they insisted "*can no longer be withheld*," while an eastern Illinois River improvement convention declared that such expenditures were "proper and expedient." Such attitudes conflicted with traditional party doctrine. In 1830, when vetoing the Maysville Road bill, Andrew Jackson had declared that the Constitution precluded the federal government from funding local internal improvement projects. Although not dismissive of this perspective, Illinois Democrats, like most western Democrats, considered federal assistance critical to commercial development.[4]

For this reason, Illinois's congressmen requested land grants for railroad construction. In 1844, Orlando Ficklin solicited federal grants for a railroad opening the eastern Illinois prairie to settlement, and in subsequent years Illinois's congressmen renewed Ficklin's appeal and also submitted petitions for other railroads. Senator Sidney Breese, for instance, repeatedly sought land grants for railroads connecting Springfield to Indiana and Cairo to Galena. However, such requests brought the state's congressmen in conflict with southern Democrats, who construed the Constitution strictly and denied the government's power to subsidize improvements in individual states. In response, Breese contended that railroad land grants to Illinois benefited all the states and thus met the strictest constitutional scruples. Acknowledging that the federal government would sacrifice revenue from land sales, he nevertheless contended that the settlement of Illinois's "broad and fertile plains" would amply compensate the country, and hence the government "should contribute in proportion to their interests thus to be advanced." Tempted by subsidies for commerce, many western Democrats like Breese sought to loosen the straitjacket of strict construction.[5]

Economic considerations also spurred the Illinois Democrats' support of the acquisition of Oregon and Texas. The United States had shared joint occupancy of Oregon with Great Britain since 1818, but by the early 1840s American settlers predominated there and many westerners wanted to lay claim to the whole territory. Meanwhile, Texas had been an independent republic since 1836, after its successful revolt from Mexico, and American expansionists, especially Southerners, considered it ripe for annexation. Eager to provide land for Illinois's emigrants, develop markets for Illinois's farmers, and stimulate urban growth in the Mississippi Valley, Illinois Democrats urged acquisition of both regions. In 1842, Illinois senator Samuel McRoberts urged Congress to facilitate settlement in Oregon by donating land to immigrant farmers. In subsequent years, Illinois's other congressmen prodded Congress to extend American law over Oregon. They felt protective of the stream of Illinoisans emigrating to Oregon, and they coveted Oregon's soil, fisheries, and ports for Asian trade. Moreover, they feared that existing British settlements in Oregon might preempt the United States from acquiring all of Oregon country. Democratic congressman John McClernand expressed typical sentiments when he declared that Asian countries offered "the great remedy of new markets, and a new and infinite commerce, matching the wants and energies of our great people." Texas offered similar inducements. A public meeting favoring the annexation of Texas in 1844 argued that Texas's cotton planters "will need a vast amount of provisions from the valley of the Mississippi." The address claimed that the South "is our best and largest home market for provisions," and would remain so as long as the slave economy remained robust. To be sure, most proannexation arguments emphasized the value of Texas to national rather than state commerce. However, Illinois's Democratic politicians believed with good reason that an expanding American empire served the economic interests of their constituents.[6]

To develop that empire, the party's leaders lobbied for a Pacific Railroad. In 1846 Sidney Breese submitted the first Senate report advocating construction of an intercontinental railroad. Breese argued that the road would increase land values, encourage settlement, promote manufacturing, develop western mineral resources, foster the Pacific fishing industry, and expand commerce within the United States and abroad. By claiming Asian "riches" for American acquisition, Breese expected to create a city in the Mississippi Valley that would "possess commercial advantages equal if not superior to those of any on the Atlantic seaboard." Stephen Douglas also urged a Pacific Railroad. In 1844 Douglas introduced bills to organize the Nebraska and Oregon territories. He wanted to survey the land, encourage rapid settlement, extend American law over the region, and construct the road in the wake of emigration. He anticipated capturing the "vast commerce of the Pacific ocean," stimulating "surplus produce" from the western settlers, and expanding the home market for eastern "goods and merchandize." Although Breese and Douglas dickered over details, they agreed that the Pacific Railroad deserved federal support.[7]

Illinois's Democratic congressmen couched their demands as westerners. They believed that the West held the key to the nation's future—to quiet sectional turmoil, they hoped, but certainly to wield economic and political leadership. The westward tide of population, the growth of western commerce, and the nation's seemingly unlimited future expansion all portended westerners' influence. Consequently, Illinois Democrats resented the federal government's high tariff rates, high land prices, and miserly disbursements for western commerce. As Breese complained in 1844, propositions beneficial to the West are "always met" by "certain parties with all the opposition that enmity could engender." That same year John Wentworth complained that western rivers, harbors, and highways "have been most outrageously neglected." He maintained that Congress bestowed "the richest adulations" on Atlantic sailors, yet hardly spent a penny on the "intrepid mariners" of the Lakes. Orlando Ficklin calculated that the government expended "[n]ineteen-twentieths" of its monies "east of the mountains." He considered the inequity unendurable and vowed that the "West will vindicate her rights." Indeed, past maltreatment caused westerners to suspect that the Polk administration would cede part of Oregon to Britain, and Illinois's legislators protested this possibility. John McClernand warned that westerners shared a "vital concern" for Oregon because the "relative political influence, wealth, and power" of the West hinged on Oregon's acquisition. These rhetorical appeals were built on a strong popular foundation. Editorials and conventions in Illinois incessantly invoked western interests and urged the state's representatives to obtain a just share of "Governmental liberality."[8]

To make their case, westerners relied on nationalist appeals. They contended that the interests of their region were national interests. This claim flowed from the region's geography. As Douglas observed, the Mississippi River connected westerners to the middle states and to the South, while the Great Lakes connected them to the Atlantic Coast. Thus he concluded that "members from all portions of the Union" should support western commerce. With the same logic, the *Illinois State Register*—central Illinois's leading Democratic newspaper—maintained that "every dollar" spent by Congress on western rivers unites "us together as one People—East, West, North, and South." The Oregon issue further conjoined western commercialism and nationalism. McClernand observed that the Columbia and Missouri Rivers constituted a great Pacific outlet for western trade. The acquisition of Oregon would therefore complete the "symmetry" of the country, tying the "interests" and "productions" of the Middle West to every portion of the country and securing "the *union* and *unity* of our great Republic." McClernand therefore vehemently opposed ceding territory in Oregon, arguing that a British colony on the Pacific Coast would hinder the nation's trade and jeopardize its security. Indeed, the possibility of warfare with Britain deepened westerners' conviction that the interests of the West and the nation coincided. In 1845,

Douglas urged federal construction of the Illinois-Michigan Canal in order to defend the Great Lakes from the British Navy. He argued that the canal would give American ships ingress and egress to the Gulf of Mexico, a harbor on the Chicago River, and a supply route for western coal, iron, hemp, timber, and food. To Douglas, "patriotism" justified construction of the canal, although he acknowledged that Illinoisans stood to benefit disproportionately from it.[9]

Yet the articulation of nationalist claims in a country divided by slavery and freedom had unanticipated risks. After all, nationalism requires adherents both to identify with the nation and to define its values and objectives. Where there is sufficient consensus, a nation unites; where there is not, it divides. Because nineteenth-century Americans could neither invoke nationalism without lauding freedom, nor laud freedom without dragging in slavery, nationalism soon would prove extremely divisive. Westerners made nationalist appeals without intending to precipitate conflict over slavery, but they were not the only arbiters of American nationalism, and they could not control its consequences. At root, conflicting definitions of freedom made nationalism profoundly combustible by the 1840s.[10]

Ironically, westerners' appeals aptly illustrated the difficulty of using nationalism to unify disparate interests. The rhetoric of western interests flowed from a common objection to perceived mistreatment, but westerners' economic interests actually diverged. As Illinois's circumstances demonstrated, settlement patterns and commercial arteries tended to divide as well as unite the state's population. The flow of the Ohio and Mississippi Rivers attached southern Illinois primarily to the South; the blossoming Great Lakes trade tied northern Illinois to the East; while the state's geography connected west-central Illinois strongly to both regions. The politicization of western trade thus tended to pit western congressmen against each other. The burgeoning Great Lakes trade, valued at $100 million annually by 1845, certainly had this effect. Southerners feared its amazing growth, the disproportionate benefits it lavished upon eastern cities, and the ties it forged between the East and West. They hoped to divert western commerce southward, and to this end they courted the aid of southern Illinoisans, who envied the growing riches and population of northern Illinois.[11]

Such regional rivalries caused Illinois's Democratic congressmen to split their votes on the rivers and harbors bills in 1844, 1845, and 1846. The bills were not identical, but the same pattern characterized each one. Chicago received money to improve its harbor, as did many other Great Lakes harbors. This benefit to the Lakes trade secured the support of northern Illinois's congressmen, despite Stephen A. Douglas's failure to acquire money for the Illinois River. However, Congress provided little funding for proposed river improvements in southern Illinois. The House struck the Wabash River from consideration on constitutional grounds and allotted small amounts for the lower Mississippi and Ohio Rivers. Worse yet, large appropriations for St. Louis's harbor disadvantaged Illinois's river towns. These factors led John McClernand to contend in 1844 that the bill violated propriety, justice, and equality. He protested that the harbor interests received a disproportionate share of the spoils, and he urged that river and harbor appropriations be separated, each "to stand upon their own merits." McClernand knew that Great Lakes shipping provided little aid to the southwestern river economy, and his critique exposed the regional rivalries within western commerce.[12]

The rivers and harbors bills also fomented sectional divisions. Southern Democrats claimed that the federal government had no constitutional power to subsidize internal commerce, and therefore they overwhelmingly opposed the bills from 1844 to 1847. Their opposition sprang partly from naked economic interest and partly from a fear of encroaching federal power. Southern jeremiads against the "Federalist" alliance of pro-tariff easterners and pro-improvement westerners indicated their hostility to federal policies that might establish antislavery precedents. Southern presidents John Tyler and James Polk reinforced strict constructionist doctrine by vetoing the 1845, 1846, and 1847 bills. Polk argued that the 1846 bill engendered sectional "prejudices." He maintained that spending federal money on "local" interests discriminated against states whose legislators did not "engage" in public plunder. And he observed that the recently begun war with Mexico required the nation to husband resources instead of wasting them on "unimportant objects." Polk's arguments indelicately privileged southern interests, and westerners could not help but to resent it.[13]

The failure of the rivers and harbors bills brought northern Illinois Democrats into an alliance with sympathetic easterners. Northern Illinois's leading newspaper, the *Chicago Democrat*, lambasted Polk's vetoes, despite its party loyalties, while Springfield's *Illinois State Register* stoutly defended him. Regional economic loyalties explained the divergence. The *State Register* had been the state's foremost advocate for the Memphis convention in 1845, when John C. Calhoun urged a southern-western trade alliance. Two years later, the *Democrat* promoted the Chicago River and Harbor Convention, which protested Polk's 1846 veto. The latter convention attracted at least ten thousand visitors to a city of sixteen thousand residents, asserted the constitutionality of improving rivers and harbors, and strengthened the commercial bond between easterners and westerners. After the convention, a committee composed largely of easterners issued a report ardently advocating improvements to enhance lake and river commerce. Unlike Southerners, easterners thought western commerce was vital to their prosperity. The absence of Southerners at the convention underscored the emerging union of easterners and westerners. Of roughly twenty-five hundred delegates, only fifty-one were Southerners, and forty-five of those were from Missouri. The convention also highlighted regional economic divisions within the state. Of 1,016 Illinois delegates, 958 hailed from the northern counties. Chicago resident Stephen A. Douglas, a prominent participant in Memphis, was conspicuously absent.[14]

Increasingly, these regional differences created dissension within the state Democratic Party. From 1844 to 1846, regional factions quarreled over instituting a property tax to pay for the completion of the Illinois-Michigan Canal. The rivers and harbors bills inflamed this infighting, as did proposals to resuscitate banks, and petty disputes among party leaders.[15] Regional antagonisms came to a head during the 1846 state convention, when a slate of candidates fought over the gubernatorial nomination. Delegates from the northern, central, and eastern counties eventually prevailed over the southern and western counties, but only after compromising on a man without strong factional allegiances. By championing the canal, opposing banks, and discreetly ignoring the rivers and harbors bill, the party's platform similarly reflected the party's regional divisions.[16]

The glue to the state party's platform was national expansion. The convention resolved that the recent annexation of Texas would "strengthen the bonds of the Union," while the occupation of Oregon would extend "liberal republican principles." Party leaders believed that territorial expansion united both northern and southern Illinois Democrats, and northern and southern Democrats throughout the nation. After all, as adherents of Manifest Destiny promised, national expansion opened new lands for westward migration, relieved overcrowding in eastern cities, spurred interregional trade, extended the nation's political institutions, and strengthened its continental grasp. To Illinois Democrats, Manifest Destiny seemed an elixir for the party's problems.[17]

⌇

The appeal of expansionism had led Illinois Democrats to support the nomination of Tennessean James K. Polk for president in 1844. Public pressure for annexing Texas during that year had created a dilemma for Henry Clay and Martin Van Buren, respective frontrunners for the nominations of the Whig and Democratic Parties. Each man feared that annexation would trigger sectional discord, and each feared opposing annexation alone. In April 1844 they both published letters opposing annexation, and both soon learned that expansionism could not be so easily shunted aside. Illinois Democrats immediately distanced themselves from Van Buren. The *Illinois State Register* and the *Quincy Herald* issued dissenting editorials, and several Democratic meetings resolved to annex Texas. Abraham Lincoln reported from Springfield that "[n]early half" of the state's Democratic leaders were vowing to overthrow Van Buren at the national convention in Baltimore. Illinois's delegates did so by voting unanimously at Baltimore to adopt the two-thirds rule, as did the Indiana and Michigan delegations. The rule required Van Buren to secure the votes of two-thirds rather than a simple majority of the delegates. But it also turned the Van Burenites against Michigan's Lewis Cass, enabling James K. Polk to prevail. Although a southwestern strict constructionist, Polk secured the votes of western Democrats because he desired to annex Texas and appeared willing to sustain American claims to Oregon. Van Burenites retrospectively dubbed Polk's nomination the first step in the southern hijacking of the Democratic Party, and after further provocation many of them jumped ship and helped to form the Free Soil Party in 1848. Their hostility to southern expansionists was not unjustified, but it did obscure the crucial votes provided by western Democrats eager for Van Buren's defeat.[18]

Support for the acquisition of both Oregon and Texas ran deep in Illinois. Agitation for Oregon started in 1842 and continued throughout 1843. At the behest of the state legislature, Illinois's congressmen in 1844 urged the federal government to assert sovereignty over Oregon by terminating a treaty of joint occupancy with Britain. However, Whigs and southern Democrats hesitated to antagonize Britain, and they defeated the Oregon resolution. The frustration of Illinois and many other western Democrats only escalated later that year, when Whig senators defeated a treaty to annex Texas. But these setbacks did allow Illinois Democrats to turn the 1844 elections into a referendum on expansion, which party leaders knew would work as a trump card in Illinois. The "Oregon question is becoming more and more exciting in this State," one southern Illinois Democrat reported to Senator Sidney Breese, and opposition to Oregon's occupation "is exciting a deep and indignant feeling." But he called the "passion" for Texas even "more exciting and more absorbing," and he promised Breese that a "strike for Texas" would "do you credit which will astonish you." This was sound advice.[19]

Illinois Democrats rode the wave of public support for expansion to a huge victory in the 1844 elections. They accumulated 54 percent of the presidential vote and won seventy-one of the state's ninety-nine counties. Only portions of central and northwestern Illinois exhibited Whig strength. Democrats triumphed in six of the seven congressional districts, with expansionists like Wentworth, McClernand, Douglas, Ficklin, and Joseph Hoge rolling to victory. But the unity the party achieved flowed from the presumption that the party cherished Oregon and Texas equally. Polk had stated his opposition to a British colony in Oregon, and party leaders like Douglas crowed that "Oregon and Texas" are "inscribed upon our banner." The Baltimore convention had recommended the occupation of Oregon and the annexation of Texas "at the earliest practicable period," and had resolved that the nation should cede "no portion" of Oregon to Britain. Polk encouraged these expectations with his bold inaugural statement that the nation's title to Oregon was "clear and unquestionable." He left no doubt that he would brook no compromise with Britain.[20]

But not only did Polk brook compromise, he brokered it. He probably intended to broker it from the start. His inaugural statement helped bluff the British into compromising. Not eager for a war with Britain, and not shy of one with Mexico, Polk chose to placate the greater power. He knew that America had little to gain by occupying all of Oregon. The nation needed Puget Sound's harbors at 49° because the forbidding Pacific Coast left no other alternatives on Oregon's shore. By contrast, the region's agricultural land north of 49° possessed comparatively little value for the United States, and therefore it was trade bait for negotiation. Given this reality, Polk maneuvered Britain into recognizing American rights at 49° by threatening war for 54°40'. Britain denied that American sovereignty extended north of 46°, but Polk gambled successfully that Britain would not risk war to maintain a somewhat dubious claim. After lengthy and convoluted negotiations, Polk secured the harbors in a treaty that the Senate ratified in June 1846. Outraged northwestern congressmen were powerless to prevent it.[21]

Compromise with Britain permitted Polk to deal harshly with Mexico. In 1845, President John Tyler had pushed through the annexation of Texas despite strenuous Whig opposition. The Whigs had feared precipitating war with a Mexican government that had never recognized Texas's independence, and Texas's border dispute with Mexico heightened their concerns. By maintaining that the Rio Grande rather than the Nueces River formed its southern boundary, Texas claimed a substantial strip of Mexico. The problem could have been peacefully adjudicated. However, the president militantly sustained Texas after Mexico refused to receive an American minister authorized to purchase the disputed land. Polk ordered the U.S. Army to the Rio Grande, virtually inviting a skirmish with Mexican troops. It occurred in April 1846, and Polk immediately pressured Congress to declare war with the misleading claim that Mexicans had "shed American blood upon American soil." His brinksmanship paid huge dividends. Cowed by the fear of being branded traitors, the Whigs acquiesced in the war bill without investigating the origins of the skirmish, which flowed primarily from Polk's desire for territorial concessions in New Mexico and California. Illinois's Democrats overwhelmingly supported the war, but resentment against Polk's betrayal of Oregon persisted among northwesterners.[22]

The contrast between Polk's actions on Oregon and Mexico aggravated regional divisions in Illinois's Democratic Party. To be sure, Illinoisans ardently supported the war. The state boasted the highest enlistment rate of any free state and filled its quota of men so quickly that a majority of the volunteers had to be turned away. Yet regional antagonisms rooted in the Oregon treaty bubbled beneath the surface. Prior to the war, Illinois's congressmen had argued in vain against a temporizing policy with Britain. Therefore, like other westerners, they felt betrayed by southern Democrats, whose interest in Oregon dwindled after the annexation of Texas in 1845. As John McClernand put it, westerners had suffered the "desolation of desertion." Yet McClernand, Douglas, and Ficklin sought to quiet their anger and preserve party unity. Douglas stated that he "never questioned" the patriotism of southern Democrats, who he knew would "rally" to the "country's standard" rather than permit "divided counsels" during a war. But other Illinoisans were neither so trusting nor so forgiving.[23]

Blaming slavery for the betrayal, two prominent Illinois congressmen arraigned the South. Chicago's John Wentworth, who represented a region with a growing population of abolitionists, criticized Southerners for reneging on Oregon once they had used northern Democratic votes to acquire Texas. He complained that such rough usage furnished arguments to "northern abolitionists" by making northern Democrats appear to be southern tools. His words echoed in the speech of Edward Baker, an expansionist Whig from central Illinois, who charged that southern Democrats abandoned Oregon because they feared that a war with Britain would "affect their 'peculiar institutions,'" and hence they had proved more eager to extend "the area of freedom" southward than northward. The politics of slavery thus united a leading northern Illinois Democrat with a prominent Illinois Whig.[24]

The nation's prospect of acquiring Mexican land deepened this emerging affinity. In August 1846, in an amendment to a funding bill, Pennsylvania's Democratic congressman David Wilmot proposed that slavery should be prohibited in any land acquired from Mexico. Wilmot's proviso did not pass, but it was reintroduced in 1847, when it failed again. The proviso revealed a growing regional split in the state. Northern Illinois's Democratic congressmen allied with Whigs against slavery, while their southern Illinois counterparts allied with the South. In the 1846 vote, four Illinois Democrats voted against the proviso, Chicago's Wentworth voted for it, and two congressmen abstained. In 1847, Illinois's three northernmost congressmen favored the

proviso, including Whig John Henry, while the four southernmost congressmen opposed it. This outcome corresponded to the results in the Illinois
legislature, which in 1847 voted against instructing the states' congressmen
to support the proviso. Only central Illinoisans were ambivalent. Abstentions
among legislators from the central counties revealed that they—unlike politicians from northern and southern Illinois—were reluctant to take a stand.
Their constituents hailed from both sections of the Union and possessed
conflicting views of slavery. In 1847 the anti-proviso forces still held sway
in Illinois. But the rapidly growing population of northern Illinois rendered
their status insecure.[25]

John Wentworth expressed the growing antisouthernism of northern Illinois Democrats. He had worried in 1844 that Southerners would abandon
Oregon, and subsequent sessions of Congress convinced him of their hostility
to northern and western interests. In 1846 Southerners opposed the rivers
and harbors bill while using western votes to reduce the tariff, and in 1847
Southerners defeated a bill to organize Oregon Territory because it contained
an objectionable antislavery provision. Wentworth's frustration boiled over
when Treasury Secretary Robert Walker proposed raising revenue for the
war by placing a 25 percent ad valorem tax on tea and coffee, which would
raise consumers' costs for those items by 25 percent. Wentworth considered
the tax another southern betrayal. In 1846 Southerners had agreed to leave
tea and coffee untaxed in order obtain northern support for the lower tariff;
now, with their tariff secure, the backstabbing began. It was "part and parcel of
the same system of legerdemain!" he cried, "a game of plunder of the North!"
But he did not stop there. For the first time, Wentworth blamed slavery for
the sins of Southern politicians.[26]

Wentworth contended that slavery threatened to destroy the northern
Democracy. He observed that Democrats since 1832 had forbidden taxation
on tea and coffee, which were consumed "hourly" by the northern poor.
Slaves did not drink tea or coffee, and Wentworth resented southern advocacy
of a bill that discriminated against "free labor." Moreover, he considered the
tax a repudiation of the Democrats' progressive tax philosophy. "I will not
vote," he said, "to tax the poor as much as the rich." His concern for free labor
led him to predict that Northerners who opposed the beverage tax would
support the Wilmot Proviso. "The poor white man's friend will always oppose
slavery," he declared, because free labor cannot afford to work for the "wages"
of a slave. Nevertheless, he expected some northern Democrats to betray
their constituents by shutting free labor "out of the Californias forever," and
he feared that their success would annihilate the northern wing of the party.
Therefore he vowed to "proclaim the alarm to the North," to sustain the "real

democracy," and to preserve "[f]ree tea and free coffee . . . and free territory." Wentworth's freesoilism doubtless revolted southern Democrats. He grafted antislavery principles to the party's equalitarian creed and virtually declared that the party should represent the white laboring class rather than slaves or their masters. For Illinois Democrats, and Democrats throughout the nation, these doctrines imperiled party unity.[27]

The seeds of this division had been sown unwittingly by the nationalistic professions of Democratic Party advocates of Manifest Destiny. Their central object had been to facilitate economic opportunity and market capitalism by acquiring new land for farms. Land acquisition had long been a Democratic Party priority, and Illinois Democrats throughout the 1840s petitioned the government to promote western settlement by reducing land prices. In keeping with this tradition, the *Illinois State Register* crowed that the acquisition of Texas will open "a more ample field of enterprise for our people." The Democrats' ambivalence about the proliferation of dependent wage laborers in factories reinforced their efforts to acquire western land. The *State Register* lamented the fate of farmers in New England, who were "driven to the factories and cotton mills for employment" and were paid "the lowest wages that will sustain animal life." Yet the Democrats' ambivalence toward wage labor did not inhibit their celebration of industrialism's products, such as railroads, steamboats, and telegraphs. Indeed, their pride in America's material progress justified their advocacy of expansion. By settling the West, they expected to stretch railroads to the Pacific, cultivate Pacific and Asian commerce, and spread civilization. Moreover, they claimed that eastern industry would benefit from the nation's new markets, and they expected that Illinois would benefit by facilitating trade between the East and far West.[28]

They also maintained—in the teeth of Whig opposition—that expansion would strengthen the nation. From 1844 to 1848, Whigs warned that territorial growth would weaken American nationality by dispersing the population, exacerbating regional divisions, and inciting conflict over slavery. Breese, Douglas, McClernand, and congressman Thomas Turner rebutted these charges. Breese and Douglas argued that steam power united the states by collapsing time and distance, enabling virtually unlimited expansion, while McClernand asserted that the nation's rivers created an "intimate relationship" among America's states, linking the people of the Mississippi Valley to both oceans and thus demonstrating Oregon's importance to the "symmetry and completeness of our Union." Contending that prior expansion had yielded incalculable national benefits, the Democrats challenged Whigs to prove how circumstances had changed. Congressman Thomas Turner avowed that westward migration ensured the "progress of civilization," and moreover he predicted that "the conservative power" of the West would check sectional antagonisms over slavery. And, in chorus with Breese, Douglas insisted that state sovereignty made the American confederacy especially well fitted to expansion, "avoiding those dissensions which have proved the destruction of former republics." To Democrats, America's progress flowed from the commercial and political benefits of relentless territorial growth.[29]

They also expected American expansion to spread civil and religious liberty throughout the globe. Wentworth declared that God intended the original states to be "the great centre from which civilization, religion, and liberty should radiate and radiate," and Douglas asserted that "North America has been set a part as a nursery for the culture of republican principles." Sharing these sentiments, another Democrat gushed that the "history of this Country is to work out the amelioration of human kind by opening a new world to the oppressed." This understanding of the nation's destiny convinced many Democrats of the nation's duty to annex California, Canada, Cuba, Texas, and Mexico in order to enlarge what they called "the area of freedom." After all, increased trade and wealth, and concomitant cultural improvements, seemed to follow irresistibly from private-property rights and individual enterprise. Thomas Turner justified expansion by comparing the progress of western cities, villages, schools, churches, farms, commerce, and manufacturing to the "wigwam and the whoop" of displaced Indians. Similarly, McClernand lionized the "[g]lorious people" in whose wake "cities have sprung up, fields have blossomed, and innumerable swarms of people have penetrated the forest and overspread the prairies." Political freedom and economic abundance flowed from American institutions and culture.[30]

Yet the Democrats' spread-eagle nationalism also incorporated slavery. In large measure this flowed from their Anglophobia. Illinois's Democratic congressmen repeatedly expressed concern that Britain sought to encircle the North American continent and limit American growth. In 1844, for instance, Senator Breese warned that Texas would form "alliances" with Britain if the United States spurned annexation, creating a hostile power on America's southwestern border. Northern Democratic nationalists like Breese did not actually advocate slavery's expansion. However, they supported the annexation of slave territory in Texas partly because they feared that British abolitionists—who in 1833 had successfully lobbied for a parliamentary law that abolished slavery throughout the British Empire—posed a serious threat to southern slavery, and thus to the nation. The same nationalist considerations impelled them to support the demand for "All Mexico" during the war, and for the purchase of Cuba whenever possible. They did not necessarily consider their support for expansion to be proslavery, even though territorial acquisitions strengthened slavery and southern political power. As Stephen A. Douglas claimed in 1850, northern Democrats annexed Texas upon the "broad national grounds" of commercial and territorial expansion, political power, national security, and glory. To him, these nationalist considerations were "totally disconnected" from slavery.[31]

However, for some northern Democrats, genuine sympathy for slavery lay behind this configuration of American nationalism. This was evident among southern and central Illinois Democrats, whose representatives tended to defend southern institutions. Orlando Ficklin, for example, disdained the antislavery agitation that slowed the annexation of Texas. He believed that free blacks were "more degraded, more addicted to crime, more stinted for food and raiment, and more miserable" than slaves. Sharing this perspective, a southern Illinois state senator excoriated abolitionists for violating the "laws of God and man," and the *Illinois State Register* declared that American slavery was "mild and merciful" compared with British industrial labor. Even these Democrats probably preferred freedom to prevail in the territories, but their tolerance for slavery and bellicose nationalism tempered their freesoilism.[32]

But many other northern Democrats could not so easily marry American nationalism to slavery. In 1847, South Carolina congressman Armistead Burt proposed an amendment that prohibited slavery in Oregon because the territory lay north of 36° 30'. Burt's extension of the Missouri Compromise line to the Pacific sought to undercut the Wilmot Proviso by establishing a precedent that would effectively reserve land taken from Mexico for the South. Burt's proposal presented a dilemma for northern Democrats who wished to conciliate southern congressmen but did not wish to promote slavery. The extent of the dilemma was made painfully clear by southern Illinois's John McClernand, who opposed the measure for contradictory reasons. His primary objection was that it promoted sectional conflict by agitating the territorial issue. He opposed "any and every agitation of the question of slavery" from the North or the South, preferring national harmony to a mad and reckless rush "upon the rocks and reefs of strife and danger." Hence he was hardly an unyielding opponent of slavery's expansion. Instead, he promised to negotiate the vexing issue of slavery's expansion, once the country had acquired new territory, in the "spirit of fairness and justice—in the spirit of the compromises of the Constitution itself." Nevertheless, he also opposed Burt's amendment on freesoil grounds. He claimed that it gave the bounty of the war with Mexico and perhaps "all future wars on this continent" to the southern states, and he objected that it would "hedge" the Northwest between southern and British empires. Then, in a cogent repudiation of southern arguments, he boldly avowed the federal government's power to prohibit slavery in the territories. The incongruence of McClernand's position reflected the northern Democrats' incongruous position between slavery and freedom. As was the case with many northern Democrats, McClernand's freesoil preferences warred with his partisan and nationalist obligations to slavery. Although he was generally tolerant of slavery, other Illinois Democrats felt no obligation to incorporate slavery into American nationalism. Emphasizing the freesoil attributes of Jacksonian ideology, they began to develop a radical critique of slavery.[33]

In the abstract, Jacksonian principles contravened slavery. Reiterating the party's egalitarian creed, the 1841 Illinois state convention address declared that the party established "its basis on the Declaration of Independence." All men were created equal, endowed with rights to life, liberty, and property, and possessed the capacity for self-government. Reasoning from these principles, the convention delegates maintained that political power is "derived from the people," and that "personal rights and not property should be the paramount object of government." Illinois Democrats clung to these ideals in the 1840s even though they knew that slavery contradicted their creed. Inevitably, their defense of slavery clashed with their ideals. For instance, abolitionists' petitions to repeal the state's black laws spurred a surprising comment from Democrat Peter Lott in 1845. Lott believed that "the day would arrive when the whites and blacks of this State would stand on the same *political* footing," but he thought that Illinois should maintain its "conservative position" until contiguous slave states adopted emancipation. Lott's anticipation of eventual abolition and black rights deviated sharply from prevailing views in the southern states. In effect, he coupled emancipation with American nationalism, and implied the superiority of free society.[34]

Illinois Democrats generally shared Lott's preference for freedom, even if they rarely expressed antislavery sentiment. Prior to Illinois's 1847 constitutional convention, southern Illinois's *Belleville Advocate* insisted that every candidate should publicly recognize that "All men are born free and equal." Although the paper abhorred antislavery politics, the editor insisted that "hereditary and involuntary slavery must not be recognized in our Constitution." Sidney Breese carefully picked his way through this minefield during the Texas annexation debates, contending that slavery's migration into Texas would eventually enable blacks to achieve "unqualified emancipation" in Central or South America. Just like Lott, he expected slavery's "total extinction, in the progress of time." Yet his claim that the annexation of Texas would promote emancipation highlighted the latent antagonism between Democratic principles and slavery. Northern Democrats suffered the unwelcome burden of defending slavery without renouncing antislavery ideals. The possibility of slavery's expansion made this problem particularly acute. For the most part, northern Democrats justified slavery where it existed in good conscience, but they were deeply ambivalent about its expansion.[35]

For some Illinois Democrats, southern hostility to western interests turned ambivalence toward slavery into an antislavery nationalism. John Wentworth epitomized this transformation. In 1845 he voted eagerly for the annexation of Texas, hoping that its admission would quell abolitionist sentiment. Like other Illinois Democrats, he paid little heed to slavery amid nationalist fervor. But the Oregon compromise, the rivers and harbors vetoes, the proposed tea and coffee tax, and Polk's suggestion that the Great Lakes cities finance their own harbors altered his outlook. He began to perceive Southerners as antinational. Rather than subordinating local considerations for the greater good, as had westerners, Southerners dragooned the government into serving slavery. Wentworth resented southern control of leading governmental and party posts, and in 1847 he charged that the "slave-power" aggressively sought to open the West to slavery. His prior conflation of western and national interests strengthened his conviction that southern antiwesternism reflected a lack of nationality, although ironically he began presenting himself and his constituents as Northerners in response to perceived southern sectionalism. He predicted that antislavery sentiment will grow "until every portion of the Union gets its deserved share of the protection and the privileges of this Government," and he insisted that Southerners keep "Hands off!" to "all territory now free." Moreover, he feared proslavery treachery. He described southern political pledges as the "kiss of Judas" and warned Southerners that opening Mexican territory to slavery would enrage "millions of wronged freemen." Just as Wentworth had previously associated western and national interests, now he elided the North and the nation. He demanded a nation whose principles, territories, and labor remained free.[36]

Divergent attitudes about slavery's relationship to the nation led Illinois Democrats to adopt contrasting territorial policies. Northern Illinois Democrats, who wished to preserve the Mexican territories for free labor, generally supported the Wilmot Proviso, which enlisted the national government in the service of the North by mandating congressional prohibition of territorial slavery. Central and southern Illinoisans preferred a doctrine more in accord with their ambivalent view of slavery, and what came to be known as popular sovereignty proved an ideal fit for them. Historically, popular sovereignty had been a proslavery policy. It had enabled Southerners to spread slavery in southern territories prior to 1820, including into Missouri, and in the 1820s Illinois's proslavery partisans had used it to justify slavery's legalization. In the ensuing two decades, however, northern whites largely ceased debating whether they should enslave blacks. But the underlying idea of popular sovereignty never disappeared. In 1844, a correspondent of John McClernand urged him to vote for the annexation of Texas, "leaving it to the people of the territory afterward to adopt such form of government as may suit their condition and circumstances." The idea reemerged forcefully in 1847, when Democratic presidential hopeful Lewis Cass of Michigan promulgated popular sovereignty as an alternative to the Wilmot Proviso. It held out the prospect of resolving the northern Democratic Party's central dilemma. Although not overtly antislavery, it appeared likely to produce free states if northern settlers predominated in national territories. At the very least, free white men would have the opportunity to establish freedom in the territories. For this reason, popular sovereignty would prove an attractive policy for Illinoisans who preferred freedom but tolerated slavery. But Cass's hopes notwithstanding, the idea ultimately accentuated the growing rift among northern Democrats. In northern Illinois, Democrats did not think that slavery had an equal claim on national territories, and they had little interest in embracing an old proslavery policy. They were not alone in the northern states.[37]

⤺

By 1847 the politics of Manifest Destiny had begun to poison the Democratic Party in the North. The toxins concentrated most heavily in New York, where the 1844 defeat of Martin Van Buren still rankled the "Bucktail" faction that Van Buren controlled. Outraged by the nomination of Lewis Cass on a popular sovereignty platform in 1848, the Bucktails would defect from the party and denounce slavery. They quickly allied with abolitionists and antislavery Whigs to form the Free Soil Party, which nominated Van Buren for the presidency on a Wilmot Proviso platform. To some extent, the Free Soil Party commenced a struggle over northern Democratic ideals. But mostly it commenced a struggle over the meaning of freedom in the nation. In that contest, many northern Illinois Democrats, antislavery Whigs, and abolitionists would find common ground.

4. Advocates for an Antislavery Nation, 1837–1848

THE FREE SOIL PARTY of 1848 sought to defend not only Northerners, but also the nation, from slavery. Its emergence marked a critical evolution in antislavery politics. For the first time, a relatively large and diverse group of Northerners mobilized politically to demand slavery's subordination to freedom. Yet precisely because the party had a broad popular base, the path to its creation was far from straightforward. Its origins lay primarily with abolitionists, who developed the concept of an antislavery nation in the preceding decade. However, its appeal flowed from persistent conflicts between slavery and freedom in Illinois over fugitive slaves, the kidnapping of free blacks, the right of whites to speak against slavery, and slavery's legal standing in the state, all of which forced Illinoisans to come to grips with the meaning of freedom. By the end of the 1840s, following precedents elsewhere in the North, a series of court decisions dedicated the state entirely to freedom. The idea behind those decisions—that slavery could exist only where local laws legalized it, such as in southern states—deeply shaped the Free Soil Party platform, which declared that federal law also owed singular allegiance to freedom. The Free Soil Party did not carry the state in 1848, but its alliance of abolitionists, antislavery Whigs, and northern Illinois Democrats in a nationalist defense of freedom posed a tremendous threat not only to slaveholders but also to northern Democratic defenders of the Union. To combat the idea of an antislavery nation, Democrats had little choice but to challenge the emerging northern understanding of freedom.

⁓

The abolitionist movement, which took root in Illinois during the mid-1830s, laid the ideological foundation for the Free Soil Party. Antislavery sentiment had percolated in the state since the 1824 convention battle, exhibited especially in sporadic attempts to organize a society for the colonization of blacks in Africa. However, abolitionism largely resulted from new immigrant streams to the state. Southern abolitionists migrated to Illinois in the early 1830s in response to growing persecution at home, and joining them were New England Yankees, who soon began to pour into central and northern Illinois. The New Englanders reproduced their institutions in Illinois as they previously had in Ohio, New York, and Vermont, bringing ministers and moral reform along with horses and plows. In this they were aided by the American Home Missionary Society, which funneled Congregational and Presbyterian ministers into central and northern Illinois. By the mid-1830s, the state's new immigrants had established a handful of antislavery communities led by ministers.[1]

Illinois's predominantly southern population did not welcome abolitionists. Their kin networks, cultural convictions, and economic interests ranged them in sharp opposition. As abolitionist minister Albert Hale put it, every "prospect of the final triumph of anti slavery principles makes them feel as did the chief priests under the first proclamation of the gospel, when they cried out—'you intend to bring that man's blood upon us.'" Hale did not exaggerate. Anti-abolitionists detested both the doctrine of racial equality, which was propounded by abolitionists and portended far-reaching changes in American society, and the abolitionists' intention of purifying the nation from the sin of slavery, which raised the specter of disunion. In 1837 abolitionists embroiled Congress in fiery debates by submitting antislavery petitions Southerners abhorred, and Illinois's slaveholding Democrat Adam Snyder tersely predicted that disunionism "will in my opinion be the result." Southerners' hostility to abolitionism ensured that it generated deep antagonisms not only in Congress but also in the northern states.[2]

From the abolitionists' perspective, conflict between slavery and freedom compelled them to act. In Illinois, the kidnapping of free and indentured blacks, who were hustled to southern states for sale, provided one stimulant. This brutal practice had been common since 1822, and southern Illinoisans largely sanctioned it. But the new antislavery settlers decried it. Their confrontations with kidnappers enlarged their compassion for blacks, hardened their antislavery attitudes, and emboldened some of them to begin assisting fugitive slaves. Yet their actions angered slavery's northern defenders, and the abolitionists themselves soon became targets of obloquy and violence, none more so than Alton's Elijah P. Lovejoy, an abolitionist minister and newspaper editor who had been driven from St. Louis to Alton because of his antislavery views. But Alton's residents—led by some of its leading citizens—strove to silence him as well, destroying three of his printing presses before mobbing and murdering him on November 7, 1837, shortly after he had organized the Illinois State Anti-Slavery Society. Lovejoy's murder proved a galvanic stimulant to abolitionism in Illinois and throughout the nation. His newspaper had more than twenty-one hundred subscribers in 1837, most of them sympathetic to the antislavery editorials flowing from his pen, as were the ministers who bulked large among his Illinois press agents, and his death spurred them and newfound sympathizers into action. Illinois abolitionists formed nineteen antislavery societies from 1838 to 1839 and countless more in the succeeding four years.[3]

The religious orientation of Illinois's abolitionists led them to promote the idea of an antislavery nation from the start. They perceived total congruence between the laws of God and the Declaration of Independence and thus advocated a divorce of the national government from slavery. Despite acknowledging that the Constitution sanctioned slavery in the states, they wanted the law of freedom to prevail wherever the federal government had jurisdiction, especially in Washington, D.C., and the national territories. For this reason, they turned fairly easily from organizing antislavery societies to establishing an abolitionist political party.[4]

In the early 1840s, in keeping with the broader politicization of American evangelicals, Illinois abolitionists shifted from moral suasion to antislavery politics. Owen Lovejoy, who had pledged his life against slavery while kneeling "alone with the dead and with God" alongside his brother's bleeding but lifeless body, preached that "we should carry our religion to the polls" to ameliorate slaves' suffering in Christ's name. Taking up this solemn duty was the Illinois Liberty Party, an offshoot of the national party established by eastern abolitionists in 1840. Illinois's Liberty Party received a few scattered votes that year but began organizing earnestly in 1842, when the state party platform demanded repeal of the state's black laws and urged the federal government to use its constitutional power to extirpate slavery "throughout the Union." To propagate these doctrines, the party hired abolitionist editor Zebina Eastman to establish the *Western Citizen* in Chicago. With his aid, the Liberty Party grew rapidly. In 1844, delegates to the state convention resolved that abolitionists must vote the Liberty ticket, and by 1846 twenty-seven counties regularly nominated Liberty candidates for district, county, and town offices. This organizing paid appreciable dividends. From 1840 to 1846 the party's statewide vote total rose from 160 to 5,154. The latter figure constituted 5.11 percent of votes cast, most of which were concentrated in the state's northern counties. Abolitionism was neither mainstream nor fully respectable by 1846, but it commanded a growing following among northern Illinoisans.[5]

By mid-decade, abolitionist ideas circulated widely in central and northern Illinois. The *Western Citizen* in 1846 had a regular circulation of more than two thousand subscribers and a campaign circulation of thirty-seven hundred subscribers. The party also sponsored lectures by its leading orators, such as Owen Lovejoy, who spoke to audiences as large as five thousand people. To drive the abolitionist message home, former slaves testified to the evils of slavery and free blacks recounted the horrors of kidnapping. Meanwhile, antislavery societies circulated thousands of petitions among Illinoisans. Mailed to Springfield and Washington, D.C., the petitions urged repeal of Illinois's black laws and severance of the federal government from slavery. The abolitionists expected civil rights to elevate free blacks, weaken prejudice, and thus undermine slavery. The voluminous number of petitions amazed one state legislator, who complained in 1845 that "abolition petitions are referred every day." Forced to respond to "this Vexd Question," the legislator knew that abolitionist ideas had found a wide hearing.[6]

The demand for the immediate abolition of slavery was one of the characteristic aspects of abolitionist thought. By this, abolitionists meant that they wanted the work of emancipation begun immediately, even though they did not expect the instantaneous freeing of two million slaves. In this regard, abolitionists differed from their gradualist forebears, who lamented slavery's violation of inalienable rights, but who expected a more measured transition to freedom. Gradualists primarily used political and legal means to chip away at slavery, sending petitions to government officials and representing blacks in court. The abolitionists denounced gradualism because they believed that any toleration of slavery postponed, if not denied, the moral accountability of man to God. Moral accountability not only rendered individuals accountable for their sins, but also entrusted Christians with a collective responsibility for reforming sinners. Abolitionists thus infused the nation's creed of inalienable human rights with what one historian called the "government of God." This conjunction of Protestant morality and natural rights informed the abolitionist belief that slaveholders, and the nation, should immediately renounce slavery.[7]

The abolitionists' commitment to freedom was also central to their idea of progress. After all, many abolitionists believed that eradicating sin in society would bring on Christ's millennium. But achieving that august end required restructuring society so that all individuals could reach their fullest potential.

As Illinois abolitionist Edward Beecher put it, God established "individual inalienable rights" not only as the "basis of all religion" but also in accordance with the "laws of the mind and the dictates of political economy." Accordingly, he urged Southerners to elevate blacks "as fast as possible, as free laborers, in the scale of intelligence and religion." Whereas slavery warred upon both the moral and economic uplift of blacks, freedom permitted competitive public striving among men while sanctifying women's private moral realm. In the sanctuary of the home, parents raised children to be morally accountable by nurturing their conscience. By contrast, Elijah Lovejoy inveighed, slavery "degraded" a man into "a brute" by prohibiting him from "reading the gospel," educating his children in "the principles of morality and religion," and acting as a "free moral agent." The idea of moral accountability thus forged an indissoluble connection between individualism, progress, and antislavery in abolitionist social thought. Imagining social progress advancing steadily through individual uplift, abolitionists could not but condemn slavery, which contradicted every prospect of moral and economic growth. Hence the nation's duty to promote freedom.[8]

Indeed, abolitionists conflated God's will and national ideals. Although some eastern abolitionists, such as William Lloyd Garrison, considered the Constitution a proslavery document, Illinois abolitionists contended that the Declaration of Independence expressed God's antislavery principles. Edward Beecher wrote that God intended individual rights to renovate the world, and that the "irresistible course" of God's providence was taking shape in the United States. Beecher conceded that slavery had intruded during "the very foundation of our nation," but he maintained that the "Spirit of God" now demanded national emancipation. The state's abolitionists concurred with Beecher. Zebina Eastman juxtaposed the Declaration of Independence and the commandment to love thy neighbor under the masthead of the *Western Citizen*, which declared "THE SUPREMACY OF GOD AND THE EQUALITY OF MAN." Such convictions soon led Illinois abolitionists to criticize southern power over the federal government. In 1836, rumors about the annexation of Texas led the pioneering abolitionist editor Benjamin Lundy to urge Northerners to resist the "domineering tyrants of the South." In 1838 he carried these ideas with him to Illinois, where he and other abolitionists regularly denounced what they termed the Slave Power. The abolitionists' veneration for American ideals eventually would help them to enlist northern whites in the antislavery cause. Their most likely converts were northern Whigs.[9]

Like abolitionists, Whigs also conjoined individualism and progress, but their devotion to the Union and expectation of slavery's demise distinctly tempered their antislavery politics. Unwilling to risk the nation, they harbored a powerful, but latent, antislavery sentiment. Nevertheless, their opposition to slavery was rooted in American nationalism. In their view, Americans' rights to liberty and property heralded a world order in which human energy unleashed moral and material progress. Springfield Whig James Conkling attributed the nation's exceptional progress to the "fearless intrepidity" that "nerves the American breast & a deep spirit of investigation" that "inflames the American mind." Individual uplift thus produced social progress. Yet Whigs did fear that liberty might descend into licentiousness and progress into anarchy. As the *Illinois Journal* pointed out, the danger of "anarchy and ruin" in a free government could only be averted "in proportion to the moral power which a people exercise over their own passions." The excesses of the French Revolution, not to mention despotism around the globe, persuaded Whigs that self-government required the masses to elevate their intellectual and moral faculties. A self-governing people needed knowledge and determination to assert their liberty, and discipline and virtue to preserve it. Whigs thus aspired to rational liberty, whereby individuals adopted moral precepts, pursued education, mastered their passions, and promoted the public good. In contrast to a licentious liberty, rational liberty ensured social order. In support of this goal, Whigs championed institutions that facilitated self-improvement, including schools, churches, asylums, prisons, libraries, lyceums, and the home. As Illinois Whig legislator Orville Hickman Browning declared, education "is a contest in fact, between poor houses, jails and penitentiaries on the one hand, and moral and intellectual culture on the other." The Whigs' aversion to intemperance and support for evangelical reform followed from the same conviction: social progress flowed from the moral and economic uplift of individuals.[10]

The idealization of rational liberty pitted northern Whigs against caste. They presumed that all men had the capacity for self-elevation. James Conkling declared that education in Africa was "startling" Africans "from the long and profound slumber of ignorance & barbarism." He predicted that both Africans and Chinese soon would enjoy freedom, peace, and independence. Conkling also decried the liquor trade with Indians, which "robbed them of their reason" and "deprived them of their lands." Like Conkling, the *Weekly North-Western Gazette* had great faith in the transformative power of the mind, copying an extract on education from New Jersey's Episcopal Bishop George Washington Doane, a leading Christian educator, who asserted that the mind bore "no mark of high or low, of rich or poor," and heeded "no bounds of time or place, of rank or circumstance." It was precisely this logic that led Whigs to insist that caste divisions were unjust. "No procrustean bed can here be established," contended the *North Western Gazette and Galena Advertiser*, "where men will extend themselves, generation after generation, to be drawn out or cut off to the same length and measure." Society was best served when incompetence relegated some men to obscurity while genius brought others to greatness; under such circumstances, enterprise, morality, and creativity thrived. In contrast, caste destroyed initiative and individual responsibility, creating a society of slackers, hedonists, and revolutionaries. Such conditions made progress impossible. Only a fluid social order spurred enterprise and ensured social stability.[11]

This individualistic ideal led Illinois Whigs, like northern Whigs generally, to condemn slavery as a profound impediment to social progress. In his 1835 travels through Missouri and Kentucky, Cyrus Edwards, a native-born Southerner and soon-to-be Whig Party gubernatorial candidate, lamented slavery's "desolating effects" on "commerce, agriculture, wealth and population." He wrote that large slaveholders gobbled up the land of small farmers by the "thousands of acres" in order to maximize profits for the purchase of "more negroes, and land." He deplored that slaveholders "forfeited" the benefits of "improved society and well regulated schools" by creating "a wilderness around them." His vision for Illinois was starkly different. He vowed to promote internal improvements and common schools in Illinois, thus encouraging population growth, developing the "physical resources" of the state, and diffusing a "salutary moral influence." To Edwards, the political economy of slavery systematically stunted individual uplift and social progress. This idea paralleled abolitionist arguments about free labor and later enjoyed wide currency among Whigs like Lincoln. Yet, unlike the abolitionists, northern Whigs did not politicize such beliefs. Despite their antislavery sentiment, they typically shied from abolition societies and antislavery politics. Paradoxically, their progressive ideology would justify political conservatism.[12]

The presumption of slavery's eventual demise tempered northern Whig antislavery. This optimistic outlook dated to the revolutionary generation, but it received reinvigoration from prominent Whig political economists such as Henry Carey and Calvin Colton. Carey claimed in 1840 that slaves "are found in great numbers, hiring their own time, and paying their owners a fixed sum for the privilege." He predicted that this practice would increase as owners "find that they can derive more advantage from granting this sort of half freedom, than from any other course." Ultimately, such slaves would accumulate capital and buy their freedom, and when similar inducements were proffered to field hands, "the progress to freedom will be rapid." Colton similarly contended that southern slavery persisted primarily because more efficient free laborers did not drive slave laborers from the cotton, rice, and tobacco fields. In his view, without the protections of a tariff system or a demand for staples that "free labor can not produce," slavery was as certain to perish "as the sun is sure to rise and set." Correspondingly, neither Carey nor Colton endorsed antislavery politics, a judgment shared by most northern Whigs. The *North Western Gazette and Galena Advertiser*, which generally ignored slavery, declared that slavery agitation had "no purpose" because the laws of political economy would "surely overthrow slavery." The editor compared "rheumatic" South Carolina, with its wasted fields, to "vigorous" Ohio, "already a giant." He ascribed the difference to apathetic slave labor, and declared that when "free labor comes in contact with slave labor, the former must overcome—the latter must fall." He predicted that slavery might be in paroxysms by the 1850s, and he considered changes "in the rise and fall of the tides" more likely than the reinvigoration of slavery. Many northern Whigs, including Lincoln, shared the conviction that slavery should be permitted to die a natural death.[13]

A desire to preserve the Union further tempered northern Whig antislavery. To be sure, northern Whig congressmen routinely opposed proslavery measures, Whig editors proved solicitous of the abolitionists' civil rights, and the Liberty Party took most of its votes from antislavery Whigs. But abolitionists scorned the conciliatory attitudes that made Unionism possible and disputed the constitutional provisions sanctioning slavery. This alarmed northern Whigs, who considered the Union a transcendent justification for a constitution that knitted together the nation's disparate interests. To them, the Union was a crowning achievement of rational liberty, representing the triumph of social order and continental peace over the centrifugal forces of local interest. Indeed, the northern founders' rationale for making concessions on slavery reflected precisely such wisdom: recognizing that slavery was a deeply rooted inheritance from the past that profoundly shaped southern society and could not easily be eradicated, they had put their trust in Providence and progress to eradicate the evil. Fifty years later, their example and conviction still commanded respect. Hence abolitionist assaults on a dying labor system appeared misguided and perhaps treasonable to Whigs.[14]

Most Illinois Whigs consequently denounced abolitionism in the 1830s. Whig state legislators overwhelmingly supported an 1837 resolution that condemned abolitionists for subverting property rights, embittering the South, and undermining the Union, and Whig leaders did little to quell anti-abolitionist violence. Prior to Lovejoy's murder, a committee of citizens headed by Cyrus Edwards, an influential Alton resident, publicly urged Lovejoy to cease publishing in order to avert violence. After Lovejoy's death, Whig governor Joseph Duncan regretted the "outrage at Alton" but expressed "decided disapprobation" over attempts "to agitate the question of abolishing slavery in this country, for it can never be broached without producing violence and discord." The leadership of southern-born politicians accentuated the anti-abolitionism of Illinois Whigs in the 1830s. This was especially evident in 1837, when Kentucky relatives of prominent Jacksonville Whig John J. Hardin brought slaves to the state. After antislavery activists prompted the slaves to run away, Hardin's brother and brother-in-law captured one of them and rushed him back to Kentucky. This act put Hardin at loggerheads with abolitionists whose antislavery sentiments he largely approved. But Hardin and Whigs like him subordinated antislavery values to the Union's perpetuation.[15]

The 1840s infusion of Yankees into northern Illinois intensified Whig antislavery but did not eradicate Whig antagonism to abolitionists. Both the Whig and Liberty Parties benefited from a growing number of antislavery voters, and the openly antislavery Whig *Chicago Journal* often courted the abolitionists. Yet, for the same reason, the Whigs' antislavery convictions also enabled Liberty Party candidates to gobble up Whig votes. In a philippic against this development, the *Alton Telegraph* argued that the consequent election of northern Democrats resulted "*practically* in defeating the very object" the abolitionists desired. Polk's 1844 election, which northern Whigs blamed on New York abolitionists, whose votes could have elevated Henry Clay to the presidency, especially embittered Whigs. The *Chicago Journal* inveighed that the abolitionists had "proved recreant to their holy trust" by enabling slavery's expansion, and leading Whigs expressed a deep sense of betrayal. This attitude reflected a growing tension between antislavery and Unionism in party ideology. Whigs continued to denounce abolitionist threats to the Union yet imperiously demanded Liberty Party votes to hem slavery into the South. This incongruity appeared elsewhere. In the late 1840s the *Alton Telegraph* alternated between publishing plans for compensated emancipation and putting a moratorium on articles about slavery. Caught between antislavery and Union, northern Whigs vacillated between the two until the 1850s, while generally viewing abolitionists with suspicion. While the Whigs' promotion of individual uplift and social progress caused them to consider slavery antagonistic to national ideals, their countervailing interest in Unionism and social order muffled their antislavery impulses in the 1830s and early 1840s. Whenever possible, they opted to ignore slavery.[16]

But they could not ignore it permanently because of conflicts between slavery and freedom. Slavery contradicted the cardinal principle of free society—the inalienable freedom of individuals—and hence the existence of slavery in Illinois, the transit of slaves through Illinois, the escape of slaves into Illinois, and the persecution of abolitionists like Lovejoy caused chronic disputes between Illinoisans over the meaning of freedom. In the 1840s, political and legal skirmishes over slavery's status in Illinois thrust these issues into public discourse and compelled Whigs to acknowledge that citizens in a free society required laws subordinating slavery. Under such stimulus their antislavery sentiment began evolving into political antislavery, and their ideological compatibility with abolitionists began transforming into partisan cooperation. By 1848, some Whigs would vote the Free Soil ticket. By the 1850s a large majority would vote Republican.

In Illinois, as Lovejoy's murder illustrated, the clash of slavery and freedom was no abstraction. Slavery persisted in southern Illinois until the 1840s, receiving the support of Illinois's jurists on numerous occasions. For instance, the state supreme court ruled in 1828 that "a registered servant" was "liable to be taken and sold on execution" for debt. Even Justice Samuel Lockwood, who opposed slavery, reluctantly concluded that indentured servants "must be regarded as goods and chattels" under state law. The flight of slaves from brutal masters precipitated even more piercing dilemmas for antislavery Illinoisans such as Lockwood. When Andrew Borders's six slaves escaped after severe beatings, threats of beatings, or threats of sale to the South in 1841 and 1842, shoemaker Matthew Chambers took in one of Borders's slaves. The state subsequently convicted him of "harboring" a fugitive. The supreme court reversed the conviction on technical grounds but held that Chambers otherwise might have been guilty. Justices William Wilson and Lockwood each wrote separate opinions, maintaining that Chambers could not be convicted without proof that he knowingly harbored a fugitive. Lockwood argued that the court's opinion made it "dangerous" for whites to extend to blacks "the most common offices of humanity," such as saving them from "perishing in the streets, with hunger, cold, or sickness," and he reproached the court for forcing whites to presume the servitude of blacks. Such a ruling violated the governing principle of a free society, where "the presumption is in favor of freedom." Yet this logic was not yet widely shared in Illinois. In 1829 the legislature enacted a law that stipulated the arrest "as runaways" of black people who could not demonstrate proof of freedom. The statute broadcast slavery's influence in Illinois: notably, no other northern state ever enacted a law presuming blacks' enslavement.[17]

Illinois's proximity to slave states intensified conflicts between slavery and freedom. In 1830 John Forrester removed his black servant Lotty to Kentucky, leading John Lockhart to contact a lawyer in hopes of assisting her. Lockhart expressed compassion for Illinois's blacks, observing that the servant's husband had pleaded for assistance, "which realy made me feel sorry for the poor fellow, as I always have been impressed with the idea that Blacks are in possession of the sence of feeling for each other as partners for life." This recognition of blacks' humanity also influenced other whites to oppose slavery. In 1843, a Missouri slave named Julia escaped from her mistress, who was visiting Jacksonville. A free black woman took Julia to college student Samuel Willard, who was not an abolitionist, but who felt "a religious duty" to assist Julia in her peril. He shepherded her away from a searching posse and deposited her safely with a local abolitionist. The next day Willard's father smuggled Julia out of Jacksonville, hoping to put her on the underground railroad to freedom. But the posse captured them and spirited Julia back to Missouri, and the courts convicted both Willards of harboring a fugitive. Yet the punishment meted out could no more quell antislavery sentiment in Jacksonville than it could efface the moral sentiments of white Illinoisans who perceived the humanity of blacks.[18]

Mob violence against abolitionists further escalated conflicts between slavery and freedom in Illinois. Promoting abolition required fortitude, because abolitionists endured repeated threats and violence beginning in the late 1830s. Even in northern Illinois, where tolerance was highest, abolitionist lecturers often found churches and schools closed to them. Anti-abolitionists were more active in central Illinois, firing off guns and cannon during abolitionist meetings, throwing eggs, stones, and bricks at the participants, and threatening personal violence. In 1842 an elder in a Methodist church in Tazewell County justified slavery from the Bible and then participated in the mobbing of an abolitionist meeting, and in 1846 a Bloomington lawyer offered $100 for the tarring and feathering of abolitionist minister Levi Spencer. Southern Illinoisans were the most hostile of all. In 1841 a Kaskaskia mob twice attacked an attorney seeking to free a black man held in servitude, and likely only the intercession of the man's neighbors and other bystanders saved his life. These acts of violence steeled many Illinoisans to preserve the rights of free society. Elijah Lovejoy's initial

mobbing made his brother John "almost determined" to become an abolitionist. John hated the "doctrine of Abolitionism" but cared deeply for
individual liberty, property rights, and the "preservation" of a government
dedicated to those ends. The Tazewell County mobbing led a correspondent
of the *Western Citizen* to write that the "question now is not merely whether
the slaves of the South shall be free, but whether *any* of the people shall
enjoy their rights unmolested." Suppression of free assembly, speech, and
press forced Illinoisans to consider whether anti-abolitionism threatened
their own freedom.[19]

Blatant attacks on the rights of nonabolitionists tipped the scales sharply in
favor of freedom. In February 1843, Peoria's abolitionists scheduled a meeting
to organize an antislavery society. In response, leading citizens declared their
intention to employ "force" if necessary "to prevent the catastrophe." On the
scheduled evening, an anti-abolitionist mob shouted down the antislavery
speaker, forcing the meeting to adjourn amid a climate of violence. But the
mob refused to stop there. In a subsequent meeting, the anti-abolitionists
demanded that local editors suppress abolitionism by censoring antislavery
material. This outrageous demand, backed up by the newspaper publishers,
caused the former slaveowning Whig editor of the *Peoria Register* to rebel.
He "thought nothing and cared nothing" for the antislavery meeting, but
he defended the constitutional right of all Americans to think, speak, and
publish for themselves. He insisted that "the surest way to make abolitionists
is to persecute and mob them." Ironically, the *Register*'s publishers forced him
to resign, and he converted to abolitionism shortly thereafter. Outcomes such
as these disgusted Bloomington's David Davis, a prominent Whig lawyer who
opposed efforts in McLean County to organize an "association" seeking to
"prevent" abolitionists from meeting. Davis wrote that abolition "cannot be
stopped in any such way as that." As he comprehended, the interests of a free
people forbade it.[20]

Most Illinoisans had, after all, indicated their preference for freedom by
their choice of residence. Southern immigrants such as Cyrus Edwards and
John J. Hardin had chosen purposefully, and without regrets, to forsake slavery. Edwards believed that slave society degraded both freemen and slaves,
and he rejoiced in 1835 that Kentucky's small farmers had "wisely sought
an asylum in our rich prairies." Lucinda Casteen, the wife of an immigrant
Kentuckian, preferred living in a "free state" because "people that have their
own work to do are happier and healthyer." Exulting in Illinois's high wages
and steady work, Maryland immigrant O. H. Wallace wrote to a southern
friend, "I don't wish myself back you may depend on it to be a slave." Swiss

immigrants visiting St. Louis in 1833 described public slave auctions as an "appalling" and "incomprehensible" contradiction of freedom, and encouraged Swiss emigrants to join them in Illinois. A German immigrant reported from St. Louis in 1837 that Southerners forbade public discussion of emancipation and that slaves were "very frequently the children of their own masters!" He chose to live permanently in Illinois. In preferring freedom to slavery, he was in accord with the vast majority of Illinoisans, who correspondingly resisted the application of slave laws to their society.[21]

The press of public opinion caused the state's politicians to begin asserting freedom's supremacy by the 1840s. In 1843 Missouri's governor requested that Illinois governor Thomas Ford extradite Richard Eells, who had been indicted in Missouri for stealing a slave. Ford initially issued a warrant for Eells's arrest but rescinded it after learning that Eells had harbored but probably not stolen the slave. Ford maintained that his "first and highest duty" was "to the people of his own state," and he refused to extradite Eells. The case thus produced the curious spectacle of a Democratic governor shielding a lawbreaking abolitionist from arrest. But Ford acted astutely, aware that "the liberty of a citizen" was of "vital interest" to the "happiness" of his constituents, and that "a hard case of oppression" would swell the ranks of abolitionism. Employing the same reasoning, state legislators in 1845 referred an abolitionist petition for repeal of the state's black laws to the House Judiciary Committee. The legislators had no intention of altering the black laws, and in fact later strengthened them, but they hesitated to table the petition and infringe the right to free speech. Eight years earlier the General Assembly had condemned the mere organization of antislavery societies, yet now it protected the right of abolitionists, "in common with other citizens, to be heard upon this floor." Indeed, the Democrat who presented the petition argued that tabling it disrespected his constituents, and a number of Whig legislators agreed. These legislators opposed abolitionism, but they agreed that freedom must reign supreme in Illinois.[22]

Despite the fitful progress common to the judiciary, Illinois's supreme court played the greatest role in establishing the supremacy of freedom in Illinois. The attempt of indentured servants and escaped slaves to establish their freedom caused a steady flow of slavery cases to come before the court. The court invalidated legally flawed indentures as early as 1825, but it only began advancing an antislavery interpretation of state law in 1836. That year, the court freed the children of black people who had been registered as servants under territorial law, but had been too young to have been indentured. The court ruled that the territorial legislature had passed no specific provision "affecting the liberty of the children of registered negroes," and thus their "natural right of freedom" remained unimpaired. The court extended the application of this doctrine in 1840, when an indentured servant claimed to be free and sued for back wages. He presented no proof of his freedom, but the defendant provided no evidence of his servitude, and although he would have been declared a slave in most southern states, Illinois's high court decided that with "us the presumption is in favor of liberty." Indeed, the court argued that the southern principle "is founded in injustice," being "contrary" to the nation's "fundamental principles" and "repugnant" to "natural right." This thinking culminated in the 1845 decision *Jarrot v. Jarrot*, in which the court freed the descendants of slaves owned by French settlers. The defendant was a slaveholder who maintained that the 1784 Virginia deed ceding Illinois territory to the United States protected French slavery. The court conceded this point but argued that sovereign states had the power to abolish slavery, as Illinois's 1818 constitution demonstrated.[23]

In these decisions, the court followed legal precedents that avowed slavery's dependence on local law. This doctrine had its origins in a 1772 decision by England's Lord Mansfield and gained acceptance in America's northern courts after 1836. Mansfield argued that slavery violated man's natural right to liberty and therefore only existed where positive law established it. Understanding the portentous implications of this idea, abolitionists argued that slaves taken to a free state reclaimed their natural liberty in the absence of slavery. Most northern states quickly adopted this rule, which prevented slaveowners from traveling through free states with their slaves. However, concern for the rights of slaveholders blunted immediate application of Mansfield's doctrine in Illinois.[24]

From 1843 to 1847, the state's judges vested slaveholders with the right of transit in Illinois. Their willingness to protect slaveholders' rights stemmed from southern Illinois's location between Kentucky and Missouri. Familial bonds ensured that slaveholders routinely crossed through Illinois or stopped in the state for extended stays. Although the right to transit contradicted the presumption of freedom in Illinois, the Supreme Court permitted it in order to promote the bonds of Union. For this reason, the Court upheld the 1843 circuit-court conviction of Julius Willard, who had smuggled the slave Julia out of Jacksonville in violation of the state's fugitive slave law. Justice Walter Scates, the subsequent author of *Jarrot v. Jarrot*, admitted that Illinois could deny the right of transit. But he preferred to enforce the law of slavery in Illinois, preserving "comity" of laws with slave states, in order to avoid "great and irremediable evils, of discord, of heart burnings, and alienation of kind and fraternal feeling" among Americans. Deliberately eschewing Illinois Supreme Court justice John Caton's reasoning in a similar circuit court case earlier that year, Scates's decision marked the last time a northern court would sustain comity. But Caton's ideas soon won out. In an 1847 circuit-court decision, Justice Wilson freed five Kentucky slaves whose master had domiciled them in Illinois, arguing that the "law of slavery is a municipal regulation, and local in its operation." The Illinois Supreme Court never countermanded Wilson, and in 1852 the court affirmed the Mansfield doctrine.[25]

By embracing the idea of slavery's dependence on local law, and by indicating a preference for freedom, Illinois's jurists endorsed the core presumption behind the abolitionists' antislavery nationalism. The abolitionists contended that the Declaration of Independence consecrated the nation to freedom by enshrining natural rights bestowed by God. For this reason they lobbied the government to divorce itself from slavery wherever constitutionally permissible. Although Illinois's jurists made no political statements about slavery and only addressed slavery in Illinois, their ideas reflected key tenets of abolitionist ideology. "All philanthropists unite in deprecating the evils of slavery," wrote Justice Scates in *Jarrot v. Jarrot*, "and it affords me sincere pleasure, when my duty under the constitution and law requires me to break the fetters of the slave, and declare the captive free." Justice Wilson wrote that slavery "is unquestionably to be deplored as a great evil in any form," and the "removal of this deforming feature from our fair and happy form of government, would leave it almost without a blemish." Like abolitionists, Scates and Wilson imagined a nation without slaves. This presumption shaped northern perceptions of abolitionists, who won far more allies than enemies when slavery clashed with freedom. Knowing this, a leading abolitionist wrote in 1846 that fugitive slaves should not be sent to Canada. "Make home the battle ground," he urged, and it will do "more to abolitionize the free states than all other instrumentalities afoot."[26]

Yet the concept of an antislavery nation still faced heated opposition. Indeed, the Illinois Supreme Court permanently embraced the idea of slavery's dependence on local law only after overruling its earlier 1843 decision that upheld Richard Eells's conviction for harboring a fugitive slave. The prosecuting attorney in that case argued that the federal Constitution's mandate for the return of fugitives created "an obligation" upon "every state, and each citizen of every state, to aid in the enforcement of that right." The court adopted this language in its decision, ruling that returning slaves was a "strict moral, political and international obligation and duty," and it "rested upon each state, to enforce the right." The court conjoined this broad constitutional construction with the remarkable argument that knowledge of the fugitive's status was irrelevant. Thus, the court implicitly departed from earlier cases establishing the presumption of freedom for all Illinoisans, and resuscitated the southern rule requiring blacks to prove their liberty, which in the territorial period and again in 1829 had been incorporated into Illinois law. In essence, the court obliged Illinoisans to establish the liberty of black people they sheltered, thereby protecting slaveowners' rights under the "national compact." This decision contradicted the precedents of virtually all northern courts, rested on tenuous legal foundations, and proposed arguments soon rejected by the court's subsequent decisions. Yet it indicated the potential for a proslavery nationalism among Illinois Unionists who were willing to incorporate black enslavement into their definition of freedom.[27]

Central and southern Illinois Democrats largely adopted this line of thinking. While the decision upholding Eells's conviction stirred objections among Whigs and northern Illinoisans, Springfield's *Illinois State Register* claimed that it did "justice" to "our southern brethren." Like the *State Register*, many central and southern Illinoisans hated "negro-stealing from our sister States," and to discourage it they prodded their representatives to fortify the state's fugitive slave laws. In 1845, the General Assembly passed a law that jailed suspected fugitives—and mandated hiring them out for one year—unless they could prove their freedom. In 1847, the delegates to Illinois's second constitutional convention approved an article mandating that the legislature "prohibit" free blacks from migrating into the state and "prevent" nonresident slaveowners from emancipating slaves in the state. Democratic delegates voted 65 to 11 in favor, with northeastern Illinois Democrats casting 9 of the 11 negative votes. By contrast, central and southern Illinois Democrats voted overwhelmingly to support it, as did the state's voters when it was submitted to them separately for approval. Like the 1845 bill, it presumed the servitude of blacks entering Illinois, and its passage demonstrated the degree to which Illinoisans' hostility to blacks increased their tolerance for slavery. Reflecting these attitudes, and sharply rebuking antislavery legal theory, a General Assembly dominated by Democrats instituted black laws in 1853 that not only made it a "high misdemeanor" for free blacks to come to Illinois, but also restored slaveholders' right of transit through the state.[28]

Nevertheless, conflicts between slavery and freedom boded ill for Illinois Democrats. While it was relatively easy for northern Democrats to sacrifice the rights of blacks, sacrificing the rights of whites was far riskier. For instance, in the absence of effective state legislation, some northern Democrats leaned toward federal enforcement of fugitive slave laws. A correspondent of Senator

Sidney Breese urged Congress to establish "officers & other machinery" in northern states to return fugitives. Despite knowing that such an unprecedented use of federal power threatened northern liberties, Breese's correspondent considered it a necessary risk to avoid "irritation and ill will between States." Illinois's Democratic congressmen would support just such a bill in 1850, indicating the party's willingness to sacrifice northern liberties to southern rights. Yet federal enforcement of the fugitive slave law also illuminated the party's dilemma. Greater application of police power could not solve a problem rooted in antagonistic moral systems. Northerners would resist laws they considered wrong. Federal enforcement of fugitive slave laws therefore was likely to rouse antislavery sentiment by escalating the conflict of slavery and freedom. Illinois's experience demonstrated that most Northerners, even many northern Democrats, were unlikely to yield up the nation's law to slavery.[29]

The clash of slavery and freedom in Illinois provided a rehearsal in defense of freedom. Forced to adjudicate between slavery and freedom, Illinois's courts ruled that slavery violated natural and national law and existed only in southern states. While recognizing southern constitutional rights to fugitives, Illinois's courts applied the law of freedom in all other circumstances. These rulings fused an implicit moral condemnation of slavery to a defense of the northern interest in freedom, creating a doctrine applicable to national politics as well as state law. But applying the precepts of antislavery nationalism to federal conflicts over slavery would prove no easy task. The shared ideological convictions of antislavery Northerners did not imply political unity. Rather, antislavery forces were incongruous, often antagonistic, and faced a phalanx of northern and southern foes. However, antislavery nationalism provided a bridge between antislavery sentiment and antislavery politics for any northern voter who wanted free land preserved for free labor. A nation dedicated to freedom could not condemn its territories to slavery without abandoning its ideals and promise of economic abundance. Accordingly, the issue of territorial expansion brought antislavery Northerners together to demand a prohibition on slavery's extension. The nationalist precepts that underlay abolitionist politics, Whig antislavery, and Democratic freesoilism created the ideological basis for the Free Soil Party.

⤸

The man most responsible for the fusion of abolitionists, antislavery Whigs, and freesoil Democrats into Free Soilers was a zealous expansionist, President James K. Polk. Illinois's abolitionists condemned him from start to finish. The territorial aggrandizement that had been his 1844 campaign watchword repelled them. In 1836 they had deprecated the annexation of Texas as a proslavery scheme, and they remained equally hostile to its annexation in 1844. They doubtless would have cheered British acquisition of Texas and the emancipation decree that would have followed. As for Oregon, they considered it little more than a distasteful bribe dangled by southern Democrats in exchange for Texas. Polk's election validated their fears. He soon precipitated a war with Mexico over a boundary dispute they considered chimerical, prompting the *Western Citizen* to excoriate the nation's "robber-rulers." Meanwhile, his turnabout on Oregon reflected "the long practiced arts of this slaveholding government to extend and strengthen slavery," and his vetoes of the rivers and harbors bills flowed from his devotion to southern interests. For these reasons the abolitionists unhesitatingly supported the Wilmot Proviso, which they considered the first step in divorcing the government from slavery. The threat of slavery's expansion therefore enabled them to find common ground with antislavery Whigs and Democrats.[30]

Illinois's Whigs castigated Polk as much as the abolitionists. For starters, the president repealed Whig economic policies. With Polk's assent, Congress reduced tariff rates by one-third and rescinded a Whig law that funneled federal land office monies to the states for internal improvements. Meanwhile, Polk sunk two rivers and harbors bills. These injuries stimulated antisouthernism among Illinois Whigs. The *Weekly North-Western Gazette* complained in 1846 that westerners had been forced to endure southern laws that degraded "free labor" and placed it "beneath the foot of slavery." The *Chicago Journal* agreed that slavery was behind "this fiery Southern opposition to Western measures and Western improvements." And Illinois Whigs particularly resented western Democrats for following southern leaders "as obediently as the beagle trots at his master's whistle." What westerners wanted, declared congressman John J. Hardin, was "an equal share of the appropriations made by the government." But the President did not share their conception of sectional equity.[31]

Polk's handling of American expansion especially angered them. Admittedly, Illinois Whigs had long been ambivalent about territorial expansion. Their antislavery sentiment, wariness of southern political power, and fear of slavery's political divisiveness conditioned them to oppose the annexation of Texas. They also shrank from waging an unjust war on Mexico and felt constrained to abide by the national Whig Party's strong opposition to annexation. Yet the expansionist urges of western settlers operated against their conservative tendencies. Southern and central Illinois Whigs perceived commercial advantages in the annexation of Texas, and most of the state's

Whigs militantly supported the nation's claim to Oregon. The result of these countervailing pressures was that Illinois's Whigs approved Oregon's occupation but opposed the annexation of Texas, war with Mexico, and the "robbery" of Mexican territory. Not only were Whig hopes dashed on every point, but Polk's decisions reeked of a southern bias. Antagonism to slavery consequently began surfacing in Whig newspapers. The *Chicago Journal's* caustic criticism of Polk and the Slave Power began in 1844 and continued throughout the war, while the *Alton Telegraph* chastely but repeatedly admonished against the "extension and perpetuation of the curse of slavery," which gave "the slave holding interest the preponderance in the nation." Cognizant of Polk's territorial ambitions, Illinois Whigs demanded that territory taken from Mexico remain free. On that point, they insisted that northern and national interests coalesce.[32]

Their hostility to slavery's expansion reflected their conviction that the nation must be dedicated to freedom. In 1845 John J. Hardin denounced the common southern argument that the government had an obligation to extend and perpetuate slavery. He claimed that slavery blighted the South by crippling its population, productivity, and morality. He called it the nation's "greatest curse," and he insisted that Washington, Jefferson, and Madison would have repelled John C. Calhoun's doctrine that "slavery and national prosperity are identical." Hardin declared that the "immense majority" of Northerners had no intention or desire to interfere with southern slavery, but they did desire "that this government keep free from any connection with slavery further than the constitution now recognises it." While Hardin discountenanced abolitionism and esteemed his "ties" to slaveholding relatives, he had embraced the Liberty Party's argument that the nation must be dedicated to freedom. He was far from alone. Northern Whigs' opposition to the annexation of Texas led Illinois Democrats to chastise their "forgetfulness of nationality." Politicians from both parties realized that the annexation issue crystallized a growing battle over the lineaments of American nationalism. But the significance of the conflict was not yet clear. Northern Democrats did not recognize the degree to which national expansion forced them to adopt proslavery positions, and northern Whigs did not realize that abolitionist ideas had driven them from the fundamental interests of the South.[33]

While a united Democratic Party likely would have benefited from the growing convergence of abolitionism and northern Whiggery, the antislavery bug also bit northern Democrats. The mutiny of antislavery New York Democrats at their party's national convention in May 1848 recast northern politics by precipitating the rise of the Free Soil Party. The New Yorkers had wielded national power during the Jacksonian years and were unwilling to cede it to the South. Their rebellion created the critical mass necessary for the formation of a broad-based antislavery party. In addition to sheer numbers, they possessed a well-oiled organization, well-honed political skills, and New York's electoral clout. Their revolt encouraged Ohio abolitionist Salmon Chase, who hoped to form a northern antislavery party, to invite the friends of "Free Territory" and "Free Labor" to a Buffalo antislavery convention in August 1848. Illinois's Liberty Party sent delegates to the convention but voted to join a new party only if it pledged to oppose slavery wherever constitutionally permissible. Antislavery Whigs joined them, angered by the Whig Party's presidential nominee, slaveholding General Zachary Taylor, and by a Whig Party platform that ignored slavery. In exchange for the nomination of New York's Martin Van Buren, the freesoil Democrats accepted an abolitionist platform. This bargain allied the most ideologically disparate groups and made coalition possible. Antislavery politics had finally arrived.[34]

The Free Soil Party unhesitatingly proclaimed an antislavery nationalism. The platform declared the party's "fixed determination to rescue the Federal Government" from the "Slave power," which sought to extend and nationalize slavery in violation of the "settled policy" of the nation's founders. Here was a ringing endorsement of the Wilmot Proviso. Moreover, the platform claimed that slavery existed only by force of local law and that the federal government had a "duty" to divorce itself from slavery wherever the "government possesses constitutional authority to legislate on that subject." This doctrine led the *Western Citizen* to proclaim that "the Liberty Platform has been adopted by the Free Soil party," and it urged abolitionists to join hands with former enemies in the battle against slavery. Abolitionists remembered that Northerners of both parties had once mobbed, stoned, and shot them for publicly declaring that slavery was wrong. Yet now some of the abolitionists' central ideas had launched an antislavery party.[35]

The Free Soil Party divided Illinois's Democrats on regional lines. Southern and central Illinois Democrats had little predilection for the Wilmot Proviso and no tolerance for the upstart party built largely on Democratic ruins. At the Democratic state convention in April, they silenced antislavery dissenters from northern Illinois by condemning "unnecessary agitation" of the slavery question. They pledged Illinois's national convention delegates to Michigan's Lewis Cass, subsequently nominated at Baltimore, who argued that the introduction of slavery into the territories was a question best left for territorial settlers. During Cass's campaign, Illinois Democrats deemphasized slavery. The *Peoria Democratic Press* largely ignored freesoilism and popular sovereignty, for instance, while the *Belleville Advocate* barely referred to slavery, the proviso, or the Free Soil revolt. Likewise, the resolutions of virtually every Democratic public meeting published by the *Advocate* in 1847 and 1848 omitted mention of slavery, and the one exception declared the expectation that slavery would never enter the territories taken from Mexico. Democrats who broached the freesoil issue expressed a characteristic ambivalence toward slavery. The *State Register* insisted that popular sovereignty would yield free soil but contended that territorial settlers had a right to slavery. Indeed, the newspaper's editor predicted that "the people of Illinois" would prove "cordial subscribers" to Cass's doctrine that whites' rights to enslave blacks followed from the nation's "original principles." Meanwhile, the *State Register* and like-minded Democrats condemned freesoil politics as disunionist. "I care not who raise the shout of disunion," declared Democrat James Shields, but "my voice will never swell the cry." Likewise, Stephen A. Douglas pledged to resign from Congress if his constituents instructed him to support the proviso. Central and southern Illinois Democrats were freesoil in preference rather than in policy.[36]

By contrast, many northern Illinois Democrats supported the Wilmot Proviso and the Free Soilers. The party's regional leader, John Wentworth, had supported the proviso since its 1846 introduction, and his 1847 rebellion against southern domination of the party only fueled his antislavery politics. Consequently, his newspaper, the *Chicago Democrat*, championed the proviso, promoted free labor, chastised "doughface" Democrats who did southern bidding, and urged northern congressmen to oppose slavery's expansion. His constituents generally encouraged his iconoclasm. Liberty Party candidates in his district commanded 16 percent of the vote, Whig conventions opposed slavery's expansion, and Democratic conventions usually endorsed his course. For instance, at a mass meeting on April 1, 1848, Chicago Democrats insisted that slavery was a local institution, declared that the founders had consecrated the nation to freedom, and urged slavery's prohibition in the territory taken from Mexico. This freesoil pressure caused Wentworth to lobby party leaders to permit district nomination of delegates to the national convention. He sought to prevent the pledging of all the state's delegates to a popular sovereignty platform at the state convention. More was at stake than northern Illinois's representation in national party councils. Wentworth sought to escape Springfield's dictation and to establish a freesoil beachhead in the party, aware that the future of northern Democratic Party, and his own career, might hang in the balance.[37]

Wentworth met a sharp rebuff. Party leaders at the state convention squashed his scheme of district nominations and called the Union's preservation "an object of paramount importance" that should never be sacrificed for "particular interests" or "abstract opinions." Unwilling to break from the party, and threatened by a rival Democratic congressional candidate nominated at a rump convention by disgruntled central Illinois delegates in his district, Wentworth ultimately endorsed Cass. But the *Democrat* largely sat the election out, rarely criticizing the Free Soilers or promoting popular sovereignty. Indeed, the *Democrat* attempted to retain the proviso with the doubtful claim that Cass "would never veto a bill having the free clause in it." Meanwhile, the *Democrat* endorsed the ideas expressed by the Free Soil platform and emphasized Wentworth's antislavery convictions. But the *Democrat*'s course left Wentworth in no-man's land. His new doctrine verged close to the anti-provisoism of Democrats who putatively supported antislavery extension in principle but preferred national harmony to the passage of antislavery law; nevertheless, the *State Register* considered Wentworth's freesoilism abominable and supported his reelection to Congress only as a "choice of evils." Given these circumstances, the antislavery Democrats Wentworth represented had good reason to vote for Van Buren.[38]

Illinois Whigs had fewer reasons to bolt their party. To be sure, they could not boast a national party platform dedicated to antislavery politics, and the Whig candidate, Zachary Taylor, refused to pledge his opposition to slavery's extension. This uncertainty drove Illinois's most ardent antislavery Whigs into the Free Soil ranks. But there were good reasons for Whigs to remain loyal. Northern Whig congressmen had strongly supported the Proviso in 1846 and 1847 and had consistently voted against proslavery legislation since the 1830s. Moreover, the 1848 contest marked the first time northern Whigs actually campaigned for antislavery policy. Whig provisoism was strongest in northern Illinois, but Whig conventions and newspapers throughout the state opposed slavery's expansion. The likelihood of Taylor's victory also appealed to Illinois's Whigs, starved as they were for success. They knew that Van Buren's popularity among Democrats was likely to damage Cass badly in the northern states, and that Taylor's slaveholding would be a tremendous asset in the South. Whig victory seemed within grasp.[39]

At the polls, antislavery politics bloodied the Illinois Democracy. Taylor won the presidency with a powerful showing throughout the country, punctuated by Free Soil–aided triumphs in the critical states of New York and Pennsylvania. Although Cass weathered the freesoil storm in Illinois, the Free Soilers gouged deeply into the Democratic vote. The *State Register*

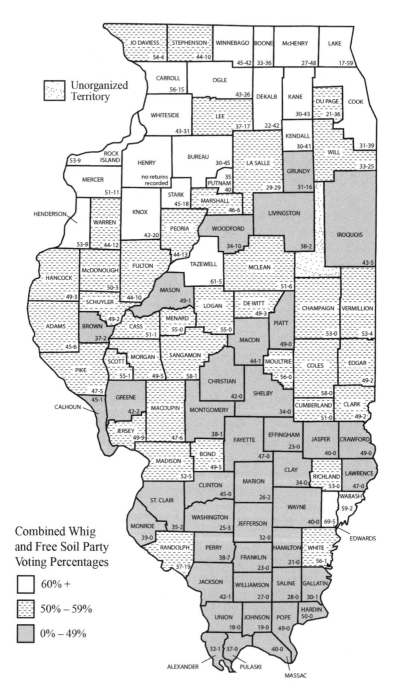

MAP 4. Combined Vote for President, Whig and Free Soil Parties, 1848

Note: Numbers represent respective Whig and Free Soil percentages of the vote (rounded).

had predicted a twenty-thousand majority for Cass, but he beat Taylor by only 3,099 votes. The Democrats won 44.9 percent of the ballots, the Whigs 42.4 percent, and the Free Soilers 12.6 percent. Although the state's total vote had increased 14.25 percent since 1844, the Democratic vote declined by 4.84 percent, with the Free Soilers gobbling up most of the difference.[40] Former Liberty Party voters cast at least forty-seven hundred of Van Buren's 15,702 ballots, and approximately seven thousand Democrats and five hundred Whigs crossed party lines to do the same. The remaining thirty-five hundred votes came from newly arrived voters in northern Illinois counties such as Cook, Lake, McHenry, Boone, Kane, DeKalb, Kendall, Putnam, and Bureau. The Free Soilers won a plurality in each of those counties, racking up a remarkable 50 percent of Van Buren's total vote in the state.[41] Indeed, the election revealed a pronounced regional divide. Free Soilers accounted for 31.2 percent of the state's vote in northern Illinois, 4.9 percent in central Illinois, and 2.6 percent in southern Illinois. But the combined votes of the Free Soilers and the Whigs, who also opposed the proviso, best illustrate the divide. Together, they accounted for 66.8 percent of the northern vote, 53.2 percent of the central, and 42.6 percent of the southern.[42] Democrats still ruled Illinois politics, but the rise of an antislavery northern region boded ill. The antislavery movement was like a locomotive gathering steam. Aware of this, the *Chicago Democrat* urged a party reunion with the freesoilers, and warned against further submission to "southern dictation."[43]

The 1848 presidential election demonstrated that the Democrats would have a difficult time resolving the antagonism between slavery and freedom. They had worked the freesoil and Unionist angles of popular sovereignty in order to claim that their policy served northern and national interests alike. Yet popular sovereignty required them to hedge the interests of freedom. They opposed using Congress's power to prohibit territorial slavery, and they insisted that the founders' principles vested white men with the right to enslave blacks. Thus they implicitly offered a legal, historical, and moral defense of slavery, which took them one long step toward the southern definition of freedom. But a majority of Illinoisans allied themselves with the northern idea of freedom and endorsed the Wilmot Proviso. Their hostility to slavery presented a long-term threat to the cohesion of both the Whig and the Democratic Parties. While not yet portending the destruction of either major party, Northerners' intensifying antislavery attitudes inevitably played out in Congress, complicating party relations with Southerners. The northern Democrats' political dilemma was especially acute. Their party loyalties and unbending Unionism conflicted with the interests of freedom, so political battles over slavery whipsawed them unmercifully. Consequently, they had strong ideological and organizational reasons to forge compromises on slavery. The fate of their party, and probably the Union, hung in the balance. By 1848, resuscitating partisan loyalties required the suppression of national conflicts over slavery. To achieve that end, Stephen A. Douglas stepped to the fore.

5. Stephen A. Douglas and the Northern Democratic Origins of the Kansas-Nebraska Act, 1849–1854

RESOLVING NATIONAL CONFLICTS OVER slavery required a man of experience, influence, power, ability, ambition, decisiveness, and prudence. Stephen A. Douglas possessed all these traits in abundance, but one. A Vermonter by birth, he had migrated to Illinois in 1833, arriving with only five dollars to his name. He rose rapidly. Endowed with a razor-sharp mind, an extraordinary memory, a friendly manner, inexhaustible energy, and a deep, clear voice that boomed from his short, rotund frame, he quickly organized the state's Democratic Party and became known as its "Little Giant." Elected in 1843 to the United States House of Representatives at age thirty and elevated to the Senate in 1846, he quickly achieved national renown, shepherding compromise measures through Congress in 1850 to pacify dangerous sectional discord. Thus by the early 1850s he had readied himself for greatness by joining experience, influence, and power to his widely recognized ability, ambition, and decisiveness. His future could not be known, but one contribution seemed likely. Territorial organization of the Great Plains, from which slavery had been barred by the Missouri Compromise in 1820, promised to aid land-hungry settlers, open a path for a transcontinental railroad, spur market exchange, augment national power, and strengthen the Democratic Party. There was only one hitch: securing the approval of southern politicians who believed that slavery had a claim on all national territories. As a partisan Democrat and an ardent Unionist, Douglas decided to serve the nation by substituting popular sovereignty for the Missouri Compromise's antislavery prohibition. His idea was highly imaginative, impressively bold, and astonishingly imprudent. By applying popular sovereignty to territories promised to freedom, Douglas ignited a national conflagration over the meaning of freedom.

〜

In 1849, the Illinois General Assembly directly challenged Douglas by instructing the state's U.S. senators to support the Wilmot Proviso. The instructions underscored the peril that divisions over slavery among northern Democrats posed to national unity. Encouraged by John Wentworth and the *Chicago Democrat*, northern Illinois Democrats leagued with Whigs in the General Assembly to pass resolutions supporting the proviso. The Whigs voted 29–0 and northern Illinois Democrats 16–1 in favor of the resolution, while central and southern Illinois Democrats voted 44–6 against. The Whigs paced the attack with a resolution urging Congress to prevent the formation of proslavery territorial or state governments, but after an initial defeat they consented to a resolution that barred only territorial slavery. Meanwhile, anti-proviso Democrats endorsed popular sovereignty with a resolution that urged the use of "constitutional and just means" against slavery's expansion. This wording was a thinly veiled critique of the proviso, which the *Illinois State Register* more bluntly called "a proposition to organize a northern party in opposition to a southern party." Like anti-proviso Democrats generally, the *State Register* valued "the perpetuity of the constitution" and "the integrity of the confederacy" far more than antislavery extension. The disjuncture between freesoilism and Unionism produced a sharp divide not only in Illinois's Democratic Party but also in the northern states generally.[1]

Indeed, the party's internal division contributed to Congress's failure to resolve the territorial crisis precipitated by the war with Mexico. Between 1846 and 1848, Southerners opposed the Wilmot Proviso in the Senate, where they had a majority of the votes, while a large majority of northern Democrats and virtually all northern Whigs supported the proviso in the House of Representatives, where they had a majority. Consequently, sectional wrangles over the proviso killed an appropriation for the Mexican War in 1846, blocked Oregon's organization as a territory in 1847, and stymied California and New Mexico's territorial organization in 1848. This standoff persisted into 1849, when freesoil congressmen sought to prohibit slavery in the land ceded by Mexico in the 1848 Treaty of Guadalupe Hidalgo. Eight days after the 1848–49 session began, House freesoilers adopted the proviso by a 109–80 vote. Northern Democrats cast thirty-nine of the proviso votes, demonstrating their indispensability to the freesoil coalition.[2]

Douglas and Wentworth illustrated the problem that Democratic divisions posed for national unity. Douglas sought to break the territorial impasse, admit California to statehood, and preserve the Union. Accordingly, he supported every conceivable solution to the territorial conflict, including the Walker amendment, which rescinded antislavery Mexican law in the ceded territories. Only four northern senators voted for the amendment, and under normal conditions the bill surely would have died in the House. However, the Senate had attached the amendment to a vital appropriations bill in the last hours of the session, when exhaustion, clamorous lobbying, and intense political struggle had weakened the resolve of antislavery congressmen. Only the adroit parliamentary maneuvers of Wentworth and several freesoil allies managed to forestall a potentially adverse vote. In the end, stalemate triumphed again, preventing the organization of California territory. Congressmen girded for a titanic struggle in 1850.[3]

Passage of the 1850 compromise measures through Congress was a brutal ten-month affair. Sectional tensions beset Congress from the start, delaying organization of the House for almost two months. President Taylor got the ball rolling in January by advocating the early admission of California and New Mexico to the Union. Taylor sought to bypass the controversial territorial stage by creating full-fledged states once settlers in California and New Mexico ratified their respective constitutions and requested admission to the Union. However, Southerners bitterly opposed what they considered the president's freesoil scheme. In late January, Senator Henry Clay superseded Taylor's plan by proposing a comprehensive settlement of sectional issues. Clay's central proposals included admitting California as a free state, establishing territorial governments in the remainder of the Mexican Cession, strengthening the fugitive slave act, abolishing the slave trade in the District of Columbia, and adjusting the disputed Texas–New Mexico boundary, with Texas relinquishing territorial claims in exchange for federal assumption of its state debt. Clay relied on a version of popular sovereignty to settle the nettlesome territorial issue, stipulating that the new territories would be organized "without the adoption of any restriction or condition on the subject of slavery." In April, the Senate approved a select committee led by Clay to propose specific legislative measures, and in early May the committee reported three bills: the first strengthening the fugitive slave law, the second abolishing the District of Columbia slave trade, and the third, called the Omnibus bill, addressing the controversies stemming from the Mexican Cession. The Omnibus brought together the territorial and boundary issues by combining two bills written by Stephen A. Douglas, the first admitting California as a state and the second establishing the Texas–New Mexico border and creating territorial governments for Utah and New Mexico. The Omnibus bill occupied the Senate for three months before failing spectacularly on July 31, the day of its expected passage. In an effort to strike an amendment from a clause, a pro-compromise senator initiated a parliamentary maneuver that resulted in a train of votes that dynamited the bill. To the shocked audience, Congress seemed back where it started eight months before.[4]

However, Douglas brokered a compromise in the wake of the Omnibus's defeat. Undeniably, he had a great stroke of fortune. President Taylor died on July 9, which elevated New York Whig Millard Fillmore into office. Unlike Taylor, who had sought to impose a freesoil solution, Fillmore wanted Congress to forge a solution satisfactory to all parties, and therefore he assisted congressional leaders who supported compromise. Douglas needed little encouragement. He gauged accurately that a Senate majority existed to pass a California statehood bill, establish territorial governments for Utah and New Mexico under the doctrine of popular sovereignty, and resolve the Texas–New Mexico boundary dispute, provided that the Senate consider each of the issues separately. With remarkable energy, Douglas orchestrated Senate passage of four corresponding bills in fifteen days and subsequently worked closely with House leaders to assure passage of his measures. The struggle in the House was severe—the boundary bill only barely passed, making every vote crucial. Indeed, it would not have passed without Fillmore's masterful use of patronage, which swayed a sizable minority of northern Whigs, especially from New York, to the support of compromise. The votes of Illinois's congressmen were equally instrumental, and every Illinois Democrat except Wentworth supported compromise. In the end, passage of the compromise measures was a triumph for both Douglas and the northern Democrats, who provided a large majority of the northern votes in favor of compromise.[5]

Popular sovereignty was essential to the settlement. Although the boundary issue was the most explosive, because Texas's determination to occupy the disputed territory could have escalated into a military confrontation between the North and South, it boiled down to "metes, bounds, and money," as one historian observed, and thus proved negotiable. Northerners and Southerners largely held nonnegotiable positions only on the issue of territorial expansion, which they presumed would determine slavery's future in the United States. Even southern Whig congressmen, whose roll calls placed them decidedly in favor of compromise, categorically rejected the Wilmot Proviso. Popular sovereignty was thus indispensable, enabling Southerners and Northerners alike to hope for auspicious territorial outcomes. Nevertheless, enactment of popular sovereignty constituted a serious reversal for antislavery Northerners. They had clung to the proviso since its introduction in Congress in 1846, but suddenly a minority of them had capitulated, binding them all to a policy that had enabled slavery's expansion since the founding of the republic. Now they had to hope that popular sovereignty would serve instead to check slavery's growth. The adoption of popular sovereignty—and the failure of the freesoilers—is thus one of the most intriguing stories behind passage of the compromise measures.[6]

Dread of disunion certainly altered northern public sentiment. During the first three months of congressional debate, Southerners arrogantly discoursed on the advantages of a separate confederacy and pledged to rebel unless propitiated. Yet despite anger at southern threats, Unionism inclined Illinoisans to compromise with Southerners. Indeed, for Democrats, Unionism *implied* compromise. The *Belleville Advocate* spoke for many central and southern Illinois Democrats when it declared itself to be a "'Democratic' Union preserving and mutual rights paper," and not a "'Free-soil' sectional triumph or ruin paper." Confident that Illinois's Whigs were beginning to embrace compromise also, Democratic congressman William Richardson concluded in May 1850 that the great mass of "our people" approved no policy that periled "our national existence." He was probably right. Despite the strong Whig preference for the proviso, somber reflection persuaded many central Illinois Whigs to elevate Unionism above antislavery extension. The *Alton Telegraph* stampeded to support Clay's compromise measures in early 1850, and the *Illinois Journal* and the *Quincy Whig* soon judged congressional nonintervention in the territories to be an acceptable alternative to the proviso. Meanwhile, Whig orators such as Springfield's James Conkling sentimentally appealed to Unionism, urging Illinoisans to sustain the Constitution "in a spirit of concession."[7]

The growing conviction that popular sovereignty likely would produce free states also altered northern sentiment. Douglas insisted in a major Senate speech that slavery could not exist in mountainous regions such as Utah and New Mexico, and virtually every Illinois Democratic congressman followed his lead. As William Bissell confided to a friend, "If, however, I really believed that a prohibitory enactment by Congress were necessary to prevent the extension of African slavery over the Territories acquired from Mexico, I should feel constrained by the highest considerations of duty to my Country to vote in favour of such prohibition. But it is not necessary, I think." Meanwhile, following the celebrated procompromise March of Seventh speech by Massachusetts Whig senator Daniel Webster, who declared that Congress did not need to "reënact the will of God" because physical geography precluded slavery's introduction into New Mexico, the Whig *Illinois Journal* soon declared that the "people of California, New Mexico, and Deseret will, under no circumstances, establish slavery in their respective territories." Even John Wentworth, who fought the compromise measures bitterly, conceded after passage of the Utah and New Mexico bills that "the chances of slavery ever going [there] are very poor indeed." Sharing this conviction, a significant minority of Whigs and antislavery Democrats sacrificed the proviso for peace.[8]

To be sure, most freesoilers refused to capitulate. The *Chicago Democrat* and the *Western Citizen* kept up a severe fire on compromise from the inception of Congress to its finish, buttressed by the intense antislavery extension sentiment in northeastern Illinois. A Chicago mass meeting in February proclaimed its "abhorrence" of compromises whereby slavery's extension "may be allowed or secured," while a Joliet convention in June blasted the compromise measures as a "conspiracy" against freedom that attempted to "reconcile good and evil." Freesoilers refused to relinquish the proviso partly because they feared that popular sovereignty would enable slavery's expansion. Prominent freesoil senator John P. Hale bluntly observed that "the friends of freedom" should not "deceive" themselves that "latitude fixes this matter" when southern congressmen declare their intention to take slaves into the territories. But as the Joliet convention indicated, freesoilers also clung to the proviso because they insisted that Congress uphold the "rights of man which form the true foundation of our Government." By their logic, popular sovereignty undermined national precepts by equating slavery with freedom. They reprehended the course of men like Bissell, who supported popular sovereignty despite acknowledging that slavery violated natural law. The freesoilers' political course was therefore plain: to resist Douglas's dangerous expedient at all hazards. Many Northerners shared their sentiments, and consequently the Utah territorial bill received the sanction of only 38 percent of northern congressmen. Northern Illinois's two congressmen, Edward Baker and John Wentworth, joined this antislavery phalanx. Even when bolstered by northern fears of disunion and a freesoil gloss, popular sovereignty did not command the sanction of a majority of northern congressmen. By and large, the southern vote sustained it.[9]

Nevertheless, the actions of the General Assembly upon convening in 1851 evinced the change in Illinoisans' political attitudes. The newly elected state legislature quickly passed ten resolutions on the slavery controversy. Each resolution passed easily, but the votes provided an index of the relative strength of Unionism and freesoilism. A resolution endorsing the Union passed 90–4, for instance, while the repeal of the legislature's 1849 proviso instructions passed 73–22. The proviso resolution constituted a test of freesoil sentiment, both as a declaration of principle and as a reflection on how the Illinois General Assembly wished future territorial acquisitions to be organized. The vote revealed an important shift in state politics. Whigs had supported the proviso instructions unanimously in 1849. However, southern and central Illinois Whigs in 1851 voted 22–4 to repeal the instructions, while northern Illinois Whigs voted 7–1 against repeal. Meanwhile, northern Illinois Democrats voted 10–6 against repeal. Regional divisions persisted, but Unionism had mastered the Whigs' antislavery sentiment in southern and central Illinois, while weakening northern Democratic freesoilism. Passage of the compromise measures had ruptured the freesoil alliance between Whigs and northern Democrats, putting antislavery politics into remission.[10]

In the absence of slavery, Unionism became the refrain of both parties by 1852. Douglas made this possible for the Democrats by repairing relations with Wentworth in 1851. In return for Wentworth's endorsement of his presidential bid in 1852, Douglas aided Wentworth's reelection to Congress and gave Wentworth considerable control over patronage in northern Illinois. The return of freesoilers to the Democratic church enabled the party to censure antislavery politics. The *Rock Island Republican* called the Free Soil Party a "contemptible" faction who preferred disunion to sectional compromise; meanwhile, party conventions approved the national platform, which vowed to preserve the "permanency of the Union" by resisting "all attempts" to renew slavery agitation. The Whig national platform and Illinois Whigs echoed these sentiments. Jacksonville's Richard Yates wrote in 1852 that "any attempt" to "disturb or repeal the compromise measures" would seriously "hazard" the Union, and Cook County's Whigs likewise expressly declared their devotion to the Union.[11]

Yet the convergence of the parties on the preservation of the Union dulled party difference and preempted discussion of salient issues. The Democratic platform advocated no positive role for the federal government, specifically limiting its powers to those "derived solely from the constitution." Lincoln justly complained that the Democratic platform "is full of declarations as to what ought *not* to be done," but "does not propose to do a single thing." Ironically, the Whig platform proposed little more, bettering the Democrats only by recognizing the constitutionality of federally funded river and harbor improvements. An insipid Unionism had replaced the distinctive Jacksonian approaches to political economy.[12]

The convergence of partisan economic policy was particularly evident in Illinois. From 1850 to 1854, Democrats and Whigs both supported a homestead grant for settlers, land grants for railroad construction, river and harbor improvements, and freer incorporation laws within the state. These measures reflected Illinoisans' determined pursuit of economic opportunity, especially through western settlement and corresponding commercial development. Even the Democrats' resistance to increased tariff rates, which did differentiate the parties, had little import. In 1850 Wentworth and Douglas willingly traded western support of the tariff for eastern support of a railroad land grant. Regional economic differences were more pronounced than partisan ones. Douglas proposed to fund western harbor construction through tonnage duties, hoping to reduce sectional friction over internal improvements. However, northern Illinois Democrats considered tonnage duties an unjust imposition on western commerce and continued to demand federal funding for improvements. State banking legislation also precipitated a regional rather than partisan split. Northern Illinois Democrats voted with Whigs in 1851 to establish free banking, which permitted any person who deposited securities with the state to establish a bank. The bill produced a titanic battle in the state legislature, but the Democrats chose not to make it a party test. Douglas conceded that the law had strong backing in northern Illinois, and therefore he urged the Democratic Party to "submit" to the "obnoxious" law. Party convergence led an unrepentant Free Soiler, rechristened a Free Democrat, to observe that "nearly every question which has divided the Whig and Democratic parties, has been settled." In large measure, he was right.[13]

The most significant indicator of partisan economic consensus was the Democrats' embrace of a diversified capitalist economy. Their reservations about corporate power, manufacturing enterprises, wage labor relations, and large-scale capitalism had receded significantly by the early 1850s. Douglas exemplified this shift. His conception of the American economy stretched beyond Illinois's prairies and encompassed New England manufactures, western minerals, southern cotton, and international exchange. Impressed by the nation's technological ingenuity and specialized economic interests, he expected free trade to yield enormous economic benefits for the United States. Just like Whigs, he celebrated the "mutual interests" of the "farmer, the planter, the grazier, the mechanic, and the manufacturer," and he advocated the production and use of "practical" agricultural, scientific, and mechanical knowledge. His belief in the symbiosis between economic development and social progress fueled his avid interest in railroad construction. He was a leading advocate for the Illinois Central Railroad, which stretched from Chicago to Cairo when completed in 1856. To fund its construction, the Illinois delegation wheedled an astounding 2.5 million-acre land grant from Congress in 1850. Douglas knew that the road would spur settlement on some of Illinois's finest farmland, which had been rendered "comparatively valueless" by "remoteness from markets," and he hoped that it would cement the Union by spurring north–south trade. It would illustrate the nation's harmony of interests.[14]

Yet Democratic support for a diversified economy destroyed the distinctive basis of party political economy. Agrarian capitalism had been the hallmark of Jacksonian ideology. Now, the party had climbed into bed with eastern capitalists, who agreed to build the Illinois Central in exchange for the state's land grant, and who employed an army of wage laborers to fulfill the pledge. Notably, a few old-line Democrats feared that the Illinois Central charted a new path for the party. "I am opposed to the Central rail Road not only on the ground of monopoly," wrote W. Edwards, but also because "I realy for see the total rout of our long cherished principles." In particular, he lamented that Democratic "land reform" had been sacrificed to the corporate "immunities" demanded by the company. Yet his protest had little resonance with Illinoisans, who welcomed the road with unmitigated excitement. Even some formerly radical Democrats conceded that large-scale capitalism contributed to social progress. "I have been taught to look upon corporations with distrust," admitted congressman James Allen, "but it is only through these associations that great enterprises are carried forward," and hence "they become necessary." This attitude led the Whig *Rock Island Advertiser* to complain that Illinois Democrats had adopted Whig "*principles* without the name." The *Advertiser* had good reason to be bitter. The triumph of Whig economics resulted not in Whig political success, but in an erosion of traditional partisan competition that disproportionately benefited Illinois's Democratic Party.[15]

In the absence of significant political debate, Illinois's voters switched parties and sometimes quit voting altogether. From 1850 to 1852, neither party had a distinctive and unwavering base of support in the Illinois electorate. For instance, the ethnic groups who supported the Democratic candidate for State Treasurer in 1850 offered distinctly less support to Democratic congressional candidates that year. Likewise, voters who supported the Democratic Party's presidential candidate in 1852 often spurned Democratic congressional candidates. A similar inconsistency among Whig voters tolled a death knell for steadfast party allegiance. Voters themselves recognized this development. After the 1850 elections, Gershom Flagg informed his son that "Whigs and Democrats voted together with no regard to the usual party lines." This nonchalance frustrated party leaders. In 1851 a Democratic politician wrote "that abolitionism, freesoilism, and other foolish issues" in northern Illinois had "so obliterated many of the ancient land marks, of the party, that any political result in districts which were formerly, and are still democratic, is now at times quite uncertain." One notable consequence of partisan breakdown was lowered turnouts. The off-year elections in 1850 produced a dreadful turnout of 53.3 percent of eligible voters. The absence of a presidential contest partly accounted for this lethargy, as did the political exhaustion produced by the protracted slavery impasse. Voter turnout rebounded to a respectable 64.6 percent in the presidential race of 1852, but even this figure reflected a steady decline. Turnout for the three prior presidential contests had been 82.0 percent, 73.3 percent, and 67.8 percent, respectively. As David Davis wrote two weeks before the 1852 election, "in Illinois there is no political excitement at all." Bereft of compelling issues, voters strayed from the polls.[16]

Illinoisans' growing interest in nativist and temperance reforms further undermined party loyalties. These issues were not entirely new, but they took on added import in the late 1840s and early 1850s, when the United States absorbed a massive influx of German and Irish immigrants. Driven from their native soil by a complex of economic and political pressures, and often poor and unskilled, the immigrants clustered together in northern cities and farming communities. Immigrants constituted more than half of Chicago's population by 1850, and Germans, who settled heavily in Illinois, also took root in Belleville, Alton, Peru, Quincy, Peoria, Galena, and many farming communities. The immigrants' predominantly Catholic faith and Democratic Party allegiances concentrated nativism among Whigs. Yet, as a specific political issue, nativism cut against existing party loyalties. Important Whigs like Lincoln, Yates, and Quincy's Orville Browning, who had little truck with nativism, considered Germans an important and desirable swing vote. Meanwhile, even a radically egalitarian Democrat like Lyman Trumbull privately expressed reservations about the German influx into his community.[17]

Temperance had even more disruptive effects on party loyalties. After all, many native-born Americans were intemperate, including Whigs, and thus the phalanxes that formed on this issue crossed party lines. Temperance took shape as a freestanding political issue much earlier than nativism, with petitions to prohibit or regulate the sale of alcohol pouring into the General Assembly in 1851. Meanwhile, temperance advocates on the local level sought to implement local prohibitions, and their initial success in the regulation of alcohol sales spurred a public movement for a statewide ban that culminated in 1855. Although neither nativism nor temperance dominated Illinois politics in the early 1850s, the two reform movements undermined party ties and gathered momentum for a forceful emergence in the mid-1850s.[18]

In Illinois, voter disaffection benefited the Democratic Party rather than its rivals. Illinois Democrats did not split significantly over whether to repeal the 1850 compromise measures, and agreement on this basic issue allowed the party to coalesce and reestablish control over state politics. The party's success was strikingly apparent in the state legislature. The 1851 General Assembly contained sixty-three Democrats, thirty-six Whigs, and one Free Soiler; two years later, it housed seventy-five Democrats, twenty-four Whigs, and one Free Democrat. The Illinois Democrats were almost as successful in congressional, gubernatorial, and presidential elections. In 1850 they won 57.4 percent of the congressional vote and elected six of their seven congressional candidates. In 1852 the Democrats' gubernatorial nominee won 52.4 percent of the vote, and the Democrats' presidential candidate, Franklin Pierce, rolled to victory with a 51.9 percent tally.[19]

Meanwhile, passage of the compromise measures virtually annihilated the Free Soil Party. Shorn of the slavery extension issue and moderate antislavery constituents, the party disintegrated and the remaining Free Soilers reverted to radicalism. The *Western Citizen* urged its readers in 1851 to revive the state's antislavery society and to work for the "total abolition of slavery." But radicalism had little appeal. The gubernatorial candidate of the newly formed Free Democratic Party won only 6 percent of the vote in 1852, indicating that antislavery politics was once again the province of abolitionists.[20]

Finally, the reunification of the Democrats returned Illinois Whiggery to its customary role as bridesmaid. Although competitive in northern and central Illinois, the Whigs in 1850 commanded only 41.4 percent of the state's congressional vote, and in 1852 won only 41.0 percent of the congressional vote and 41.8 percent of the presidential vote. Meanwhile, northern and central Illinois Whigs did not see eye to eye on slavery. In 1852, Whig candidates for Congress won three races in the northern half of the state, but only by recruiting Free Democratic votes with freesoil pledges. However, central Illinois's Richard Yates won reelection that same year only by skillfully advocating both Unionism and antislavery. This stark regional division reflected the persisting consequences of the nation's debate over slavery and underscored the profound problem that any further debate over slavery would pose for northern Whigs.[21]

The crisis of the Union also left its mark on Stephen A. Douglas. Although Illinois's Democratic Party weathered the storm over slavery's expansion more successfully than its rivals, Douglas understood that the disunity of Illinois Democrats, and of northern Democrats more generally, posed profound perils to the national Democratic Party and the Union. He certainly was aware that voter apathy, partisan feuds, and divisions over slavery plagued most other northern states, especially New York, and that new issues like temperance were further roiling party loyalties. Moreover, Douglas knew that neither the Whigs nor the Democrats could long subsist on Unionist politics—which brought the parties together rather than driving them apart—and that issues of a predominantly local character, such as temperance, were unlikely to invigorate national politics. To revitalize partisan loyalties, Congress had to address national issues that resonated with the entire American electorate. There was no better issue with which to unify the Democratic Party than expansion, presuming that some workable solution could be found to resolve the problem of slavery. Certainly Douglas could not fail to notice the continued attractions of expansion for inhabitants of western states. Illinois's economic and social development proved conclusively that men wanting cheap land had to go west.

$$\backsim$$

The state's booming economy made railroads the obsession of state politics in the early 1850s. Tantalized by the idea of lucrative markets, farmers throughout Illinois demanded alternatives to muddy roads. As one farmer observed, there was a "Rail Road feever" in the state. Perhaps the most notable aspect of railroad politics was the unrelenting demand for charters. Illinoisans built more than two thousand miles of track between 1850 and 1856, a total matched by no other state. Roads sprang up in northern Illinois with particularly astonishing speed. The region's well-capitalized farmers gave Chicago's first road a boost when they snapped up railroad stock. From that point on, market incentives did the rest. Railroads gave Chicago an insuperable commercial advantage over western rivals like St. Louis because of Chicago's ties to New York City, which enabled Chicago's merchants to pay high prices for grains and to sell manufactured products cheaply. Consequently, almost all of Illinois's railroad track wound its way to Chicago by 1856, when more than one hundred trains chugged into the city every day.[22]

Chicago's insatiable markets precipitated dramatic economic growth throughout the state. The long-awaited opening of the Illinois-Michigan Canal in 1848 promptly demonstrated the economic symbiosis between the city and the state. The canal immediately directed much of the Illinois and Mississippi River trade to Chicago, boosting the city's corn exports almost 800 percent by the end of the year and substantially increasing its lumber and mercantile business. Railroads enlarged Chicago's western hinterland even more dramatically. The Galena and Chicago Union Railroad began operating its first ten miles of track in 1848, and by 1853 the track stretched almost to the northwest corner of the state. In like manner, a network of other railroads soon transported Illinois and Wisconsin farm products to Chicago, expanding trade by slashing transport costs. From 1847 to 1852, Chicago's wool, flour, and pork exports doubled, and its animal hide exports sextupled. Incredibly, corn, oat, and lead ore exports respectively increased 4,000 percent, 5,200 percent, and 19,000 percent.[23]

The state's settlement marched in tune. From 1845 to 1855, Illinois's population increased from 661,999 to 1,300,480. Almost half of the increase was in northern Illinois, where the population expanded by 311,269 people. This 189.5 percent growth was fueled by Chicago, which grew from 12,088 to 83,509 residents, a remarkable 590.8 percent increase. The state's second-most dynamic region was east central Illinois, galvanized by the Illinois Central Railroad and growing at a 94.3 percent clip. Meanwhile, the population grew by a respectable 64.6 and 56.6 percent in west central and southern Illinois.[24] About half of the new migrants to Illinois during the 1850s emigrated from other northern states. Many of them owned considerable capital and purchased land near railroads or the Illinois-Michigan Canal. Witnessing the "astonishing" numbers of these emigrants in 1852, David Davis called them "a much better class than we usually find on the road." He and countless other Whigs expressed less enthusiasm about the new waves of foreigners, who constituted about 40 percent of the migrants, especially the unskilled Irish laborers imported from the East for canal and railroad construction. Nevertheless, the diversity of the migrant pool and the varied social positions taken by immigrants testified to the growing complexity of a state transformed by economic and demographic expansion.[25]

The newly laid railroad tracks and newly arrived immigrants quickly raised land prices. Amid rampant speculation, especially along railroad corridors, land values doubled between 1849 and 1851. "The Country is bare of money," wrote David Davis in 1852, "every cent that any body could raise, having gone into the land office." By 1855 speculators and settlers had almost extinguished Illinois's available public lands, and by 1857 the Illinois Central already had sold half of its 2.5 million acre grant. Farmland sold for high prices. Prime locations near Springfield and Ottawa, respectively, brought $100 and $150 per acre, while most land owned by the Illinois Central sold for at least $8 per acre. At such prices, farm machinery became a paying proposition, and consequently Illinois's improved acreage and value of farm implements almost tripled during the 1850s, while the value of farms more than quadrupled.[26]

Despite rising land prices, young men could still acquire a farm. It was not easy, because starting a forty-acre farm on unbroken prairie cost roughly $1,000 in 1850, and Illinois farm laborers earned only $150 per year. How laborers acquired the capital to begin farming for themselves is thus not entirely clear, but the number of farms in the state doubled between 1850 and 1860. Some of these new farmers hailed from the East and brought capital with them, but others succeeded through toil, struggle, and thrift. Because farm owners provided room and board in addition to paying wages, frugal farm laborers could purchase and outfit a farm in seven to ten years. Other strategies included making a down payment on a reaper and using it to command high wages during the harvest season, or leasing land or share-cropping, both of which permitted renters to turn their labor into capital through the sale of surpluses. Certainly, local farmers with large acreage engaged landless farmers to work for them. For instance, in Sugar Creek and northern Illinois's DuPage County, the top 20 percent of the population owned more than 50 percent of the land by 1860, while the bottom 40 percent owned only 12 percent in Sugar Creek and none in DuPage County. In such circumstances, laboring for others was a necessary stepping-stone to independent proprietorship.[27]

To be sure, the hint of a permanent wage class could be seen in the state's cities. From 1850 to 1860 the state's urban population increased from 64,000 to 246,000 people, with approximately 45 percent residing in Chicago throughout the decade. The grain, lumber, meatpacking, and railroad industries spurred Chicago's demographic growth, stimulating a host of subsidiary industries and expanding employment. But laborers garnered only a small portion of the wealth produced. In 1860 the top 10 percent of property owners possessed approximately 74 percent of the city's property, while less than one-quarter of skilled and unskilled laborers owned property, and that usually in small amounts. Skilled laborers certainly climbed into the middle class, but this required luck and pluck. German immigrant Nikolaus Schwenck, for instance, found a coppersmith's job after arriving in Chicago in 1855, securing a steady income that eventually enabled him to speculate in land and open his own shop. But, as he observed to a German relative soon after arriving, some immigrants "are much more wretched here than in Germany," and two years later he reported Chicago's widespread "misery" when thousands of unemployed workers faced "the approaching winter" with empty bank accounts and "fearful hearts." Such circumstances were perilous, he explained, because in America "nobody gives a damn . . . Help yourself is the only rule." Fortunately for some families, the German Society in Chicago responded to this "unparalleled emergency situation" with food, fuel, and clothing, but the society's "limited means" made this a difficult task, and in 1858 its officials reported that many "craftsmen and their families" who had pawned their goods still faced foreclosure. Even during good times, the long work hours, expensive housing, relatively low wages, and irregular employment spurred sporadic attempts at union organizing in the 1850s. But these efforts had little effect, and the large pool of immigrant workers restrained wage increases and inhibited capital accumulation among laborers throughout the decade.[28]

However, the overwhelmingly rural character of the state in the 1850s predisposed Illinoisans toward land reform—not unionization—as the solution to perceived economic challenges. The most radical land reformers argued that laborers required vindication from the oppression of slaveholders, landlords, and capitalists, whose control of land and capital enabled them to extort wealth from others. Believing that the product of labor was fit for sale, but not the laborer or the labor itself, land reformers excoriated both slavery and wages. By their estimation, the wealth of slaveholders and capitalists was "obtained from the toil of others and unjustly held." Following this logic, Peoria County land reformers petitioned the legislature to limit future acquisitions of land in Illinois to either 160 or 320 acres in order to prevent monopolists from fastening "dependence, degradation and misery" on cultivators. This position, however, was too extreme for most Illinoisans, who wanted no limits on property accumulation and had no need for radical politics. They married land reform to capitalism by pruning away the more radical land reform policies, while enthusiastically endorsing the key concept of free homesteads for settlers. For this reason, Illinois' Whigs and Democrats both supported a homestead law by the early 1850s.[29]

As the homestead issue illustrated, proposals to confront the nation's labor problem were more likely to emphasize antislavery than anticapitalism. Most notably, Professor Jonathan Turner of Illinois College proposed that the state establish an industrial university for the education of farmers and mechanics. He believed that education promised the "INDUSTRIAL and SOCIAL salvation" of labor, and he dreamed of the day that "millions" of independent "free laborers" would work the "vast plains" of the Great West with all the "knowledge and science" requisite to their vocation. Many farmers, mechanics, and politicians rallied behind Turner, and in 1853 the General Assembly petitioned Congress to fund the construction of industrial state universities with land grants. This idea differed radically from that of land reform. Turner presumed no necessary conflict between labor and capital because he thought that unequal access to knowledge caused social inequality. For this reason, he hoped that "the practical industrial intellect" would enable laborers to reach their "ultimate goal of destiny and renown." His proposal reflected the nation's individualistic ethos better than did land reform. Most Northerners in the 1850s did not perceive the growth of wage-labor relations, or the conditions of labor, as a crisis in capitalism. Instead, they argued that wages fostered economic opportunity.[30]

The ideal of upward mobility became a cultural icon in the 1850s. To be sure, Whigs had trumpeted the idea for several decades, and Democrats had embraced it in practice. But never before had it so thoroughly penetrated the public mind and private behavior. Democrats like Lyman Trumbull counseled family members that the "secret of success in ninety nine cases out of a hundred in every branch of business is energy & perseverance," and Whigs like James Conkling lectured youngsters that success depended on "their own efforts" in "surmounting every difficulty" with "the most strenuous efforts." Likewise, Democrat J. C. Dickerson proclaimed in 1851 that Stephen A. Douglas would "touch the popular cord" if nominated for president in 1852 because he was "a self-made man, a perfect type & embodiment of the West & indeed of our whole country." This celebration of economic individualism profoundly shaped how Illinoisans responded to the growth of wage labor. For instance, Chicago Democrat William Bross spoke before the Mechanics Institute in 1852, didactically relating the parable of a "sober, industrious" young blacksmith who saved "a little capital" as a journeyman, then opened his own shop, and finally achieved "a competency." Meanwhile, for the emerging class of white-collar workers, waged positions were becoming a highly desirable end in themselves. A bookkeeping position in a Chicago mercantile firm could start as high as $600 annually in 1851 and could double over time. For these reasons, innumerable Northerners believed that wages contributed to the nation's economic order by lubricating the social hierarchy. In this respect, wages were the precise inverse of slavery, and they deepened the distinctions between northern and southern society.[31]

The social and economic development of Illinois in the 1850s thus reinforced antislavery sentiment. The state's growth testified to the astounding dynamism of free society, driven by the industry of free men, and slave states seemed moribund by contrast. In a letter published by the *Chicago Tribune*, one frustrated but not ill-meaning visitor to the South reported that "Indolence, inconstancy of will, improvidence, extravagance and reckless carelessness, are almost necessities of their labor system." The *Alton Telegraph* concurred, arguing that Missouri's prosperity would be incalculably advanced if all the state's slaves ran away. Illinoisans' growing willingness to discuss slavery's debilitating effects reflected both their desire for freesoil expansion and the glaring disparity in economic development between Illinois and contiguous slave states. The rapid settlement of Illinois's vast prairies by land-hungry immigrants—and the almost instantaneous growth in economic productivity that ensued—conclusively proved that the nation's remaining western territories should be reserved for free men. Expectations for continued economic opportunity therefore merged powerfully with intensifying celebrations of upward mobility to condemn the expansion of slavery. "In our own favored land," declared James Conkling, "the child of most humble parentage may assume a most distinguished position in Society." Yet he and countless others actually believed that only northern society fully realized this ideal, and thus the triumph of economic individualism strengthened the girders of antislavery ideology. Despite the quiescence of antislavery politics in the early 1850s, antislavery sentiment continued to mount. If flouted, it might erupt volcanically.[32]

∽

As 1853 came to an end, Stephen A. Douglas was not particularly concerned with the subterranean movements of antislavery ideology. Preoccupied with the "distracted condition" of the Democratic Party, he desired to "consolidate" the party's power and "perpetuate its principles" in the upcoming congressional session. His policy objectives were clear: he sought to reduce the tariff, pass a tonnage bill for harbor improvements, secure a land grant for the Pacific Railroad, and organize Nebraska Territory. The last two measures were intimately linked because no land grant could be made through unorganized territory. His measures for western expansion boldly addressed the central political and social problems of the period. The Pacific Railroad promised to revolutionize national commerce in much the same way the Illinois Central would transform eastern and southern Illinois, while the organization of Nebraska would open the western plains for settlement, enabling the crowded North to pour its excess population into the grasslands between the Missouri River and the Rocky Mountains. Douglas therefore had good reason to expect his policies to revivify party loyalties. The tonnage bill would bind up a festering sectional wound; the western measures would rededicate the Democratic Party to the expansionist ideals of Manifest Destiny; and the Nebraska bill would establish popular sovereignty as a permanent solution to the problem of slavery's expansion. With popular sovereignty, Douglas could surmount southern opposition to the accession of free states. Truly, this was a grand plan to aid the nation and mend the "distracted condition" of his party.[33]

The organization of Nebraska Territory had long been part of Douglas's larger plan for national expansion. As a congressman, he had sought to organize the territory in 1844, and he had renewed the attempt as a senator in subsequent Congresses. His objectives never wavered. He wanted to foster western commerce, build a Pacific Railroad, and drive Britain from the Americas, all of which required the establishment of settlements from the Missouri River to the Pacific Rim. He considered Nebraska Territory a sluice gate to the West, and opening it thus constituted a key element of his agenda for continental empire. But like many of his territorial bills, his Nebraska bills languished for years. Congress never really considered organizing the territory until 1853; and when his bill passed the House that year, southern senators laid it on the table by recording almost every one of their votes against it. They would hold the western territories hostage rather than permit the continued growth of free states. In fact, southern unanimity indicated the possibility of an extended sectional stalemate over Nebraska unless Douglas overrode the Missouri Compromise's prohibition on slavery in Louisiana Purchase territory north of 36° 30'. But this he was predisposed to do. In a December 1853 letter to a Nebraska convention in Missouri, he maintained that the "Indian barrier must be removed" to permit "the tide of emigration and civilization" to "roll onward" to the Pacific. In his view, "the highest national" interests "imperiously demanded" the erection of settlements, railroads, and telegraphs across the West. Southerners' intransigence combined with his commitment to national expansion prepared him to make concessions on slavery.[34]

Southern congressmen certainly influenced those concessions. They knew that the proposed territory—which stretched west of Missouri to the Continental Divide and north to the Canadian border—was an incubator of future free states, protected from slavery by provisions in the Missouri Compromise that Douglas's initial Nebraska bill, reported on January 4, 1854, did not directly repeal. The bill organized Nebraska Territory with language adopted from the Utah and New Mexico Acts of 1850, vesting settlers with power over slavery and providing that the territory should be received into the Union with or without slavery, as its inhabitants decided. These provisions substantially repealed the Missouri Compromise's antislavery prohibition. However, Douglas likely intended the existing restriction on slavery to remain in force unless the territorial legislature chose otherwise, thus stacking the deck in favor of freedom. But Southerners refused to accept what might prove a mere shadow of repeal. Three weeks of intricate public and private maneuvering followed, with Douglas, the Pierce administration, and southern senators from both parties hashing out the bill's wording. On January 23, Douglas introduced a new bill. It organized the same geographic area into two territories, Kansas as well as Nebraska, the former territory lying west of the slave state Missouri, and the latter lying west and north of the free state Iowa. This change came at the behest of Iowa and Missouri congressmen who were jockeying to influence the future route of the Pacific Railroad. However, to suspicious freesoilers, it seemed to reserve Kansas for slavery in light of the bill's more momentous change. The bill also declared that the "principles of the legislation of 1850" had "superseded" the antislavery eighth section of the Missouri Compromise, which was now "inoperative." Douglas later amended this wording to read that the eighth section was "inconsistent" with the 1850 law, which more credibly justified repeal of the 1820 compromise. Pushed by southern congressmen, Douglas had decided to mount an open attack on the Missouri Compromise.[35]

Douglas undertook this task willingly and fearlessly because it converged with his core beliefs. He had attempted to avoid explicitly repealing the Missouri Compromise for political reasons, but he had no intellectual or moral attachment to prohibitions on territorial slavery. He argued that settlers had a right to slavery if they desired it, and a right to reject it if they did not, and hence the policy of running "a geographical line, in violation of the laws of nature, and climate, and soil," stripped their choice away. By his logic, popular sovereignty was preferable to a prohibition on slavery. He therefore urged Congress to "trust the people with the great, sacred, fundamental right of prescribing their own institutions." He testily denied that Southerners had forced him to repeal the Missouri Compromise. He reminded senators that he had advocated popular sovereignty since the late 1840s, and he informed them that only time constraints prevented him from reporting a similar Nebraska bill in 1853. He likely spoke the truth. He had been pressed for time in 1853 and probably had desired to establish the principle of popular sovereignty, especially because the organization of Nebraska Territory required him to endorse either congressional nonintervention with territorial slavery or congressional prohibition of it. Popular sovereignty had settled the raging storm over national expansion in 1850, and Douglas evidently expected the Kansas-Nebraska Act to reinforce that precedent. Indeed, his expectations were nothing short of idealistic. "I desire to see this principle recognized as a rule of action in all time to come," he stated in March when concluding the Senate's debate over the bill, because it will "destroy all sectional parties and sectional agitations" and will assure "the peace, the harmony, and perpetuity of the Union." To a northern Democrat like Douglas, popular sovereignty seemed a perfect fusion of democracy and Union.[36]

Beneath it lay a characteristic northern Democratic tolerance for enslaving blacks. Popular sovereignty appealed to Douglas partly because he did not believe that enslaving blacks was a moral wrong. He did not share Lincoln's conviction that all men were created equal, with inalienable rights to life, liberty, and property. Instead, he believed that only men who established self-government had the right to its fruits. "The civilized world have always held," he argued in 1850, "that when any race of men have shown" themselves to be "utterly incapable of governing themselves, they must, in the nature of things, be governed by others, by such laws as are deemed applicable to their condition." To Douglas, Africans had shown just such incapacity throughout the "history of the world," and so the preservation of white liberty required black subordination in America. The method of subordination mattered little. By his logic, northern black codes and southern slavery differed in degree but not in kind. Both were necessary systems of race control instituted by sovereign political communities of white men. Comparing blacks to women and children, who also lacked the capacity for self-government, Douglas observed that all were dependent on and subject to white men. On that account the racial differences that he called the "real gist of the matter" in 1854 justified repeal of the Missouri Compromise's antislavery provisions. "I do not understand that it requires any higher degree of intelligence, virtue, or civilization," he judged, "to legislate for the negro than for the white man." If the white man was capable of legislating for the black man, but the black man was incapable of legislating for himself, then the moral choice was clear to Douglas. Slavery had a justifiable, even necessary, political existence. These ideas were not alien to other northern Democrats. As one of Douglas's correspondents wrote in February of 1854, slavery was "a great blessing" to blacks "in comparison" to their condition in Africa "or in a state of freedom amongst us."[37]

Douglas found further justification for slavery in the American political tradition. This was no simple matter for a northern politician. Abolitionists and freesoilers had argued for decades that the Declaration of Independence and the Northwest Ordinance had dedicated the nation to liberty. Northern Democrats had never contested this claim, but opposition to the Kansas-Nebraska bill compelled Douglas to take issue with it. In January, abolitionist congressmen published a widely distributed manifesto called the *Appeal of the Independent Democrats*, which arraigned the bill "as a criminal betrayal" of the founders' antislavery policy. Stung by the attack, Douglas propounded a competing version of national history, contending that the founders had venerated local self-government, not antislavery idealism, and therefore had permitted slavery's expansion by prescribing "a line of demarkation" between free and slaveholding territories, enabling slavery to expand south of the Ohio River into Mississippi and Louisiana. He maintained that this policy had worked admirably until 1848, when freesoil opposition to an extension of the line through the Mexican Cession forced Congress to organize Utah and New Mexico territories with popular sovereignty. But he expressed no sorrow at the change. Considering popular sovereignty a return to the colonial principle of self-government, he touted its power to preserve the Union, urging Congress in 1854 to return "to the doctrines of the Revolution," leaving the people "to do as they may see proper in respect to their own internal affairs." Although his formulation of popular sovereignty justified the enslavement of black people, Douglas averred that this "principle" formed the basis of the nation's "entire republican system." His interpretation of American freedom carried a southern mark.[38]

Douglas also valued slavery's contribution to America's economic development. Unlike freesoilers, he never criticized what they called the "blight of slavery" or so much as hinted that slave labor degraded free labor. Instead, he argued that southern agriculture indispensably contributed to American economic growth. He particularly lauded cotton, calling it the "most powerful lever of the commerce of the world." He maintained that it broke down English tariff barriers to American products, generated export monies to offset foreign imports, fueled northeastern textile production, and expanded northern agricultural markets. Other southern products, such as tobacco, sugar, and rice, likewise enhanced the export economy and enlivened domestic trade. For these reasons Douglas asserted that Americans benefited from regional differences in soil and climate, and he celebrated the "common interest" that characterized American industries. Douglas's convictions about regional diversity influenced his conception of how free and slave labor interrelated. He believed that slavery flourished where white men found it profitable, normally in hot, lowland climates. To the extent that free and slave laborers worked in close proximity, he appeared to consider their relations harmonious. More typically, he bypassed this troubling issue by focusing on the slaveholder's relationship to slave labor, which subtly adopted the southern presumption that slaveownership was the route to upward mobility. Douglas's support for slavery wherever it paid encouraged him to abet slavery's expansion wherever white men wanted it. Advocacy of popular sovereignty followed logically from the idea that slavery complemented, rather than undermined, the free labor economy.[39]

Douglas's tolerance of slavery emboldened him to risk the possibility of slavery's expansion. To be sure, he probably did not expect slavery to take hold in Kansas or Nebraska. He reminded Congress that the people of Utah and New Mexico had not instituted slavery since the inception of popular sovereignty in 1850, and he declared that he had "no idea" that the new territories could be a slaveholding region "permanently." He also claimed, although disingenuously, that "candid men" agreed that climate, production, and physical geography "excluded slavery" from the new territories. Yet he could not himself deny the possibility of slavery's expansion, especially in Kansas. He admitted that some slaveowners already had established residence in the territory, and he conceded that slavery would "continue for a little while" until

settlers poured in. He even argued that the diffusion of slavery, to the extent
it occurred, was beneficial for the slave. Reviving an old proslavery argument,
he maintained that the removal of slaves to rich new soil improved their
"temporal condition" by assuring them "an abundance of provisions." These
statements highlighted an awkward fact that Douglas could not obscure: the
soil and climate of eastern Kansas mirrored that of neighboring Missouri.
This knowledge was not lost on the Missourians. Senator Atchison of Missouri urged repeal of the antislavery provisions of the Missouri Compromise
in order to enable his constituents to take slaves to Kansas, and he steeled
the nerves of southern congressmen with arguments that Kansas was ripe
for the taking. Atchison made the double game of popular sovereignty all
too evident, and anti-Nebraskites justifiably weighted southern intentions
more heavily than Douglas's freesoil promises. They knew that a rush of
slaveholders across the border likely would put a proslavery stamp on popular
sovereignty, Douglas's climatic argument notwithstanding. Northerners had
consented to popular sovereignty as a Union-saving expedient in 1850, but
it lost its charms when it opened free territory to slavery.[40]

Ironically, the mobilization of anti-Nebraska freesoil sentiment deepened
Douglas's resolve to pass the bill. He understood before submitting his revised
bill that repealing the Missouri Compromise's antislavery provisions would
engulf the North in protests, but he trusted that the "storm will soon spend
its fury." He considered antislavery politics a threat to the Democratic Party
and the Union, and he intended to break its power permanently. Moreover,
he thought that popular sovereignty was the nation's only hope for last-
ing sectional peace, and therefore he was willing to undergo a fiery trial to
engrave the principle of self-government on the public mind. This course of
action reflected his incomprehension of antislavery sentiment. He perceived
neither the depth of Northerners' opposition to slavery nor their hostility
to its economic and political aggrandizement. Rather, he repeatedly denied
that antislavery sentiment had abiding roots in northern society and culture.
He instead blamed extremism. In 1848 he had contended that "abolitionism"
resulted from incendiary southern speeches, and now he argued that abolitionists had raised the "tornado" of anti-Nebraskism by falsifying "the law
and the facts." This conviction led him to dismiss the salience of northern
public meetings that burned him in effigy, even though such exhibitions
deeply wounded him. Abolitionist politicians "make the people believe" that
the bill is a hideous crime, he explained, which caused them to protest "under
the delusion that they have been wronged." Certain of his rectitude, Douglas
expected the whipped-up crisis to fade quickly. He had tamed a Chicago mob
incensed by the 1850 fugitive slave law, and he thought he could again stem

the tide. In concert with his correspondents, he predicted that the Act "will be as popular at the North as at the South" once its principles were understood, because "you cannot convince" Northerners that self-government "deprives a people of the right of legislating for themselves." On this point he was sure that he and the northern people saw eye to eye.[41]

Yet Douglas was further from public sentiment on this matter than he imagined. Indeed, he was far distant from the sentiment of many other northern Democrats. He was willing, perhaps even eager, to purify the northern Democracy by ridding it of unreliable antislavery elements. He knew that his bill would force freesoil Democrats to declare their loyalties, and he probably anticipated some party reorganization in the 1854 elections, particularly freesoil Democrats swapping allegiances with Unionist Whigs. Nevertheless, he expected the Democracy to emerge "united upon principle" and "stronger than ever," and predicted that the Kansas-Nebraska Act would then "impart peace to the country & stability to the Union." This rosy view accounted neither for virulent freesoil sentiment nor for conservative Whigs' and Democrats' deep-seated hostility to slavery agitation. Douglas apparently never considered that some of his erstwhile allies would blame him for the sectional agitation, but he soon learned that even some southern and central Illinois Democrats considered the Missouri Compromise repeal an abomination. They did not object to popular sovereignty per se, but to the incendiary use it was put. Freesoilers' anger burned even hotter. After all, the Nebraska bill deliberately destroyed a legal barrier to slavery's expansion. But Douglas returned their anger with contempt, calling them abolitionists because he considered them toxic to the Union's perpetuity. He defied their creed that slavery was freedom's antithesis. Instead, he counseled tolerance for slavery, claiming that its legalization should be left "to the arbitrament of those who are immediately interested in and alone responsible for its consequences." His principle of popular sovereignty thus took sharp issue with the growing antislavery nationalism that a generation of antislavery activists had developed and begun to popularize in the North. By advocating popular sovereignty, he gambled that antislavery ideology had shallow roots in the northern public mind. He was profoundly mistaken.[42]

The portents of looming disaster were quickly evident in Illinois. Only a handful of Democratic journals supported the Nebraska bill, led by the *State Register* and *Quincy Herald*. The loyal few met stiff opposition from mutinous Democratic editors throughout the state. The *Chicago Democratic Press*, *Chicago Democrat*, *Alton Courier*, *Belleville Advocate*, *Chester Herald*, *Greenville Journal*, *Urbana Union*, *Salem Advocate*, *Rock River Democrat*, *Galena Jeffersonian*, and *Aurora Guardian* all went on record against the bill, as did virtually all Whig newspapers. Political disenchantment with Douglas was especially evident in the state's cities. In Chicago, Ottawa, Rockford, Alton, and Belleville, residents mounted massive protests against what they considered Douglas's treachery. Chicago Democrats participated in an anti-Nebraska assembly on February 8, and the city's Germans participated in a mass meeting on March 16 that culminated with the burning of Douglas's effigy. Political arousal also reached the pulpit. Ministers delivered hundreds of anti-Nebraska sermons and sent signed protests to Congress "in the name of Almighty God."[43] These denunciations put a chill into Democratic ranks. In February, Democratic legislators in the General Assembly only reluctantly obeyed Douglas's instructions to endorse the bill. Although the public had yet to mobilize in opposition, 38.7 percent of the party's legislators voted against the resolutions or abstained. This figure likely understated Democratic opposition to the bill. Lincoln later reported that only three of the seventy-five Democratic legislators approved of the bill in a February party caucus. Even more ominous than Democratic opposition was the renewal of the antislavery alliance between Whigs and northern Illinois Democrats, who together opposed the resolutions 24–7. The signs were unmistakable. Most Northerners reviled the bill.[44]

But Northerners' hostility to the bill could not prevent its passage. Support from three of the state's five Democratic representatives marked Illinois as one of the more steadfast Democratic states. Democratic congressmen John Wentworth and William Bissell joined Illinois's four Whig congressmen to fight the bill. The delegations from most northern states exhibited even greater resistance. Only four of thirteen state delegations controlled by the northern Democratic Party cast a majority of their ballots for the measure, and not even pressure from President Pierce could bring 50 percent of the House's northern Democrats to sanction the bill. This resistance, combined with implacable northern Whig opposition, rendered House passage of the bill difficult. Nevertheless, the aye votes of almost 90 percent of Southerners from both parties offset northern opposition. The Southerners' allegiance to slavery was particularly evident in the House. New York Democrats led the revolt against the bill by bottling it up in the Committee of the Whole, which prevented a floor vote on the measure for six weeks. Once the bill's supporters overcame this obstacle, the opposition filibustered with long speeches and an avalanche of dilatory motions. After two weeks of obstructionism that threatened passage of the bill, Georgia Whig Alexander Stephens rescued the bill with a parliamentary stratagem that shut off debate. Shortly thereafter, his phalanx of southern Whigs provided key votes to pass the bill. Stephens's guileful strategy trampled northern political opposition as surely as Douglas's bill flouted northern public opinion. It was a fitting end to an inglorious bill.[45]

～

The Kansas-Nebraska Act epitomized the national clash of slavery and freedom. Although its introduction and passage rested to a degree on contingencies largely unrelated to broad historical forces, such as Douglas's psychology, it owed its conception and execution to the problem of slavery in American social and political life. Westward migration posed calamitous political troubles for antebellum Americans only because of proslavery expansionism. This was as true for Nebraska as it had been for Missouri, Utah, New Mexico, and California. Similarly, slavery made bi-sectional political alliances necessary for the Union's preservation, even while making them very difficult to maintain. The related problems of national expansion and partisan breakdown induced Douglas to attempt to eradicate the incommensurability of slavery and freedom with the principle of popular sovereignty. His momentous decision was neither irrational nor incomprehensible. It reflected his loyalty to a party that was uniquely interested in ending tensions over slavery and uniquely positioned to do so. Northern Democrats always had considered their party a shield for the Union, and for that reason they vigorously opposed antislavery politics. Measures sponsored by the northern Democracy had helped pacify the nation in 1850, and Douglas expected no less from his 1854 bill. The Kansas-Nebraska Act was thus no mystifying aberration in antebellum politics; rather, it culminated the northern Democrats' attempt to blunt the clash of slavery and freedom. But Douglas never comprehended that his party's power to destroy as well as to enact slavery compromises invested it with as great a potential for disunion as for union. This was the paradox of a party located at the intersection of slavery and freedom in America. That passage of Douglas's bill almost annihilated the northern Democratic Party speaks tellingly of slavery's incongruity in a nation dedicated to freedom.[46]

The act also transformed northern politics. That it did so should come as no surprise. After all, it administered two bracing shocks to the northern people: it represented a betrayal of staggering proportions by southern politicians, and it nakedly challenged most Northerners' understanding of American freedom. In doing so, it forced them to come to grips with slavery. Few Northerners willingly defended slavery's morality, the growth of slaveholders' political power, or the opening of new territory to slave labor. Yet the Kansas-Nebraska Act implicitly did all these things, on principle. Douglas informed Georgia's Howell Cobb in April 1854 that the North would never "decide that the principle upon which our whole republican system rests is

vicious & wrong."[47] But Douglas failed to comprehend that many Northerners considered slavery vicious and wrong, and countless others considered
it, at the very least, injurious and regrettable. Certainly, a majority of them
considered it an absolute contradiction of freedom. While some Northerners
had accepted popular sovereignty in 1850 as an expedient freesoil policy to
save the Union, very few had elevated it to a national ideal. The repeal of the
Missouri Compromise in 1854 created a radically different context for popular
sovereignty. Most Northerners deemed the repeal an execrable proslavery
sin, damned it for reopening the slavery controversy, and trembled for the
fate of Kansas and the nation. Shocked by popular sovereignty's new creedal
claims—and its alarming new application in Kansas Territory—Northerners
vowed to defend freedom. The Kansas-Nebraska Act thus backfired cata-
strophically. It destroyed the freesoil reputation of popular sovereignty and
precipitated a remorseless national struggle to determine slavery's relationship to freedom.[48]

6. The Collapse of the Douglas Democracy, 1854–1860

NORTHERN DEMOCRATS HAD ONLY barely possessed sufficient strength to lead the forces of compromise to victory in 1850. The crisis produced by the Kansas-Nebraska Act would tax their remaining strength to the utmost. Had northern Democrats crushed their opposition in the 1854 elections, Douglas's gambit to marginalize antislavery politics might have succeeded. But just the reverse occurred, and the emergence of a vibrant antislavery political movement, which crystallized into the newly founded Republican Party in 1856, created severe problems for northern Democrats. The Republicans' insistence on halting slavery's growth not only increasingly forced Democrats to justify popular sovereignty by defending slavery, but also caused southern politicians to inflict unyielding proslavery demands on northern Democrats in a search for validation and security. The fundamentally different understandings of freedom in the North and South necessarily produced a clash in national policy. Republicans sought to preserve freedom by prohibiting slavery in the territories, while Southerners insisted on protecting the property rights of territorial slaveholders for the same reason. This irreconcilable conflict imperiled the northern Democrats' standing in both sections of the Union, making it difficult for leaders like Douglas to maintain the unity and power of the party. But he could have no other goal, believing that only the Democratic Party could keep the nation together. By decade's end, however, debate over the meaning of freedom had sundered not only northern Democrats from southern Democrats, but also northern Democratic politicians from their constituents. Most Northerners rejected both the core concept of popular sovereignty—that whites' freedoms included the power to enslave

blacks—and its nationalist corollary—that freedom in America was inseparably intertwined with slavery.

⮩

The sustained outrage against the Nebraska Act was unprecedented in
American political history. In Illinois, as in the rest of the North, protests
against the act soon gathered steam and lasted until the elections in November. As early as January 22, a Carlinville editor reported that the "Nebraska
question is absorbing the public," and a few weeks later in Jacksonville Democrats broke up an anti-Nebraska meeting called by freesoilers, which precipitated a protest that one observer described as the "largest I have ever seen."
Illinoisans continued agitating during the spring and summer, punctuated
by a massive Fourth of July celebration in Chicago that resolved itself into
an anti-Nebraska convocation. In August raucous crowds greeted Douglas
on his return to Illinois, and in September ten thousand hissing Chicagoans
prevented him from making a Nebraska speech. Public animosity followed
him like a plague during his travels through northern and even central Illinois
that fall. As Democratic senator James Shields concluded glumly in October,
"The Anti Nebraska feeling is too deep—more than I thought it was."[1]

The political upheaval upset party ranks. This was not entirely unexpected.
Whig congressman Richard Yates had predicted in March that the bill would
rend party ranks, leaving only a "northern party and a southern party," and
he was quickly proved prescient. Anti-Nebraska meetings were often non-
partisan and produced incongruous spectacles, such as Whig leader O. H.
Browning writing anti-Nebraska resolutions that angry Democrats endorsed
in Quincy. Such phenomena led a Jacksonville newspaper editor to marvel
at the "perfect independence among men of all parties in the expression of
their sentiments on this question." One notable consequence of the bill was
the immediate attempt of abolitionists and Free Democrats to fuse with
other anti-Nebraskites into an antislavery Republican Party. Although this
effort failed at the state level, it partly succeeded in northern Illinois, laying
groundwork for the Republicans' successful emergence in 1856. Of equal
significance was the disruption of Illinois's Democratic Party. A bevy of leading Democrats ranged themselves against the Nebraska Act, most notably
Lyman Trumbull, John M. Palmer, and John McClernand. They were joined
by thousands of their constituents, who expressed two central reasons for
their apostasy. Some anti-Nebraska Democrats, including the German population, opposed the extension of slavery into free territories and condemned
Nebraska Democrats as being "recreant to the interests of freedom." Other
Democrats, such as John McClernand, criticized the disruptive political

consequences of the act rather than its proslavery implications. He repudiated the Nebraska Act as an "unreasonable" party test, complained that it
exacerbated rather than suppressed slavery agitation, and warned that it
endangered the party's survival. In the wake of the act, party stalwarts faced
besiegers from without and sappers from within.[2]

The politicization of temperance in 1854 compounded the Democrats'
troubles. The temperance movement had been growing since the early
1850s, when the General Assembly passed a law limiting liquor sales. When
the law proved ineffective, temperance advocates established a Maine Law
Alliance in 1853, which petitioned the General Assembly to follow Maine's
example and prohibit alcohol sales. After meeting a rebuff from legislators,
prohibitionists elected Maine Law advocates to the legislature in 1854. The
temperance movement soon blended with anti-Nebraskism, largely because
many evangelicals endorsed both causes. One voter instructed his legislator
to inscribe on his banner "An exterminating war against Intemperance—&
restoration of the Missouri Compromise." In northern Illinois, temperance
conventions seconded the nominations of local and regional anti-Nebraska
organizations. One observer perceptively noted that the "politicians are getting *orfully skeered*, with anti-Nebraska on one hand, and anti-whiskey on
the other."[3]

Nativism also threatened the Democrats' control of Illinois politics. Hostility to the massive waves of preponderantly Catholic and often impoverished
German and Irish immigrants who arrived on American shores from 1846
to 1854 had been growing throughout the nation since the mid-1840s, but
nativist sentiment did not generate a powerful political organization until the
Kansas-Nebraska Act created a vast pool of disgruntled voters. From May to
October 1854, membership in the secretive nativist organization known as
the Know Nothings grew from about fifty thousand to one million people,
mostly in the northern states. The movement expressed Protestant animus
toward Catholicism, native-born laborers' hostility to increased competition
and lower wages, and widespread disenchantment with the growth of poverty,
alcoholism, and crime in immigrant neighborhoods. The Democratic Party's
vigorous championing of immigrants' naturalization and suffrage rights,
which successfully captured the immigrant vote, also shaped the nativist
movement, pitting temperance and antislavery reformers sharply against the
Irish, who drank whiskey, despised blacks, and unapologetically endorsed
pro-southern measures such as the Kansas-Nebraska Act. The Know Nothing
movement flourished in Chicago, home to many immigrants, where leading
Whig and Free Soil journals regularly flayed Irish Catholics and approved
of nativist reforms. In a typical article, Chicago's *Free West* judged that the

Democratic Party opposed nativist reforms because Irish Catholics were the "standard bearers of the slavery and whiskey banner." The *Free West* was not alone in conjoining nativism, antislavery, and temperance. In fact, one nativist anonymously testified that a "majority" of the Know Nothings he knew considered antislavery more important than nativism. He vowed that he would "sooner see the whole order, and its principles blown higher than the *seven stars*, than see it perverted to the support of the Slave power." But he had little to fear in the wake of the Nebraska Act, when antislavery attitudes helped fuel the rising movement.[4]

The Nebraska Democrats—as Democratic Party stalwarts were now christened—deployed a series of arguments to counter voter backlash in 1854. Unionism was their leading appeal. Douglas warned that anti-Nebraskites sought to establish "a great northern, sectional party" on "the abolition platform" in order "to carry on an offensive war" against the South. Likewise, the *State Register* trumpeted that there were "but two parties in the land— a UNION PARTY and an ABOLITION PARTY." Douglas expected these extreme claims to inhibit partisan defections and to attract conservative, southern-born Whig voters. With this strategy uppermost, he vilified northern Whigs as abolitionists, enlisted southern Whigs to speak for the Nebraska Act in Illinois, and instructed the editor of the *Chicago Times* to treat the multitudinous anti-Nebraskites as one "great abolition Party." The *State Register* followed this lead, repeatedly warning central Illinois Whigs that the coalition of anti-Nebraska elements into "fusion" tickets would eventuate in abolitionism and disunion.[5]

The Democrats also attacked nativism. They sought to tar the anti-Nebraskites with nativism and thus blunt the appeal of antislavery politics among immigrants and Catholics. Douglas therefore denounced the "alliance" of nativists with anti-Nebraskites and condemned the Know Nothings' proscriptive politics. He protested that ethnic and religious discrimination violated the Constitution and profaned American ideals of "civil and religious freedom." In cadence with Douglas, the *State Register* charged that the Know Nothings intended to destroy the Democratic Party in order to exclude immigrants and Catholics from the political process. Off the stump, Douglas more prosaically urged the *Chicago Times* to charge into the Know Nothings "boldly and disputedly" in an effort to "bring the Germans and all other foreigners and Catholics to our side."[6]

The Democrats also sporadically advanced a freesoil interpretation of popular sovereignty. Democratic editors and orators occasionally claimed that popular sovereignty would produce freesoil in Kansas, Nebraska, and possibly the entire West. For instance, the *Quincy Herald* contended that very few southern congressmen believed that slavery could go to Kansas, and the *State Register* argued that settlers from the South "would be more likely than northern emigrants, to oppose it, because they better appreciate the evils attending the institution." Meanwhile, Senator James Shields proclaimed that popular sovereignty, if applied fully and fairly, would "work with such powerful force and effect that no man would ever see another slave territory on this continent." These freesoil appeals doubtless attracted some voters who were torn between the values of antislavery and Union, such as Elder Benjamin Bradbury, who wrote Douglas that he had "suported the measure from the start" despite suffering much reproach, "having always the fullest belief that neither of those Teritories when mad[e] states would be made slavestates." Freesoil appeals thus helped to combat what Douglas called the "allied forces of abolitionism, whigism, nativeism, and religious intolerance."[7]

But northern Democrats advocated popular sovereignty far more frequently than they did freesoilism. Douglas declared that the principle of the Nebraska Act involved "the right and capacity of the people to make their own laws and manage their own local and domestic concerns," or what he called "self-government." Acknowledging that some Americans considered slavery to be immoral, he observed that "it is not the only wrong upon which the people of each of the States and Territories of this Union are called upon to act and decide for themselves." Necessarily, the people had to establish standards of morality. Other Democrats followed his lead. Observing that the Nebraska Act "recognizes the right of the people to adopt slavery or reject it as they may see fit," the *State Register* insisted that Northerners "have no right to speculate upon the morality or immorality of slavery in any such connection." Consequently, the *Register* stated that freesoilism had "nothing to do" with the central question the Nebraska Act presented: that of "state and territorial rights, of domestic tranquillity, national safety, and the integrity of the Union."[8]

Almost inevitably, the Nebraska Democrats' adherence to popular sovereignty compromised their freesoilism. The *Eastern Illinoisan* wrote that the Nebraska bill was "just the thing to smoke the freesoilers" out of their holes. If "it is right" that Southerners can choose slavery, reasoned the editor, "then it is equally just" that Northerners "should have the same privilege." The *State Register* similarly concluded that "there is no danger of the introduction of slavery into Nebraska, but if a majority of the settlers of the territory desire it they have a right to it under our constitution." At root, the freesoilism of Nebraska Democrats rarely flowed from insuperable objections to slavery, and indeed some of them took sharp issue with the freesoilers' reasoning and objectives. Former senator Sidney Breese wrote to a correspondent that he would consider the rise of an antislavery party as "an event more disastrous to our confederacy" than the "absolute legislation of slavery had Congress the power, into territories now free." Looking "at this question of Slavery, in a practical and patriotic point of view," he asked, "How can its extension into Nebraska or any other territory affect us?" He denied that slavery's expansion harmed slaves or strengthened slavery, contending that as "you extend the area" of slavery, "you better the condition of the Slave" and eventually "fit him for the enjoyment of freedom." Here were statements to shock the millions of northern voters with growing freesoil inclinations, and something no northern Democrat was likely to state publicly, yet in fact the sentiment harmonized well with the *State Register*'s less inflammatory judgment that slavery was a "much smaller evil than civil war and dismemberment." The Nebraska Act thus activated the latent northern Democratic tendency toward both conditional freesoilism and unconditional Unionism, which in subsequent years would cause northern Democrats to retreat from freesoil politics as the nation neared disunion. But challenging Northerners' freesoil sentiment was dangerous. As Bradbury presciently observed after the election, "should Kansas be brought in as a slave state I perdict troubles to meet that we have never yet seen."[9]

Nevertheless, the alarming intensity of anti-Nebraska politics in 1854 led Douglas to advance explicit arguments in defense of slavery. For instance, like Breese, Douglas repeated the half-century-old southern argument that slaves taken to Kansas or Nebraska would improve their "temporal condition" by removal "from poor lands to rich ones." Strikingly, however, unlike Breese or Illinois's proslavery advocates in the 1820s, he did not pair this argument with the claim that slavery's diffusion promoted emancipation. To be sure, that claim had worn threadbare given that slavery's earlier diffusion had anchored the institution in the trans-Appalachian West and spawned a generation of fiery proslavery politicians, but that outcome only underscored Douglas's willingness to abet slavery's expansion and perpetuation. He certainly could not have more clearly expressed his conviction that slavery's expansion was good for slaves. Few Northerners would have dared make such a declaration in a widely published public letter.[10]

Douglas also advanced a proslavery interpretation of the Constitution in a major Fourth of July speech in Philadelphia. Disputing the claim of some abolitionists that the Constitution was "an anti-slavery instrument," Douglas replied that representatives from the "twelve slaveholding States" at the Constitutional Convention did nothing "to abolish slavery." As he correctly observed, slaveholders had sought and received constitutional concessions for slavery. Yet Douglas further argued that the founders never imagined "extending or circumscribing slavery" by the "action of the federal government." This contention disregarded both the constitutional provision enabling Congress to ban the importation of slaves in 1808 and the Confederation Congress's prohibition of slavery in the Northwest Territory, a law informed by the antislavery sentiments of many framers and later ratified by the new federal government in 1789. Both provisions illustrated clearly that the founders did conceive of circumscribing slavery, and, as Lincoln would later show, most of the Constitution's authors also acknowledged Congress's power over territorial slavery.[11]

But Douglas's objects were exactly the reverse of Lincoln's. Seeking to claim the founders' mandate for popular sovereignty, Douglas argued that the framers designed the Constitution "to recognise and protect whatever institutions each State acting for itself, had or should establish," which mandated the federal government's "duty" to protect slavery in "the several States" as it was "found to exist." Furthermore, argued Douglas, the constitutional provision that new states entered the Union "on an equal footing" with existing states meant that "every new State which shall be admitted in all time to come" had the right to "exercise every power" secured to the original states by the Constitution. In Douglas's novel constitutional interpretation, territories were infant states, and therefore Congress had no right to forbid territorial inhabitants from legalizing slavery. Much turned on his argument. If the federal government owed protection to territorial slavery, should settlers establish it, as well as to slavery in the states, then the Union would be safe for slavery, and slavery for the Union. For this reason, Douglas would vigorously develop his constitutional interpretation in subsequent years. In 1854, however, Douglas thought that these arguments would triumph immediately. In June he told a New York audience that if "the north is to be arrayed against the south" after the anti-Nebraskites "form a party upon geographical and sectional lines," then "there will be found enough patriotic men to meet the issue." And in September he confidently predicted, "We will gain more votes than we will lose on Nebraska and No Nothingism" and will "*carry the State.*"[12]

But the election results were an overwhelming rebuke. Anti-Nebraska candidates took five of the state's nine congressional seats, losing two contests by razor-thin margins, and won control of the state's House of Representatives. Two of the five anti-Nebraska congressmen were Know Nothings, and the others had generally received Know Nothing support. Voters in other northern states shed Democratic blood even more freely. After the election the Democrats controlled only two northern state legislatures, and the number of their northern congressmen plummeted from seventy-nine to twenty-four, with further severe losses pending in states that elected congressmen

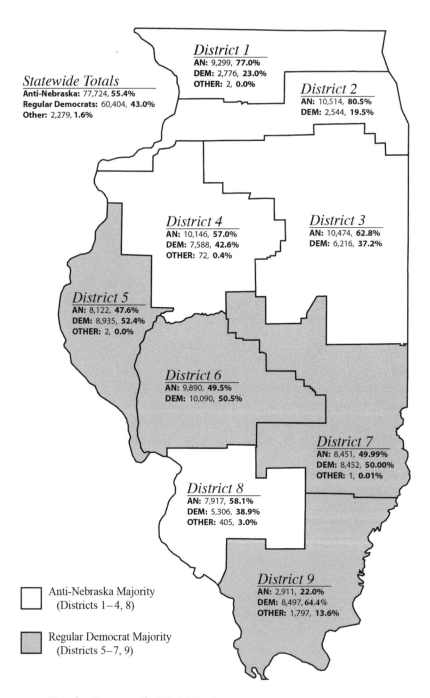

Statewide Totals
Anti-Nebraska: 77,724, **55.4%**
Regular Democrats: 60,404, **43.0%**
Other: 2,279, **1.6%**

District 1
AN: 9,299, **77.0%**
DEM: 2,776, **23.0%**
OTHER: 2, **0.0%**

District 2
AN: 10,514, **80.5%**
DEM: 2,544, **19.5%**

District 4
AN: 10,146, **57.0%**
DEM: 7,588, **42.6%**
OTHER: 72, **0.4%**

District 3
AN: 10,474, **62.8%**
DEM: 6,216, **37.2%**

District 5
AN: 8,122, **47.6%**
DEM: 8,935, **52.4%**
OTHER: 2, **0.0%**

District 6
AN: 9,890, **49.5%**
DEM: 10,090, **50.5%**

District 7
AN: 8,451, **49.99%**
DEM: 8,452, **50.00%**
OTHER: 1, **0.01%**

District 8
AN: 7,917, **58.1%**
DEM: 5,306, **38.9%**
OTHER: 405, **3.0%**

District 9
AN: 2,911, **22.0%**
DEM: 8,497, **64.4%**
OTHER: 1,797, **13.6%**

☐ Anti-Nebraska Majority
(Districts 1–4, 8)

▨ Regular Democrat Majority
(Districts 5–7, 9)

MAP 5. **Vote for Congress, by District, 1854**
Note: Numbers reflect votes and rounded percentages of the vote for anti-Nebraska candidates, Democrats, and other candidates. The anti-Nebraska vote aggregates Republicans, Whigs, and anti-Nebraska Democrats.

in odd-numbered years. Illinois's new state legislature did its part, replacing Democratic senator James Shields with anti-Nebraska Democrat Lyman Trumbull, passing anti-Nebraska resolutions through the House, and driving a Maine Law referendum through the General Assembly. The Democratic Party's northern opposition, although divided, was formidable: Know Nothings, Republicans, and the remaining Whigs generally opposed slavery.[13]

The election returns indicated that Illinois's Democratic Party could no longer rely on its traditional voting base. Many northern Illinois Democrats defected to anti-Nebraskism or abstained from voting, contributing to decisive antislavery victories in Illinois's northernmost congressional districts. In southern Illinois, the defections of anti-Nebraska German Democrats put Lyman Trumbull into Congress from the region's Eighth District before the state legislature elevated him into the United States Senate.[14] Fortunately for the Democrats, voters with native southern ties joined the party in central and southern Illinois, cushioning the party's fall. These were the Unionist Whigs so ardently wooed by the *State Register*. But the bulk of northern voters without southern ties were much less sympathetic to the party's course. Illinois's immigrants illustrated this tendency well. Although the Democrats retained the allegiance of the Irish, only about 30 percent of German voters supported the Democratic Party, in contrast to the roughly 90 percent who had done so in 1852, a stunning decline produced by their strong antislavery sentiments, and this despite their hostility to the nativists in the anti-Nebraska movement. Northern Illinois's faster rate of growth combined with the growing regionalization of voting behavior meant that the Democratic Party needed to recapture the anti-Nebraska immigrant vote. The party's traditional strength in central and southern Illinois could not salvage its fortunes alone.[15]

⁂

Douglas did not back down from this challenge. He had known that repealing the antislavery provisions of the Missouri Compromise would provoke a response from antislavery Northerners, and he scorned the idea of conceding their primacy in northern politics and thus putting the Union at risk. Therefore he pressed on with the same ideas that had motivated his introduction of the bill, and presumed that anti-Nebraska sentiment would not long sustain antislavery politics. This was not as unrealistic as later events would come to suggest. As Bradbury wisely judged after the election, "I canot yet think that the ship is to be given up if Kansa[n]s will but speadly do their work in making a state and that free all may be well and I think will." Bradbury comprehended that a freesoil outcome in Kansas would rehabilitate popular sovereignty's reputation and severely undercut the anti-Nebraska movement. In the meantime, as Douglas predicted shortly after the election, the "incongruous and irreconcilable" factions of the anti-Nebraska movement would likely come to blows; and, indeed, in early 1855 differences between anti-Nebraska state legislators hampered their efforts to pass antislavery resolutions in the General Assembly. Moreover, Douglas expected the nativist movement to undermine antislavery politics, especially given the prominence of the temperance issue in the upcoming state and local elections. "The Nebraska fight is over," he wrote to Charles Lanphier of the *Illinois State Register* in December 1854, "and Know Nothingism has taken its place as the chief issue in the future." If this were true, the Democrats could lure back disaffected immigrants and stabilize the party. These prospects encouraged Douglas to advocate support of "Democratic principles and the regular organization of the Party," purging anti-Nebraska Democrats and cutting "loose now and forever from abolitionism." This decision, which reflected both the Democrats' practice of enforcing party discipline and Douglas's original determination to purify the party, doubled down his bet on the Kansas-Nebraska Act. Dissenters could only return by endorsing popular sovereignty.[16]

Correspondingly, Douglas sought to maintain party ties with southern Democrats. He needed their support to validate his Unionist appeals, establish popular sovereignty as the party creed, and ensure that southern politicians supported an evenhanded application of popular sovereignty in Kansas and elsewhere. Accordingly, he displayed sensitivity to southern attitudes, turning down an 1855 invitation to lecture on slavery in Boston, writing that his "tastes" and "public duties" precluded him from speaking about "a domestic regulation" over which "neither the federal government nor the citizens or authorities of other States have any right to interfere." More significantly, he indicated his willingness to shield territorial slavery with the same constitutional protections guaranteed to slavery in the states. During a Democratic Party meeting in Chicago on October 12, 1855, he introduced a resolution that "congress has no rightful authority to establish, abolish or prohibit slavery in the states or territories." This resolution did not undermine his belief that settlers could exclude slavery during the territorial period, which southern politicians derisively called "squatter sovereignty," but it did eviscerate his prior argument that popular sovereignty was merely a preferable alternative to congressional restriction. Since at least 1845 he had acknowledged Congress's authority over territorial slavery, but now he claimed that Congress could not rightfully prohibit it. This was a significantly pro-southern step, distinctly moving him toward the southern understanding of freedom.[17]

Popular sovereignty was the key to Douglas's partnership with Southerners. Few Americans denied Congress's power to prohibit territorial slavery prior to 1819, when zealous southern defenders of slavery unveiled the argument during the Missouri crisis. Consequently, to freesoilers, Douglas's newest proclamation meshed forebodingly with southern claims that the Constitution carried slavery into the territories. Douglas did not adopt that position, but his resolutions did represent an attempt to find common ground with Southerners on popular sovereignty. He had coauthored the resolutions in cooperation with border-state allies in order to produce "unity of action between the free & slave states" at the 1856 Democratic national convention. He termed the resolutions the "*Illinois Platform*," urged his lieutenants to "get every county & Town to concur in them," and predicted that Illinois would "have the honor of making the national Platform." As he had informed Georgia moderate Howell Cobb on October 6, the Democracy must be "consolidated" upon a platform that is "specific on all controverted points," in "such language that it cannot be construed one way south and another way north." If he could persuade Southerners to endorse squatter sovereignty despite the likelihood that Kansas would then enter the Union as a free state, Unionist politics likely would bear fruit for the Democratic Party in the North, while slavery's interests could be served elsewhere, most notably through expansion into the Caribbean and Central America. Such an agreement would have constituted a genuine alliance, and one scholar has called it the "southern strategy" of the northern Democratic Party. One way or the other, Douglas had to propitiate the slave interest in order to preserve party unity, as his correspondence with Southerners illustrated clearly.[18]

But as Douglas well knew, southern politicians had never sanctioned his interpretation of popular sovereignty. Most of them had claimed since 1850 that the federal constitution protected territorial slavery, which Douglas denied, and they resolved their difference with him and other northern Democrats on this point in 1850 and 1854 only by ceding jurisdiction of the constitutional issue to the Supreme Court. Consequently, their feelings about popular sovereignty were mixed. It had their sanction if it protected slave property in the territories until statehood, but if it did not, they considered it a thinly disguised freesoil policy, and they did not intend to yield their opposition to it unless compelled by the Supreme Court.[19]

Thus the dramatic failure of popular sovereignty in Kansas quickly undermined Douglas's plans. During the inaugural election for territorial legislators in March 1855, proslavery Missourians crossed the border and elected politicians who soon established draconian proslavery laws. Only 2,905 legal voters resided in Kansas, but the Missourians swelled the vote to 6,178. Outraged freesoilers organized a competing government in late 1855. They adopted a constitution by a vote of 1,731 to 46, and in early 1856 their legislature submitted it to Congress and requested statehood. Sporadic violence followed from this contentious beginning, and although the territorial governor managed to avert a potentially ugly conflict in December 1855, the smoldering antagonisms relit in the spring. An attempt by a proslavery posse to arrest several freestate political leaders in May 1856 resulted in the infamous Sack of Lawrence, in which drunken Missourians ransacked or burned a handful of buildings in the leading freestate city. Almost simultaneously, South Carolina congressman Preston Brooks clubbed Massachusetts senator Charles Sumner senseless in punishment for his vitriolic antislavery speech, "The Crime Against Kansas." Three days later an enraged abolitionist, John Brown, hacked five proslavery Kansans to death, sparking several months of guerrilla warfare in what became known as Bleeding Kansas. The governor eventually pacified the territory by deploying the army, but his forcible dispersal of the freestate legislature alienated freesoil settlers. Only the September arrival of a territorial governor who exercised a stronger and more impartial hand stopped the bloodletting that year. But he could not heal the wounded reputation of popular sovereignty. After two years, the balance sheet of popular sovereignty included two hundred deaths, $2 million in property damage, competing territorial governments, and a polarized citizenry. Worse yet, the bloodshed and disorder precipitated a struggle over Kansas in Congress that forced Douglas to adjudicate between northern and southern congressmen. As the architect of the Nebraska Act, he could not ignore the growing crisis.[20]

Douglas threw his lot in with the South. By December 1855, the pressing question confronting legislators was the pacification of Kansas. In a special message to Congress on January 24, 1856, President Pierce urged lawmakers to pass a statehood-enabling bill, which would speed Kansas through the troubling territorial period. Douglas promptly prepared a report on the Kansas conflict, which he paired with an enabling bill. The report defended the actions of the proslavery settlers, and the bill sought to continue them in power. Douglas blamed the Kansas violence on the New England emigrants, palliated the vote frauds, defended the legitimacy of the proslavery legislature, and lambasted the "revolutionary" freestate government. He argued that the freestaters were in "undisguised rebellion," and he maintained that "rebellion should be put down—that insurrection should be suppressed," and that the Government should employ "whatever force may be necessary to maintain the supremacy of the laws." His bill very likely would have perpetuated the power of the proslavery element. Under his plan, the existing territorial legislature would have authorized the election of delegates to a constitutional convention, after which the convention would have submitted the constitution to Congress without popular ratification. Understandably, anti-Nebraska congressmen reviled this proposal, and New York's prominent Republican senator, William Seward, quickly wrote a competing bill that admitted Kansas to statehood under the constitution submitted to Congress by the freestaters. Predictably, the Democrats in the Senate backed Douglas, the anti-Nebraska majority in the House championed Seward, and both bills died stillborn, leaving Kansas to fend for itself.[21]

Douglas also leagued with southern politicians by pressuring Pierce to recognize the proslavery regime of William Walker, a southern filibuster who had overthrown the Nicaraguan government in 1855. Filibusters, who raised private armies to overthrow the governments of Mexico and Central America and Caribbean countries, enjoyed widespread public support in the late 1840s and early 1850s, although support for filibustering after 1854 concentrated among Southerners, who dreamed of establishing slave states in Central America. To curry favor with Southerners, Walker established slavery in Nicaragua in September 1856. For his part, Douglas needed no such inducements. He cherished expansion into Central America, slavery or not, and welcomed allies against British influence in the Americas. The Walker issue thus provided sure ground for the cultivation of his southern alliance.[22]

Douglas's prosouthernism convinced many Northerners that he was proslavery. His apparent abandonment of popular sovereignty in Kansas confirmed suspicions they had harbored since 1854. If Southerners forced slavery on Kansas, abetted by Douglas, then the Nebraska Act stood exposed as a proslavery measure and perhaps as a diabolical plot. As Edwardsville's Joseph Gillespie, a Know Nothing leader, fulminated in January 1856, the "unparalleled outrages committed not only upon the natural rights of the People of that Territory but also upon the principles pretended to be advocated by the bill have shocked most persons." Such skepticism took deep root in the North. Anti-Nebraska Democrat Ebenezer Peck dismissed popular sovereignty as a "delusion," and although he expected the Democratic convention to "sustain Douglas & Co," he wondered if northern voters would endorse the "propriety of extending" a "great political social and moral evil." Even Douglas's "old friend" Samuel Mills, who wrote to him after visiting Kansas, bewailed the Missourians' determination to usurp "by violence and fraud the control of the ballot-box" and to "oppress worry and drive [out]" the "earnest" settlers "from the eastern and middle states." Mills pleaded with Douglas to protest these abuses in order to preserve his career and "restore harmony" to the nation, observing that such a "monstrous perversion of the doctrine of popular soveregnty" eventually would shock "the moral sense of the country."[23]

Douglas's failure to promote legislation that enabled Kansans to exclude slavery deepened northern contempt and bitterness. Lyman Trumbull hounded Douglas on this point throughout the session. In July he reported to Lincoln that the Democrats had been forced "to vote squar[e]ly against the right of a territorial legislature to regulate slavery, & also against the proposition that slavery in the absence of local laws cannot go into the territories." This knowledge confirmed Trumbull's belief that popular sovereignty meant "the opening of all territories to the introduction of slavery." Correspondents from throughout the North deluged Trumbull with congratulatory epistles after he lambasted Douglas in a March speech, and many of them denounced Douglas as a traitor to freedom. Anti-Nebraska newspapers sometimes put the matter even more bluntly by denouncing Douglas as a slavery propagandist, and the Illinois Republican state convention sternly judged Douglas to be "recreant to the free principles of this Government." By their logic, popular sovereignty could not be reconciled with freedom. Unquestionably, Douglas paid a high price for throwing his lot in with the South.[24]

Southern Democrats, however, did not help him fight the antislavery movement by relaxing their opposition to squatter sovereignty. Admittedly, Southerners supported his nomination for the presidency at the party's national convention in Cincinnati. The contenders for the prize included Douglas, Pierce, and Pennsylvania's James Buchanan, a former minister to Great Britain. In the initial ballots, Douglas commanded about half of the northwestern and border-state vote, Pierce dominated New England and the South, and Buchanan controlled the eastern seaboard states and the other half of the northwestern vote. The Southerners adopted Douglas after Pierce faltered, and only Douglas's inability to control his own region kept the prize out of reach. To the rue of southern delegates, Douglas withdrew his candidacy and ceded place to Buchanan, who was preferred by Northerners because he had lived abroad in 1854 and bore no responsibility for the Nebraska Act. But Southerners' support for Douglas did not soften their stance on popular sovereignty. The platform declared that the Nebraska Act embodied "the only sound and safe solution of the 'slavery question,'" namely, "NON-INTERFERENCE BY CONGRESS WITH SLAVERY IN STATE AND TERRITORY," which essentially repeated the equivocal language that had papered over party divisions since 1850. Southerners endorsed his nomination because they appreciated his faithful support of the South, which dated to his early years in Congress, and his willingness to repeal the Missouri Compromise's antislavery provisions. They expressed less enthusiasm for the Nebraska Act, however, because they feared the antislavery possibilities of squatter sovereignty. Their reservations put Douglas in a bind. In order to strengthen the northern and national Democratic Party, he needed Southerners to affirm that popular sovereignty could actively operate in favor of freedom, and this they refused to do. Douglas therefore relinquished his desire for an unequivocal position, endorsed the platform, and hoped for a favorable outcome in Kansas.[25]

The Illinois Democratic Party's proslavery tendencies grew increasingly evident during the 1856 campaign. To be sure, Democrats did not echo slavery's southern advocates. They rarely applauded slavery's merits, never called slavery superior to freedom, and most of them probably silently harbored reservations about slavery. Nevertheless, under the press of political necessity, they began weaving slavery into every aspect of their party philosophy and campaign appeals. For instance, Douglas's claim that Congress had no power to exclude slavery from the territories took deep root. Illinois's district and state conventions dutifully proclaimed the new doctrine, and Democrats reasoning from this assumption contended that the Republicans sought to destroy the Constitution. In a typical appeal, the *State Register* contended that northern voters must choose between the "constitution or anarchy, disunion and perpetual war." Such appeals united Unionist sentiment—now more than ever the lodestar of Democratic politics—to a constitutionalism that acknowledged the right of political communities to slavery. The *Quincy Herald* more bluntly expressed this relationship, asserting that the "Union is so fraught with priceless interests and grand hopes that 'it must and will be preserved,' though fifty more slave States must be added." Meanwhile, the *Peoria Weekly Democratic Press* fleshed out Douglas's view of the founders, contending that Washington and Jefferson endorsed proslavery policy. Behind this proslavery Unionism lay a tolerance for slavery and an increasing willingness to articulate its suitability for blacks. The *Herald* printed a letter from a visitor to the South who described the slave as "the most happy, cheerful and contented being on earth," whose "task is less than half that of a white laborer at the North," and cited a Virginia newspaper that deprecated blacks' capacity to live in freedom without "fast verging to pauperism." Informed by similar convictions, and warning that free slaves would migrate north, the *Cairo City Times* asserted that "some strange perversion of feeling" made Republicans ready to "sacrifice the welfare and happiness of the white race for the imaginary benefit of the black." But the most compelling evidence of the party's proslavery evolution stemmed from what the Democrats left unspoken. From August 1 until October 31, 1856, amid a frenzied presidential contest and baited unceasingly by the Republican Party, the *State Register*,

the *Cairo City Times,* and the *Peoria Democratic Press* on only a handful of
occasions maintained that popular sovereignty was a freesoil policy, and in
most instances they did so by reprinting articles from papers outside Illinois.
A better gauge of the party's diminishing freesoil sentiment can hardly be
imagined.[26]

Yet northern voters wanted freesoil politics. To the Democrats' chagrin,
the Republican Party made a powerful showing throughout the North. The
Republicans won 45.2 percent of Northerners' votes, the Democrats 41.4
percent, and the American Party, the newly created refuge for many former Know Nothing voters, only 13.4 percent. Astonishingly, the nativists
had been largely destroyed as an independent political force, swamped as
badly as the Democrats by the power of antislavery politics. The antislavery convictions of many nativist voters had swallowed up their nativism.
Nevertheless, the nativists remained a crucial swing vote. In Illinois, for
instance, the Republicans had needed nativist support to win. The Republicans' gubernatorial candidate, former Democrat William Bissell, attracted
roughly fifteen thousand nativist votes, and with that aid edged the Democratic candidate by a five-thousand-vote margin. However, Illinois's nativists
did not support Republican presidential candidate John C. Fremont, whom
they considered too radical; instead, they voted for former President Millard
Fillmore, the American Party candidate with conservative Whig antecedents.
Consequently, Buchanan defeated Fremont in Illinois by more than nine
thousand votes. Nevertheless, Buchanan's narrow victory in Illinois reflected
the Democrats' weakness in the North, where he won only five of sixteen
states. The clash between slavery and freedom in Kansas and Congress convinced Northerners that freedom's preservation required the subordination
of slavery—and hence they rallied to the Republican standard. Portentously,
this alarming development deepened the northern Democrats' increasing
dependence on southern political power.[27]

But Buchanan's election did at least create hope among northern Democrats for an evenhanded Kansas policy. Since freestaters predominated in the
territory by 1856, a fair application of popular sovereignty meant a freesoil
result. Northern Democrats desperately needed this outcome. With it they
could silence antislavery protests about the profaning of a free land, demonstrate independence from southern dictation, renew freesoil arguments,
and promulgate the principle of popular sovereignty with more favorable
prospects. Yet without it they were sunk. They could never justify a slave
regime in Kansas. As Lyman Trumbull reported from Washington, D.C.,
after the election, the northern Democrats "feel that their political salvation
depends on making Kansas a free State." Unfortunately for Douglas and the

northern Democrats, the new year would ring in all they feared and nothing they hoped.[28]

⌇

Soon after the 1856 election, the Supreme Court's Dred Scott decision drove a deep doctrinal wedge between southern and northern Democrats. The landmark case began in 1846, when a Missouri slave named Dred Scott sued for freedom in a St. Louis County circuit court. Scott argued that his 1830s residence in the free state of Illinois and in the free territory of Minnesota legally emancipated him. In March 1857, after ten years of legal wrangling, the Supreme Court decided the case. Much hinged on the decision because the Court was likely to rule on both black citizenship rights and the constitutionality of the Missouri Compromise. Aware of the case's significance, President Buchanan privately ascertained the verdict before imploring the American people in his inaugural address to "cheerfully submit" to it. Two days later, Chief Justice Taney read his majority decision, which denied that blacks could be American citizens and concluded that Congress could not prohibit slavery in the nation's territories.[29]

Taney's reasoning undercut not only the Republicans' but also Douglas's position. Determined to eradicate the legal ambiguities of popular sovereignty, Taney had added that Congress could not legally "authorize a territorial government" to exclude slavery either. If the Constitution protected slave property in all territories until statehood, no territorial legislature could exclude slavery. The Dred Scott case did not raise this issue, and thus Taney's contention was *obiter dictum*, an argument that had no force in law. Nevertheless, the chief justice deduced the point from his established premises and indicated the court's future course in any related matter. This was no trivial matter. Should Taney's interpretation prevail, the federal government would endorse and enforce the southern definition of freedom in national territories.[30]

The Supreme Court's decision forced Douglas into a rebellion against the South. As Lincoln later jibed, Taney had "squatted out" squatter sovereignty. But Douglas resisted that conclusion, arguing in a major address to his constituents in June that territorial legislatures could still exclude slavery by refusing to pass positive laws for the protection of slavery. The constitutional right to carry slaves into a territory, he judged, "remains a barren and a worthless right, unless sustained, protected and enforced by appropriate police regulations and local legislation." This idea directly contradicted the Constitution as expounded by Taney. After all, territorial legislators had no power to flout property rights guaranteed by the Constitution. But Douglas was in no position to observe legal niceties. He feared with good reason that Taney's doctrine, if endorsed as the party creed, would produce a Republican Party triumph in the northern states that would precipitate secession and civil war. So he risked the unity of the national Democratic Party in a bid to save the Union.[31]

Douglas carefully hedged his new position. In order to palliate his heresy against the Supreme Court, he reaffirmed his friendship to the South and his tolerance of slavery. This required delicate maneuvering. First, he endorsed the Dred Scott decision and emphasized that constitutional "duty" required all good citizens to "marshal" themselves under the "banner of the Union" against "whoever resists the final decision of the highest judiciary." He did not count himself among the resistors. On the basis of his police regulations theory, he claimed that the decision "sustained and firmly established" squatter sovereignty. This pretense enabled him to avoid an immediate, catastrophic break with the South. Second, he emphasized that southern and northern Democrats shared common ground on the race question. He wholeheartedly supported the court's argument prohibiting black citizenship, calling it the "main proposition decided by the Court," and he used it to attack the Republican Party's dogma that the Declaration of Independence contradicted slavery. Douglas contended that the Declaration "referred to the white race alone," indeed, only to the equality of "British subjects" residing in America and Great Britain. In thus portraying the Declaration solely as a revolutionary political document, Douglas entirely rejected its philosophical basis. He justified this cramped construction by asserting that the nation's founders considered blacks incapable of self-government and never intended to make blacks equal. Instead, they had subordinated blacks, following the "civilized and christian" doctrine that government should provide "for the protection of the insane, the lunatic, the idiotic, and all other unfortunates." These arguments aligned him with the South, and particularly with the southern idea of American freedom.[32]

Leveraging the racial issue enabled Douglas to build solidarity between northern and southern Democrats at the least possible political cost in the North. After all, Republican Party racial doctrine contradicted not only proslavery political thought but also northern racial practice. "If the negro is the equal of the white man, and was thus created by the Almighty," Douglas questioned Republicans, what justified either white Southerners or Northerners from reducing "him to a condition of inequality?" Douglas's answer was emphatic and reassuring: the Almighty had neither created blacks equal nor endowed them with inalienable rights. Hence, they could claim only those rights that white men in the states and territories deemed "consistent with the good and safety of society." With this argument, Douglas collapsed moral distinctions between slavery and the northern color line, and also strengthened the moral and political justifications for popular sovereignty. His friend Murray McConnel quickly saluted his strategy and recommended that the party subsequently should raise the proposition of black equality whenever "we are called to speak upon or discuss the principles of the two political parties" in order to recruit all voters who are "not debased and sunk in the cespool of fanaticism." The doctrine of black inferiority was a powerful political currency, enabling Douglas and other northern Democrats to express sympathy for slavery without abandoning squatter sovereignty and forsaking northern freesoilism. Despite the risk of reinterpreting the Declaration of Independence to legitimate slavery in America, no other argument was more likely to persuade Northerners to adopt the southern idea that freedom incorporated slavery.[33]

The *Chicago Times* best indicated Douglas's plans to foster party unity in the wake of the Dred Scott decision. Douglas established the *Times* in 1854 after the anti-Nebraska tide swept away Chicago's Democratic newspapers. The *Times* articulated Douglas's positions on specific issues, such as the Dred Scott case, but also advanced his broader agenda. In 1857 the paper's editor labored to patch up party relations by developing positions to attract both northern and southern Democrats. For the former, the *Times* promised that fair elections would yield a free Kansas. This proved to be a disastrous prediction, but it seemed realistic in the fall of 1857. In May, President Buchanan had appointed Mississippi's Robert J. Walker as Kansas's territorial governor. Walker was Douglas's close friend and accepted the position only after Buchanan pledged that Kansas's voters would be given the opportunity to ratify or reject any state constitution prior to its submission to Congress. Walker subsequently published this agreement in a letter to the press, and in his inaugural gubernatorial address restated the policy twice. His stipulation protected the freestaters from the proslavery legislature, which in February had authorized the assembly of a constitutional convention at Lecompton. Pessimists feared the power of the proslavery legislature, but the *Times* trusted the administration and repeatedly assured its readers that slavery would not be forced on Kansas.[34]

Yet the *Times*, like Douglas, also appealed to southern Democrats. Most notably, articles by "Z" defended slaveholder paternalism, lauded the use of slave labor in the cotton South, and justified use of the lash. These were strong words for a Chicago paper, and in printing them the *Times* offered striking evidence of Douglas's devotion to the South and the Union. In return, the *Times* asked Southerners to exhibit equivalent concern for the North. In an unusual communiqué, "Z" reminded Southerners that northern Democrats were "the wall of adamant" between the Republicans and southern slavery. Citing our "faithful and toilsome service," the author pleaded with Southerners not to "sever themselves" from northern Democrats. "Z" perceived that such a course would "blindly" discard the fruits of Buchanan's election for "an impracticable idea." The Dred Scott decision was not named, but "Z" evidently referred to the "impracticable" prospect of Southerners demanding protection for territorial slavery where settlers did not want it. This remarkable plea to the South possibly expressed Douglas's innermost thoughts, years before southern intransigence forced him to make similar supplications on the Senate floor, and evinced how completely the Dred Scott decision put him at the mercy of the South. After Taney's verdict, Douglas more than ever needed a free pass on party doctrine from Southerners. Yet he was also far less likely to receive it.[35]

The Lecompton Constitution soon dramatically exacerbated the threat to party unity. It was a product not of Kansas's settlers, but of the territory's proslavery party, which represented no more than a quarter of the electorate, and perhaps as little as a tenth, but which had controlled the territorial legislature since 1855. Alarmed by the influx of settlers who supported the freestate movement, proslavery legislators resolved to make Kansas a slave state no matter the cost in justice or blood. They ordered a census and voter registration in preparation for the June 1857 election of delegates to the Lecompton Constitutional Convention, intending to produce a proslavery document that the Democratic Party could ram through Congress. The tabulations consequently disenfranchised freestaters. Census takers deliberately ignored nineteen of Kansas's thirty-eight counties and the registrars skipped fifteen, while the legislature's gerrymandering ensured that eight of Kansas's counties elected 62 percent of the convention delegates. Despite his determined impartiality, Governor Walker had no power to alter these arrangements. Angry freestaters therefore refused to vote in the elections, which resulted in the election of proslavery delegates.[36]

The delegates unapologetically sought to root slavery in Kansas. After they had completed their work, they submitted two constitutions for popular ratification and required the people to select one. The constitution "with slavery" fully established slavery, while the constitution "without slavery" prohibited the future importation of slaves but protected existing slavery in perpetuity. This was not the choice Walker had imagined. In the December referendum angry freestaters again withheld their ballots, and the constitution "with slavery" passed with a total of 6,226 votes, most of them fraudulent. The freestaters, however, had a card up their sleeve. In October, Kansans had elected their first freestate legislature, which, after assembling, promptly authorized a plebiscite allowing voters to either ratify or reject the Lecompton Constitution. The voters rejected it by ten thousand votes. However, as was customary in American politics, the delegates to the Lecompton convention had been elected directly by the people and exercised sovereign power while in convention, and thus they could not be countermanded by the state legislature. Consequently, only the December proslavery verdict had legal force. As Kansas's proslavery party had hoped, the Democratic Party had an opportunity to make Kansas a slave state. Democratic congressmen simply had to endorse the constitution.[37]

But Douglas could not endorse the Lecompton Constitution without destroying the northern wing of the Democratic Party. He had announced in June that voting rights in Kansas would be "efficiently and scrupulously protected," and he had even predicted a freesoil result "provided all the free state men will go to the polls." Douglas probably advanced these pledges in good faith. Perhaps he knew about the rigged delegate elections, but he could not have anticipated such a barefaced fraud, presuming at the very least that Kansans could reject the constitution if they disliked it. Hence, despite being importuned by southern politicians, Douglas could not support passage of a fraudulent constitution that forced slavery on a people against their will. Doing so would utterly discredit popular sovereignty and unmercifully expose the Democratic Party to the antislavery sentiment that Douglas had hoped to exploit with a freesoil outcome. As James Washington Sheahan had told him in December 1857, passage of the constitution "would be destructive of everything in Illinois." Hardly blind to his own reelection prospects in 1858, Douglas fought the Lecompton Constitution in Congress at every turn.[38]

Unfortunately for Douglas, Buchanan and the southern Democrats made Lecompton a party test. This was a stunning reversal on Buchanan's part, treacherous and momentous, and it unleashed a savage party struggle. The pro-Lecompton forces were sixteen votes short of a House majority, and therefore the president needed to break the ranks of the anti-Lecompton Democrats, who numbered about twenty-two and hailed mostly from the northwest. To do so, he applied the whip and marshaled patronage positions from almost every department in the government. He also sought to destroy Douglas, dismissing Douglas postmasters in three major cities, including Chicago, and instructing the new Chicago postmaster to wrest control of the state party from Douglas. Buchanan's abortive schemes achieved nothing. Rank-and-file voters from throughout the North, and some even from the border states, deluged Douglas with letters praising his opposition to

Lecompton. Thus bolstered, he and his Democratic allies blocked Kansas's admission by voting with the Republicans. By late March, a humiliating defeat loomed for the president, who therefore approved a face-saving bill that rejected the Lecompton Constitution on the pretext that the federal land grant stipulated in the constitution was irregular. The bill permitted Kansans to resubmit the constitution if they ratified a smaller land grant, but Kansans had no desire to take the constitution on any terms, and they rejected the proposition at the polls in August 1858.[39]

But for Democrats, the Lecompton farce had long since become tragedy. Southern Democrats denounced Douglas for betraying them and destroying party unity, and he fully returned the sentiment. But their reaction was more portentous. Douglas's political objectives depended on southern support, and he would seek reconciliation. But Southerners had the alternative of disunion, and their break with Douglas increased its attractions. As one Southerner stated, Douglas's defection "has done more than all else to shake my confidence in Northern men on the slavery issue, for I have long regarded him as one of our safest and most reliable friends." This distrust, widely shared among southern Democrats after Lecompton, would prove deep and unyielding.[40]

Yet Douglas's northern followers were equally angry. Like Douglas, they willingly tolerated slavery's expansion when white men desired it, but beyond that point they would not go. Indeed, their freesoilism reverberated most strongly in the context of Buchanan's tricky dealing. Northern Democrats could not believe that he had sacrificed them in order to sanction proslavery frauds in Kansas. Grimly, they began to show their teeth to the South. "I assure you nothing avails here now but *submission to administration or southern dictation*," wrote an Illinois congressman to a fellow Democrat. The Lecompton test had been established by disunionists, he reported, "who see no obstacle to their wishes but the Destruction of the democratic party." A "life of devotion to equal rights in every section," he concluded bitterly, means "nothing" to them. Other Democrats shared his sense of betrayal. County conventions throughout the state endorsed Douglas for reelection without exception, and Buchanan's attempt to establish a competing state Democratic party failed dismally. With justifiable satisfaction, Douglas observed in early 1858 that "[t]he Party in Ills is better united today than it ever was." Yet the great outpouring of public support paradoxically represented a party crisis of the highest magnitude. After all, freesoilism remained Douglas's enemy rather than his ally, and the ardent mobilization of northern Democrats against slavery's expansion and southern political influence augured badly for party reconciliation. To preserve the Union, he needed northern voters to accept, not reject, slavery's claim to American nationality. Instead, the South's northern allies were beginning to resent slavery's influence on the party and the nation. Hence, Douglas's triumphant victory over Buchanan ironically camouflaged a far more profound defeat. For the first time, northern Democratic voters had abandoned the South, and reuniting the two wings of the Democracy would be extremely difficult.[41]

Douglas responded to this challenge in his famous 1858 Senate contest with Abraham Lincoln by appealing to Northerners and Southerners alike. Unquestionably, he sought first and foremost to beat Lincoln, without which all else was lost. He therefore maintained his positions on Dred Scott and Lecompton, which he could not safely relinquish. But on virtually every other issue he made overtures to the South or advanced arguments that facilitated party reconciliation.

Indeed, the relative absence of freesoilism was the most striking aspect of Douglas's campaign. He did not initiate discussions of the subject, and he never claimed that popular sovereignty deliberately served freesoil ends. Instead he lionized popular sovereignty as a Unionist measure and incorporated it into his broader argument that northern Democrats sought to rescue the nation from impending disruption. To be sure, Douglas did not totally abandon freesoilism. He clung to squatter sovereignty both by claiming that slavery could not "exist a day in the midst of an unfriendly people with unfriendly laws," and by declaring his opposition to a congressional slave code in the territories. But abandoning squatter sovereignty would have ensured defeat, and thus his refusal to heed the Dred Scott decision or to endorse a slave code did not constitute a strongly freesoil position. Instead, it met the minimum standard of freesoilism required for reelection.[42]

By contrast, he labored diligently to rehabilitate slavery's reputation. Faced with Lincoln's repeated argument that the Declaration of Independence expressed the nation's ideals, and thus mandated an antislavery territorial policy, Douglas decisively and repeatedly repudiated human equality. He deemed black people inferior to whites and incapable of self-government, and accordingly he reasoned that blacks "must always occupy an inferior position" in society. He insisted also that the founders had referred only to white men when they declared that "all men are created equal." By his lights, black subordination was "only a question of degree and not a question of right," and involved a "moral question" only if blacks were equal. Hence he proclaimed "the right of each State, and territory, to decide this slavery question for itself, to have slavery or not, as it chooses," and he looked "forward to a time when each State shall be allowed to do as it pleases," even if it "chooses to keep slavery forever." This was the milder version of his forcefully stated intention "to knock in the head this Abolition doctrine of Mr. Lincoln's, that there shall be no more slave States, even if the people want them." Douglas's language starkly illustrated the shift in northern public attitudes since the slavery convention debate of the 1820s, when even the ardent convention-ists hesitated to defend slavery so frankly. But by 1858 the sustained national conflict over slavery and freedom had compelled some Northerners, like Douglas, to defend black enslavement as a legitimate product of whites' freedom in America.[43]

Indeed, Douglas bluntly stated his conviction that national expansion and slavery's growth went hand in hand. He argued that the immigrants flooding the country required "more territory upon which to settle," the acquisition of which he favored "without reference to the question of slavery." He specifically suggested acquiring Cuba, but also expected that Americans would eventually acquire portions of "Mexico or Canada" or other land on "this continent or the adjoining islands." The bulk of his imagined empire lay southward and possessed a climate he considered congenial for slavery. Conceptualizing a symbiotic relationship between climate, crops, slavery, and the law, he repeatedly stated that "great varieties of soil, of production and of interests" required "different local and domestic regulations." To Douglas, geographical and climatic differences made popular sovereignty especially useful to the expanding nation. If Congress clothed every territory with the power to reject or adopt slavery, then the republic would "expand until it covers the whole continent" and could "exist forever divided into free and slave States." Only five years earlier the *State Register* had approvingly printed a colonization circular that promoted a plan for eventual emancipation. Now Douglas promulgated his readiness to use popular sovereignty as slavery's handmaiden, enabling slavery's expansion and guaranteeing its perpetuity in the western hemisphere. This doctrine was indeed "bold," as one Republican solemnly stated during the debates, but it was not freesoil.[44]

Voters proved less receptive to Douglas's boldness than he would have liked. To be sure, the election results had much to recommend them. He defeated Lincoln and secured six more years in the Senate. In addition, he whipped the Buchananites and proved conclusively that northern Democrats followed his ideas and leadership, rather than the president's. Clearly, he would be the North's leading candidate for the party's presidential nomina-tion in 1860, and with border-state support he likely would be the party's strongest candidate. Yet darker tidings could be perceived in the returns. In the state's first election without nativist candidates since 1854, the Republicans dominated the fast-growing region of northern Illinois, won two statewide offices, and attracted 52.3 percent of the popular vote in the state legislative contests that determined the Senate race. By contrast, the Democrats won 45.2 percent of the vote in the state legislative contests, while the Buchananites, who had sought to hamstring Douglas by running competing Democratic candidates, took the leavings. Douglas was reelected despite this differential both because the state's apportionment favored the Democrats and because he won some close victories in Whig districts in central Illinois. Overall, Democrats captured forty-six of the state legislature's eighty-seven open seats and controlled fifty-four of the legislature's one hundred votes. In other states, Democrats also fared poorly. In New Jersey, Pennsylvania, Indiana, and Illinois, the four states likely to be critical in the 1860 election, the number of Democratic congressmen dropped from twenty-nine to sixteen. These numbers testified not only to the northern Democratic Party's waning influence, but also to the cavernous breach between northern and southern Democrats that had put the party in deep disarray.[45]

⌒

As 1858 wound to a close, Douglas's predicament was painfully clear. He had embittered Southerners by opposing the Lecompton Constitution and the Dred Scott decision. This had been unavoidable, but they were unforgiving. To make matters worse, he had made insufficient friends in the North despite his stand against the Lecompton Constitution; instead, his brief rebellion had simply staved off an otherwise certain defeat. If anything, his political appeal was shrinking, in his home state and throughout the North. Unionist Whigs had enabled his reelection in Illinois, yet these southern-born conservatives lived only in the Ohio River Valley states. In other northern states he would be hard pressed to find another population so sympathetic with slavery and so prone to Unionist pleas. He thus faced the prospect, already partly realized, of growing unpopularity in both the North and the South, along with increasing hostility to popular sovereignty, which was the only policy likely to preserve a middle ground between slavery and freedom. Worse yet, sectional irritations had advanced to such a degree that measures to soothe one constituency almost inevitably irritated the other. To resolve this dilemma, he somehow had to persuade Northerners to tolerate slavery's expansion where Southerners predominated, while convincing Southerners to relinquish their inflexible opposition to squatter sovereignty. To accomplish the latter, he embarked on a southern tour soon after the debates, championing his idea of proslavery expansion and seeking to patch up the party's rift.

At last untethered from the northern electorate, Douglas courted southern favor on his trip back to Washington, D.C., giving speeches in St. Louis, Memphis, New Orleans, and Baltimore. Most notable was his implicit defense of slavery's morality. In St. Louis he stated that Illinoisans had tried slavery but had abolished it because "we could make no money out of it." In Memphis, he generalized that whites "accept and protect" slavery when climate, soil, and crops "encourage" slave labor, which reduced the matter of slavery's expansion to "a mere question of dollars and cents." He also mockingly stated that antislavery radical Joshua Giddings would "advocate" slavery if relocated to the South, and for himself confessed that "if the people desire slavery, they are entitled to have it, and I am content with the result." In New Orleans and Baltimore he contended that had early Illinoisans lived in the black-belt districts, "we would have seen just as much virtue in slave labor as you do" and would have adhered to it "with the same tenacity." Moreover, Douglas promoted proslavery expansionism. He urged the acquisition of Cuba in every speech, insisting in Memphis that "we will be compelled to take it, and can't help ourselves," and asserting in New Orleans that the "same is true of Central America and Mexico." Far from expressing reservations about slavery's expansion, he insisted that it would benefit the nation's trade and consequently would help the United States to become the greatest planting, manufacturing, commercial, and agricultural power "on the globe." All in all, Douglas made a clear bid for southern support.[46]

Yet he found southern Democrats hostile and unrelenting. After disembarking in New York, he learned that the Democratic Senate caucus had stripped him of his chairmanship of the Committee on Territories, an unprecedented action given his absence, and a vindictive punishment calculated to drive him from the party. Clearly, the president and many Southerners wanted to rid the party of squatter sovereignty, not to mention its sponsor. Political animosity soon spread into personal pettiness. Douglas bore the abuse with a decorum he rarely showed to Republicans, and he quietly sought to avoid conflict. He continued to attend party caucuses and even supported southern attempts to purchase Cuba. It was all to no avail. Near the end of the session, southern Democrats finally precipitated an acrimonious and portentous debate with Douglas by threatening disunion if Congress did not provide a slave code for the territories. They insisted that Taney had recognized their right to carry slaves into the territories, and consequently they demanded territorial or congressional laws to protect that right. This demand met the approbation of both southern moderates and Republicans, who agreed that the Dred Scott decision, if considered valid, obliged the legislative branch to protect slaveholders' property. In the end, Douglas was reduced to special pleading, obstinately refusing to vote for a slave code in the territories because it would destroy the northern Democracy and the Union. But this incontrovertible political argument had no legal standing, and after the session Douglas set out to justify his constitutional position more persuasively. But an ugly precedent had been set. Douglas had offered Southerners an olive branch, and they had responded with blows. His determination to solidify his position was likely only to inflame the conflict.[47]

Indeed, the party split widened significantly after Congress adjourned. In September 1859, Douglas published his attempt to defend the constitutionality of popular sovereignty in a widely read *Harper's Magazine* article. He argued that Congress could confer—but not exercise—powers over "the domestic affairs" of a territory. He thus eschewed the idea of territorial sovereignty but still maintained that the territorial legislatures possessed the only valid power over slavery. Douglas grounded this argument in both history and law. He contended that American colonists had battled Britain for the right to control their domestic affairs, that the founders had established constitutional protections for local self-government, and that Jefferson's Ordinance of 1784 had authorized self-rule in the territories. Moreover, Douglas asserted that Congress's power to administer territorial governments stemmed not from the plenary power of the Constitution's territorial clause, but rather from the clause regulating the admission of new states. However, the latter clause did not authorize Congress to establish laws for the territories, and therefore Douglas claimed that the people of the territories retained that legislative power.[48]

These arguments brought Douglas into collision with Taney. The Dred Scott decision claimed that the Constitution "distinctly and expressly affirmed" the right of slave property, and on this basis Taney had denied Congress's right to exclude it from the territories; after all, the Fifth Amendment prohibited the government from depriving individuals of property without due process of law. Douglas finessed this problem with a remarkable sleight of hand. He claimed that Taney had decided that the government possessed a distinct and express power to return fugitive slaves, but its authority over slavery in the "States or Territories" went no further. This specious reading of Taney excited the contempt of Southerners and precipitated a widely publicized three-month pamphlet war between Douglas and Buchanan's attorney general, Jeremiah Black, who spurned Douglas's reading of Taney and disdained the idea that a territorial legislature could vitiate constitutional rights. When the hubbub finally died down, Douglas's bold attempt to recruit southern support had backfired badly; it not only had accentuated but also had publicized his unwillingness to meet the southern standard for Democratic politics.[49]

Undeterred, Douglas extended a conciliatory hand to the South throughout the ensuing congressional session. In late December 1859, he wrote the resolutions for Illinois's Democratic state convention, which effectively announced the position he intended to take at the 1860 Democratic national convention in Charleston. The resolutions were as prosouthern as possible, denouncing the Republicans for precipitating abolitionist John Brown's shocking attempt to spark a massive, armed uprising of Virginia's slaves on October 16, 1859— which had aroused hysteria and rage in the South—and correspondingly lambasting Brown's "treasonable conspiracy" to "incite a servile insurrection." The resolutions also promised to abide by the party platform established at Charleston and to support the party nominee. Moreover, although the convention's delegates rejected "new issues and tests," such as a slave code, they conceded the legal primacy of the Supreme Court and pledged to abide by future Supreme Court decisions on the power of territorial legislatures over slavery. Douglas was equally conciliatory in the Senate. In mid-January he introduced a bill to suppress conspiracies against slavery. Technically, the bill sought to protect any state from invasion by any other state, but Douglas clearly indicated his intention to crush out what he called antislavery "conspiracies," such as John Brown's raid into Virginia. Douglas planned to stop such "sectional warfare" by making "examples" of the leaders in order to "strike terror into the hearts of the others." In February, Douglas severely censured antislavery politics, blaming freesoilers for fomenting conflict over slavery since 1848 and denouncing the Republicans' condemnation of slavery. He insisted that slave labor was as well suited to the South as free labor was to the North, and he endorsed the newly established slave codes in New Mexico, stating that if "the people of New Mexico want slavery, let them have it, and I never will vote to repeal their slave code." Short of abandoning popular sovereignty, Douglas would have been hard pressed to devise more attractive overtures to Southerners. He was abundantly willing to adopt the southern idea of freedom, provided only that Southerners not force slavery on unwilling Northerners.[50]

Yet Southerners continued to spurn him. They were no less determined than he to shape the Charleston platform and determine the party nominee, and therefore southern radicals sought to brand him a heretic prior to the April convention. A handful of leading southern senators launched biting attacks on popular sovereignty in January, culminating in the submission of slave-code resolutions by Mississippi's senators. Alarmed by the public quarreling precipitated by the resolutions, border-state Democrats referred the issue to a party caucus, which promptly endorsed Congress's obligation to "insure adequate protection to constitutional rights in a Territory." The easy adoption of the resolutions indicated Douglas's unpopularity in the South, an unwelcome fact soon confirmed by the southern Democratic state conventions, which rejected Douglas's candidacy and demanded protection for territorial slavery. The Alabama convention instructed the state's delegates to secede from the national convention unless the platform provided for a federal slave code, and other southern delegations intended to greet Douglas's nomination with the same response. His overtures once again had gone for naught.[51]

The southern Democrats consummated their break with Douglas at Charleston. The story of the disruption of the Democracy is a familiar one. Delegates from the North and South gathered in late April in Charleston, where the tempers, like the temperature, boiled over. Prior to the opening of the convention, the Georgia, Mississippi, Florida, Alabama, Louisiana, Texas, and Arkansas delegations agreed to demand a slave-code platform. Yet the northwestern Democrats, who stood for Douglas like iron, adhered just as fiercely to popular sovereignty. Paralyzed by this dissension, the platform committee deliberated fruitlessly for several days before reporting three platforms to the convention. The Douglasites controlled a majority of the delegates and accordingly adopted the platform they had proposed, which affirmed the resolutions adopted at the 1856 Democratic convention and promised to abide by future Supreme Court decisions on territorial slavery. Reacting instantly, the Gulf states, joined by South Carolina, bolted the convention amid fiery oratory and deafening applause. The next day, New York and border-state delegates, still hoping for a compromise, prevented Douglas's nomination, and Douglas's representatives soon proposed a six-week recess of the convention, preparatory to reassembly in Baltimore. During the interim, both sides marshaled their forces. Douglas men in Alabama, Georgia, and Louisiana scrambled to appoint delegates to the Baltimore convention, and Douglas himself vowed to exclude the bolting delegations from readmission. Meanwhile, southern Democrats repledged themselves to a slave code and southern rights.[52]

The Southerners proved more obdurate than Douglas. At Baltimore, Douglas's managers ultimately agreed to seat many of the bolters, and Douglas himself, wracked by fears of disunion, offered to withdraw in favor of a "reliable, Non-Intervention, and Union loving Democrat." But the Southerners spurned the majority report of the credentials committee because it failed to admit all the bolting delegations, and they preemptively torpedoed the possible candidacy of Georgian Alexander Stephens, later vice president of the Confederacy. Douglas would have gladly withdrawn in favor of Stephens, but this last southern snub strengthened the determination of Douglas's managers to stick to their man until the end. The suspense, however, did not build very long. Following the adoption of the majority report of the credentials committee, most of the southern delegates protested with their feet and filed from the hall. The remaining delegates nominated Douglas for the presidency, an honor dulled by the absence of the bolters, who gathered in a nearby hall and nominated Kentucky's John C. Breckinridge for president on the Charleston slave-code platform. The South had finally abandoned Douglas.[53]

Yet Douglas did not abandon the South. The breakup of the Democracy ironically intensified his Unionist politics and encouraged his conciliatory impulses. In an exchange with Jefferson Davis on the Senate floor after the Charleston convention, Douglas reassured Southerners of his constancy despite his adherence to popular sovereignty. In particular, he promised to obey a subsequent Supreme Court decision on the power of territorial legislatures over slavery. "We differ only on a law point," he observed, and "only as to what the decision of the court will be; not as to whether we will obey it when made." Indeed, he declared that once the court rendered a direct judgment on the issue in dispute, its decision "must be carried out in good faith" with "all the power of this Government—the Army, the Navy, and the militia." Given the court's evident direction, this concession gave up virtually the whole ground. Douglas also reiterated his support for the New Mexico slave codes and documented the proslavery consequences of popular sovereignty. "Under this doctrine," he asserted, New Mexicans "have introduced and protected slavery in the whole of that Territory," converting "a tract of free territory into slave territory, more than five times the size of the State of New York." He observed that no other free territory had been turned into slave territory since the Revolution, and he asked Southerners, "will not the same principle protect you in the northern States of Mexico when they are acquired, since they are now surrounded by slave territory; are several hundred miles further South; have many degrees of greater heat; and have a climate and soil adapted to southern products?" These were breathtaking words from a northern senator, and they testified both to his toleration for slavery where it would pay, especially if it abetted national expansion, and to his profound interest in conciliating the South to preserve the Union.[54]

In this regard he was not alone among northern Democrats. Remarkably, even after the Southerners had bolted at Baltimore, the Douglasites still reached out to them, pledging in their party platform that Supreme Court decisions on territorial slavery should be "enforced with promptness and fidelity by every branch of the general government." The Baltimore platform also urged the acquisition of Cuba and denounced northern laws that impeded the recovery of fugitive slaves. Never before had northern Democrats so openly avowed proslavery politics, but never before was the need so great.[55]

The penetration of proslavery thought into northern Democratic politics appeared starkly in Illinois during the ensuing campaign. In large part this reflected Douglas's influence. His arguments about race, slavery, and Unionism had taken root, and now constituted the basis for northern Democratic political thought. The *Shawneetown Mercury*, for instance, followed Douglas's historical arguments to the letter, denying that the founders opposed slavery. Instead, the *Mercury* maintained that the founders knew that blacks would not labor without "force," estimated blacks "only in a pound shilling-pence point of view," and considered blacks' "natural" condition "ten times worse than bondage." Similarly, Democratic state senator Orlando Ficklin asserted that blacks benefited from slavery, which elevated them from "the level of the beast." Also echoing Douglas, prominent Belleville Democrat J. L. D. Morrison rejected the Republicans' claim that the Northwest Ordinance had excluded slavery from Ohio, Indiana, and Illinois, emphasizing instead that "climate, soil and production" regulated slavery's adoption, making it "a question of dollars and cents." And, like Douglas, Morrison implicitly argued that black racial inferiority justified slavery, declaring to his audience of "free white men" and "day laborers" that the slave should "be upon the plantation—let him be engaged in raising tobacco—let him be engaged in raising hemp—let him be engaged on the farms of the country, where he is," because he "belongs to an inferior race—he is not your equal—he never can be admitted with you upon terms of equality without lowering you." Morrison thus judged, as did Douglas, that popular sovereignty made sense to any man "whose brain has not been addled by this miserable humanitarianism that proclaims the freedom and equality of all men, without regard to quality or condition." The old Jacksonian doctrine of human equality was but a shell of its former self, into which had crawled the southern definition of freedom.[56]

The *State Register* also occupied proslavery ground. To be sure, Illinois's leading Democratic newspaper did not defend slavery per se. Nevertheless, dread of secession characteristically propelled its editor toward the southern position. Alarmed by reports of a slave revolt in Texas, the *State Register* blamed Lincoln for having incited the slaves with his "most unfounded" contention that slavery was "wholly unjustifiable." The "effect of such information upon minds not familiar with the falsehoods and hypocrisy of the day," explained the editor, "can well be imagined." Under the conviction that Lincoln's election would provoke a general slave uprising, the *State Register* assessed the relative merits of Republican and Democratic politics. "The republican party assert that slavery is an evil of the greatest magnitude," it observed, "that it is a curse to the state where it is permitted, a curse to the society which tolerates it, and a curse to all men who participate in it as masters." Impliedly dissenting from these ideas, and deadly hostile to politics based upon them, the *State Register* warned that the Republicans' attempt to produce slavery's "ultimate extinction" might result in mass emancipation. To avert this calamity, it urged Northerners to support the Democracy, which would not destroy the "harmony of the Union" in order to gratify "abolition demagogues." Instead, Democrats proposed to subordinate blacks permanently, leaving the "entire question of slavery and negroism" to the "interests" of whites. The *State Register* promised that under this policy the "country will not be overrun with millions of free negroes" but will continue "to be a nation of free white people." Deliberately and profoundly, the *State Register* thus grafted slavery to American nationalism. Meanwhile, it did not print a single antislavery argument from August to October 1860. Wavering voters might easily have concluded that Democrats subordinated free soil along with free blacks.[57]

Indeed, Douglas's tireless advocacy of Unionism distracted him from economic issues relevant to northern voters. He spent his time justifying popular sovereignty historically, legally, and politically, and accordingly largely ignored economic issues, which did not incubate Unionist sentiment. Given the Republicans' aggressive promotion of homesteads, the Pacific Railroad, and internal improvements in the service of free labor, this was no small disadvantage. One Illinois Democrat wrote to McClernand in June that the Republicans "are harping considerable on the Homestead Bill and I fear if that Bill dont become a law during the Session of this Congress that they will defeat us on Nov next." The bill "is very popular," he reported, "among the Masses." Southern politicians, however, resisted it, and after Republicans and northern Democrats drove it through Congress, Buchanan's veto reflected the Southerners' influence. Coming on the heels of successful southern opposition to a Pacific Railroad bill, Buchanan's veto underscored the Democratic Party's insensitivity to northern voters.[58]

Northern Democratic politicians deeply resented the course of southern Democrats. Having made countless sacrifices for slavery in order to promote the welfare of the party and the Union, northern Democrats had expected southern Democrats to make similar concessions. In particular, they had needed southern Democrats to cease demanding a slave code. For this reason, the Democratic delegates to Illinois's state convention in January 1860 had only very reluctantly pledged to accept the resolutions and the nominee adopted by the Charleston convention. On that point, wrote Charles Lanphier of the *State Register* to McClernand, a mere "spark would have lit up an awful conflagration." Expressing similar frustrations, Orlando Ficklin regarded "the fire eaters" as "disunionists" who had no greater loyalty than to "the continuance and extension of African slavery." In response to their schemes, which he believed would ensure the Democratic Party's defeat in "every free state," Ficklin declared that the time had come for northern Democrats to "preserve our manhood, by boldly asserting and standing by our measures and our men." Such militancy intensified after Southerners broke up the party. One of Douglas's correspondents aptly captured northern party feeling after Charleston, writing that Maine Democrats were "*uniform* in their *indignation* at the course pursued by the Southern disunion leaders and the pro-slavery administration." The disaffection of northern Democrats illustrated the fatal consequences of the party's abandonment of the North. When antisouthernism brimmed among leading northern Democratic politicians, Douglas could hardly hope to find conciliatory sentiment in the North at large.[59]

Douglas and the northern Democratic Party's retreat from the North opened up extensive ground for antislavery politics. While Douglas wooed the South, the burgeoning Republican Party laid exclusive claim to northern society and popularized an antislavery nationalism. Popular sovereignty aided their efforts by endorsing the right of whites to enslave blacks, thus largely adopting the southern idea of freedom. Even though popular sovereignty did not meet the southern standard for proslavery politics, it justified slavery's morality, expansion, and perpetuity, warranted national policies that treated slavery and freedom equally, and thus married slavery to American nationalism. Many Northerners recoiled at those ideas, including Abraham Lincoln, who believed that slavery debased the idea and practice of liberty. Lincoln understood the Declaration of Independence to chart the development of a national future profoundly different than that envisioned by Douglas. For this reason, after passage of the Kansas-Nebraska Act, Lincoln began to build an antislavery coalition in Illinois that sought to preserve, protect, and promote freedom in America.

7. Abraham Lincoln and the Triumph of an Antislavery Nationalism, 1854–1860

A KENTUCKIAN BY BIRTH, and the son of an illiterate farmer, Abraham Lincoln had come to Illinois in 1830. Self-taught, he had steadily risen to distinction in law and politics, serving as a Whig state legislator from 1834 to 1841, and congressman from 1847 to 1849, before leaving politics to focus on his legal career, precluded from aspiring to higher office by the Whig Party's statewide torpor. Wedded to Whig ideas of individual uplift and social progress, he opposed slavery in theory and practice and voted repeatedly in Congress for the Wilmot Proviso. Yet, like most northern Whigs, he had made peace with popular sovereignty in 1850, grateful for the Union's preservation, and in the tranquil years that followed seemed to enter the sunset of his political career. But the Kansas-Nebraska Act, as he subsequently recalled, "aroused him as he had never been before" and provoked his return to politics. Still, he had little discernible prospect of election to high political office in a state dominated by Democrats, and thus he indifferently agreed to campaign for a seat in the state legislature. In this, he later wrote, he had "no broader practical aim or object" than to help reelect his friend Richard Yates to Congress. But he did harbor a profound philosophical objective that he shared with anti-Nebraskites throughout the state: the preservation of an antislavery nation. Believing that slavery threatened the ideals and practice of freedom, he fashioned a powerful and partisan antislavery nationalism to combat it. Over the next six years, his efforts to engrave the northern understanding of freedom into national policy spearheaded the Republican Party's rise to power in Illinois, the North, and the nation—and elevated him into the White House. But the triumph of antislavery politics came at a great cost. Lincoln's nationalism spurred the South to secede.[1]

⌒

From the first, anti-Nebraskites believed that the Nebraska Act would spread slavery. Given the repeal of the antislavery provisions of the Missouri Compromise, any other conclusion seemed ludicrous. As Richard Yates dryly observed in Congress, the territory "is already free," and his constituents would "not ask for the right to make it slave." Anti-Nebraskites therefore listened impatiently to Douglas's claim that Kansans would reject slavery. Lincoln called this argument a *"palliation—a lullaby,"* and southern Illinois Democrat Lyman Trumbull emphasized that "time alone" would determine "whether slavery shall go into those territories." More pugnacious anti-Nebraskites, such as the *Quincy Whig,* asserted that Douglas and his southern allies *"intended to extend Slavery* to Kansas." The Quincy newspaper documented the migration of Missouri's slaveholders into Kansas and quoted a leading southern journal that supported the act because it opened *"new outlets to slavery."* Lincoln concurred, arguing that the Missourians' "disposition" toward slavery extension would likely decide the issue in the absence of a legal prohibition. After all, slavery had taken root in virtually every territory not protected by the Northwest Ordinance and had been thrust out of Illinois only with difficulty. From this fact Lincoln and many other Illinoisans drew the obvious lesson: preserving freedom in Kansas required stalwart opposition to the Nebraska Act.[2]

Most opponents of the Nebraska Act strongly opposed slavery's expansion. Certain that slavery's "admission" into the territories excluded free men for "all coming time," the newly formed Republican Party in northern Illinois's Second Congressional District resolved to reconsecrate the territories "to the ennobling occupation and use of Free Labor and Freemen." Meanwhile, Yates declared on the House floor that obligations to "country, God, and humanity" required him to oppose slavery's extension. Although he refused to discuss the "social evils" of slavery in deference to southern congressmen, he bluntly stated that slavery stigmatized manual labor, reduced wages, drove out free workers, and retarded "prosperity." Thus, the relatively conservative position of one of central Illinois's leading Whigs neatly meshed with the newfound Republicans' determination to prevent slavery's expansion. Under press of Nebraskism, antislavery sentiment quickly begat antislavery politics.[3]

However, the varying intensity of political antislavery inhibited the formation of a unified movement in 1854. The state's abolitionist phalanx, now calling themselves Free Democrats, bitterly denounced the Nebraska Act and recruited other antislavery Illinoisans to join the Republican Party. Yet the Free Democrats did not always find a receptive audience among anti-Nebraskites, especially among central and southern Illinoisans, many of whom still harbored suspicions of radical politics. For instance, anti-Nebraska

Democrat John Palmer declared his unwillingness to aid a party that would wage "a war of legislative retaliation" against the South. By contrast, northern Illinoisans showed a greater readiness to cooperate. The Whig district convention in northeastern Illinois advocated repeal of the Nebraska Act, prohibition of slavery's expansion, revision of the fugitive slave law, abolition of slavery in territory controlled by Congress, repeal of the state's black laws, and fusion with the fledgling Republican Party. In the same district, anti-Nebraska Democrats voted heavily for the Republican candidate in the November election. Such actions were unthinkable in central Illinois, where a correspondent of Yates warned him against supporting repeal of the fugitive slave law, which local Whigs opposed. Appalled by the prospect of their party being "abolitionized," Whig voters such as Bloomington's David Davis feared "that a sectional issue will be made disastrous to this country." Central Illinoisans like Davis and Palmer wanted to calm the growing national crisis and supported neither men nor measures they perceived as radical. They helped stymie concerted action against slavery.[4]

Partisan loyalties also worked against the formation of an anti-Nebraska organization. In a few instances party leaders cooperated to elect antislavery politicians, most notably in southern Illinois, where the otherwise impotent Whigs rallied behind anti-Nebraska Democrats. However, old antagonisms, mutual suspicions, and jostling for power usually spoiled attempts at interparty unity. Anti-Nebraska Democrats in Greene County, for instance, refused to vote for Yates because they believed that "abo[l]itionism" had mastered Whiggery. Even the strongly antislavery Whigs of northeastern Illinois failed to fuse with the Republicans. Both the Whigs and the Republicans hoped to select the congressional nominee for the Second District, which frustrated their intention to fuse. Even more frequently, party leaders and followers simply spurned the idea of joining a new party. After all, Whig leaders hoped to attract antislavery voters and revivify their party, while most anti-Nebraska Democrats intended to beat down the Nebraska test and eventually rejoin their party. In 1854 most Illinois politicians were anything but committed to creating an antislavery party.[5]

The hostility between Illinois's Germans and antislavery nativists also inhibited the fusion movement. The Germans had been a trusty Democratic vote, but they rebelled spectacularly against the Nebraska Act. The possible extension of slavery offended them, as did a proposed amendment to the bill that limited suffrage and other political rights in Kansas and Nebraska to American citizens. Although ultimately defeated, the amendment had received strong support from southern senators, who sought to protect territorial slavery from immigrant political power. Consequently, Chicago

Germans denounced the bill for nationalizing slavery, augmenting southern political power, and discouraging immigrant "pioneers." Yet despite their fierce hostility to the Nebraska Act, antislavery Germans refused to fuse with nativist freesoilers. The Germans could hardly be blamed for their mistrust. The state's leading freesoil organs, the *Free West* and the *Chicago Tribune*, regularly lambasted Catholics, Irish, and intemperance, and in so doing represented the many anti-Nebraskites who intended to pass a prohibitionist law in 1855. The nativist overtones of prohibitionism, not to mention prohibitionism itself, thus steeled the Germans to abjure nativist freesoilism.[6]

For these reasons, the Free Democrats' attempt to unify anti-Nebraskites into a broad-based antislavery party largely failed. Despite the efforts of abolitionist Ichabod Codding, who spoke throughout the state from July to October in support of all anti-Nebraska candidates, efforts at fusion succeeded in only two of northern Illinois's three districts and never got off the ground in the state's six other districts. Anti-Nebraska Whigs dominated central Illinois, dedicated Democrats like Trumbull led anti-Nebraskism in southern Illinois, and both groups disclaimed association with radicals like Codding. The failure of fusion at the local level doomed statewide efforts. The first Republican state convention, held in Springfield, attracted little support despite passing moderate antislavery resolutions. The *Illinois State Journal* virtually ignored it, and Lincoln declined affiliation with the new party, probably unaware that the convention had pursued a moderate course. His reaction epitomized fusion's failure in Illinois. Mistrust, misinformation, political differences, party loyalties, and ethnic prejudices created unbridgeable divisions between the anti-Nebraskites in 1854.[7]

Yet the anti-Nebraskites did share a common devotion to the national idea of freedom. Like the political abolitionists and the Free Soilers before them, the anti-Nebraskites contended that the founders had established a government that nationalized freedom and localized slavery, and virtually all anti-Nebraskites demanded a return to the founders' nationalism. The Democratic *Oquawka Plaindealer* wrote that "the framers of our Constitution" attempted to "circumscribe" slavery because they desired to enhance the "welfare" of future generations. "Are you prepared, Democrats!" the *Plaindealer* exclaimed, "to reverse this long-settled, wise and wholesome policy of our Government." Northeastern Illinois's Whigs were no less emphatic, resolving in their district convention that the federal government must "use all constitutional means" to prevent slavery's expansion, thus returning the nation to the "redeeming principles" enshrined in the Declaration of Independence. Meanwhile, the Republican state convention called the Nebraska Act "a complete surrender" of the government's antislavery policy, and asserted that slavery's violation of natural law obliged Congress to prohibit its extension. The resonance of these nationalist appeals flowed from most Northerners' opposition to slavery. They believed that slavery endangered their freedoms and the nation's progress, and therefore they wanted national policy to privilege freedom. Reflecting these convictions, the state's leading anti-Nebraska politicians all claimed that national ideals and national interests coincided on this crucial point.[8]

Both anti-Nebraska Democrat Lyman Trumbull and abolitionist Ichabod Codding contended that the nation's antislavery ideals justified northern antislavery politics. Trumbull argued throughout southern Illinois that the Nebraska Act warred with the "[sett]led policy of the government." He observed that the founders had sought to prevent slavery's expansion because they considered it "an evil," whereas Douglas had invited slavery into territories previously free. Trumbull charged that popular sovereignty gave no rights to territorial settlers other than "the right to *introduce* slavery," and thus he maintained that it undermined the principles of liberty "established" by the Declaration of Independence. Trumbull's anti-Nebraska politics were thus ostensibly conservative. Far from perceiving himself as radical, he scorned the charge of "abolitionism" and termed it an odious "mad dog cry." Yet Codding found Trumbull's conservatism entirely congenial. In his estimation, the Declaration of Independence formed the basis of government policy because it recognized "*all that goes to make up our common nature*," including "*reason, conscience, will, sensibility, immortality*." Hence, he maintained that constitutional rights derived "sanctity" from natural law and existed to "provide for the needs of our *common* humanity." Although he conceded that the Constitution recognized slavery in the states, he argued that it localized slavery in all other respects. To Codding, the nation's heritage and "principles" thus contradicted popular sovereignty. Douglas had reversed the founders' policies and had "nationalized Slavery." In this, he and Trumbull agreed.[9]

Abraham Lincoln developed the idea of an antislavery nation even more extensively. Directly challenging the principle of popular sovereignty, which he called "despotism," Lincoln bitingly observed that Jefferson never conceived of "the liberty of making slaves of other people." Like Trumbull and Codding, Lincoln claimed that the founders had opposed slavery on principle and tolerated it only from necessity, which placed them in opposition to Douglas, whose popular sovereignty policy treated slavery as a "moral right." Therefore Lincoln considered the founders' legacy to be the best antidote to Douglas's popular sovereignty. "If the negro is a *man*," Lincoln argued, "then my ancient faith teaches me that 'all men are created equal'; and that there can be no moral right in connection with one man's making a slave of another." To Lincoln, the idea of equality gave meaning to American nationalism because it justified a government based on consent rather than force. Consequently, he urged all Americans to "repurify" the nation's ideals by implementing the antislavery extension policies that harmonized with the Declaration of Independence. In doing so, they would "not only have saved the Union," but would have made it "forever worthy of the saving." This was a position that Lincoln considered "no less than National."[10]

The 1854 elections demonstrated that these antislavery nationalist appeals resonated strongly with Illinois's voters. Anti-Nebraska candidates in the congressional contests racked up 77,724 votes to the Democrats' 60,404, winning 55.4 percent of the total vote. Trumbull's impromptu election to Congress also demonstrated the movement's power. He did not publicly oppose the Nebraska Act until late in the year, but after a brief campaign he rolled up 58 percent of the vote in an overwhelmingly Democratic district and justifiably concluded that "the mass of the People" opposed Nebraskism. The state legislative contests also decisively favored the anti-Nebraska candidates. Lincoln calculated after the election that anti-Nebraska legislators controlled fifty-seven of the legislature's one hundred seats, making the election of an anti-Nebraska senator likely. His own hopes turning toward that prospect, Lincoln declined the seat he had won in the statehouse. Antislavery politics had notched its first major triumph in Illinois.[11]

Yet the partisan disruption evident in the election returns also indicated the uncertain future of antislavery politics. After all, despite its brutal beating, the Democratic Party was in better condition than its three rivals in the wake of the election. In northern Illinois, many Whigs were well on their way to Republicanism, having more in common with radicals like Codding than conservatives like David Davis. Meanwhile, in downstate Illinois, southern-born Whigs went in the opposite direction, sitting out the election or perhaps even voting for Democratic candidates. The Know Nothing movement complicated the Whigs' quandary. After all, Whigs of all regions had a taste for nativism, and continued Whig defections to Know Nothingism seemed a distinct possibility in 1854. But the fate of the Know Nothings was no clearer than that of the Whigs. The nativist party probably had a sizable following, but it was hardly a dominant political force. Know Nothings had yet to perfect an organization and would soon face the vexing problem of disentangling nativism from antislavery. Meanwhile, the fledging Republican Party had a strong toehold in northern Illinois, but in order to become a dominant statewide organization it needed to absorb the Know Nothings, the anti-Nebraska Democrats, the downstate Whigs, and the non-Catholic immigrants. Yet none of these groups was especially eager to join the party.

So the Republicans, who were sometimes called fusionists, confronted the difficult task of bringing discordant groups together and melding them into a unified party.[12]

⟿

The newly elected Illinois General Assembly quickly showcased both the impressive power and the persisting divisions of the anti-Nebraska movement. In February, antislavery legislators elected Trumbull to the U.S. Senate and passed House resolutions that demanded slavery's prohibition in all national territories, including Kansas and Nebraska. The 41–32 House vote revealed that the Whigs' longstanding antislavery alliance with northern Illinois Democrats had continued in new guise, now with northern Illinois's upstart Republicans. Northern Illinois's legislators supported the resolutions by a vote of 25–0, and central and southern Illinois Whigs and Republicans added a 15–0 tally. Downstate Democrats voted 32–1 against. Remarkably, the House had more Republican than Whig members, which highlighted the dramatic shift in partisan loyalties and the burgeoning strength of antislavery politics.[13]

Yet the divisions within the anti-Nebraska ranks were also notable. In the senatorial election, Trumbull defeated Lincoln only because five anti-Nebraska Democrats refused to vote for a Whig. Lincoln's adherents bitterly resented such partisanship, but Lincoln knew that retaliatory Whig partisanship would result in the election of a Democrat who had craftily stayed neutral on the Nebraska bill. Hence Lincoln gave his votes to Trumbull, refusing to "let the whole political result go to ruin, on a point merely personal to myself." Meanwhile, the more radical anti-Nebraskites urged repeal or modification of the fugitive slave law and prohibitions against the admission of all future slave states that central Illinois Whigs and some conservative Republicans opposed, considering them impolitic if not unconstitutional. Such contrasting attitudes demonstrated that the antislavery movement was not yet an antislavery party.[14]

The temperance issue further roiled state politics in 1855. Support for temperance reform had been building steadily since 1851, and many anti-Nebraska legislators strongly supported temperance. These men proposed a Maine Law to prohibit the sale of alcohol in Illinois and secured passage of the bill by agreeing to permit a public vote on the law in a June 1855 referendum. Electioneering on this volatile issue subsequently consumed Illinois politics from March to May, and the antitemperance forces proved more powerful than the reformers ever imagined. Immigrants organized to protect dram shops and beer halls; southern Illinois's corn farmers mobilized to protect a valuable market; and liquor dealers bankrolled resistance to what they considered a threat to liberty. But the reformers did not quail from the conflict, outraged by the groggeries, slums, and impoverished children they attributed to the liquor trade. Intemperance was "an evil," declared one temperance committee, and thus "society has a right" to abate the evil by "any means proper and necessary." However, the large number of Illinoisans who enjoyed libation felt differently, and their vigorous opposition defeated the temperance bill, which won only 46 percent of the vote. The temperance movement reshuffled the electorate strikingly. Anti-Nebraska immigrants abandoned their former antislavery allies, some temperate southern Illinoisans joined their erstwhile antislavery opponents, a sizable number of prior voters abstained, and a horde of new voters came forth to vote no. Clearly, the antislavery and temperance electorates were not identical.[15]

The Know Nothing movement, which by 1855 had transformed into the American Party, exacerbated the political confusion. Although nativism per se was neither antislavery nor protemperance, many nativists supported both reforms. Chicago's nativists, for instance, won the city's March 1855 mayoral election by attracting antislavery and temperance voters. But the coalition was fragile. In payment of his temperance debt, the new mayor, William W. Danenhower, successfully urged the City Council to increase license fees for taverns. The ensuing protest by Chicago's Germans ended in violent riots, which undermined the coalition by sharpening the political conflict between antislavery and nativism. The antislavery nativists valued the German vote too much to tolerate the mayor's policies, and consequently they inaugurated a successful struggle for party supremacy that culminated in July at the party's state convention, where they passed resolutions demanding restoration of the Missouri Compromise, affirming Congress's power over the territories, and condemning "assaults upon the elective franchise in Kansas." Their action challenged not only Danenhower, who lamented sectional animosities and hoped that the American Party could ignore slavery, but also the party's National Council, which had met in June at Philadelphia and had endorsed the Kansas-Nebraska Act. Most of the northern delegates at Philadelphia had rebelled, as did Illinois's antislavery nativists, many of whom by midsummer had joined the Republicans. This knowledge cheered anti-Nebraskites, but much uncertainty remained. The nativist movement was not yet dead, and even if it were, no one could foresee the future allegiances of nativist voters, or how their political course would influence the politics of antislavery immigrants.[16]

Party loyalties proved a further obstacle for the beleaguered fusionists in 1855. Codding's indefatigable labors to organize the Republican Party yielded little downstate. In late 1854, for instance, Trumbull supported an alliance of anti-Nebraskites in the state legislature, provided that the radicals stopped "at the proper point," but he had no intention of immediately organizing a new party with them. As he informed Republican Owen Lovejoy a year later, southern Illinois Democrats opposed fusion because many of them opposed slavery's extension, abolitionism, and Know Nothingism "equally." Trumbull gauged that these "old party associations & side issues" inhibited consolidation of the antislavery movement, and he recommended against a state fusion convention in 1855. Downstate Whigs also stood aloof from fusion. They were loath to disturb slavery despite opposing its spread, and many probably agreed with Quincy's O. H. Browning that "the good of whites & blacks is alike consulted by preserving the present relations between them." Consequently they continued to look suspiciously on Republican Party antislavery politics, which Springfield's *Illinois Journal* called a "one-idea crusade against the South." The downstate Whigs' preference for a relatively conservative antislavery protest partly explained the success of Know Nothingism in central Illinois; to some anxious Whigs, Know Nothingism seemed safer than Republicanism. Aware of this Whig predisposition, Lincoln, like Trumbull, discouraged an 1855 Republican state convention, writing to Lovejoy in August that an "open push" to get the Know Nothings might "tend to prevent our ever getting them." Thus rebuffed by two of the state's leading anti-Nebraska politicians, the Republicans postponed a second state convention.[17]

Yet, only a few months later, the tumult in Kansas improved the prospects for Illinois's fusionists. Thousands of Illinoisans had traveled to Kansas for cheap land, and thousands of emigrants from other states had traveled through Illinois to Kansas. Sharing a sense of solidarity, most Illinoisans resented proslavery aggressions in a territory once promised to freedom and now vital to their interests. The fraudulent election of the territorial legislature, the imposition of draconian proslavery laws, the threats and acts of violence against freestate settlers, and President Pierce's unwillingness to protect the integrity of the electoral process and the rights of freestate settlers convinced many Illinoisans that the Nebraska Act actually had been a proslavery plot. In late 1855 and early 1856, correspondents of Yates and Trumbull rued the "practical exposition" of popular sovereignty and indicated that the "Kansas troubles" had created an "immense" majority against slavery's extension in large portions of central Illinois. Meanwhile, Chicago's leading Democratic newspapers took strong ground against border ruffianism and slavery's expansion, as did a Chicago Democratic meeting in October, when one of Douglas's former associates condemned the "stupendous scheme for the extension of slavery" in Kansas. The struggle between slavery and freedom in Kansas had a similar effect even in parts of southern Illinois, where Know Nothing leader Joseph Gillespie reported that the "horrible crimes" in Kansas had "waked up" the "People." Indeed, public agitation reached such a pitch that anti-Nebraskites circulated a petition urging the governor to assemble the legislature for the purpose of taking measures to protect Illinoisans in Kansas from the "armed and lawless invaders from Missouri." The circulation of this petition indicated the profound shift in public sentiment since 1837, when Alton's citizens had killed Elijah Lovejoy for publicly opposing slavery. Now Illinoisans sought to protect freedom from slavery.[18]

The Kansas crisis moved anti-Nebraskites from ideological agreement toward organizational unity. In August letters to Lovejoy, both Lincoln and Trumbull had stated their desire to fuse. By January, Trumbull largely had decided to support the Republican national ticket, and in February Lincoln helped write the resolutions for an anti-Nebraska conference at Decatur. They were not alone. By early 1856, many of Illinois's leading anti-Nebraskites desired fusion. Republican congressman Elihu Washburne indicated his unwillingness "to be beaten by our internal divisions," Gillespie hoped that "we shall be able to unite," and Chicago Democrat Ebenezer Peck opposed a state convention only because he feared it would "disunite" rather than "amalgamate." But they all wanted to fuse, which made a great deal of difference. In Alton, Whigs graciously supported a Democratic congressional nominee; in Chicago, Republicans joined with Germans against nativism; and in Springfield, a gathering of leading politicians agreed to run anti-Nebraska Democrat William Bissell for governor. And, contrary to Peck's widely shared fear that the radicals "would insist upon extreme abolition avowals," Lovejoy and Codding gladly fell into line. They certainly preferred strong doses of antislavery, but they had a firm grasp of political realities. The stage was set for unification.[19]

The statewide Republican Party took shape with surprising ease in 1856. Anti-Nebraska newspaper editors joined Lincoln in Decatur to establish a suitable "line of policy" for the party and endorsed resolutions emphasizing the nation's antislavery heritage. Maintaining that the federal government recognized freedom as "the *rule*" and slavery as "the *exception*," they advocated slavery's restriction "to its present authorized limits." They then organized a Republican state central committee and issued a call for a state convention in Bloomington. To be sure, the conservative anti-Nebraskites feared a radical coup at Bloomington, but their fears proved overblown. Two hundred and seventy cheering delegates, mostly from central and northern Illinois, vowed to return the government "to the principles and practices" of the Revolution by prohibiting slavery's spread "into territories heretofore free." All agreed on this doctrine, and thus the delegates strictly subordinated secondary issues. Most notably, they promised to "proscribe no one" on account of religion or nativity. Freesoil nativists swallowed the plank in a spirit of concession, recognizing the need for the immigrant vote. Meanwhile, the Republicans let downstate Illinoisans dictate the convention resolutions and monopolize party offices, while the Whigs awarded a disproportionate share of party positions to Democratic leaders who could deliver the anti-Nebraska Democratic vote. The anti-Nebraskites had truly fused into a new party.[20]

The anti-Nebraskites' fear that slavery imperiled free society had facilitated fusion at Bloomington. The state convention met immediately after the Sack of Lawrence and Massachusetts senator Charles Sumner's caning, and in this moment of heightened emotion the delegates listened to the gripping oratory of Kansas's freestate governor, who had fled the territory in fear of his life, and whose appalling stories of proslavery violence swayed the emotions of even conservative Whigs. Henceforth, Kansas affairs received detailed newspaper coverage, and the returning tide of Illinoisans who had been violently driven from Kansas by proslavery partisans reinforced anti-Nebraskites' building sense of outrage and wrong. In this context, anti-Nebraska conventions vowed to resist the "extinction of Constitutional Liberty" by "slavery propagandists" and anti-Nebraska newspapers decried southern politicians who called the Declaration of Independence an "*abstraction*," southern editors who claimed that "*free society has proved a failure*," and southern declarations that slavery "is the natural condition of the laboring man, whether white or black." To astonished anti-Nebraskites, such pronouncements must have seemed a belated declaration of the war already begun in Kansas.[21]

In response, the anti-Nebraskites unapologetically proclaimed the superiority of free society. As Lincoln's speeches illustrate, the North's economic dynamism, burgeoning wealth, fluid social structure, and progressive self-image pitted antislavery advocates implacably against proslavery social philosophy and political economy. Lincoln attributed the nation's extraordinary "prosperity" to the "cause" that "every man can make himself," and he contended that "to give up that one thing, would be to give up all future prosperity." Consequently he concluded that Northerners had "an interest" in maintaining "the principles of the Government," and "without this interest" the government "is worth nothing." He reported to his northern audiences that southern newspapers, such as the *Richmond Enquirer*, claimed that "their slaves are far better off than Northern freemen." Lincoln ridiculed this idea because no fixed class of labor existed in the North. "The man who labored for another last year," he declared, "this year labors for himself, and next year he will hire others to labor for him." Lincoln therefore disdained any moral comparison between free and slave labor, or between free and slave society; in his estimation, no credible basis existed for the southern defense of slavery on "principle." Accordingly, he urged Northerners to keep "the Territories free for the settlement of free laborers" by defeating southern attempts to make slavery "a ruling element in our government." Lincoln, along with other antislavery Northerners, was beginning to conflate northern society and American nationalism.[22]

The crystallization of the contest between slavery and freedom pushed nativism to the margins of northern political debate during the 1856 campaign. This development had been evident in Illinois since March, when the Democratic candidate for Chicago's mayoral election had defeated a fusion candidate endorsed by the Know Nothings. Anti-Nebraska Germans had decided the election by voting Democratic, and their defection gave a nasty shock to the fusionists, who realized afresh that nativism could seriously undermine antislavery politics. The Bloomington delegates took this admonition to heart when writing the 1856 Republican state platform, and the antislavery nativists knuckled under in order to make fusion possible. Their willingness to do so partly stemmed from the recent breakup of their party's second national convention, which had disgruntled them by again adopting a pro-Nebraska plank. In May, a leading nativist summed up the attitude of many former Know Nothings, promising Trumbull that party members would give "all their votes" to Republican John Palmer provided only that he "did not *abuse* them." For the most part, nativism in Illinois was a spent political force. Nevertheless, politicians from both major parties knew that the remaining Know Nothings likely held the balance of power.[23]

The 1856 elections gave Lincoln and the Illinois Republicans encouragement for the future. Democratic presidential candidate James Buchanan carried Illinois, primarily because American Party candidate Millard Fillmore attracted former Whig and Know Nothing voters whose fear of disunion drove them from the Republican Party. Yet, about 40 percent of Fillmore's voters supported Illinois's victorious Republican gubernatorial candidate, William Bissell, suggesting that many nativists had underlying antislavery tendencies. The regional distribution of Republican votes also augured well for the party's future. The party's presidential candidate, John C. Fremont, won 67.3 percent of the vote in northern Illinois, 31.2 percent in central Illinois, and 13.0 percent in southern Illinois, so the party clearly would continue to benefit from northern Illinois's rapid population growth. Moreover, Fremont attracted approximately 60 percent to 70 percent of the German vote and as many new voters as the Democrats and Know Nothings combined. This knowledge energized Republicans in Illinois and throughout the

MAP 6. Vote for President, by Party, 1856

Note: Numbers reflect respective Republican and American percentages of the vote (rounded).

MAP 7. Combined Vote for President, Republican and American Parties, 1856
Note: Numbers reflect combined Republican and American percentages of the vote (rounded).

North. Lincoln observed in December that Fremont and Fillmore voters in the North had a four-hundred-thousand-vote majority over Buchanan men, if they would put aside their past differences, and Trumbull reported from Washington, D.C., that party members were in "great spirits" and "feel that they will certainly win next time."[24]

To win next time, Illinois Republicans and the national party faced an identical challenge. Illinois Republicans needed to recruit additional voters in central and southern Illinois—the conservative regions of the state—just as the national party needed to secure electoral votes in Pennsylvania, New Jersey, Indiana, and Illinois—the conservative regions of the North. Fillmore Whigs thus loomed large not only in Illinois but also in the North generally. Since the Republicans needed to carry virtually every northern state to win the presidency in 1860, they needed to defuse the Fillmore Whigs' fear of radicalism. This was not an easy task. Fillmore Whigs dreaded sectional conflict, and those with southern ties likely had more tolerance for slavery than did most other Northerners. Converting their antislavery sentiment into antislavery politics thus required Republicans to show that Douglas, the northern Democracy, and the principle of popular sovereignty posed as grave a danger to free society as did proslavery Southerners. During the next four years, no Republican in Illinois, or the nation, would do that more effectively than Abraham Lincoln.

⤿

Douglas's response to the Dred Scott decision in a June 1857 speech in Springfield created a tremendous opportunity for Lincoln to step to the fore. Douglas's endorsement of the Supreme Court's denial of citizenship rights to blacks—including Taney's dictum that blacks had no rights that whites were bound to respect—increasingly aligned northern Democratic political thought with the southern definition of freedom. Douglas's course reflected his intense hostility to the idea of black equality, his political ties to southern Democrats, and his intention, as Lincoln observed, to "fasten the odium" of black equality on the Republicans. Knowing that Lincoln considered human equality to be the nation's "*central idea*," from which subordinate ideas "radiate," Douglas likely anticipated his long-term Springfield foil giving battle on the critical racial issue. If so, northern Democrats stood to profit dramatically from white racism in negrophobic Illinois.[25]

Yet the Little Giant's racial gambit also enabled Lincoln to collapse distinctions between Douglas and the South. In an impassioned protest several weeks later, Lincoln challenged Douglas's interpretation of the Declaration of Independence. Lincoln maintained that the founders sought to establish "a standard maxim for free society, which should be familiar to all, and revered by all," thereby "spreading and deepening its influence, and augmenting the happiness and value of life to all people of all colors everywhere." Lincoln conceded that equal rights might never be "perfectly attained," but he insisted that the founders had declared "the *right*, so that the *enforcement* of it might follow as fast as circumstances should permit." Consequently, he deplored both the Democrats' refusal to acknowledge blacks' inalienable rights and the Democrats' determination to roll back the few political privileges blacks possessed. To Lincoln, the Taney and Douglas racial doctrine culminated a long-developing retreat from the idea of equality proclaimed in the Declaration of Independence by providing an intellectual and legal capstone to the nation's increasingly discriminatory racial practices. He observed that while Republicans insist "that the negro is a man," and resist enlargement of "the field of his oppression," Democrats "deny his manhood; deny, or dwarf to insignificance, the wrong of his bondage," and "call the indefinite outspreading of his bondage 'a sacred right of self-government.'" Thus Lincoln identified the principles and objectives Douglas and the southern Democrats shared, and in so doing laid bare the points at issue between Republicans and northern Democrats.[26]

Lincoln intensified this nationalist critique after Douglas helped prevent passage of the Lecompton Constitution. Douglas's break with the South led some prominent eastern Republicans to laud him as a freesoil champion and to support his reelection to the Senate in 1858. Indignant Illinois Republicans responded by nominating Lincoln for the Senate in their June 1858 state convention. Nevertheless, Douglas's revolt against Lecompton had obscured distinctions between Republicans and northern Democrats. Clarifying the difference, Lincoln emphasized that Republicans "think slavery is wrong" and "ought to be prohibited" from expansion, while Douglas "cares not" whether slavery in Kansas is "voted down or voted up." Hence Lincoln maintained that the Republicans could not adopt Douglas's position without destroying the party and encouraging "the people of the nation to not care anything about slavery." That outcome, he observed, "is Nebraskaism in its abstract purity—in its very best dress." He utterly opposed it.[27]

Lincoln inaugurated the senatorial campaign with a dramatic attempt to distinguish himself from Douglas. In his House Divided speech, delivered to the Republican state convention on June 16, 1858, he advanced his famous charge that Douglas, Pierce, Buchanan, and Taney had conspired to nationalize slavery. By his estimate, the Kansas-Nebraska Act and the Dred Scott decision were bookends to the nefarious scheme, and he anticipated a subsequent Supreme Court decision striking down antislavery laws in the northern states. This aspect of Lincoln's argument rested on a careful analysis of the Dred Scott decision, which had in fact established a legal basis for the Supreme Court subsequently to invalidate state as well as territorial prohibitions on slavery. Yet Lincoln's central argument rested on the biblical metaphor that a "house divided against itself cannot stand." Reasoning from this proposition, Lincoln argued that either Republicans would place slavery in the "course of ultimate extinction" or Democrats would "push it forward, till it shall become alike lawful in *all* the States." Lincoln's polarization of the slavery question eradicated any middle ground between slavery and freedom, while the conspiracy charge allied Douglas with proslavery expansionists. Lincoln could not have drawn the contrast between himself and Douglas any more sharply.[28]

However, the House Divided speech in some respects overshot its mark and made him vulnerable to counterattack. It did differentiate him from Douglas, but it also channeled him away from his most effective arguments for the first three and a half months of the campaign. In no small part this reflected the political skill of Douglas, who disparaged Lincoln as an abolitionist and disunionist and thus put him on the defensive. Lincoln had much to fear from Douglas's bid for conservative voters. The editor of the antislavery *Chicago Daily Democratic Press*, John L. Scripps, informed Lincoln only six days after the House Divided speech that the ultimate extinction doctrine alarmed some of "my Kentucky friends who want to be Republicans, but who are *afraid* we are not sufficiently conservative." Although they "hate" the Democrats "most cordially," wrote Scripps, they deemed that aspect of Lincoln's speech "*ultraism*." Scripps did not ask Lincoln to renounce his position but did recommend that he state his views subsequently on "the general question of federal interference with slavery in the states," including "the policy of the Republican party," in order to persuade conservative voters that Republicans did not intend "to make war" upon slavery "where it now exists." Lincoln followed this advice, stating "again and again" that he would not "disturb the institution of slavery," but his protests against Douglas's "misrepresentation" only reinforced his defensive position, leading the concerned editor of the *Chicago Tribune*, Charles Ray, to urge him in late August to inflict "the deadliest thrusts," drawing Douglas's "blood" at the close of each sentence.[29]

But Lincoln's tireless and ultimately tedious repetition of the conspiracy charge did not have the desired effect. His desire to diminish Douglas's freesoil reputation was understandable, but the gravity of the charge required better evidence than he possessed, especially because Douglas's leadership in combating the Lecompton Constitution made it hard for most voters to believe that he had been at the center of a sinister proslavery plot. Nevertheless,

Lincoln groped toward a more effective argument over the course of the campaign. In October he finally grasped how to best distinguish Douglas's politics from the principles and policies of the Republican Party.[30]

In the last three debates, Lincoln reemphasized the moral appeal he had first articulated in 1854. He repeatedly argued that the Republicans, in contrast to Douglas, considered slavery "a moral, a social and a political wrong." He judged that this was the "real difference" between the parties, from which sprung the Republicans' determination to treat slavery as a wrong by making "*provision that it shall grow no larger.*" As always, Lincoln emphasized the antislavery character of the Declaration of Independence, which enabled him to root his moral argument in nationalism rather than theology. Indeed, he used the Declaration as a bridge to the founding fathers, claiming that they likewise considered slavery immoral and sought to place it in "the course of ultimate extinction" by abolishing the slave trade and prohibiting slavery's expansion. Calling this "the peaceful way" of cutting slavery from the body politic, he maintained that Republican antislavery extension policy "proposed nothing more than a return to the policy of the fathers." These were not entirely new ideas with Lincoln, but he had begun to assemble them into a cohesive, powerful, and partisan antislavery nationalism that Douglas totally rejected.[31]

Lincoln's distillation of the moral argument also enabled him to utilize his conspiracy charges effectively as an adjunct argument. In the House Divided speech, he had argued that Douglas's "care not" policy constituted a part of the conspiracy to nationalize slavery, serving to "*educate* and *mould*" northern public opinion "to not *care* whether slavery is voted *down* or voted *up.*" This was the most persuasive aspect of the conspiracy charge because it accurately described the consequences of Douglas's ideas, even if not his motives. Lincoln strengthened this argument in the last three debates by pairing it with a legal syllogism that demonstrated the likelihood of slavery's nationalization. Lincoln observed that nothing in the "laws of any State" could destroy a right "expressly affirmed" in the Constitution; the Dred Scott decision "expressly affirmed" the "right of property in a slave"; therefore, nothing in the "laws of any State" could "destroy the right of property in a slave." By deemphasizing the alleged political conspiracy, this argument narrowed Douglas's culpability for slavery's nationalization yet still permitted Lincoln to call Douglas the man most culpable for "preparing the public mind" to take the next Supreme Court decision "when it comes." Lincoln did not charge that Douglas considered slavery to be right; but he did claim that moral indifference would cause Douglas to endorse southern jurists who thought it right. Like Southerners, Douglas would willingly put slavery on the "*cotton gin basis*" of self-interest, which Lincoln believed would lead to slavery's nationalization rather than to its ultimate extinction.[32]

Like Douglas's, Lincoln's appeals proved only a partial success. His failure to attract enough conservative voters in central Illinois resulted in a painfully narrow defeat. However, the contest was so close that the Democrats lost Illinois's statewide offices because a vengeful President Buchanan—embittered by Douglas's opposition to the Lecompton Constitution—had spurred pro-Lecompton candidates to challenge the Democratic nominees of the state party Douglas controlled. The Lecompton Democrats won few votes, but it was enough to change the outcome. As in 1856, Illinoisans had not decisively supported either the Democrats or Republicans, and therefore the state would be a crucial battleground in the 1860 campaign.[33]

Cognizant of these facts, Lincoln developed a political strategy to win the state in 1860. His planning centered on the defeat of Douglas. Presciently, Lincoln predicted that southern demands for a territorial slave code would soon create another "blow up" in the Democracy, forcing Douglas to break with southern Democrats. But Lincoln's comprehension that the politics of slavery had almost consumed the Democratic Party did not make him complacent. If Douglas did break with the South, he observed, "the struggle in the whole North will be, as it was in Illinois last summer and fall, whether the Republican party can maintain it's identity, or be broken up to form the tail of Douglas' new kite." Such a contest might not redound to the Republicans' advantage. Conservative Whigs and Know Nothings in contested states like Illinois would likely hold the balance of power in 1860, and an independent Douglas would make a strong bid for just those voters. Faced with this possibility, Lincoln redoubled his efforts to persuade them to adopt the party's antislavery extension policy, while convincing the party's radical wing to unify harmoniously with the conservative recruits. As the 1856 election had demonstrated, the Republicans imperatively needed them.[34]

For these reasons, Lincoln widely propagated an antislavery nationalism in the sixteen months after his defeat. He believed that the doctrine, battle tested in Illinois, could both unify the party and attract conservatives; and he used his newly acquired national reputation—forged by the nationwide publicity of the debates—to disseminate his ideas. His efforts to unify the party initially concentrated in Illinois. He urged Chicago Republicans not to demand radical policy from downstate Republicans, and meanwhile scolded central Illinois Republicans who censured the "ultra" antislavery men of the North. Lincoln soon branched out to national affairs. He urged Ohio Republicans to drop their opposition to the fugitive slave law, informed

Massachusetts Republicans that nativism undermined liberty, instructed Kansas Republicans to steer clear of popular sovereignty, and encouraged a leading Indiana Republican to keep "explosive" issues out of the party's 1860 national platform. Disdaining the idea that every party member should agree "upon every minor point," Lincoln instead urged party members to rally around the "great principle" of slavery's wrong and the central object of "preventing the *spread* and *nationalization* of Slavery." He was beginning to put his distinctive stamp on Republican Party ideology.[35]

Lincoln refined his nationalist ideology in response to Douglas's September 1859 essay in *Harper's Magazine*. In a series of speeches given in Ohio, Indiana, and Wisconsin in September, and Kansas in December, Lincoln took issue with Douglas's historical argument that the founders had enshrined the principle of local self-government in the Constitution and early territorial law. At Columbus, he developed ideas broached briefly in a speech at Carlinville a year earlier, claiming that the Republicans' "original and chief purpose" was the "eminently conservative" object of preventing slavery's nationalization. He explained that the Republicans promised "to restore this government to its original tone," desiring no more in relation to slavery "than that which the original framers of the government themselves expected." Despite his professed conservatism, these arguments were no more than a freshly minted version of his ultimate extinction doctrine. After all, Lincoln argued that "the fathers of this government did not make it part slave and part free to remain permanently so." Instead, they had passed the Northwest Ordinance to promote slavery's gradual extirpation.[36]

Lincoln built on this argument by fusing antislavery nationalism to the interests of free society. He pointed out that Indiana's settlers unsuccessfully petitioned the government at an early date to suspend the antislavery provision of the Northwest Ordinance, and he argued that Ohio, Indiana, and Illinois likely would all have become slave states had the Ordinance not warded off slaveholders. Reasoning from this proposition, Lincoln invoked free labor arguments to demonstrate the need for antislavery law. Comparing the "*mudsill*" theory of labor, in which laborers were fixed in their position for life, and free labor, in which laborers accumulated capital throughout their lives, Lincoln contended that free labor was a "just and generous, and prosperous system, which opens the way for all—gives hope to all, and energy, and progress, and improvement of condition to all." To Lincoln, slavery deliberately destroyed the "inspiration of hope" required for "human exertion," while free labor encouraged men to innovate and excel. Given these considerations, he urged Northerners to return to the ideals that served their interests. In his estimation, progress was "the order of things" only in "a society of equals." Never before had Lincoln so completely conflated northern interests and American nationalism.[37]

Lincoln brought antislavery nationalism to its zenith in his Cooper Union address of February 1860. Invited to talk in New York City, as he had been invited earlier to speak throughout the Northwest, Lincoln accepted with alacrity. The invitation marked his growing stature and provided him with an unparalleled opportunity to present his views to some of the nation's most powerful Republicans. He pondered the subject of his address in light of both John Brown's recent raid at Harper's Ferry, which had dramatically polarized the nation, and his growing chances for the party's presidential nomination. The first required him to defend the Republican Party from charges of incendiarism, and the second encouraged him to use words that calmed skittish northern Whigs. His characteristic cloaking of antislavery policy in a putatively conservative nationalism was perfectly suited to the occasion. His task was to indelibly associate the founders with antislavery values, showing that slavery contradicted the ideals of a nation that slave-holders did much to form.[38]

Lincoln's argument was a masterpiece of misdirection. He ostensibly argued for a conservative antislavery extension policy that comported with the will of the founders, yet he in fact issued a radical manifesto against slavery that denounced disunionism and importuned Republicans to resist it at any cost. Lincoln achieved this startling result with means as covertly radical as his ends. His tone resonated with reasonableness, and with a set of ingeniously misleading arguments he breathed a spirit of conservatism into the three portions of his speech, successively addressed to Douglas, Southerners, and Republicans. His initial argument locked horns with the *Harper's Magazine* essay and conclusively demonstrated that a majority of the signers of the U.S. Constitution believed that Congress possessed the power to prohibit slavery in the nation's territories. This carefully researched contention was straightforward, but in a masterful sleight of hand Lincoln inferred from it that the founders intended to put slavery in the course of ultimate extinction, a conclusion that did not follow from the premises. After all, as Lincoln conceded in a different context in the speech, the power to prohibit territorial slavery did not imply the expediency of doing so. This was no small discrepancy considering that Lincoln's idea of an antislavery nation rested upon his historical argument.[39]

The founders' thinking on slavery was considerably more complex than Lincoln acknowledged. While most founders professed antislavery ideals, and hoped for slavery's end, their expectations of its death typically amounted to little more than a progressive faith in free labor political economy. Meanwhile, the Constitution they created was preeminently a practical document designed to establish a governance structure suitable for the diverse interests and extensive size of the infant United States. Determined to protect slavery in the new government, some southern delegates demanded concessions from northern delegates as the price of union. These southern delegates had no desire whatsoever to promote the "ultimate extinction" of slavery, and especially not through the auspices of the new federal government, whose potential power to destroy slavery gravely concerned them. Consequently, northern delegates hostile to slavery, such as Gouverneur Morris, ultimately had to sacrifice their antislavery convictions in order to create the Union. Meanwhile, some New England delegates proved quite willing to make concessions to slavery. In stark contrast to the Constitution's authors, the Republicans sought to contain and ultimately destroy slavery—a policy that risked disunion—because they feared slavery's vitality and expected it to expand. Their assumptions and intentions therefore differed radically from those of the founders. Lincoln's claim that Republican antislavery policy descended directly from the founders flowed from a distinctly selective reading of the nation's past.[40]

Lincoln very likely flattened out the historical record deliberately. Admittedly, no historian can identify the intent of a historical actor with certainty. Perhaps Lincoln believed that every iota of the historical record justified his interpretation. However, his extensive preparation for the Cooper Union address combined with his logician's mind and masterful command of language strongly suggests that his conservative cloaking of antislavery policy was deliberate and shrewd. With finely honed lawyerly skill, he made the best case possible for his position.

Lincoln elaborated his ingenious argument by pinning the odium of radicalism on the South. This was a logical deduction from his premises. If Republicans contended for the "old policy" of the government, as he maintained, then Southerners "reject, and scout, and spit upon that old policy." By refusing to adopt antislavery extension politics, as had the founders, Southerners branded themselves as unworthy heirs to the national patrimony. Lincoln consequently characterized their threats to destroy the union as a "great crime." They had neither legal nor moral right to take such action. Although Lincoln's argument against disunion had much to recommend it, he had again shifted the grounds of the debate. In effect, he combated charges of Republican radicalism by charging that crime upon the South. In truth, both Southerners and Republicans bore responsibility for polarizing the slavery issue, but Lincoln insisted that "the greater prominence" of the slavery issue since the nation's founding stemmed solely from proslavery "innovation" on the "old times." By advancing this argument with a seemingly transcendent objectivity, Lincoln skillfully adapted his ideas to the scruples of conservative Whigs.[41]

This line of reasoning enabled Lincoln to claim that antislavery nationalism was eminently conservative. In the final segment of his speech, he urged Republicans to promote *"peace"* and *"harmony"* even *"though much provoked,"* and to *"yield"* to southern demands if *"we possibly can."* This passage immediately followed his critique of disunion and seemingly testified to his conciliatory spirit. Yet his deft use of the moral argument soon indicated that he had issued the conciliatory sentiments in order to harden Republican resolve. Much as he had done with Douglas, he insisted that Southerners thinking slavery right, "and our thinking it wrong, is the precise fact upon which depends the whole controversy." He conceded that if slavery was right, Southerners could justifiably ask for its nationalization, but if it was wrong, they could not demand its extension. Thus Republicans could not, after all, "yield" to the South, but instead must stand by their duty inflexibly and unflinchingly. Remarkably, Lincoln's conciliatory beginning culminated in a steely peroration in which he commanded Republicans to oppose slavery's extension "TO THE END," daring "TO DO OUR DUTY AS WE UNDERSTAND IT." Lincoln's exquisite framing of antislavery politics turned the moralism of the abolitionists into the duty of the nation.[42]

Lincoln's exposition of Republican thought contributed decisively to his presidential nomination in Chicago. In the parlance of politics, it made him an available candidate, adapting him ideally to the party's needs. The Republicans' one vexing problem in 1860 was the absence of a suitable nominee. None of the party's leading lights precisely fit the bill. New York's William Seward and Ohio's Salmon P. Chase seemed too radical to win the critical states of Pennsylvania, Indiana, and Illinois; Pennsylvania's Simon Cameron had too many enemies in his own state and too few principles and scruples to inspire the confidence of men elsewhere; Missouri's Edward Bates had an overly strong nativist heritage and little antislavery pedigree; and age bowed down Supreme Court Justice John McLean. The lack of a strong candidate highlighted the continuing divisions within Republican ranks. The national party, like the Illinois state party, needed to unify a discordant mix of radicals, moderates, conservatives, immigrants, and nativists in a manner appealing to voters in the crucial Lower North states. Under the circumstances, as Lincoln's advisors quickly discovered in Chicago, the man most responsible for uniting Illinois's state party had perfect credentials for the presidential nomination. The antislavery nationalism he had fashioned to bring Illinoisans together proved ideally suited to the entire North. Indeed, his representatives at the convention—a northern Illinois Democrat, a German, and two conservative Whigs—suggested his unusual capacity to bridge ideological divides. Perhaps not surprisingly, the convention delegates refused "lightly to throw away," as Lincoln had once remarked of Douglas's wide-ranging appeal, this "power to perform wonders." Illinois politics had produced a man uniquely suited for national leadership of the Republican Party.[43]

The 1860 election confirmed the wisdom of the delegates at the Republican convention. Lincoln won all electoral votes in every free state except New Jersey, demonstrating strength across the ideological spectrum. He edged out Douglas in Illinois by taking three-fourths of the 1856 Fillmore vote, two-thirds of the German vote, and two-thirds of the newly eligible voters. In Pennsylvania he attracted an astonishing 87 percent of the Fillmore men and virtually all of the newly eligible voters who cast a ballot. These patterns held, somewhat more moderately, for the North at large. The Republicans' success in attracting the support of such disparate groups while holding on to their 1856 antislavery constituency in no small part reflected Lincoln's appeal, and the tightness of the contest in the crucial Lower North states indicates that the Republicans might well have lost their majority in the electoral college had they instead nominated New York's William Seward, Lincoln's chief rival at Chicago. The Republicans' campaign mythologizing of Lincoln's rise from frontier poverty to political distinction proved apt indeed. Lincoln was, after all, an ideal representative of free society.[44]

Yet Lincoln's devotion to free society was thoroughly nationalist. To Lincoln, universal liberty represented the nation's guiding principle; self-government represented its greatest achievement; free labor represented its prodigious strength; and northern society represented its true character. Imbued with these convictions, Lincoln considered slavery unjust, slave society antiprogressive, and proslavery politics antagonistic to the idea of liberty and the existence of free society. Consequently, his radical opposition to slavery took the cast of national preservation from the inception of the anti-Nebraska movement. Lincoln was not entirely unique in this regard. The Nebraska Act's wanton aggression on freedom clothed the antislavery movement in a preservationist mantle that it had never before enjoyed and would never later relinquish. Certainly the movement could not have taken shape as it did without such a shocking assault on the interests and prerogatives of freedom.[45]

MAP 8. Vote for President, Republican Party, 1860
Note: Numbers reflect Republican percentage of the vote (rounded).

Nevertheless, Lincoln united antislavery radicalism with national preservation more powerfully than perhaps any other Republican. This stemmed from his unusual antislavery perspective. Although his critique of slavery was fundamentally moral, and although he frequently used biblical metaphors and language, he did not primarily think of slavery as a sin against God. Nor did he centrally concern himself with the naked struggle over sectional political power or the promotion of free labor political economy, as did some other Republicans. Instead, he perceived slavery as a moral challenge to American citizens. After all, slavery had been nurtured in American soil, propagated by American slaveholders, and protected, to an extent, by the American Constitution. This nationalist outlook placed him nearer to the political abolitionists than to any other group of Republicans. But many of them sought to make the national Constitution into an antislavery instrument, hoping to turn the law and the courts in favor of freedom. Lincoln, by contrast, rested his hopes solely on the moral sentiments of the people and sought to turn the people in favor of freedom. Accordingly, he told Northerners that the Declaration of Independence articulated the moral foundations of free society and the moral obligations of American government, and he urged Northerners to do their duty by halting slavery's advance and preserving freedom. The precepts of an antislavery nation, and the progress of free society, required no less.

As Lincoln comprehended, advocacy of an antislavery nationalism sharply distinguished Republicans from northern Democrats. Neither Stephen A. Douglas nor any other leading northern Democrat could sanction an ideology that condemned slavery as un-American without precipitating a southern Democratic rebellion that would destroy the Democratic Party and probably the Union. For this reason, Douglas adamantly contested Lincoln's reading of American history, claiming instead that the founders had made the country half-slave and half-free and pillorying Lincoln as a radical whose doctrines threatened to rend the Union. In this way, Douglas sought to attract the same northern conservative swing voters pursued by Lincoln and the Republicans. A variety of reasons explain why he was unable to win their loyalty: their abiding bitterness at his role in driving the inflammatory Kansas-Nebraska Act through Congress in 1854; their deep hostility to the Irish Catholic voters who so strongly supported him; southern delegates' demand for congressional protection of territorial slavery at the 1860 Democratic National Convention in Charleston, which tore the Democratic Party asunder and eroded Douglas's claim to represent the interests of both Northerners and Southerners; and Northerners' increasing hostility to perceived southern high-handedness. Indeed, the violence of proslavery settlers in Kansas Territory, South Carolina

representative Preston S. Brooks's vicious beating of Massachusetts senator Charles Sumner, Kansas's fraudulent Lecompton Constitution, and the
destruction of the Democratic Party at Charleston all pushed swing voters
toward the Republicans.

Yet the precepts of an antislavery nationalism played probably the most
critical role in driving the votes of conservative Northerners to Lincoln rather
than Douglas. After all, the founding generation *had* articulated universal
claims for human liberty in order to justify the Americans' revolutionary
struggle for freedom, and therefore the idea of a nation dedicated to liberty
was surely compelling to any Northerner who considered freedom superior
to slavery. Moreover, the logical deduction from this premise was that the
interests of freedom should continue to predominate in the country, slavery's
continued existence notwithstanding. Hence the Republicans' fusion of the
past, present, and future in a nationalist ideology that justified antislavery
politics philosophically and instrumentally had tremendously persuasive
power. Although radical in practice, it seemed thoroughly justified, deeply
moral, and eminently reasonable, and furthermore it unhesitatingly promised
to favor the interests of the North.

Such considerations attracted both conservative Whigs and former Know
Nothings. A large majority of northern Whigs and Know Nothings opposed
slavery, even if Unionist or nativist convictions blunted, and in some cases
precluded, their participation in antislavery politics. Moreover, northern
Know Nothings had developed a strong nationalist creed, promoting national
regeneration through nativist reforms and antislavery policy. Such attitudes
made them susceptible to Lincoln's antislavery nationalism, which touched
directly on one of their central concerns. Finally, Lincoln's seeming moderation surely swayed some Whigs who had voted for Millard Fillmore in 1856;
after all, the American Party had promoted sectional conciliation that year as
avidly as nativism. By thus attracting a crucial cadre of conservative recruits,
the Republicans' nationalist appeals helped bring their party to power with
remarkable speed.[46]

Yet antislavery nationalism also helped propel the nation to war. Republicans had gambled by organizing a party on antislavery principles. The idea
of a nation dedicated to freedom, and pledged against slavery, challenged
the South as sharply as Douglas's Kansas-Nebraska Act had challenged the
North. Southerners considered slavery to be a positive good and imagined a proslavery past: they remembered southern founders who secured
constitutional protections for slavery, facilitated slavery's expansion, and

censured antislavery agitation. Consequently, Southerners clung fiercely to their political and economic interests in slavery and pronounced slavery to be an exemplary method of social organization. They even deprecated free labor political economy and claimed that northern exactions, such as the tariff, plundered southern wealth. Given their growing conception of a proslavery nation, the election of a president who claimed that the founders' mandate required slavery's ultimate extinction provoked them to secede. Here the dialectic of irreconcilable antislavery and proslavery nationalisms exerted a profound political influence. Certain of their conservative intent, Republicans considered secession not only a subversion of constitutional order but also a perversion of national ideals. By their lights, secession desecrated the democratic process and shattered the Union in order to promote a social system that repudiated the nation's core principles. Imbued with Lincoln's nationalism, Republicans refused to countenance it. Millions of soldiers—and four bloody years of war—arbitrated the dispute.[47]

Conclusion

The Northern Democrats' Dilemma over Slavery

ON APRIL 21, 1838, in Washington, D.C., Adam Snyder took a moment from his day to scribble some observations about slavery. The Democratic congressman from Illinois had never opposed slavery. Born impoverished in Pennsylvania, he had migrated to Illinois in 1817 and had risen rapidly due to talent, industry, and ambition—and the patronage of Illinois's prominent proslavery politician, Jesse B. Thomas. Thomas deeply influenced Snyder's views of slavery. Snyder supported Illinois's proslavery movement, purchased four slaves, and abhorred abolitionism. Such a background makes his letter from Washington, D.C., in 1838 all the more fascinating. He noted that "a poor man came the other day to get some information from me in regard to the country," doing so "with his hat off stooping and cringeing into my room, more humble than one of my negroes comes before me, it is so with all of them." By contrast, every white Illinoisan "however poor he may be is proudly independent," wrote Snyder, "the equal of the richest and the highest," but in slave country the poor "are a different race," miserable "amongst the proud slave holders." Certain that poor whites would be respected if they were "in the far west the owners of their own homes," he thought that "they ought to go to Illinois" even if "they took it on foot and lived all the way on parched corn." Snyder did not criticize every aspect of slavery, or slavery everywhere, but he levied a damning indictment nonetheless.[1]

Snyder's appraisal contrasts sharply with South Carolina senator John C. Calhoun's defense of slavery on the floor of Congress in 1837 and 1838. Calhoun claimed that slavery was a "positive good" and deserved to be protected at all hazards against northern antislavery sentiment. Slavery had "inseparably united" blacks and whites, he argued, securing "the peace and happiness of both." Blacks had benefited especially, rising from a "low, degraded, and savage condition" to a relatively "civilized condition" under slaveholders' "fostering care." This portrayal apparently did not persuade Snyder, who observed in his letter that "many of these Maryland & Virginia people" survive only due to "the Shad & Herring fisheries," and cannot adequately "feed their negroes," who consequently are "red headed and husky red skins," not "black & glossy." The gulf between Calhoun's public declaration and Snyder's private views encapsulate the northern Democrats' dilemma over slavery. Although northern Democrats prized the Union, Southerners prized both slavery and the Union, typically in that order. Consequently, just as Calhoun's positive good defense of slavery became southern orthodoxy over the next two decades, so too did his declaration that his "first duty" was to the "slaveholding States" rather than to the Union, and his insistence that the Constitution protected slavery in the nation's territories. Northern Democrats like Snyder could not easily swallow these doctrines. Protecting slavery against abolitionism was one thing; promoting its expansion and perpetuity in concert with Southerners at the expense of northern whites was altogether another. In this sense, Snyder's criticism of slavery was a harbinger of a very serious crisis in the Democratic Party.[2]

Almost twenty years later, in February 1856, a letter to Stephen A. Douglas by his boyhood friend Samuel Mills demonstrated that southern and northern Democrats' contrasting attitudes toward slavery had come home to roost. Mills wrote that Douglas's "powerful support" for repeal of the antislavery provisions of the Missouri Compromise had led Northerners to misapprehend his "real position on the vexed question of slavery." While declaring that he had not "ceased to believe" that Douglas's "leading motive" for the Kansas-Nebraska Act was devotion to the principle of popular sovereignty, Mills reported that most Northerners regarded Douglas "as foremost among those most active and desirous to extend the institution of slavery to the New Territories." This, as Mills recognized, was a dangerous state of affairs, especially since his own faith in Douglas partly rested on the presumption "that with *an open field* and *a fair trial*" popular sovereignty would exclude slavery from national territories. Yet popular sovereignty in Kansas was receiving neither an open field nor a fair trial, and slavery's legalization there under such circumstances probably would deeply erode Douglas's northern support. Indeed, Mills's "greatest fear" was that southern plaudits and northern censure of Douglas's seemingly proslavery course would inadvertently drive Douglas into the South's "embrase," whatever Douglas's private attitudes toward slavery. To forestall this calamitous possibility, Mills urged Douglas to defend Kansas's maligned and persecuted free state settlers, who were "earnest" men seeking to better "their condition," and who deserved protection against the Missourians' "monstrous" and indefensible "perversion" of popular sovereignty. "Under these circumstances," he asked, "has not a favorable time arrived when in justice to yourself as well as the great interests of the country, you may openly take ground" against such abuses, "safely" trusting "to the better judgment and good sense of the people of every section of the country to rally around & sustain you?" To Mills, such a principled stand would be consistent with Douglas's "former course," and the Missourians' atrocious conduct would enable Douglas to support the free-state settlers without alienating the South.[3]

But Douglas's southern correspondence showed that such a course would be very risky. As early as 1852, when Douglas was first considered for the party's presidential nomination, a southern Democratic supporter demanded his position on various slavery-related issues because "[w]e of the south have been imposed on long enough and the time has come we should know the views of those who may be presented for our support." Southerners' determination to support only those northern politicians who served southern interests had not altered by 1856. Georgia's Lyman Hall association honored Douglas that year for his "Gallant" advocacy of "the interest of the South," William Vaughan gratefully acknowledged that Douglas had "gone further" in defending the South than "many" southern politicians, and Horatio Boxley observed that Southerners "look to such men as you, Cass & Buchanon with a kind of a reverential awe." These correspondents were hardly threatening Douglas, but he could surely perceive the dangers that lurked behind their commendations. After all, disunionism was always the southern alternative to seeking security in the Union. As Southerner James N. Shine bluntly observed in February 1856, in sharp counterpoint to Mills, "We have already seen armed Bands in Kansas commencing as it were the dissolution and destruction of this Glorious Confederacy," and Boxley observed that without "that kindred feeling" shown by northern politicians such as Douglas, "the Union of the States would not exist a 12 month," for why should Southerners endure "injustice & inequality & pretend to be bound together by the ties & rights of the same laws[?]" Mills was thus more perceptive than he knew in fearing that public perceptions would drive Douglas southward. After all, as Mills desired, Southerners did consult their "better judgment and good sense" in assessing the country's "great interests" in 1856. However, they concluded that Douglas's unwavering support of the South was precisely what made him a Northerner worthy of commendation. Douglas truly faced a terrible dilemma, one rooted deeply in the country's past.[4]

↬

The seeds of the northern Democrats' dilemma had been planted at the country's founding. The delegates to the Philadelphia Constitutional Convention had, like Douglas, struggled with the problem of incorporating slavery into the Union. Unlike him, they did not attempt to resolve the problem permanently. While acknowledging the contradiction between slavery and the nation's founding ideals, their agreements on slavery stopped there, and their disagreements prevented them from fashioning a long-term solution that ensured slavery's abolition. They subsequently swept their disagreements under the rug as much as was possible during the struggle to ratify the Constitution. This strategy succeeded, but their collective silence about slavery's status in the nation forced their descendants to decide the issue. Meanwhile, southern delegates' successful negotiation of a fugitive slave clause, a twenty-year moratorium on laws to prohibit the Atlantic slave trade, and the partial inclusion of the slave population in congressional apportionment significantly raised the stakes of that future decision. Northern delegates probably could have driven a harder bargain, but they wanted to forge a stronger federal government and needed southern support to do it. Hence, deciding how hard to bargain was a delicate matter. Although antislavery delegates perhaps consoled themselves with the hope that economic changes in the new nation would result in voluntary emancipation, the bargain they struck had exactly the opposite effect. Subsequent generations of Americans learned that the concessions consolidated and polarized existing northern and southern attitudes toward slavery, thus precluding the possibility of a national response to a problem the Constitution had rooted in federal law. In particular, slave representation in Congress and the fugitive slave law vested slaveholders with political power and legal privileges that Northerners came to resent, while white Southerners perceived such provisions as evidence of an unwritten constitutional right to slavery that served as a foundation for the Union. The founders made many sagacious judgments about political theory and institutions. However, their establishment of a nation that sanctioned and ultimately strengthened slavery created an incipient regional division in American politics. Most Americans living outside the South abstractly opposed the institution but had little connection to it; by supplying the connection, the new nation both justified the subsequent northern attack on slavery and established the sovereign power necessary to assault it. Here was the political basis for future escalation of northern and southern conflicts over slavery.[5]

Economic competition between slavery and freedom over land compounded the problem of slavery in American politics. In the wake of the American Revolution, slaveholders used the doctrine of inalienable property rights and proto-industrial techniques of mass production to satisfy the demands of northern and European wage laborers for sugar, tobacco, and cheap clothing. Consequently, slavery grew in leaps and bounds. Although slave states and free states developed strong economic ties, as was evident in the cotton trade between northern textile manufacturers and southern planters, America's economic integration of slavery and freedom created a unique problem usually associated with the clash of rival powers: northern and southern states both desired exclusive control of national territories because chattel slavery required laws inimical to free labor. In this particular respect, a radical economic antagonism existed between slavery and freedom. Not easily amenable to compromise, this antagonism forcefully penetrated the political system whenever the nation acquired more territory, creating a chronic problem in American political economy.[6]

The social and cultural differences between free and slave society made resolution of the problems in politics and political economy particularly difficult. In the South, the presence of many people who lacked significant social standing or legal rights influenced every aspect of society. Fugitive slaves, kidnapped free blacks, slave patrols, the slave trade, the disciplining of slaves, and the sexual abuse of black women, to name just some notable aspects of southern life, all stemmed from slavery. Such social and cultural practices appalled many Northerners. For instance, Abraham Lincoln paid a substantial sum in 1857 to free a black resident of Springfield who had been arrested in New Orleans after mistakenly leaving his free papers on a steamboat. Injustices like these, which slavery necessarily produced, disturbed Northerners and led them to contrast their society favorably with the South. Admittedly, abolitionists spearheaded most critiques of the South, while northern Democrats, who had vastly more political power, avoided invidious regional contrasts whenever possible. But the abolitionists' growing influence on northern culture meant that the Democrats' attitudes became less typical of northern society over time, sharpening the Democrats' dilemma over slavery.[7]

The fate of America's churches perhaps best illustrates how cultural conflicts over slavery influenced northern politics. Doctrinal differences over slavery's sinfulness split every major Protestant denomination by the mid-1840s, and the war over biblical hermeneutics both hastened and justified the later war of steel and lead. The Protestant churches, a once-powerful bond of Union, became an even more powerful tool of its undoing. With men of the cloth defending both freedom and slavery in the name of God, pressure mounted on northern and southern politicians to align public policy with God's will. By the 1850s, northern evangelicals unhesitatingly pitted their organizational resources and moral convictions against northern Democratic defenders of the South.[8]

As theological divisions over slavery suggest, public discussion of slavery and freedom exacerbated southern and northern social and cultural differences. Even Stephen A. Douglas, who never publicly criticized slavery, found it difficult to equate free and slave societies morally. In an 1848 exchange with southern senators, he insisted that northern Democrats be permitted to defend Southerners' constitutional rights without having to defend slavery. If Northerners agreed that slavery was a positive good, he said, "it would be a very pertinent inquiry, Why do you not adopt this institution?" Douglas's preference for freedom, so obliquely phrased, and moderated by his tolerance for slavery, posed no danger to the Union. But other Northerners' blunter assessments about freedom's superiority both stiffened northern voters' resistance to proslavery politics and poisoned national politics by wounding southern sensibilities. Meanwhile, southern radicals' zealous defense of the South and vitriolic denunciations of abolitionists and antislavery politics angered Northerners while strengthening southern voters' determination to maintain their equality in the Union. Hence Unionists like Douglas understood perfectly that the social and cultural tensions produced by the intersection of slavery and freedom could conceivably inflame the problems in politics and political economy past any prospect of resolution or mitigation.[9]

⮎

In the northern states, the Whigs' antislavery tendencies ensured that the delicate task of managing the nation's conflict over slavery fell largely to the Democrats. Not surprisingly, as Snyder's letter suggests, it was a task they viewed with some ambivalence. Although their marriage to proslavery southern Democrats strengthened their contempt for and hostility toward blacks, whom they typically considered irredeemably inferior to whites, northern Democrats represented citizens of a free society, often opposed slavery in the abstract, and in any case could hardly flout northern preferences for freedom with impunity. Consequently, from the 1830s to the early 1850s northern Democrats sought to subordinate slavery as a social and political issue. In doing so, they carefully differentiated between antislavery sentiment and antislavery politics. They generally did not challenge antislavery sentiment, the widespread sense among many Northerners that slavery was wrong. Instead, they fiercely resisted the intrusion of antislavery sentiment into social reform and politics, fearing that an antislavery political movement would drive Southerners from the Union. In this regard, northern Democrats differed considerably from most northern Whigs, who sympathized with the antislavery movement. To be sure, northern Whigs also promoted tolerance for existing slavery, abhorred the idea of disunion, and criticized abolitionism, but they invariably took the antislavery position when slavery penetrated politics. A thin line separated the northern Whigs' antislavery sentiment from antislavery politics, forcing Democrats to take the lead in subordinating the slavery issue in the North.[10]

Yet, precisely because of the northern Democrats' greater tolerance for slavery, the national Democratic Party ultimately played the greatest role in injecting slavery into northern political debate. Over Whig objections, Democrats dramatically expanded America's territorial domain in the 1840s, precipitating a traumatic sectional contest over expansion from 1846 to 1850. They did not intend to create this crisis. The proximate cause of northern Democratic expansionism was the nationwide depression in the early 1840s, which significantly exacerbated Democratic Party fissures over the propriety of both state banking and state subsidies for market development. To frustrated northern Democratic Party leaders, expansionism promised the party's unification on a patriotic platform as well as the acquisition of land stretching from the Mississippi River to the Pacific Ocean. This seemingly perfect solution to the party's vexing economic problem served the Democrats' agrarian constituency and the country's swelling population, which was carrying wave after wave of land-hungry settlers to the West. Nevertheless, the northern Democrats' alliance with proslavery Southerners deeply colored their expansionist politics. Most northern Democrats in the 1840s contended that national expansion enlarged the area of American freedom, regardless of slavery's expansion, and some northern party members disingenuously repeated proslavery arguments that America's southwestern expansion would advance the cause of emancipation by draining southern slaves into Central America. Eager for expansion, Illinois Democrats, like almost all western Democrats, undercut the nomination of New York's Martin Van Buren at the 1844 Democratic national convention, which opened the door for Tennessee's James K. Polk, whose expansionist policies as president put slavery at the forefront of political debate.[11]

The possibility of slavery's expansion into newly acquired territories almost inevitably catalyzed the antislavery movement. This was hardly surprising. Since the government's inception, Northerners had repeatedly indicated their preference for freedom's expansion, yet southern Democrats during the 1840s did not hide their desire to spread slavery. Thus the war with Mexico precipitated not only antislavery fusillades from abolitionists and northern Whigs, but also a rebellion of freesoil Democrats, whose Wilmot Proviso sought to exclude slavery from any territory acquired in the war. The predictably stiff resistance put up by southern congressmen to the proviso ultimately induced most northern Democrats to support popular sovereignty as a compromise by 1848, but not without driving freesoil Democrats into an alliance with abolitionists and antislavery Whigs in the Free Soil Party. However unwittingly, Democratic Party expansionism had let the genie of antislavery politics out of its bottle.[12]

The rise of antislavery politics set the stage for Stephen A. Douglas's Kansas-Nebraska Act of 1854, a bold attempt to resolve—rather than to subordinate—the nation's slavery problem. To be sure, no immediate crisis over slavery impelled Douglas's bill. The Compromise of 1850 had largely silenced the slavery debate summoned by the war with Mexico. However, Southerners remained hostile to a proliferation of free states, and in the early 1850s they blocked the organization of western territories that Douglas wanted to make into states. By 1854, therefore, he felt an urgent need to organize western territories because orderly settlement and the construction of a transcontinental railroad depended on it. Moreover, he wanted to consolidate the northern Democratic Party by resolving divisions that dated to the Free Soilers' revolt, and doing so required the party to clearly define its policy on slavery. And he knew that only meaningful partisan conflict could resuscitate eroding Democratic and Whig Party loyalties, which were threatened in the North by the politics of slavery, the declining salience of economic debate over banking and tariff policy, and the rise of temperance reform and nativist politics. For these reasons, the Kansas-Nebraska Act made a great deal of sense. Douglas hoped that popular sovereignty would attract southern support for western expansion, resolve the northern Democrats' dispute over slavery, and reinvigorate party conflict. But there was a catch: his initiative radically departed from the northern Democrats' traditional effort to subordinate slavery as a political issue. Instead, the act struck down existing antislavery law and put slavery and freedom on an equal moral footing in the service of a new national principle: slaveholders' equal access to all the nation's territories. Although a risky change in strategy, Douglas's decision still reflected the central tenets of northern Democratic politics: zeal to expand American ideals and empire, celebration of the people's sovereignty, indifference to the fate of blacks, contempt for antislavery politics, support for the South, and determination to perpetuate the Union. Influenced by these presumptions, Douglas boldly decided to rid the Democratic Party, and the nation, of its dilemma over slavery. The Kansas-Nebraska Act was the capstone of the politics of slavery in the northern Democratic Party.[13]

The ensuing whirlwind, which spread rapidly from Washington, D.C., to the northern states, and from thence to the nation's territories and the South, revealed the profound difficulty of reconciling slavery and freedom in America. A majority of Northerners repulsed Douglas, refusing to define freedom as the right of whites to enslave blacks. Indeed, recognizing no such right, Abraham Lincoln, Douglas's great Illinois antagonist, condemned popular sovereignty as a despotic threat to the philosophical basis of northern society. With most Northerners siding with Lincoln, conflict over the Kansas-Nebraska Act increased exponentially. After all, the act was no mere exercise in political thought; it also profoundly altered the nation's territorial policy. Both the Northwest Ordinance in 1787 and the Missouri Compromise in 1820 had partitioned slavery and freedom, prohibiting slavery in northern territories while permitting its legalization in southern ones. This approach mitigated sectional competition over land and political power. However, popular sovereignty thrust slavery and freedom into the same territories and primed them to fight like pugilists for the victory. These circumstances precipitated a bloody struggle in Kansas and strife in Congress. Dissatisfied with Douglas's willingness to leave the fate of slavery in the hands of territorial legislatures, most northern congressmen sought to prohibit territorial slavery and most southern congressmen demanded protection for it. Their competing arguments turned on whether the state should sanction property rights in man, and thus divergent moral and cultural attitudes heavily freighted the political debate. This elemental contrast between slavery and freedom inseparably fused sectional ideologies to sectional interests, virtually eradicated a middle ground for moderates, and thereby profoundly sharpened the conflict. At stake was the existing constitutional order, the future of American social and economic development, and the meaning of free society and American nationalism.

Brought into being by the Kansas-Nebraska Act, the Republican Party vowed to end the nation's long struggle over slavery by nationalizing freedom. To do so, Republicans borrowed heavily from the abolitionists, who maintained that the affirmation of human equality in the Declaration of Independence consecrated the nation to freedom. Contending that northern society was the only true representative of American political ideals and social practices, the abolitionists insisted that federal policies should discriminate in favor of freedom. Despite its abolitionist origins and implications, the idea of a nation dedicated to freedom proved to be the linchpin of Republican politics. It enabled Northerners like Lincoln to bridge the divide between the party's radical and conservative wings by fusing the principle of human equality to the duty of national preservation. Although neither Douglas nor white

Southerners had ever perceived a fundamental antagonism between slavery and freedom, the northern definition of freedom seemed alluringly logical in Lincoln's formulation: slavery was wrong; the nation's destiny hinged on treating it as a wrong; and therefore Northerners needed to purify the nation by uniting northern interests with national ideals. This antislavery nationalism propelled Lincoln to the presidency. It also drove a wedge deeply into the Democratic Party.[14]

Southerners ratcheted up their demands on northern Democrats in response to the Republicans' emergence. By 1857, southern Democrats demanded an unambiguously proslavery popular sovereignty policy—one in which territorial settlers could not exclude slavery until they requested admission to the Union as a state—and from that point until 1860 Douglas faced the virtually impossible challenge of simultaneously battling with Republicans and southern Democrats alike. Over time, the South's growing radicalism forced him to adopt an increasingly proslavery position, which sharply differentiated northern Democratic and Republican politics. In particular, he denounced the core principles of antislavery nationalism. Claiming that the founders had made the nation half-slave and half-free, he contended that American nationalism united slavery and freedom. He correspondingly condemned the Republicans as a "sectional" party and insisted that the success of their policies would destroy the Union. Yet Douglas's tolerance for slavery and his hostility toward the Republicans did not win over Southerners. With increasing imperiousness, they scorned his version of popular sovereignty and demanded that northern Democrats support statutes protecting territorial slavery. This Douglas could never voluntarily do without destroying his party. Nevertheless, in one of his last gestures to the South, he promised to abide by a Supreme Court decision mandating legislative protection for slavery in the territories. Here slavery exacted what promised to be its greatest price from freedom, but it was a price that the northern electorate refused to pay. They did not permit Douglas to retreat unscathed from the interests of freedom, and in the 1860 election their votes gave Lincoln almost every northern state.[15]

↩

But Douglas can hardly be blamed for failing to solve his party's dilemma over slavery. The problem was beyond one person, one party, one state, or one moment in time. From the inception of the country, Americans had struggled to define and practice freedom. Slavery's relationship to freedom posed an especially pernicious problem, so momentous that it remained unresolved until the Union Army destroyed slavery in a brutal, remorseless, and revolutionary civil war. Although America rose phoenix-like from the ashes of war, it only did so, as Lincoln realized by 1865, after "every drop of blood drawn with the lash" largely had been paid with "another drawn with the sword." Southerners' long and almost implacable resistance to emancipation assured that in the end only the alchemy of war could turn slavery into freedom. Such was the final fashioning of an antislavery nation.[16]

Acknowledgments

JUST AS THE ILLINOIS frontiersmen needed friends and family to help carve out homesteads, so have I relied on others in the often solitary endeavor of researching and writing this book. James Oakes supervised the house raising, and his intellectual influence profoundly marks the finished work. I am deeply grateful also to T. H. Breen, Laura Hein, Tom Hall, Gerald Henig, and Hank Reichman, inspiring mentors who guided my development with wise and generous counsel.

Putting my hands to the plow in the primary sources was made much easier by a phalanx of librarians, funders, and research assistants. Raymond Collins, Greg Cox, James Edstrom, Kim Efird, Debbie Hamm, Kathryn Harris, John Hoffman, David Joens, Jenny Marie Johnson, Anita Morgan, Sheila Murphy, Cheryl Pence, Ryan Ross, and Cheryl Schnirring are librarians and scholars par excellence, and generously responded to every inquiry. I received grants from Northwestern University, the J. L. Kellogg Graduate School of Management Dispute Resolution Research Center, the Illinois State Historical Society, the Andrew Mellon Foundation, and Saint Xavier University, whose provost, Kathleen Alaimo, has been a wellspring of support and friendship for many years. In addition, I gratefully acknowledge the careful archival research performed by Karen Biggs, Claire Doherty, Michael Gott, B. J. Ross, and Glenna Schroeder-Lein, whose findings improved this book.

Many scholars contributed to the tilling by reading portions of the work. For stimulating my thinking, answering my questions, permitting me to use their ideas, suggesting primary sources, or providing encouragement, I thank Howard Bodenhorn, Michael Burlingame, Richard Carwardine, Rodney Davis, Dan Feller, Jonathan Glickstein, Ryan Hall, Theodore Karamanski,

Lewis Lehrman, Robert May, Jane Ann Moore, William F. Moore, Paul Pas-
koff, Thomas F. Schwartz, Amanda Seligman, Rebecca Shereikis, Silvana
Siddali, Adam I. P. Smith, Michell Snay, the late Robert H. Wiebe, Douglas
L. Wilson, and Stewart Winger. My intellectual debt to Eric Foner, Michael
F. Holt, John Ashworth, and the late William E. Gienapp and Don E. Fehrenbacher runs especially deep. Their distinguished work on the origins of
the Civil War stirred my interest, ambition, and engagement; this book is
my reply.

A final group of contributors helped bring in the harvest. Nathan Peck—
artist, colleague, and marvelous friend—fashioned the illustrations, adapting
maps from freevectormaps.com and following William Gienapp's design in
The Origins of the Republican Party, 1852–1856. Jim Huston's two detailed critiques as a reviewer for the University of Illinois Press significantly improved
the manuscript. In particular, he and an anonymous reviewer convinced
me to articulate the argument more explicitly. Laurie Matheson, acquisitions editor and now director of the press, earns plaudits for her patient and
staunch support of the project, as does Julie Gay, a congenial and scrupulous
copyeditor. The David Davis Mansion Foundation permitted use of Patricia
Kasbohm Schley's transcriptions from the David and Sarah Davis Family
Correspondence (Illinois Wesleyan University), a collection available at
http://collections.carli.illinois.edu/cdm/landingpage/collection/iwu_davis.
Most of the text in chapter 7 was previously published in "Abraham Lincoln
and the Triumph of an Antislavery Nationalism," *Journal of the Abraham
Lincoln Association* 28 (Summer 2007), 1–27, and some of the evidence in the
manuscript was previously published in "Was There a Second Party System?
Illinois as a Case Study in Antebellum Politics," *Practicing Democracy: Popular
Politics in the United States from the Constitution to the Civil War*, edited by
Daniel Peart and Adam I. P. Smith (Charlottesville: University of Virginia
Press, 2015), 145–69. The journal and the press have kindly authorized reuse
of that material. I hope that the many colleagues and contributors listed
here—and others whom memory lamentably has failed to bring to mind—
find pleasure in what their hands and minds have shaped. They certainly bear
no responsibility for any errors or misinterpretations; that yoke is mine to
bear alone.

Friends and family deserve the greatest gratitude. As if devoted friendship
and countless laughs were not enough, Ira Silver compellingly presented his
interpretation of the book's key contribution in proposing most of the title.
I will use the royalties to repay him handsomely. Much of the remainder of
the title was suggested by another treasured friend and gifted scholar, Jared
Orsi, whose close readings sharpened this book incalculably; his generosity

of spirit is a profound gift for others. In similar ways, my wife's parents, Helen and Jerry Martin, have enriched my life immeasurably, notwithstanding Jerry's constant refrain: "Finish the book." My own parents, Brian and Nicola, nurtured me with love and discipline, and freely permitted me to follow my muse into the past. My dear mother, now departed, made me a lover of language; this book bears her special mark. It also bears the marks of my daughter Nicola, who is developing into a writer herself and worked with me on the final edit. Yet of all the gifts I have received, the greatest has been my wife, who has stood by me steadily and patiently and lovingly despite my imperfections, and who gave life to vibrant girls who have filled our lives with joy. To Rosemary, Nicola, and Sylvia, I tender profound thanks and love.

Appendix
Illinois Voting Tables

Table 1. Party Vote for President, 1844 to 1848

Political Party	Total Vote 1844	Percent Vote 1844	Total Vote 1848	Percent Vote 1848	Change in Total Vote 1844 to 1848	% Change in Total Vote 1844 to 1848
Democrats	58,795	53.91%	55,952	44.91%	−2,843	−4.84%
Whigs	45,854	42.05%	52,853	42.42%	6,999	15.26%
Liberty/Free Soil	3,469	3.18%	15,702	12.60%	12,233	352.26%
Other	939	0.86%	89	0.07%	N/A	N/A
State Totals	109,057	100.00%	124,596	100.00%	15,539	14.25%

Source: Howard W. Allen and Vincent A. Lacey, eds., *Illinois Elections, 1818–1990: Candidates and County Returns for President, Governor, Senate, and House of Representatives* (Carbondale: Southern Illinois University Press, 1992), 115, 123. I have corrected errors Allen and Lacey made in calculating the 1844 Whig vote, the percentage of the 1844 Whig vote, and the total of the 1844 state vote.

Table 2. Regional Party Vote for President, 1844 to 1848

Political Party	Northern Illinois		Central Illinois		Southern Illinois	
	% Vote 1844	% Vote 1848	% Vote 1844	% Vote 1848	% Vote 1844	% Vote 1848
Democrats	49.9%	33.1%	51.1%	46.7%	62.0%	57.4%
Whigs	41.1%	35.6%	46.6%	48.3%	35.5%	40.0%
Liberty/Free Soil	9.0%	31.2%	1.6%	4.9%	0.7%	2.6%
Other	—	0.1%	0.7%	0.1%	1.8%	—
Regional Totals	100.0%	100.0%	100.0%	100.0%	100.0%	100.0%

Source: Data compiled from Allen and Lacey, *Illinois Elections, 1818–1990*, 113–15, 121–23. Southern Illinois's northern boundary included Madison, Bond, Fayette, Effingham, Jasper, and Crawford Counties; and northern Illinois's southern boundary included Mercer, Henry, Stark, Marshall, La Salle, Grundy, and Will Counties.

Table 3. Vote on General Assembly Resolutions Instructing Illinois's Senators to Vote for the Wilmot Proviso, 1849

Party	Region	Voted Yea	Voted Nay	Absent/Abstained
Independent	North	1	0	0
Whig	North	5	0	0
Whig	Central	17	0	0
Whig	South	7	0	0
Democratic	North	16	1	1
Democratic	Central	5	26	0
Democratic	South	1	18	2
Totals	N/A	52	45	3

Sources: E. Rust, "A List of the Members Composing the Illinois State Legislature, Assembled at the Capitol in Springfield, Monday, January 1st, 1849," B-124, BC-ALPLM; 16th Gen. Ass., 1st Sess., *Senate Journal* (2, 3, 4, 5, 6, and 8 Jan 1849), 16–17, 22–23, 25–26, 32–35, 38–39, **42–44**; *House Journal* (2, 5, 6, 8, and 9 Jan 1849), 18, 19, 34–35, 38–42, 47, 52, **54–55**. Boldface pagination indicates location of resolutions and votes used to make the table.

Table 4. Vote on General Assembly Resolutions Rescinding Wilmot Proviso Instructions, 1851

Party	Region	Voted Yea	Voted Nay	Absent/Abstained
Free Soil	North	0	1	0
Whig	North	1	7	1
Whig	Central	16	4	0
Whig	South	6	0	0
Democratic	North	6	10	0
Democratic	Central	21	0	3
Democratic	South	23	0	1
Totals	N/A	73	22	5

Sources: E. Rust, "A List of the Members Composing the Seventeenth General Assembly of the State of Illinois, Session of 1851," B-309, BC-ALPLM; 17th Gen. Ass., 1st Sess., *Senate Journal* (6, 14, and 23 Jan 1851), **4–6**, **52–57**, 101–2; *House Journal* (15 and 22 Jan and 14 Feb 1851), 69, 71–72, **126–34**, 445–46. Boldface pagination indicates location of resolutions and votes used to make the table.

Table 5. Illinois Voter Turnout, 1840 to 1860

Election	Eligible Voters	Votes Cast	% Voter Turnout
1840 Presidential Election	113,656	93,175	82.0%
1841 Congressional Elections	122,434	69,419	56.7%
1843 Congressional Elections	139,990	93,833	67.0%
1844 Presidential Election	148,768	109,057	73.3%
1846 Congressional Elections	166,324	99,565	59.9%
1848 Presidential Election	183,880	124,596	67.8%
1850 Congressional Elections	195,380	104,222	53.3%
1852 Presidential Election	240,004	154,964	64.6%
1854 Congressional Elections	284,628	140,407	49.3%
1856 Presidential Election	328,615	239,337	72.8%
1858 Congressional Elections	371,961	252,025	67.8%
1860 Presidential Election	415,307	339,666	81.8%

Sources and Methodology: Data compiled from *Compendium of the Enumeration of the Inhabitants and Statistics of the United States, as Obtained at the Department of State, from the Returns of the Sixth Census* (Washington: Thomas Allen, 1841), 3:84; *The Seventh Census of the United States: 1850* (Washington: Robert Armstrong, 1853), 1:694–98, 717; *Population of the United States in 1860; Compiled from the Original Returns of the Eighth Census* (Washington: GPO, 1864), 1:78–81, 102–4; *Illinois State Register* (Springfield), 16 Oct 1855; 3 and 5 Jan 1856; Allen and Lacey, *Illinois Elections, 1818–1990*, 108–45. To estimate voter turnout from 1840 to 1848, I divided the number of votes cast in the presidential and congressional elections by the number of white males who were twenty years or older at the time of the election (AWM). Federal census tabulators reported the number of AWM at the end of each decade, and I interpolated to estimate the number of AWM in intervening years. To estimate the number of eligible voters in Illinois from 1850 to 1860, which required calculating estimates of naturalized voters, I used the methodology explained by William E. Gienapp in *The Origins of the Republican Party: 1852–1856* (New York: Oxford University Press, 1987), 475–76. I am indebted to Gienapp for sharing the percentage of naturalized voters among Iowa's foreign-born population in 1856 (.1824476), which I used to estimate the number of naturalized voters in Illinois during the 1850s. To improve the accuracy of the interpolations, I used Illinois's 1855 state census returns, and I also corrected an error Allen and Lacey made in calculating the Lake County 1850 congressional vote.

Table 6. Vote on General Assembly Resolutions Endorsing the Kansas-Nebraska Bill, 1854

Party	Region	Voted Yea	Voted Nay	Absent/Abstained
Free Democratic	North	0	1	0
Whig	North	0	6	0
Whig	Central	3	6	5
Whig	South	1	2	1
Democratic	North	3	10	4
Democratic	Central	22	4	6
Democratic	South	21	1	4
Totals	N/A	50	30	20

Sources: E. Rust, "A List of the Members Composing the Eighteenth General Assembly of the State of Illinois, Convened in Extra Session, February 9, 1854," B-175, BC-ALPLM; 18th Gen. Ass., 2nd Sess., *Senate Journal* (9, 10, 20, 21, and 23 Feb 1854), 21, 25–27, **49–50**, 57–58, 71, **78–81**; *House Journal* (25 and 27 Feb 1854), 96, 162–63, **166–68**. Boldface pagination indicates location of resolutions and votes used to make the table.

Table 7. Democratic Vote for Congress and State Treasurer, Districts 1, 2, and 8, 1854

District Election	Congressional Election	State Treasurer	Aggregate Change	Percent Change
One	2,776	3,638	862	31.1%
Two	2,544	3,896	1,352	53.1%
Subtotal	5,320	7,534	2,214	41.6%
Eight	5,711	8,371	2,660	46.6%
Statewide Totals	60,809	68,917	8,108	13.3%

Sources and Methodology: Congressional data compiled from Allen and Lacey, *Illinois Elections, 1818–1990*, 135; and State Treasurer data from *Illinois Election Returns, 1818–1861*, roll 30–45, KALVAR, 100–101, ALPLM. For District Eight, I combined the "Democrat" and "Other" congressional votes compiled in *Illinois Elections* because Lyman Trumbull indicated that all his opponents, not just the regular Democratic nominee, supported the Nebraska Act.

Table 8. Vote on Illinois House of Representatives Resolutions to Prohibit Slavery in All United States Territories, 1855

Party	Region	Voted Yea	Voted Nay	Absent/Abstained
Republican	North	18	0	0
Republican	Central	3	0	0
Republican	South	1	0	0
Whig	North	4	0	0
Whig	Central	11	0	0
Whig	South	0	0	1
Democratic	North	3	0	0
Democratic	Central	0	17	0
Democratic	South	1	15	1
Totals	N/A	41	32	2

Sources: E. Rust, "A List of the Members Composing the Nineteenth General Assembly of the State of Illinois," B-172, BC-ALPLM; 19th Gen. Ass., 1st Sess., *House Journal* (29 Jan and 2, 3, 5, 6, 7, 10, and 14 Feb 1855), 197, 210–11, 234–36, 265–67, **283–84**, 286–87, **306–09**, 391–97, 625, 711–12. The resolutions did not pass the Senate. *Senate Journal* (6 Jan and 6, 8, and 13 Feb 1855), 32, 201, 206–7, **239**, 326–28, **330–31**. Boldface pagination for the *House Journal* indicates location of resolutions and votes used to make the table. Boldface pagination for the *Senate Journal* indicates location of the resolution and the votes tabling it.

Notes

I have sought to reproduce quotations exactly. Therefore, I have neither added emphasis in italics nor corrected authors' capitalization, spelling, or grammar. I have, however, rendered both underlined and italicized words in italics.

Almost all citations to the *Congressional Globe* reference the volumes of the *Globe* held in Northwestern University's Government and Geographic Information Collection. The pagination for Northwestern's volumes does not always correspond to the pagination of the *Congressional Globe* volumes on the Library of Congress's Web site. To assist researchers, citations to the Northwestern volumes are denoted *CG-NU*; citations to the online Library of Congress version are denoted *CG-LOC*.

Abbreviations

LIBRARIES AND ARCHIVES

ALPLM	Abraham Lincoln Presidential Library and Museum
ISA	Illinois State Archives
LOC	Library of Congress
UChicago SCRC	Special Collections Research Center, University of Chicago
UIUC	University of Illinois Library at Urbana-Champaign

JOURNALS, SERIES, COLLECTIONS, AND TRANSACTIONS

CISHL	*Collections of the Illinois State Historical Library*
CWH	*Civil War History*
FHS	*Fergus Historical Series*
IHJ	*Illinois Historical Journal*
IHLC	*Illinois History and Lincoln Collections*

JAH	*Journal of American History*
JER	*Journal of the Early Republic*
JIH	*Journal of Illinois History*
JISHS	*Journal of the Illinois State Historical Society*
JSH	*Journal of Southern History*
MCHST	*Mclean County Historical Society Transactions*
MVHR	*Mississippi Valley Historical Review*
TISHS	*Transactions of the Illinois State Historical Society*
WHQ	*Western Historical Quarterly*
UISSS	*University of Illinois Studies in the Social Sciences*

SOURCES

BC-ALPLM	Broadsides Collection, Abraham Lincoln Presidential Library and Museum
CG-LOC	*Congressional Globe* (Library of Congress American Memory Web site)
CG-NU	*Congressional Globe* (Northwestern University Government and Geographic Information Collection)
CW	*The Collected Works of Abraham Lincoln*, edited by Roy P. Basler, 9 vols.
IE	*Illinois Elections 1818–1990: Candidates and County Returns for President, Governor, Senate, and House of Representatives*, edited by Howard W. Allen and Vincent A. Lacey
LSAD	*The Letters of Stephen A. Douglas*, edited by Robert W. Johannsen
RD	*Register of Debates*

Introduction

1. Henry Cleveland, ed., *Alexander H. Stephens in Public and Private: With Letters and Speeches before, during, and since the War* (Philadelphia: National Publishing, 1866), 721.

2. *CW*, 4:262–63, 267.

3. *CW*, 2:461, 4:151.

4. *CW*, 2:276.

5. On the concept of antislavery nationalism, see Graham Alexander Peck, "Abraham Lincoln and the Triumph of an Antislavery Nationalism," *Journal of the Abraham Lincoln Association* 28 (Summer 2007): 1–27; Suzanne Cooper Guasco, *Confronting Slavery: Edward Coles and the Rise of Antislavery Politics in Nineteenth-Century America* (DeKalb: Northern Illinois University Press, 2013), 7–8; Padraig Riley, *Slavery and the Democratic Conscience: Political Life in Jeffersonian America* (Philadelphia: University of Pennsylvania Press, 2016), 199–255. For the emergence of a kindred "moral nationalism" in antebellum reform efforts, consult Kyle G. Volk, *Moral Minorities and the Making of American Democracy* (New York: Oxford University Press, 2014), 11–36.

6. William M. Wiecek, *The Sources of Antislavery Constitutionalism in America, 1760–1848* (Ithaca, N.Y.: Cornell University Press, 1977), 40–83; Patrick Rael, *Eighty-Eight Years: The Long Death of Slavery in the United States, 1777–1865* (Athens: University of Georgia Press, 2015), 1–3, 69–79, 242.

7. Kenneth M. Stampp, *The Imperiled Union: Essays on the Background of the Civil War* (New York: Oxford University Press, 1980), 223–45.

8. William W. Freehling, *The Road to Disunion*, vol. 1, *Secessionists at Bay, 1776–1854* (New York: Oxford University Press, 1990), 119–61; James Oakes, *The Scorpion's Sting: Antislavery and the Coming of the Civil War* (New York: Norton, 2014), 56–60; Peter B. Knupfer, *The Union As It Is: Constitutional Unionism and Sectional Compromise, 1787–1861* (Chapel Hill: University of North Carolina Press, 1991); Matthew Salafia, *Slavery's Borderland: Freedom and Bondage along the Ohio River* (Philadelphia: University of Pennsylvania Press, 2013).

9. Leon F. Litwack, *North of Slavery: The Negro in the Free States, 1790–1860* (Chicago: University of Chicago Press, 1961).

10. For an earlier effort on my part to define the meaning of proslavery and antislavery, see "Was Stephen A. Douglas Antislavery?" *Journal of the Abraham Lincoln Association* 26 (Summer 2005): 1–21.

11. Russel B. Nye, *Fettered Freedom: Civil Liberties and the Slavery Controversy, 1830–1860* (East Lansing: Michigan State College Press, 1949), v–vi, 177–251; Eric Foner, *The Story of American Freedom* (New York: Norton, 1998), xiii–xxii, 86–97; James Oakes, "Conflict vs. Racial Consensus in the History of Antislavery Politics," in *Contesting Slavery: The Politics of Bondage and Freedom in the New American Nation*, ed. John Craig Hammond and Matthew Mason (Charlottesville: University of Virginia Press, 2011), 291–303. The terminology of freedom presents a challenge because both Southerners and Northerners used it to describe their beliefs. To alleviate confusion in the pages that follow, my use of the term will reflect its antislavery usage unless I indicate otherwise.

12. Michael F. Holt, *Political Parties and American Political Development from the Age of Jackson to the Age of Lincoln* (Baton Rouge: Louisiana State University Press, 1992), 10–12, 26, persuasively argues that only chronological narratives incorporating contingency can adequately explain the origins of the Civil War. In contrast to Holt's scholarship, however, this book will use that approach to make the case for slavery's central role in destroying the Union.

13. *CW*, 3:301, 313.

14. Historians of the early Republic increasingly are emphasizing slavery's significance to early national political history, as the essays in Hammond and Mason's *Contesting Slavery* testify.

15. For studies that do root the Civil War in the early Republic, see Sean Wilentz, *The Rise of American Democracy: Jefferson to Lincoln* (New York: Norton, 2005); Elizabeth R. Varon, *Disunion! The Coming of the American Civil War, 1789–1859* (Chapel Hill: University of North Carolina Press, 2008); Donald J. Ratcliffe, "The Decline of Antislavery Politics, 1815–1840," in Hammond and Mason, *Contesting*

Slavery, 267–90; Christopher Childers, *The Failure of Popular Sovereignty: Slavery, Manifest Destiny, and the Radicalization of Southern Politics* (Lawrence: University Press of Kansas, 2012).

16. Scholars emphasizing the significance of the collapse of the Second Party System include Michael F. Holt, *The Political Crisis of the 1850s* (New York: Wiley, 1978); William E. Gienapp, *The Origins of the Republican Party: 1852–1856* (New York: Oxford University Press, 1987); Holt, *The Rise and Fall of the American Whig Party: Jacksonian Politics and the Onset of the Civil War* (New York: Oxford University Press, 1999); Joel H. Silbey, *Party over Section: The Rough and Ready Presidential Election of 1848* (Lawrence: University Press of Kansas, 2009). For an interpretive framework that even more radically truncates the periodization of the war's origin and consequently focuses almost exclusively on contingency as an explanation for it, see Edward L. Ayers, *In the Presence of Mine Enemies: War in the Heart of America, 1859–1863* (New York: Norton, 2003), xvii–xxi, 3–187, 416–18. John L. Brooke and Michael E. Woods have advanced cultural explanations to bridge the divide between structural and contingent explanations of the rise of antislavery politics, but the core periodization of their work still focuses on the 1850s. See John L. Brooke, "Party, Nation, and Cultural Rupture: The Crisis of the American Civil War," in *Practicing Democracy: Popular Politics in the United States from the Constitution to the Civil War*, ed. Daniel Peart and Adam I. P. Smith (Charlottesville: University of Virginia Press, 2015), 72–95; and Michael E. Woods, *Emotional and Sectional Conflict in the Antebellum United States* (New York: Cambridge University Press, 2014), 1–7, 119–80.

17. Just some of the most notable recent work on abolitionism and antislavery includes John Stauffer, *The Black Hearts of Men: Radical Abolitionists and the Transformation of Race* (Cambridge: Harvard University Press, 2002); Richard S. Newman, *The Transformation of American Abolitionism: Fighting Slavery in the Early Republic* (Chapel Hill: University of North Carolina Press, 2002); Frederick J. Blue, *No Taint of Compromise: Crusaders in Antislavery Politics* (Baton Rouge: Louisiana State University Press, 2005); James Brewer Stewart, *Abolitionist Politics and the Coming of the Civil War* (Amherst: University of Massachusetts Press, 2008); Edward Bartlett Rugemer, *The Problem of Emancipation: The Caribbean Roots of the American Civil War* (Baton Rouge: Louisiana State University Press, 2008); Corey M. Brooks, *Liberty Power: Antislavery Third Parties and the Transformation of American Politics* (Chicago: University of Chicago Press, 2016); Manisha Sinha, *The Slave's Cause: A History of Abolition* (New Haven, Conn.: Yale University Press, 2016).

18. The important exceptions are Robert E. May, "A 'Southern Strategy' for the 1850s: Northern Democrats, the Tropics, and the Expansion of the National Domain," *Louisiana Studies* 14 (Winter 1975): 333–59; May, *Slavery, Race, and Conquest in the Tropics: Lincoln, Douglas, and the Future of Latin America* (New York: Cambridge University Press, 2013); John Ashworth, *Slavery, Capitalism, and Politics in the Antebellum Republic*, vol. 1, *Commerce and Compromise, 1820–1850* (New York: Cambridge University Press, 1995), 323–50, and vol. 2, *The Coming of the Civil War, 1850–1861* (New York: Cambridge University Press, 2007), 399–436; and, to a limited degree, Leonard L. Richards, *The Slave Power: The Free North and Southern Domination*

(Baton Rouge: Louisiana State University Press, 2000), 109–13. Michael Todd Landis, *Northern Men with Southern Loyalties: The Democratic Party and the Secession Crisis* (Ithaca, N.Y.: Cornell University Press, 2014), has also made this case, although not persuasively. For other significant treatments of the Democratic Party, see Roy Franklin Nichols, *The Disruption of American Democracy* (New York: Macmillan, 1948); Jonathan H. Earle, *Jacksonian Antislavery & the Politics of Free Soil, 1824–1854* (Chapel Hill: University of North Carolina Press, 2004); Wilentz, *Rise of American Democracy*.

19. James Oakes, *Freedom National: The Destruction of Slavery in the United States, 1861–1865* (New York: Norton, 2013), ix–xxiv, 1–48; and Oakes, *Scorpion's Sting*.

20. *CW*, 2:276. For the significance of Republican Party moral appeals, see Richard J. Carwardine, *Evangelicals and Politics in Antebellum America* (New Haven, Conn.: Yale University Press, 1993), 235–323, and *Lincoln* (Harlow: Pearson Longman, 2003), 43–130. The leading treatments of the Republican Party more generally include Eric Foner, *Free Soil, Free Labor, Free Men: The Ideology of the Republican Party before the Civil War* (New York: Oxford University Press, 1970); Richard H. Sewell, *Ballots for Freedom: Antislavery Politics in the United States, 1837–1860* (New York: Oxford University Press, 1976); and Gienapp, *Origins of the Republican Party*. Each of these historians, in different ways, recognizes the significance of the nation to Republican Party politics, but none puts nationalism at the center of the party's antislavery appeal. For a valuable interpretation of Republican Party nationalism that traces the emergence of an "antisouthern ideology," see Susan-Mary Grant, *North over South: Northern Nationalism and American Identity in the Antebellum Era* (Lawrence: University Press of Kansas, 2000), 8–18 (quote, 9).

21. Slaveholders' political conduct to no small degree reflected the necessity of controlling unwilling bondsmen, which was the root conflict between freedom and slavery. An important guide to the slaveholders' mindset is Freehling, *Road to Disunion*; a corresponding guide for slaves and free blacks is Ira Berlin, *The Long Emancipation: The Demise of Slavery in the United States* (Cambridge, Mass.: Harvard University Press, 2015).

Prelude

1. Natalia Maree Belting, *Kaskaskia under the French Regime* (Urbana: University of Illinois Press, 1948; reprint, Carbondale: Southern Illinois University Press, 2003), 39.

2. Paul Finkelman, "Slavery and the Northwest Ordinance: A Study in Ambiguity," *JER* 6 (Winter 1986): 343–70; N. Dwight Harris, *The History of Negro Servitude in Illinois and of the Slavery Agitation in that State, 1719–1864* (Chicago: McClurg, 1904; reprint, New York: Haskell, 1969), 1–15; Francis S. Philbrick, ed., *The Laws of Indiana Territory, 1801–1809* (Springfield: Illinois State Historical Library, 1930), vol. 21, *CISHL*, 42–45, 136–37.

3. Paul Finkelman, "Evading the Ordinance: The Persistence of Bondage in Indiana and Illinois," *JER* 9 (Spring 1989): 24–33, 39–40; John Craig Hammond, *Slavery, Freedom and Expansion in the Early American West* (Charlottesville: University of

Virginia Press, 2007), 96–123; Andrew R. L. Cayton, *Frontier Indiana* (Bloomington: Indiana University Press, 1996), 246.

4. Francis S. Philbrick, ed., *The Laws of Illinois Territory, 1809–1818* (Springfield: Illinois State Historical Library, 1950), vol. 25, *CISHL*, 35–36, 91–92, 157–58 (quote).

5. John Reda, "Joining the Union: Land, Race, and Sovereignty in the Illinois Country, 1763–1825" (PhD diss., University of Illinois at Chicago, 2009), 156–57; Solon J. Buck, *Illinois in 1818* (Springfield: Illinois Centennial Commission, 1917; reprint, Urbana: University of Illinois Press, 1967), 232–61, 277–83; Charles N. Zucker, "The Free Negro Question: Race Relations in Ante-Bellum Illinois, 1801–1860" (PhD diss., Northwestern University, 1972), 39–56; *Illinois Intelligencer* (Kaskaskia), 17 June and 1 and 22 July 1818; 16 July 1824; George Churchill Journal, vol. 3, 25 April, 3 May, 5 June, and 3, 16, 17, 18, and 19 July 1818, SC 290, George Churchill Papers, ALPLM; "Letter of George Churchill of Madison County, ILL., to Mr. Swift Eldred, Warren CT.," *JISHS* 11 (April 1918): 65 (quote); Rev. Thomas Lippincott, "The Conflict of the Century," typescript, (mss. note on p. 2), Thomas Lippincott Papers, *IHLC*, UIUC. The convention's proceedings are skeletal and thus preclude the drawing of firm conclusions. Lippincott's notes report Edward Coles's belief that the proslavery delegates did not constitute a majority at the convention, an important observation if accurate.

6. Emil Joseph Verlie, ed., *Illinois Constitutions* (Springfield: Illinois State Historical Library, 1919), vol. 13, *CISHL*, 38 (quotes); Buck, *Illinois in 1818*, 277–83, 311–15; Finkelman, "Evading the Ordinance," 45–51; 15th Cong., 2nd. Sess., *Annals of Congress* (23 Nov 1818), 307 (quote).

Chapter 1. The Nation's Conflict over Slavery in Miniature: Illinois, 1818–1824

1. Jay Monaghan, ed., "From England to Illinois in 1821: The Journal of William Hall," *JISHS* 39 (March and June 1946): 23 (quote), 24, 67 (quote); Richard Lyle Power, *Planting Corn Belt Culture: The Impress of the Upland Southerner and Yankee in the Old Northwest* (Indianapolis: Indiana Historical Society, 1953), 26–30; Douglas K. Meyer, *Making the Heartland Quilt: A Geographical History of Settlement and Migration in Early-Nineteenth-Century Illinois* (Carbondale: Southern Illinois University Press, 2000), 136–41; Solon J. Buck, *Illinois in 1818* (Springfield: Illinois Centennial Commission, 1917; reprint, Urbana: University of Illinois Press, 1967), 98–100; George Flower, *History of the English Settlement in Edwards County, Illinois*, 2nd ed. (Chicago: Fergus, 1909), vol. 1, *CHSC*, 145–46.

2. W. P. Strickland, ed., *Autobiography of Peter Cartwright: The Backwoods Preacher* (New York: Methodist Book Concern, 1856), 244–45; James Oakes, *Slavery and Freedom: An Interpretation of the Old South* (New York: Vintage, 1990), 80–84, 104–8.

3. Morris Birkbeck, *Letters from Illinois*, 3rd ed. (London: Taylor and Hessey, 1818), 22 (quote), 71 (quotes); George Flower to his mother, 24 Oct 1816, BV 66-39, George Flower Letterbook, Flower Family Papers, ALPLM.

4. Clarence Walworth Alvord, ed., *Governor Edward Coles*, vol. 15, *CISHL* (Springfield: Illinois State Historical Library, 1920), 22–30, 41–47 (quotes, 42, 45, 46), 354–55;

Kurt E. Leichtle and Bruce G. Carveth, *Crusade against Slavery: Edward Coles, Pioneer of Freedom* (Carbondale: Southern Illinois University Press, 2011), 69–72.

5. Charles N. Zucker, "The Free Negro Question: Race Relations in Ante-Bellum Illinois, 1801–1860" (PhD diss., Northwestern University, 1972), 67–68, 157–64; Paul Finkelman, "Evading the Ordinance: The Persistence of Bondage in Indiana and Illinois," *JER* 9 (Spring 1989): 41; *Spectator* (Edwardsville), 12 Oct 1822 (quotes); James Simeone, *Democracy and Slavery in Frontier Illinois: The Bottomland Republic* (DeKalb: Northern Illinois University Press, 2000), 115–16; Theodore Calvin Pease, *The Frontier State, 1818–1848* (Springfield: Illinois Centennial Commission, 1918; reprint, Urbana: University of Illinois Press, 1987), 48–50; 3rd Gen. Ass., 1st Sess., *House Journal* (9 and 10 Dec 1822), 32–33, 36; *Illinois Intelligencer* (Vandalia), 21 Dec 1822.

6. John Woods, *Two Years' Residence in the Settlement on the English Prairie, in the Illinois Country, United States* (London: Longman, Hurst, Rees, Orme, and Brown, 1822), 244; Michael J. Bakalis, "Ninian Edwards and Territorial Politics in Illinois: 1775–1818," (PhD diss., Northwestern University, 1966), 223–38; James Simeone, "Ninian Edward's Republican Dilemma," *IHJ* 90 (Winter 1997): 260–61; Simeone, *Democracy and Slavery in Frontier Illinois*, 82–96; Ninian W. Edwards, *History of Illinois, from 1778 to 1833; and Life and Times of Ninian Edwards* (Springfield: Illinois State Journal Company, 1870), 29 (quotes), 30 (quote), 32 (quotes).

7. Ninian Edwards campaign document, 10 Sept 1818, folder 2, SC 447, Ninian Edwards Papers, ALPLM; *Spectator* (Edwardsville), 25 April 1820; 20 and 27 March 1821; Daniel Feller, *The Public Lands in Jacksonian Politics* (Madison: University of Wisconsin Press, 1984), 18–30, 35–36; R. Carlyle Buley, *The Old Northwest: Pioneer Period, 1815–1840* (Indianapolis: Indiana Historical Society, 1950), 1:135; Payson Jackson Treat, *The National Land System, 1785–1820* (New York: Treat, 1910), 145–52, 408–9; *Illinois Gazette* (Shawneetown), 3 Aug 1822; 1 July 1826; Daniel Pope Cook, "Reply to Brutus, To the People of Illinois," 23 July 1822, B-569, BC-ALPLM; Franklin William Scott, *Newspapers and Periodicals of Illinois, 1814–1879* (Springfield: Illinois State Historical Library, 1910), vol. 6, *CISHL*, xxxv.

8. Governor Thomas Ford, *A History of Illinois: From Its Commencement as a State in 1818 to 1847* (Chicago: Griggs, 1854; reprint, Urbana: University of Illinois Press, 1995), 13; William Coffin, *Life and Times of Samuel D. Lockwood* (Chicago: Knight and Leonard, 1889), 39; *Illinois Intelligencer* (Vandalia), 7 Dec 1822; 22 Feb 1823; *Spectator* (Edwardsville), 27 July 1822; Evarts Boutell Greene and Clarence Walworth Alvord, eds., *The Governors' Letter-Books, 1818–1834*, vol. 4, *CISHL* (Springfield: Illinois State Historical Library, 1909), 86 (quote), 99–107, 136–38; Barbara Lawrence and Nedra Branz, eds., *The Flagg Correspondence: Selected Letters, 1816–1854* (Carbondale: Southern Illinois University Press, 1986), 17.

9. John Mack Faragher, *Sugar Creek: Life on the Illinois Prairie* (New Haven, Conn.: Yale University Press, 1986), 54–55, 62–67; Robert Leslie to David Robson, 13 Dec 1821, and David Robson to William Shepherd and Robert Leslie, 16 Feb 1822, folder 1, SC 432, James and John Dunlop Papers, ALPLM; Christiana Holmes Tillson, *A Woman's*

Story of Pioneer Illinois, ed. Milo Milton Quaife (Chicago: Donnelley, 1919; reprint, Carbondale: Southern Illinois University Press, 1995), 13 (quotes); James Flint, *Letters from America, Containing Observations on the Climate and Agriculture of the Western States, the Manners of the People, the Prospects of Emigrants* (Edinburgh: Tait, 1822; reprint, Cleveland: Clark, 1904), vol. 9, *Early Western Travels, 1748–1846*, ed. Reuben Gold Thwaites, 232–36; Lawrence and Branz, *Flagg Correspondence*, 25; Timothy Mahoney, *River Towns in the Great West: The Structure of Provincial Urbanization in the American Midwest, 1820–1870* (New York: Cambridge University Press, 1990), 28–36; Stephen Aron, *How the West Was Lost: The Transformation of Kentucky from Daniel Boone to Henry Clay* (Baltimore, Md.: Johns Hopkins University Press, 1996), 58–81, 102–23; *Republican Advocate* (Kaskaskia), 27 Jan 1824.

10. Power, *Planting Corn Belt Culture*, 28–34; Susan Gray, *Yankee West: Community Life on the Michigan Frontier* (Chapel Hill: University of North Carolina Press, 1996), 11–13; Morris Birkbeck, *Notes on a Journey in America*, 4th ed. (London: Severn, 1818), 134.

11. Horatio Newhall to Isaac and Joel Newhall, 22 March 1823, folder 1, SC 2100, Horatio Newhall Papers, ALPLM; Flower, *History of the English Settlement*, 239–40.

12. Lawrence and Branz, *Flagg Correspondence*, 28; Malcolm J. Rohrbough, *The Land Office Business: The Settlement and Administration of American Public Lands, 1789–1837* (New York: Oxford University Press, 1968), 139; Buley, *Old Northwest*, 1:124–28, 137; Pease, *Frontier State*, 176; Ford, *History of Illinois*, 24.

13. William H. Brown, "An Historical Sketch of the Early Movement in Illinois for the Legalization of Slavery," vol. 4, *FHS* (Chicago: Fergus, 1876), 11–13; Lawrence and Branz, *Flagg Correspondence*, 27, 37 (quote); Buley, *Old Northwest*, 1:126–32; *Illinois Intelligencer—Extra* (Vandalia), 1 Oct 1824.

14. George William Dowrie, *The Development of Banking in Illinois, 1817–1863*, vol. 2, no. 4, *UISSS* (Urbana: University of Illinois, 1913), 24–35; Pease, *Frontier State*, 57–58; Ford, *History of Illinois*, 25–28.

15. Buck, *Illinois in 1818*, 97–101, 235–37; *Illinois Intelligencer* (Vandalia), 8 March 1823. Notably, advocates for a proslavery state constitution in 1818 also had contended that legalizing slavery would promote the settlement of slaveholders in the state.

16. Harris, *History of Negro Servitude in Illinois*, 27–30; Alvord, *Governor Edward Coles*, 333, 339–44; Glover Moore, *The Missouri Controversy, 1819–1821* (Lexington: University of Kentucky Press, 1953), 281–87; Zucker, "Free Negro Question," 86–94; Pease, *Frontier State*, 72–74; *Spectator* (Edwardsville), 11 July 1820 (quote); and "Address of the Board Managers of the ST. CLAIR SOCIETY to prevent the further introduction of Slavery in the state of Illinois," 12 April 1823; Merton L. Dillon, "The Antislavery Movement in Illinois, 1809–1844" (PhD diss., University of Michigan, 1951), 74.

17. Alvord, *Governor Edward Coles*, 345–47; Zucker, "Free Negro Question," 94–97, 153–54; Pease, *Frontier State*, 74–76; *Illinois Intelligencer* (Vandalia), 3 July 1821 (quotes); Merton Dillon, "The Antislavery Movement in Illinois, 1809–1844," 75–79; *IE*, 3.

18. Brown, "Historical Sketch," 16–19; Rev. Thomas Lippincott, "The Conflict of the Century," typescript, 6–9, Thomas Lippincott Papers, *IHLC*, UIUC; *Spectator* (Edwardsville), 12 April 1823; *Illinois Gazette* (Shawneetown), 6 April 1822 (quote); Horatio Newhall to Isaac and Joel Newhall, 11 May 1822, folder 1, SC 2100, Horatio Newhall Papers, ALPLM; Alvord, *Governor Edward Coles*, 319–20; Pease, *Frontier State*, 77–80; Simeone, *Democracy and Slavery*, 118–30; Leichtle and Carveth, *Crusade against Slavery*, 100–108.

19. Horatio Newhall to Isaac and Joel Newhall, 14 April 1824, folder 1, SC 2100, Horatio Newhall Papers, ALPLM; Brown, "Historical Sketch," 24; Ford, *History of Illinois*, 11, 32–33; John Reynolds, *My Own Times: Embracing Also the History of My Life* (Belleville, Ill.: Perryman and Davison, 1854; reprint, Chicago: Chicago Historical Society, 1879), 155; Linda Jeanne Evans, "Abolitionism in the Illinois Churches, 1830–1865" (PhD diss., Northwestern University, 1981), 250–58.

20. *Illinois Intelligencer* (Vandalia), 8 March 1823 ("great and fundamental" quotes); *Republican Advocate*, clipped by *Illinois Intelligencer* (Vandalia), 30 January 1824 ("people" quotes); *Republican Advocate* (Kaskaskia), 21 Feb ("A Kaskaskian") and 29 May ("OE") 1823; John Craig Hammond, *Slavery, Freedom and Expansion in the Early American West* (Charlottesville: University of Virginia Press, 2007), 55–75, 161–66; Floyd Calvin Shoemaker, *Missouri's Struggle for Statehood, 1804–1821* (New York: Russell and Russell, 1916; reprint, 1969), 81–134; Sean Wilentz, "Jeffersonian Democracy and the Origins of Political Antislavery in the United States: The Missouri Crisis Revisited," *Journal of the Historical Society* 4 (Fall 2004): 383–95; Matthew Mason, *Slavery and Politics in the Early American Republic* (Chapel Hill: University of North Carolina Press, 2006), 195–207.

21. Flower, *History of the English Settlement*, 195–96; *Illinois Gazette* (Shawneetown), clipped by *Illinois Intelligencer* (Vandalia), 30 Jan 1824; *Republican* (Kaskaskia), 13 (Orr quotes) and 20 ("Ames") July 1824; Charles R. King, ed., *The Life and Correspondence of Rufus King*, vol. 6 (New York: Putnam's, 1900), 532 (Ohioan quote); David Robson to William Shepherd and Robert Leslie, 6 August 1823, folder 1, SC 432, James and John Dunlop Papers, ALPLM; Lippincott, "The Conflict of the Century," typescript, 17, Thomas Lippincott Papers, *IHLC*, UIUC.

22. *Illinois Intelligencer* (Vandalia), 21 Dec 1822 (Conrad Will quotes); *Republican Advocate* (Kaskaskia), 7 Aug 1823 ("Veritas" quotes); *Republican* (Kaskaskia), 30 March 1824; Richard S. Newman, *The Transformation of American Abolitionism: Fighting Slavery in the Early Republic* (Chapel Hill: University of North Carolina Press, 2002), 96–97; Isaac Joslin Cox, ed., "Selections from the Torrence Papers, VII: Early Illinois Politics, As Illustrated by the Sloo Letters," *Quarterly Publication of the Historical and Philosophical Society of Ohio* 6 (July–Sept 1911): 60 ("slave party" quotes).

23. *Illinois Intelligencer* (Vandalia), 8 March 1823 (quotes); Lippincott, "The Conflict of the Century," typescript, 10–16, Thomas Lippincott Papers, *IHLC*, UIUC; Alvord, *Governor Edward Coles*, 117–54, 166–67, 335; Dillon, "Antislavery Movement in Illinois, 1809–1844," 100–113.

24. *Illinois Intelligencer* (Vandalia), 17 May 1823 ("Aristides" quotes); Morris Birkbeck, "An Appeal to the People of Illinois on the Question of a Convention," *TISHS* 10 (1905): 154 ("Freedom" quotes), 161 ("power" quote); Flower, *History of the English Settlement*, 181 ("unworthy" quotes); *Republican Advocate* (Kaskaskia), 26 June 1823 ("Martus" quote); *Spectator* (Edwardsville), 12 April 1823 ("An Old Resident of Illinois" quotes).

25. *Illinois Intelligencer* (Vandalia), 24 May 1823 ("Aristides" quotes); 2 and 30 July 1824; "Laocoon" and Thomas Lippincott, in *To the People of Illinois* (n.p.), 24 May 1824; *The Injurious Effects of Slave Labour: An Impartial Appeal to the Reason, Justice, and Patriotism of the People of Illinois on the Injurious Effects of Slave Labour* (London: Ellerton and Henderson, 1824), 5–18; Alfred Cowles to Stephen B. Munn, 29 March 1823, box 5, folder 11, Lyman Trumbull Family Papers, ALPLM.

26. *Illinois Intelligencer* (Vandalia), 28 May ("new and fertile" quotes), 4 June ("new and imposing" quotes), and 16 July ("our state" quote) 1824; Birkbeck, "Appeal to the People of Illinois," 158 (quote).

27. *Illinois Intelligencer* (Vandalia), 5 July 1823 ("Brutus" quote); 16 July 1824 ("Spartacus" quotes); *Spectator* (Edwardsville), 19 April 1823 ("Q" quote).

28. Birkbeck, "Appeal to the People of Illinois," 152, 160 (quote); *Spectator* (Edwardsville), 19 April 1823 ("A friend to Freedom" quote); *Illinois Intelligencer* (Vandalia), 15 May (Coles quote) and 30 July 1824 (Warnock quote); *Republican* (Kaskaskia), 15 June 1824 ("G. H." quote).

29. *IE*, 90–91; Theodore Calvin Pease, ed., *Illinois Election Returns, 1818–1848*, vol. 18, *CISHL* (Springfield: Illinois State Historical Library, 1923), 27; Simeone, *Democracy and Slavery*, 245–46.

30. Horatio Newhall to Isaac and Joel Newhall, 21 May 1823, folder 1, SC 2100, Horatio Newhall Papers, ALPLM; *Illinois Intelligencer* (Vandalia), 22 Nov 1823.

31. Zucker, "Free Negro Question," 132–35, 150–51, 153–56. I used Zucker's 1822 and 1824 election tables to make my calculations, although I corrected the addition error Zucker made in computing Franklin County's 1824 total vote.

32. Historians have recognized that the tide of immigration into northern Illinois aided the anticonvention party, but none have precisely calculated the impact of the migrant stream. For instance, see Harris, *History of Negro Servitude in Illinois*, 44; Dillon, "Antislavery Movement in Illinois: 1809–1844," 118; Zucker, "Free Negro Question," 150–151n72; Robert M. Sutton, "Edward Coles and the Constitutional Crisis in Illinois, 1822–1824," *IHJ* 82 (Spring 1989): 45; David Ress, *Governor Edward Coles and the Vote to Forbid Slavery in Illinois, 1823–1824* (Jefferson, N.C.: McFarland, 2006), 154. Historians have emphasized other explanations for the defeat of the convention movement. For the anticonventionists' more skillful rhetorical appeals, see Pease, *Frontier State, 1818–1848*, 86–89; Harris, *History of Negro Servitude*, 43–47; and Peter S. Onuf, *Statehood and Union: A History of the Northwest Ordinance* (Bloomington: Indiana University Press, 1987), 123–32; for the anticonventionists' superior organizing, see Dillon, "Antislavery Movement in Illinois: 1809–1844," 85–122; for their advocacy of free labor values, see Zucker, "Free Negro Question," 84–156; Suzanne

Cooper Guasco, "'The Deadly Influence of Negro Capitalists': Southern Yeomen and Resistance to the Expansion of Slavery in Illinois," *CWH* 47 (March 2001): 7–29; for their appeal to the democratic aspirations of poor whites, see Simeone, *Democracy and Slavery*, 133–57; and for the importance of Edward Coles's leadership, see Leichtle and Carveth, *Crusade against Slavery*, 130.

Chapter 2. Democrats, Whigs, and Party Conflict, 1825–1842

1. John William Ward, *Andrew Jackson: Symbol for an Age* (New York: Oxford University Press, 1955), 3–10; Robert V. Remini, *The Life of Andrew Jackson* (New York: Harper and Row, 1988), 86–128; Michael F. Holt, *The Rise and Fall of the American Whig Party: Jacksonian Politics and the Onset of the Civil War* (New York: Oxford University Press, 1999), 6; Robert V. Remini, *The Legacy of Andrew Jackson: Essays on Democracy, Indian Removal, and Slavery* (Baton Rouge: Louisiana State University Press, 1988), 7–44.

2. Alfred Cowles to Stephen B. Munn, 10 Nov 1828, box 5, folder 11, Lyman Trumbull Family Papers ("interests" quotes); Henry Eddy to William Orr, 16 Feb 1827; Singleton H. Kimmel to Eddy, 7 Nov 1827 ("measures" quotes), box 1, folder 4, Henry Eddy Papers; J. C. Mitchell to Sidney Breese, 26 April 1827, box 1, folder 3, Sidney Breese Papers; Ninian Edwards to John Mason Peck, 18 June 1829; Edwards to Henry Eddy, 3 Aug 1829, folder 1, SC 447, Ninian Edwards Papers, ALPLM; E. B. Washburne, ed., *The Edwards Papers: Being a Portion of the Collection of the Letters, Papers, and Manuscripts of Ninian Edwards* (Chicago: Fergus, 1884), 408–11.

3. Samuel D. Ingham to Singleton H. Kimmel, 1 Aug 1829, box 1, folder 6, Henry Eddy Papers, ALPLM; Washburne, *Edwards Papers*, 483; Robert V. Remini, *The Election of Andrew Jackson* (Philadelphia: Lippincott, 1963), 51–120; Richard Hofstadter, *The Idea of a Party System: The Rise of Legitimate Opposition in the United States, 1780–1840* (Berkeley: University of California, 1969), 212–71.

4. Robert V. Remini, *Andrew Jackson and the Bank War: A Study in the Growth of Presidential Power* (New York: Norton, 1967).

5. Charles Manfred Thompson, *The Illinois Whigs before 1846*, vol. 4, no. 1, UISSS (Urbana: University of Illinois, 1915), 39–40; Don E. Fehrenbacher, *Chicago Giant: A Biography of "Long John" Wentworth* (Madison, Wisc.: American History Research Center, 1957), 12–13, 28; Thomas Ford, *A History of Illinois: From Its Commencement as a State in 1818 to 1847* (Chicago: Griggs, 1854; reprint, Urbana: University of Illinois Press, 1995), 139–41; *LSAD*, 12, 16–17 (quote), 69; Robert W. Johannsen, *Stephen A. Douglas* (New York: Oxford University Press, 1973; reprint, Urbana: University of Illinois Press, 1997), 29–31.

6. Remini, *Legacy of Andrew Jackson*, 26–42.

7. John S. Roberts, Prospectus of the *Illinois Republican* (Springfield), 25 Feb 1835, B-562, BC-ALPLM (quotes); *LSAD*, 12 ("cause" quote), 21 (other Douglas quotes), 25 ("embody" quote), 29–30 (other convention quotes).

8. 9th Gen. Ass., 1st Sess., *Senate Journal* (16 Jan 1835), 263; John Francis Snyder, *Adam W. Snyder and His Period in Illinois History, 1817–1842* (Springfield: Illinois

State Historical Library, 1906; reprint, Ann Arbor: University Microfilms, 1968), 179 ("extortionate" quote); *Illinois State Register* (Springfield), 14 Dec 1839 (Breese quotes).

9. Jonathan H. Earle, *Jacksonian Antislavery and the Politics of Free Soil, 1824–1854* (Chapel Hill: University of North Carolina Press, 2004), 123–45; Sean Wilentz, *The Rise of American Democracy: Jefferson to Lincoln* (New York: Norton, 2005), 509–18.

10. Thompson, *Illinois Whigs before 1846*, 29–55; Holt, *Rise and Fall*, 38–49; *IE*, 103; Gerald Flood Leonard, *The Invention of Party Politics: Federalism, Popular Sovereignty, and Constitutional Development in Jacksonian Illinois* (Chapel Hill: University of North Carolina Press, 2002), 137–42. The Whig candidate in South Carolina was Willie P. Mangum, but he was not popularly elected.

11. Kenneth J. Winkle, *The Young Eagle: The Rise of Abraham Lincoln* (Dallas, Tex.: Taylor, 2001), 186–92; *CW*, 1:5–8 (quotes); Daniel Walker Howe, *The Political Culture of the American Whigs* (Chicago: University of Chicago Press, 1979), 9–10, 181–209; 264–68.

12. Holt, *Rise and Fall*, 44; Daniel Walker Howe, *What Hath God Wrought: The Transformation of America, 1815–1848* (New York: Oxford University Press, 2007), 510–15.

13. Milo Milton Quaife, ed., *Growing Up with Southern Illinois, 1820 to 1861: From the Memoirs of Daniel Harmon Brush* (Chicago: Donnelley, 1944; reprint, Herrin: Crossfire, 1992), 8–9, 11–12, 22, 30–33, 41–42, 54, 78–98, 102–4, 110–11, 166–72; Winkle, *Young Eagle*, 12–21, 28–29, 52, 96–111; Susan E. Gray, "Local Speculator as Confidence Man: Mumford Eldred Jr., and the Michigan Land Rush," *JER* 10 (Fall 1990): 389–406; Gray, *Yankee West: Community Life on the Michigan Frontier* (Chapel Hill: University of North Carolina Press, 1996), 13–14; David Schob, *Hired Hands and Plowboys: Farm Labor in the Midwest, 1815–60* (Urbana: University of Illinois Press, 1975), 250–72.

14. *Illinois Intelligencer* (Vandalia), 9 and 22 December 1825; 9th Gen. Ass., 2nd Sess., *House Journal*, tabular statement appended after page 372. In 1835, Knox County's returns included Henry County. For that year, I corrected tabulation errors for Edwards, Fulton, and Vermilion Counties, and the total state population; and I divided the regions as follows: southern Illinois's northern boundary included Madison, Bond, Fayette, Effingham, Jasper, and Crawford Counties; and northern Illinois's southern boundary included Mercer, Henry, Putnam, La Salle, and Will Counties.

15. William Vipond Pooley, *The Settlement of Illinois from 1830 to 1850* (Madison: Bulletin of the University of Wisconsin History Series, 1908), 358–59, 382–87, 390–93, 402–12, 440–42; Theodore L. Carlson, *The Illinois Military Tract: A Study of Land Occupation, Utilization, and Tenure*, vol. 32, no. 2, *UISSS* (Urbana: University of Illinois Press, 1951), 65–73; Theodore Calvin Pease, *The Frontier State, 1818–1848* (Springfield: Illinois Centennial Commission, 1918; reprint, Urbana: University of Illinois Press, 1987), 173, 188–93; *LSAD*, 7 (quote), 11, 18–19, 23; John C. Abbott, ed., *Journey to New Switzerland: Travel Account of the Koepfli and Suppiger Family to St. Louis on the Mississippi and the Founding of New Switzerland in the State of Illinois* (Carbondale: Southern Illinois University Press, 1987), 180 (quotes), 184 (quote).

16. Pooley, *Settlement of Illinois*, 309–11, 358, 538–44, 567–68; Josiah Francis to Charles Francis, 4 May 1832, SC 525, Simeon Francis Papers, ALPLM; Richard Lyle

Power, *Planting Corn Belt Culture: The Impress of the Upland Southerner and Yankee in the Old Northwest* (Indianapolis: Indiana Historical Society, 1953), 28–34, 92–100; Susan Sessions Rugh, *Our Common Country: Family Farming, Culture, and Community in the Nineteenth-Century Midwest* (Bloomington: Indiana University Press, 2001), 24.

17. Lewis E. Atherton, *The Pioneer Merchant in Mid-America*, vol. 14, no. 2, *University of Missouri Studies* (Columbia: University of Missouri, 1939), 78–81; Timothy R. Mahoney, *River Towns in the Great West: The Structure of Provincial Urbanization in the American Midwest, 1820–1870* (New York: Cambridge University Press, 1990), 215–16, 196, 244–45; Abbott, *Journey to New Switzerland*, 165 ("area" quote), 189 ("ready" quote); William Cronon, *Nature's Metropolis: Chicago and the Great West* (New York: Norton, 1991), 31–63; Bessie Louise Pierce, *A History of Chicago*, vol. 1, *The Beginning of a City, 1673–1848* (New York: Knopf, 1937), 50–55; Josiah Francis to Charles Francis, 4 May 1832, SC 525, Simeon Francis Papers, ALPLM.

18. Quaife, *Growing Up with Southern Illinois*, 53–56, 60, 110–11, 113–14; Atherton, *Pioneer Merchant*, 25, 30–34, 54–58, 72–76, 83, 90–102; Rugh, *Our Common Country*, 21–25; Winkle, *Young Eagle*, 50–55, 77–79, 96–102; Credit Agency of Griffin, Cleaveland, and Campbell to Henry Eddy, 4 Sept 1835, box 1, folder 15, Henry Eddy Papers, ALPLM; Barbara Lawrence and Nedra Branz, eds., *The Flagg Correspondence: Selected Letters, 1816–1854* (Carbondale: Southern Illinois University Press, 1986), 41; Stephen J. Buck, "Political and Economic Transformation in the Civil War Era: DuPage County, Illinois, 1830–1880" (PhD diss., Northern Illinois University, 1992), 30–34; Paul W. Gates, *Landlords and Tenants on the Prairie Frontier: Studies in American Land Policy* (Ithaca, N.Y.: Cornell University Press, 1973), 58–59, 144–47; LSAD, 19.

19. Quaife, *Growing Up with Southern Illinois*, 60, 110–11; W. P. Strickland, ed., *Autobiography of Peter Cartwright: The Backwoods Preacher* (New York: Methodist Book Concern, 1856), 251–54; Atherton, *Pioneer Merchant*, 44–46.

20. Abbott, *Journey to New Switzerland*, 149, 163–64 (quote), 170–72 (quote); Gates, *Landlords and Tenants*, 198, 201–3; Helen M. Cavanagh, *Funk of Funk's Grove: Farmer, Legislator, and Cattle King of the Old Northwest, 1797–1865* (Bloomington: Pantagraph, 1952), 44–47, 65–69; Winkle, *Young Eagle*, 45; Stephen J. Tonsor, ed., "'I Am My Own Boss'—A German Immigrant Writes from Illinois," *JISHS* 54 (Winter 1961): 392–404; *Illinois Intelligencer* (Vandalia), 13 April 1826.

21. Pease, *Frontier State*, 176–77; Charles R. Clarke, ed., "Sketch of Charles James Fox Clarke with Letters to His Mother," *JISHS* 22 (Jan 1930): 563; Allan G. Bogue, *From Prairie to Corn Belt: Farming on the Illinois and Iowa Prairies in the Nineteenth Century* (Chicago: University of Chicago Press, 1963; reprint, Ames: Iowa State University Press, 1994), 31–39; Carlson, *Illinois Military Tract*, 54–59.

22. *Illinois Intelligencer* (Vandalia), 23 March 1826. For an excellent study of the market orientation of frontier settlers during these years, see Jeff Bremer, *A Store Almost in Sight: The Economic Transformation of Missouri from the Louisiana Purchase to the Civil War* (Iowa City: University of Iowa Press, 2014).

23. John H. Krenkel, *Illinois Internal Improvements, 1818–1848* (Cedar Rapids, Iowa: Torch, 1958), 28–40; John Reynolds to Alexander F. Grant, 1 Jan 1830, box 1, folder 7, Henry Eddy Papers, ALPLM.

24. Krenkel, *Illinois Internal Improvements*, 51–61; William K. Ackerman, "Early Illinois Railroads," vol. 23, *FHS* (Chicago: Fergus, 1884), 16–19; 9th Gen. Ass., 1st Sess., *Senate Journal* (13 Jan 1835), 229–30, 243–48; Daniel Feller, *The Public Lands in Jacksonian Politics* (Madison: University of Wisconsin Press, 1984), 86–91, 101–5, 176.

25. Johannsen, *Douglas*, 49–51; Krenkel, *Illinois Internal Improvements*, 45–46, 69–70, 75; Rodney Owen Davis, "Illinois Legislators and Jacksonian Democracy, 1834–1841" (PhD diss., University of Iowa, 1966), 217–21; Daniel Wood to Henry Eddy, 2 Feb 1837, box 2, folder 2, Henry Eddy Papers, ALPLM.

26. Krenkel, *Illinois Internal Improvements*, 80–109, 113–23, 128–29, 146, 149; Peter Temin, *The Jacksonian Economy* (New York: Norton, 1969), 136–47.

27. *IE*, 5; Sidney Breese to Alexander F. Grant, 6 June 1834; John Reynolds to Henry Eddy and R. W. Clark, 6 July 1834, box 1, folder 13; Nathaniel Pope to Eddy, 23 Sept 1834 ("Ultra-Jackson" quotes); Grant to Henry L. Webb, 8 Nov 1834, box 1, folder 14, Henry Eddy Papers, ALPLM; *Illinois Advocate and State Register* (Vandalia), 26 July 1834 (Casey quotes); Davis, "Illinois Legislators and Jacksonian Democracy," 101–24, 329–31. I calculated Whig and Democratic legislators' support for state and local banking from Davis's tabulation of roll call votes, or items 1, 3, and 5 in table 1 and items 2, 3, and 4 in table 2 of the appendix.

28. George William Dowrie, *The Development of Banking in Illinois, 1817–1863*, vol. 2, no. 4, *UISSS* (Urbana: University of Illinois, 1913), 61–64; Davis, "Illinois Legislators and Jacksonian Democracy," 111–22, 329–31; *Illinois Advocate and State Register* (Vandalia), 31 Jan 1835.

29. 10th Gen. Ass., 1st Sess., *House Journal* (23 Feb 1837), 680–83, (25 Feb 1837), 721–22; *Senate Journal* (6 Feb 1837), 353–56; Dowrie, *Development of Banking in Illinois*, 78–83; Davis, "Illinois Legislators and Jacksonian Democracy," 132–40, 336–41; 11th Gen. Ass., 2nd Sess., *Senate and House Reports* (21 Jan 1840), 329; Temin, *Jacksonian Economy*, 31–34; Howard Bodenhorn, *State Banking in Early America: A New Economic History* (New York: Oxford University Press, 2003), 48–52. The voting percentages are derived from the roll-call vote on a bill to increase capital stock in the state bank, or item 4 in table V and item 2 in table VI of Davis's appendix.

30. Dowrie, *Development of Banking in Illinois*, 104–12; David Davis to William P. Walker, 1 July 1837, box 1, folder A-1, David Davis Family Papers, ALPLM; Ford, *History of Illinois*, 193 (quote), 278.

31. The $700,000 figure is an estimate. The bank approved 1,875 loans of less than $200, and 1,408 loans ranging from $200 to $500. Dowrie, *Development of Banking in Illinois*, 93–94.

32. *Illinois State Gazette and Jacksonville News* (Jacksonville), 3 August 1837; Adam Snyder to James Semple, 4 April 1836, box 29, folder 4, John Francis Snyder Papers; John A. McClernand to Henry Eddy, 19 Feb 1837, box 2, folder 2; A. G. S. Wight to Eddy, 4 Aug 1839, box 2, folder 4 (quote); Samuel D. Marshall to Eddy, 19 Dec 1839,

box 2, folder 4; A. Burnam and John Hynes to Kirkpatrick and Eddy, 22 Sept 1840, box 2, folder 5, Henry Eddy Papers, ALPLM; Dowrie, *Development of Banking in Illinois*, 90–95, 105; Gates, *Landlords and Tenants*, 57; 11th Gen. Ass., 2nd Sess., *Senate and House Reports* (21 Jan 1840), 257, 283–84, 288–90, 307.

33. Temin, *Jacksonian Economy*, 155–59; Dowrie, *Development of Banking in Illinois*, 105, 109–10; Adam Snyder to James Semple, 6 April 1840, box 29, folder 6, John Francis Snyder Papers; David Davis to William P. Walker, 19 Jan 1840, box 1, folder A-2, David Davis Family Papers, ALPLM.

34. Michael F. Holt, "From Center to Periphery: The Market Revolution and Major-Party Conflict, 1835–1880," in *The Market Revolution in America: Social, Political, and Religious Expressions, 1800–1880*, ed. Melvyn Stokes and Stephen Conway (Charlottesville: University Press of Virginia, 1996), 234–38, 245–46; *Illinois State Register* (Springfield), 23 and 30 (Lee County quote) Nov and 21 Dec 1839 ("channels" quote); 27 Nov 1840 (Carlin quote); 11th Gen. Ass., 2nd Sess., *Senate and House Reports* (21 Jan 1840), 257–58; Davis, "Illinois Legislators and Jacksonian Democracy," 177, 186; Dowrie, *Development of Banking in Illinois*, 112–26.

35. *Illinois State Register* (Springfield), 26 Feb and 14 (Carlin quotes) Dec 1839; 14th Gen. Ass., 1st Sess., *Senate Journal* (3 Dec 1844), 10–11 (Ford quotes).

36. Snyder, *Adam Snyder*, 204–7, 230; William L. Burton, "James Semple: Prairie Entrepreneur," *IHJ* 80 (Summer 1987): 68–71, 80; Adam Snyder to James Semple, 4 and 22 April, 12 Nov, and 25 Dec 1836; 3 June ("degrading" quotes) and 28 Aug ("healthy" quote) 1837; Snyder to unknown correspondent, 18 April 1838, box 29, folder 5, John Francis Snyder Papers, ALPLM; Evarts B. Greene, ed., "Letters to Gustav Koerner, 1837–1863," *TISHS* (1907): 229 ("reform" quote).

37. *Illinois State Register* (Springfield), 30 Nov (Lee and La Salle County quotes) and 18 Dec 1839 (Democratic Address quotes); 1 Jan (Williamson County quote) and 3 July 1840 (Reynolds quotes); Davis, "Illinois Legislators and Jacksonian Democracy," 160.

38. Douglass C. North, *The Economic Growth of the United States, 1790–1860* (Englewood Cliffs, N.J.: Prentice-Hall, 1961), 151; Alice E. Smith, *George Smith's Money: A Scottish Investor in America* (Madison: State Historical Society of Wisconsin, 1966), 58–61, 98–101; F. Cyril James, *The Growth of Chicago Banks*, vol. 1, *The Formative Years, 1816–1896* (New York: Harper and Brothers, 1938), 203; Arthur Charles Cole, *The Era of the Civil War, 1848–1870* (Springfield: Illinois Centennial Commission, 1919; reprint, Urbana: University of Illinois Press, 1987), 92–97. Technically Smith's banknotes were certificates of deposit, and thus legal.

39. *IE*, 5–6, 106, 111; Thompson, *Illinois Whigs before 1846*, 47–70, 93–94; "CONSIDERATIONS &c, No. 2," [1840], *Register—Extra* (Mount Carmel), B-563, BC-ALPLM; *Sangamo Journal* (Springfield), 2 and 9 Feb and 11 Oct 1839; *CW*, 1:180–81, 201–3; Ford, *History of Illinois*, 146–47; Pease, *Frontier State*, 279–80; 11th Gen. Ass., 2nd Sess., *Senate and House Reports* (21 Jan 1840), 253–59; William Pickering to J. Marshall, 18 April 1843, box 2, folder 7, Henry Eddy Papers, ALPLM.

40. On the subsidence of antislavery politics, also see Donald J. Ratcliffe, "The Decline of Antislavery Politics, 1815–1840," in *Contesting Slavery: The Politics of*

Bondage and Freedom in the New American Nation, ed. John Craig Hammond and Matthew Mason (Charlottesville: University of Virginia Press, 2011), 267–90.

Chapter 3. Manifest Destiny, Slavery, and the Rupture of the Democratic Party, 1843–1847

1. James Christy Bell, *Opening a Highway to the Pacific, 1838–1846* (New York: Columbia University, 1921), 120–26; Mason Brayman to Daniel and Nancy Brayman, 4 Sept 1844, box 1, folder 3, Bailhache-Brayman Family Papers (quotes), ALPLM; Milo Milton Quaife, ed., *Growing Up with Southern Illinois, 1820 to 1861: From the Memoirs of Daniel Harmon Brush* (Chicago: Donnelley, 1944; reprint, Herrin, Ill.: Crossfire, 1992), 113–14, 117.

2. William Cronon, *Nature's Metropolis: Chicago and the Great West* (New York: Norton, 1991), 55–63; Douglass C. North, *The Economic Growth of the United States, 1790–1860* (Englewood Cliffs, N.J.: Prentice-Hall, 1961), 151; Bessie Louise Pierce, *A History of Chicago*, vol. 1, *The Beginning of a City, 1673–1848* (New York: Knopf, 1937), 124–42.

3. 9th Gen. Ass., 2nd Sess., *House Journal*, tabular statement appended after page 372; 15th Gen. Ass., 1st Sess., *House Reports* (2 Jan 1847), 46–48. In 1835, Knox County's returns included Henry County. For that year, I corrected tabulation errors for Edwards, Fulton, and Vermilion Counties, and the total state population. For 1845 I divided the regions as follows: southern Illinois's northern boundary included Madison, Bond, Fayette, Effingham, Jasper, and Crawford Counties; and northern Illinois's southern boundary included Mercer, Henry, Stark, Marshall, La Salle, Grundy, and Will Counties.

4. North, *Economic Growth of the United States*, 146; Pierce, *History of Chicago*, 1:90–95, 106–8; James Conkling to Mercy Ann Levering, 18 April 1843, box 1, folder 1, Conkling Family Papers ("Miserable" quote); Hezekiah Morse Wead Diary (typescript), 1, SC 2458, ALPLM; John Reynolds, *My Own Times: Embracing also the History of My Life* (Belleville, Ill.: Perryman and Davison, 1854; reprint, Chicago: Chicago Historical Society, 1879), 379; 28th Cong., 1st Sess., *CG-NU* (4, 15, and 29 Jan 1844), 107, 149, 206, (9 Jan 1844), *Appendix*, 55–58, (17, 18, 19, and 20 April 1844), 550–51, 559, 563–64, 567–68, (June 1844), *Appendix*, 611–12; 28th Cong., 2nd Sess., (31 Jan 1845), 229; *Illinois State Register* (Springfield), 5 and 19 Jan, 5 and 12 April, and 8 Nov (Bond County quotes) 1844; 17 Oct 1845 ("proper" quote); James D. Richardson, comp., *A Compilation of the Messages and Papers of the Presidents, 1789–1908*, vol. 2 (Washington, D.C.: Bureau of National Literature and Art, 1909), 490.

5. 28th Cong., 1st Sess., *CG-NU* (25 March 1844), 443; *The Report of Mr. Breese, accompanying bill S. No. 52*, 24 February 1846 (quotes, 3–4, 7), box 2, folder 7, Sidney Breese Papers; *Report of Mr. Breese to accompany bill S. No. 355, proposing a land grant to the State of Illinois*, 19 December 1848, ALPLM.

6. 27th Cong., 3rd Sess., *CG-NU* (30 Dec 1842 and 9 Jan 1843), *Appendix*, 86–91; 28th Cong., 1st Sess., (24 Jan 1844), *Appendix*, 89–92, (27 Feb 1844), 335–38, (3 June 1844), 680–81 and *Appendix*, 598–602; 28th Cong., 2nd Sess., (6, 27, and 30 Jan 1845),

Appendix, 65–68, 134–37, 202–6, (23 Jan 1845), 182–84, (31 Jan 1845), 225–27; 29th Cong., 1st Sess., (8 Jan 1846), *Appendix,* 273–79 (McClernand quote, 278), (6 Feb 1846), *Appendix,* 171–76; *Illinois State Register* (Springfield), 14 June 1844 ("provisions" quotes); 13 June 1845; 23 Jan and 27 Feb 1846. For more extended treatments of the relationship between the Democrats' commercial objectives and mid-nineteenth-century American expansion, see Thomas Hietala, *Manifest Design: Anxious Aggrandizement in Late Jacksonian America* (Ithaca, N.Y.: Cornell University Press, 1985), 55–94, and Norman Graebner, *Empire on the Pacific: A Study in American Continental Expansion* (New York: Ronald, 1955).

7. 29th Cong., 1st Sess., *Serial Set no. 478,* Senate Document no. 466 (31 July 1846), *Senator Breese's Report accompanying Bill S. No. 246, to construct a Pacific Railroad,* 19, 25 (quotes); 29th Cong., 1st Sess., *CG-NU* (24 Feb 1846), 414; *LSAD,* 130–31 (quotes).

8. 28th Cong., 1st Sess., *CG-NU* (9 Jan 1844), *Appendix,* 55–56 (Wentworth quotes), (27 Feb 1844), 337 (Breese quotes), (June 1844), *Appendix,* 612 (Ficklin quotes); 28th Cong., 2nd Sess., (30 Jan 1845), *Appendix,* 202 (McClernand quotes); *Illinois State Gazette,* clipped by the *Illinois State Register* (Springfield), 5 Jan 1844 ("liberality" quote); *Illinois State Register,* 9 Feb, 12 April, and 8 Nov 1844; 13 June, 11 July, 1 Aug, 17 Oct, and 7, 21, and 28 Nov 1845.

9. *Illinois State Register* (Springfield), 19 Jan 1844 (first Douglas quote); 13 June (second Douglas quote) and 7 Nov 1845 ("dollar" quotes); 29th Cong., 1st Sess., *CG-NU* (8 Jan 1846), *Appendix,* 277, 279 (McClernand quotes). For other nationalist appeals by Illinois congressmen that session, see *CG-NU* (2, 3, 14, and 27 Jan 1846), 126, 136–37, 205–7, 258–60, (6 Feb 1846), *Appendix,* 171.

10. For the development of an antislavery nationalism in New England, see Joanne Pope Melish, *Disowning Slavery: Gradual Emancipation and "Race" in New England, 1780–1860* (Ithaca, N.Y.: Cornell University Press, 1998), 210–37. On the origin of such sectional nationalisms, see Peter S. Onuf, "Federalism, Republicanism, and the Origins of American Sectionalism," in *All Over the Map: Rethinking American Regions,* ed. Edward L. Ayers, Patricia Nelson Limerick, Stephen Nissenbaum, and Peter S. Onuf (Baltimore, Md.: Johns Hopkins University Press, 1996), 11–37.

11. *Belleville Advocate,* clipped by *Illinois State Register* (Springfield), 15 Oct 1841; Theodore Carlson, *The Illinois Military Tract: A Study of Land Occupation, Utilization, and Tenure,* vol. 32, no. 2, *UISSS* (Urbana: University of Illinois Press, 1951), 96–97; Mentor L. Williams, "The Background of the Chicago River and Harbor Convention, 1847," *Mid-America* 30 (Oct 1948): 220–21, 224–28; Mark Egnal, *Clash of Extremes: The Economic Origins of the Civil War* (New York: Hill and Wang, 2009), 101–22.

12. 28th Cong., 1st Sess., *CG-NU* (20 April 1844), 562–68 (quote, 567); 28th Cong., 2nd Sess., (28 Feb 1845), 369; 29th Cong., 1st Sess., (20 March 1846), 530–31; *Telegraph* (Alton), 3 Aug 1844.

13. Don E. Fehrenbacher, *Chicago Giant: A Biography of "Long John" Wentworth* (Madison: American History Research Center, 1957), 46–47, 56, 66–67; 28th Cong., 2nd Sess., *CG-NU* (28 Feb 1845), 369; 29th Cong., 1st Sess., (3 Aug 1846), 1182 (Polk

quotes), 1187 (Federalist quote); 29th Cong., 2nd Sess. (20 Feb 1847), 472; 30th Cong., 1st Sess. (15 Dec 1847), 30–33.

14. Fehrenbacher, *Chicago Giant*, 67–68, 76–78; *Illinois State Register* (Springfield), 1 Aug and 28 Nov 1845; 21 Aug 1846; 15 July 1847; *Weekly Democrat* (Chicago), 4 and 18 May and 15 June 1847; Robert Fergus, comp., "Chicago River-and-Harbor Convention: An Account of Its Origin and Proceedings," vol. 18, *FHS* (Chicago: Fergus, 1882), 18–30, 52–68, 81–86; Mentor L. Williams, "The Chicago River and Harbor Convention, 1847," *MVHR* 35 (March 1949): 608–12, 618–23; Pierce, *History of Chicago*, 1:396; Robert W. Johannsen, *Stephen A. Douglas* (New York: Oxford University Press, 1973; reprint, Urbana: University of Illinois Press, 1997), 171, 210–11. Pierce calculated the number of Illinois delegates from "northern counties," but she did not identify the counties. Hence her calculations probably do not correspond exactly to the counties I have denominated "northern Illinois."

15. For regional battles over repudiation and the canal, see the *Illinois State Register* (Springfield), 12 April, 1 Nov, and 6 Dec 1844; 17 and 24 Jan, 28 Feb, 7 and 14 March, and 28 Nov 1845; 23 Jan and 27 Feb 1846; *Telegraph* (Alton), 1 Feb 1845. For discussions of banking, see the *State Register*, 6 Dec 1844; 22 and 29 Aug 1845; 9 and 23 Jan, 27 Feb, and 16 Oct 1846. For the rivers and harbors bill, see the *State Register*, 11 July 1845; 6 March and 3 and 17 April 1846. For squabbles over offices and power, see James Shields to Sidney Breese, 7 Jan 1844, box 1, folder 6, Sidney Breese Papers, ALPLM; Theodore Calvin Pease, *The Frontier State, 1818–1848* (Springfield: Illinois Centennial Commission, 1918; reprint, Urbana: University of Illinois Press, 1987), 293–301.

16. William A. Richardson to Augustus French, 14 Nov 1845; Peter Sweatt to French, 18 Dec 1845; Josiah McRoberts to French, 1 Jan 1846; John Calhoun to French, 13 Jan and 22 Feb 1846; Thomas Ford to French, 11 Feb 1846; William Walters to French, 15 Feb 1846; Charles Oakley to French, 19 Feb 1846; A. G. Galloway to French, 21 Feb 1846; W. D. Latshaw to French, 4 Oct 1846, box 1, folder 1, French-Wicker Family Papers, ALPLM.

17. *Illinois State Register* (Springfield), 27 Feb 1846.

18. Charles Sellers, *James K. Polk, Continentalist, 1843–1846* (Princeton, N.J.: Princeton University Press, 1966), 55–107; Clement Eaton, *Henry Clay and the Art of American Politics* (Boston: Little, Brown, 1957), 172–78; Glyndon G. Van Duesen, *The Life of Henry Clay* (Boston: Little, Brown, 1937), 364–67; Michael F. Holt, *The Rise and Fall of the American Whig Party: Jacksonian Politics and the Onset of the Civil War* (New York: Oxford University Press, 1999) 169–72; *Illinois State Register* (Springfield), 17 and 24 May 1844; *CW*, 1:336 (quote); Johannsen, *Douglas*, 143–45; Eric John Bradner, "The Attitude of Illinois to Western Expansion in the 1840s" (PhD diss., Northwestern University, 1942), 90–91; Willard Carl Klunder, *Lewis Cass and the Politics of Moderation* (Kent, Ohio: Kent State University Press, 1996), 119–44; Leonard L. Richards, *The Slave Power: The Free North and Southern Domination, 1780–1860* (Baton Rouge: Louisiana State University Press, 2000), 141–56; Michael A. Morrison, "Martin Van Buren, the Democracy, and the Partisan Politics of Texas Annexation," *JSH* 61 (Nov 1995): 695–724.

19. Bradner, "Attitude of Illinois to Western Expansion," 28–41, 68–84, 95–96; Norman E. Tutorow, *Texas Annexation and the Mexican War: A Political Study of the Old Northwest* (Palo Alto, Calif.: Chadwick House, 1978), 117; *Illinois State Register* (Springfield), 15 and 29 March, 12 and 19 April, 17, 24, and 31 May, and 7 June 1844; 27th Cong., 3rd Sess., *CG-NU* (30 Dec 1842 and 9 Jan 1843), *Appendix*, 86–91; 28th Cong., 1st Sess., (24 Jan 1844), *Appendix*, 89–92, (27 Feb 1844), 335–38 and *Appendix*, 216–26, (3 June 1844), 680–81 and *Appendix*, 598–602; James Shields to Sidney Breese, 12 April 1844, box 1, folder 6, Sidney Breese Papers, ALPLM (quotes).

20. *IE*, 113–15; Charles Manfred Thompson, *The Illinois Whigs Before 1846*, vol. 4, no. 1, *UISSS* (Urbana: University of Illinois, 1915), 130–31; Sellers, *James K. Polk*, 99 (convention quotes), 210 (Polk quote); 28th Cong., 1st Sess., (3 June 1844), *Appendix*, 600, 602 (Douglas quotes).

21. Graebner, *Empire on the Pacific*, 22–32, 55–64; Sellers, *James K. Polk*, 235–58, 357–415; Daniel Walker Howe, *What Hath God Wrought: The Transformation of America, 1815–1848* (New York: Oxford University Press, 2007), 715–22.

22. Frederick Merk, *Manifest Destiny and Mission in American History* (New York: Vintage, 1966), 62–63, 80–95 (quote, 88); Mark J. Stegmaier, *Texas, New Mexico, and the Compromise of 1850: Boundary Dispute and Sectional Crisis* (Kent, Ohio: Kent State University Press, 1996), 5–20; Howe, *What Hath God Wrought*, 708, 731–43.

23. Tutorow, *Texas Annexation and the Mexican War*, 130–31, 133–35, 137, 155, 280; Bradner, "Attitude of Illinois to Western Expansion," 153–55; 29th Cong., 1st Sess., *CG-NU* (8 Jan 1846), *Appendix*, 277, (6 Feb 1846), *Appendix*, 171, (13 May 1846), *Appendix*, 903 (Douglas quotes), (16 June 1846), 983 (McClernand quote).

24. 29th Cong., 1st Sess., *CG-NU* (14 Jan 1846), 207 (Wentworth quote), (29 Jan 1846), *Appendix*, 152 ("area" quote), 153 ("peculiar" quote).

25. Bradner, "Attitude of Illinois to Western Expansion," 154–63; *Journal* (Chicago), 15 Nov 1847; 17 April and 1 May 1848; Tutorow, *Texas Annexation and the Mexican War*, 143–46, 155, 282, 288; 15th Gen. Ass., 1st Sess., *House Journal* (13 Feb 1847), 384–85, *Senate Journal* (27 Jan 1847), 170–71.

26. Fehrenbacher, *Chicago Giant*, 49–50, 64–70, 72–74; Delva Peter Brown, "The Economic Views of Illinois Democrats, 1836–1861" (PhD diss., Boston University, 1970), 86; John Wentworth, *Free Tea, Free Coffee, Free Harbors, and Free Territory*, remarks of Mr. John Wentworth, of Illinois, delivered in the House of Representatives, 2 Feb 1847, ALPLM, 5 (quotes).

27. Wentworth, *Free Tea*, 2–13 (quotes).

28. *Illinois State Register* (Springfield), 9 Feb (factory quotes), 19 April (Texas quote), and 13 Sept 1844; 17 Jan 1845; 27 Feb 1846; 28th Cong., 1st Sess., *CG-NU* (27 Feb 1844), *Appendix*, 225–26, (3 June 1844), *Appendix*, 600–602; 28th Cong., 2nd Sess., (27 Jan 1845), *Appendix*, 135; 29th Cong., 1st Sess., (27 Jan 1846), 258–60; 30th Cong., 1st Sess., (6 April 1848), *Appendix*, 512. The most penetrating analysis of Manifest Destiny drew heavily on the speeches of Illinoisans and presented conclusions similar to those presented in this paragraph and those that follow. See Hietala, *Manifest Design*, 55–214, and "'This Splendid Juggernaut': Westward a Nation and Its People,"

in *Manifest Destiny and Empire: American Antebellum Expansion*, ed. Sam Haynes and Christopher Morris (College Station: Texas A&M University Press, 1997), 48–67.

29. Hietala, *Manifest Design*, 186–88; Michael A. Morrison, *Slavery and the American West: The Eclipse of Manifest Destiny and the Coming of the Civil War* (Chapel Hill: University of North Carolina Press, 1997), 22–26; Morrison, "Westward the Curse of Empire: Texas Annexation and the American Whig Party," *JER* 10 (Summer 1990): 230–41; Morrison, "'New Territory versus No Territory': The Whig Party and the Politics of Western Expansion, 1846–1848," *WHQ* 23 (Feb 1992): 36–51; 28th Cong., 1st Sess., *CG-NU* (27 Feb 1844), *Appendix*, 220; 28th Cong., 2nd Sess., (6 Jan 1845), *Appendix*, 68, (31 Jan 1845), 225 (Douglas quote); 29th Cong., 1st Sess., (8 Jan 1846), *Appendix*, 279 (McClernand quotes); 29th Cong., 2nd Sess., (23 Feb 1847), *Appendix*, 210; 30th Cong., 1st Sess., (14 Feb 1848), *Appendix*, 350, (6 April 1848), *Appendix*, 512 (Turner quotes).

30. 28th Cong., 1st Sess., *CG-NU* (3 June 1844), *Appendix*, 601 (Douglas quote); 28th Cong., 2nd Sess., (27 Jan 1845), *Appendix*, 135 (Wentworth quote), 137; 30th Cong., 1st Sess., (6 April 1848), *Appendix*, 512 (Turner quote); James Shields to Sidney Breese, 12 April 1844, box 1, folder 6, Sidney Breese Papers, ALPLM ("history" quote); *Illinois State Register* (Springfield), 13 June and 25 Dec 1845; 2 and 23 Jan and 10 July 1846; Prospectus of the *Jackson Standard*, ed. J. S. and E. W. Roberts, 10 June 1845, B-1950, BC-ALPLM; McClernand's autobiography, 35–36, 1846, box 1, folder 4, John A. McClernand Papers, ALPLM (quotes).

31. 28th Cong., 1st Sess., (24 Jan 1844), *Appendix*, 92, (3 June 1844), *Appendix*, 543 (Breese quote), 598–602; 28th Cong., 2nd Sess., (23 Jan 1845), 184; 29th Cong., 1st Sess., (26 March 1846), 559; 31st Cong., 1st Sess., (13 and 14 March 1850), *Appendix*, 365 (Douglas quotes); *Illinois State Register* (Springfield), 19 April, 24 May, and 14 June 1844; 11 July and 25 Dec 1845; 2 Jan 1846; Sam Haynes, "Anglophobia and the Annexation of Texas: The Quest for National Security," in Haynes and Morris, *Manifest Destiny and Empire*, 115–45.

32. 28th Cong., 2nd Sess., *CG-NU* (23 Jan 1845), 184 (Ficklin quote); *Illinois State Register* (Springfield), 19 April 1844 ("mild" quote); 17 Jan 1845 ("laws" quote).

33. 29th Cong., 2nd Sess., *CG-NU* (15 Jan 1847), *Appendix*, 102–3. For the tensions that Manifest Destiny produced in the Democratic Party, see Sean Wilentz, *The Rise of American Democracy: Jefferson to Lincoln* (New York: Norton, 2005), 562–64, 575–76.

34. *Illinois State Register* (Springfield), 21 Dec 1839; 24 Dec 1841; 17 Jan 1845.

35. *Advocate* (Belleville), 4 March 1847; 28th Cong., 1st Sess., *CG-NU* (3 June 1844), *Appendix*, 543.

36. Fehrenbacher, *Chicago Giant*, 57; Wentworth, *Free Tea*, 9–12 (quotes).

37. Christopher Childers, *The Failure of Popular Sovereignty: Slavery, Manifest Destiny, and the Radicalization of Southern Politics* (Lawrence: University Press of Kansas, 2012), 9–39, 102–49; James Shields to John McClernand, 26 Dec 1844, box 1, folder 4, John A. McClernand Papers; A[lexander] B[ryan] Johnson to Sidney Breese, 23 and 29 June 1848, box 1, folder 8, Sidney Breese Papers, ALPLM; Johannsen, *Douglas*, 227–28.

Chapter 4. Advocates for an Antislavery Nation, 1837–1848

1. Merton Lynn Dillon, "The Antislavery Movement in Illinois: 1824–1835," *JISHS* 47 (Spring 1954): 154–66; Dillon, "Abolitionism Comes to Illinois," *JISHS* 53 (Winter 1960): 389–403; Dillon, "The Antislavery Movement in Illinois, 1809–1844" (PhD diss., University of Michigan, 1951), 155–66, 179–80, 314; Bessie Louise Pierce, *A History of Chicago*, vol. 1, *The Beginning of a City, 1673–1848* (New York: Knopf, 1937), 1:177–78, 402–3; Susan Gray, *Yankee West: Community Life on the Michigan Frontier* (Chapel Hill: University of North Carolina Press, 1996), 9–13; Lois Kimball Mathews, *The Expansion of New England: The Spread of New England Settlement and Institutions to the Mississippi River, 1620–1865* (Boston: Houghton Mifflin, 1909; reprint, New York: Russell and Russell, 1962), 206–19.

2. Albert Hale to Asa Turner, 26 Jan 1838, SC 622, Albert Hale Papers; Adam Snyder to Jesse B. Thomas, 23 Dec 1837, box 29, folder 4, John Francis Snyder Papers, ALPLM.

3. N. Dwight Harris, *The History of Negro Servitude in Illinois and of the Slavery Agitation in that State, 1719–1864* (Chicago: McClurg, 1904; reprint, New York: Haskell House, 1969), 52–61, 128–29; Joseph C. and Owen Lovejoy, *Memoir of the Rev. Elijah P. Lovejoy; Who Was Murdered in Defence of the Liberty of the Press, at Alton, Illinois, Nov. 7, 1837*, with an introduction by John Quincy Adams (New York: Taylor, 1838), 117–295; Merton L. Dillon, *Elijah P. Lovejoy, Abolitionist Editor* (Urbana: University of Illinois Press, 1961), 121; Dillon, "Antislavery Movement in Illinois, 1809–1844," 189, 195, 198, 205–6, 210, 230–33.

4. *Proceedings of the Ill. Anti-Slavery Convention: Held at Upper Alton on the Twenty-Sixth, Twenty-Seventh, and Twenty-Eighth October, 1837* (Alton, Ill.: Parks and Breath, 1838; NIU Libraries Digitization Projects), 20, 28–33, http://lincoln.lib .niu.edu/file.php?file=ilantislav.html (accessed April 3, 2010); Harris, *History of Negro Servitude in Illinois*, 142–45.

5. William F. Moore and Jane Ann Moore, eds., *His Brother's Blood: Speeches and Writings, 1838–64* (Urbana: University of Illinois Press, 2004), 24 (quote), 28–32, 34–42 (quote, 39), 48–49, 56–57, 61–64, 66–68; Richard J. Carwardine, *Evangelicals and Politics in Antebellum America* (New Haven, Conn.: Yale University Press, 1993), 1–49; Harris, *History of Negro Servitude in Illinois*, 142–60 ("Union" quote, 148n3); Reinhard O. Johnson, *The Liberty Party, 1840–1848: Antislavery Third-Party Politics in the United States* (Baton Rouge: Louisiana State University Press, 2009), 191–98; *IE*, 7.

6. Harris, *History of Negro Servitude in Illinois*, 149–60, 138–39; Dillon, "Antislavery Movement in Illinois, 1809–1844," 293–302; Thomas S. Hick to Benjamin Hinch, 29 Jan 1845, folder 1, SC 1763, Benjamin P. Hinch Papers, ALPLM (quotes).

7. Richard S. Newman, *The Transformation of American Abolitionism: Fighting Slavery in the Early Republic* (Chapel Hill: University of North Carolina Press, 2002), 1–38; Gilbert H. Barnes and Dwight L. Dumond, eds., *Letters of Theodore Dwight Weld, Angelina Grimké Weld, and Sarah Grimké, 1822–1844*, vol. 1 (American Historical Association, 1934; reprint, Gloucester: Peter Smith, 1965), 98; Moore and Moore, *His Brother's Blood*, 28–32; Lewis Perry, *Radical Abolitionism: Anarchy and*

the Government of God in Antislavery Thought (Ithaca, N.Y.: Cornell University Press, 1973; reprint, Knoxville: University of Tennessee Press, 1995), 32–54.

8. Richard S. Taylor, "Beyond Immediate Emancipation: Jonathan Blanchard, Abolitionism, and the Emergence of American Fundamentalism," *CWH* 27 (Sept 1981): 261; John Ashworth, *Slavery, Capitalism, and Politics in the Antebellum Republic*, vol. 1, *Commerce and Compromise, 1820–1850* (New York: Cambridge University Press, 1995), 125–91; Amy Dru Stanley, "Home Life and the Morality of the Market," in *The Market Revolution in America: Social, Political, and Religious Expressions, 1800–1880*, ed. Melvyn Stokes and Stephen Conway (Charlottesville: University Press of Virginia, 1996), 74–96; Ronald G. Walters, *The Antislavery Appeal: American Abolitionism after 1830* (Baltimore, Md.: Johns Hopkins University Press, 1976), 55, 68, 91–110, 121–27; James Brewer Stewart, *Holy Warriors: The Abolitionists and American Slavery* (New York: Hill and Wang, 1976), 37–39; Edward Beecher, *Narrative of Riots at Alton* (Alton, Ill.: Holton, 1838; reprint, New York: Dutton, 1965), 23 (quote), 70–71 (quotes); Lovejoy, *Memoir*, 198.

9. Beecher, *Narrative of Riots at Alton*, 73 ("irresistible" quote), 90–91 ("foundation" quotes); *Western Citizen* (Chicago), 26 July 1842; 27 July 1843 (masthead quote); 8 April, 13 May, and 30 June 1846; Harris, *History of Negro Servitude*, 126–27; George Lawrence, "Benjamin Lundy, Pioneer of Freedom," *JISHS* 6 (July 1913): 198–99 (Lundy quote); Johnson, *Liberty Party*, 315–22; *Illinois State Register* (Springfield), 7 June 1844. An important guide to the abolitionists' racial egalitarianism is Paul Goodman, *Of One Blood: Abolitionism and the Origins of Racial Equality* (Berkeley: University of California Press, 1998), 54–64.

10. James Conkling, Speech at Springfield Lyceum, 5 Jan 1839, p. 4, box 1, folder 2, Conkling Family Papers, ALPLM; *Illinois Journal* (Springfield), 28 Oct 1847 (quotes); 6, 13, and 20 April 1848; *Sangamo Journal*, clipped by the *North Western Gazette and Galena Advertiser* (Galena), 10 Feb 1843 (Browning quote); Daniel Walker Howe, *The Political Culture of the American Whigs* (Chicago: University of Chicago Press, 1979), 150–80; Carwardine, *Evangelicals and Politics in Antebellum America*, 110–11.

11. James Conkling, Speech at Springfield Lyceum, 5 Jan 1839, p. 4 (African quote), and Speech at Vandalia State House, 4 July 1839, p. 12 (Indian quote), box 1, folder 2, Conkling Family Papers, ALPLM; *Weekly North-Western Gazette* (Galena), 19 Dec 1845 (Doane quotes); 20 Nov 1846; *North Western Gazette and Galena Advertiser* (Galena), 7 July 1843; 12 April, 31 May, and 1 Nov 1844; 10 Jan 1845 ("procrustean" quotes); *Daily Journal* (Chicago), 29 Nov 1844; 17 Dec 1845.

12. Cyrus Edwards to Joseph Gillespie, 14 April 1835, folder 1, SC 558, Joseph Gillespie Papers, ALPLM. See Eric Foner, *Free Soil, Free Labor, Free Men: The Ideology of the Republican Party before the Civil War* (New York: Oxford University Press, 1970), 1–72, for the significance of these ideas in the 1850s.

13. H. C. Carey, *Principles of Political Economy, Part the Fourth*, vol. 3 (Philadelphia: Lea and Blanchard, 1840; reprint, New York: Kelley, 1965), 95–96, 202–3 (quotes); Louis S. Gerteis, *Morality and Utility in American Antislavery Reform* (Chapel Hill: University of North Carolina Press, 1987), 68–71; Calvin Colton, *Public Economy for*

the United States (New York: Barnes, 1848), 308–10, 420–21 (quotes); *North Western Gazette and Galena Advertiser* (Galena), 7 March 1845; Ashworth, *Slavery, Capitalism, and Politics,* 1:358–61; *CW,* 1:347–48.

14. Thomas B. Alexander, *Sectional Stress and Party Strength: A Study of Roll-Call Voting Patterns in the United States House of Representatives, 1836–1860* (Nashville, Tenn.: Vanderbilt University Press, 1967), 216; *Daily Journal* (Chicago), 18 Dec 1844; Samuel H. Davis, *Free Discussion Suppressed in Peoria,* 18 Feb 1843, ALPLM; Richard H. Sewell, *Ballots for Freedom: Antislavery Politics in the United States, 1837–1860* (New York: Oxford University Press, 1976), 62–64; Stewart Winger, *Lincoln, Religion, and Romantic Cultural Politics* (DeKalb: Northern Illinois University Press, 2003), 111–20.

15. 10th Gen. Ass., 1st Sess., *House Journal* (12 Jan 1837), 242, 309–11; *Senate Journal* (12 Jan 1837), 195–98, 297; *CW,* 1:74–76; Beecher, *Narrative of Riots at Alton,* 43–45, 52; Elizabeth Duncan Putnam, "The Life and Services of Joseph Duncan, Governor of Illinois, 1834–1838," *TISHS* 26 (1919): 160 (quotes); Don Harrison Doyle, "Chaos and Community in a Frontier Town: Jacksonville, Illinois, 1825–1860" (PhD diss., Northwestern University, 1973), 105–7. For Hardin's connections to slavery, see Richard Lawrence Miller, *Lincoln and His World: The Early Years, Birth to Illinois Legislature* (Mechanicsburg, Penn.: Stackpole, 2006), 189–98.

16. *Telegraph* (Alton), 30 Dec 1843 (quote); 13 Nov and 11 Dec 1846; 19 March 1847; *Journal* (Chicago), 19 (quote) and 22 Nov 1844; 15 and 22 March 1845; *CW,* 1:347. In *Liberty Power: Antislavery Third Parties and the Transformation of American Politics* (Chicago: University of Chicago Press, 2016), 47–72, Corey M. Brooks ably documents the efforts by political abolitionists to draw Whigs into national antislavery politics.

17. *Nance v. Howard, Illinois Reports* (Breese), 242–47 ("servant" quotes, 242, 246); *Chambers v. The People of Illinois,* ibid. (4 Scammon), 351–60 (Chambers quotes, 353, 359); Carol Pirtle, "*Andrew Borders v. William Hayes*: Indentured Servitude and the Underground Railroad in Illinois," *IHJ* 89 (Autumn 1996): 151; John Codman Hurd, *The Law of Freedom and Bondage in the United States,* vol. 2 (Boston: Little, Brown, 1862), 135 ("runaways" quote); Thomas D. Morris, *Free Men All: The Personal Liberty Laws of the North, 1780–1861* (Baltimore, Md.: Johns Hopkins University Press, 1974), xi–xii.

18. John Lockhart to Henry Eddy, 4 May 1830, box 1, folder 7, Henry Eddy Papers; Mat Stacy to Richard Yates and John Henry, 23 Feb 1843, box 1, folder 1, Yates Family Papers, ALPLM; Mark E. Steiner, ed., "Abolitionists and Escaped Slaves in Jacksonville: Samuel Willard's 'My First Adventure with a Fugitive Slave: The Story of It and How It Failed,'" *IHJ* (Winter 1996): 232 (quote); Don Harrison Doyle, *The Social Order of a Frontier Community: Jacksonville, Illinois, 1825–70* (Urbana: University of Illinois Press, 1978; reprint, Urbana: Illini Books, 1983), 54–58. For additional accounts of slaves kidnapped from Illinois, see Lea Vandervelde, *Redemption Songs: Suing for Freedom before Dred Scott* (New York: Oxford Press, 2014), 66–116.

19. Dillon, "Antislavery Movement in Illinois, 1809–1844," 293–325; Owen W. Muelder, *The Underground Railroad in Western Illinois* (Jefferson, N.C.: McFarland, 2008),

21–22; Charles N. Zucker, "The Free Negro Question: Race Relations in Ante-Bellum Illinois, 1801–1860" (PhD diss., Northwestern University, 1972), 266–68; Jonathan Blanchard, *Memoir of Rev. Levi Spencer: Successively Pastor of the Congregational Church at Canton, Bloomington, and Peoria, Illinois* (Cincinnati, Ohio: American Reform Tract and Book Society, 1856), 96–99; John W. E. Lovejoy to Elizabeth Lovejoy, 26 July 1836, box 2, folder 7, Elijah Parish Lovejoy Papers, Wickett-Wiswall Collection, Texas Tech University Southwest Collection/Special Collections Library; *Western Citizen* (Chicago), 26 July 1842. For the salience of these issues in the nation at large, consult Russel B. Nye, *Fettered Freedom: Civil Liberties and the Slavery Controversy, 1830–1860* (East Lansing: Michigan State College Press, 1949), 94–176.

20. Davis, *Free Discussion Suppressed in Peoria*, 2 (quotes); Dillon, "Antislavery Movement in Illinois, 1809–1844," 268; David Davis to William P. Walker, 7 Dec 1843, box 1, A-2, David Davis Family Papers, ALPLM. For a more extended discussion of the free-speech issue in Peoria, see Dana Elizabeth Weiner, *Race and Rights: Fighting Slavery and Prejudice in the Old Northwest, 1830–1870* (DeKalb: Northern Illinois University Press, 2013), 81–85, 108–25. Weiner extensively documents a wide range of conflicts between slavery and freedom in the Old Northwest.

21. Cyrus Edwards to Joseph Gillespie, 14 April 1835, folder 1, SC 558, Joseph Gillespie Papers; Lucinda Casteen to Elisa Tomson, undated, folder 2, SC 2056, Lucinda Casteen Papers, ALPLM; J. W. Clinton, ed., "Letters from Ogle and Carroll Counties, 1838–1857," *TISHS* (1907): 259 (Wallace quote); John C. Abbott, ed., *Journey to New Switzerland: Travel Account of the Koepfli and Suppiger Family to St. Louis on the Mississippi and the Founding of New Switzerland in the State of Illinois* (Carbondale: Southern Illinois University Press, 1987), 193 (Swiss quotes), 206; Theodore Engelmann to Gretchen Hilgard, 21 Jan 1837, box 2, folder 1, Engelmann-Kircher Family Papers, ALPLM (German quote).

22. Evarts Boutell Greene and Charles Manfred Thompson, eds., *Governors' Letter-Books, 1840–1853*, vol. 7, *CISHL* (Springfield: Illinois State Historical Library, 1911), 69–78 (quotes 76, 73, 75, and 77); *Illinois State Register* (Springfield), 17 Jan 1845 ("common" quote); David Davis to William P. Walker, 31 Dec 1844, box 1, A-3, David Davis Family Papers, ALPLM. For other examples of interstate conflict over fugitive slaves, see Stanley Harrold, *Border War: Fighting over Slavery before the Civil War* (Chapel Hill: University of North Carolina Press, 2010), 72–93.

23. *Cornelius v. Cohen, Illinois Reports* (Breese), 131–32; *Fanny v. Montgomery*, ibid., 247–50; *Choisser v. Hargrave*, ibid. (1 Scammon), 318–20; *Boon v. Juliet*, ibid., 259 ("affecting" quotes); *Kinney v. Cook*, ibid. (3 Scammon), 232–33 ("presumption" quotes); *Jarrot v. Jarrot*, ibid. (2 Gilman), 30; Harris, *History of Negro Servitude in Illinois*, 117–18, 121.

24. William M. Wiecek, *The Sources of Antislavery Constitutionalism in America, 1760–1848* (Ithaca, N.Y.: Cornell University Press, 1977), 20–39; Paul Finkelman, "Slavery, the 'More Perfect Union,' and the Prairie State," *IHJ* 80 (Winter 1987): 253–54.

25. *Willard v. The People of the State of Illinois, Illinois Reports* (4 Scammon), 472, 476 (quotes); *Illinois State Register* (Springfield), 10 Dec 1847 (Wilson quote); Harris,

History of Negro Servitude in Illinois, 110–12; Finkelman, "Slavery, the 'More Perfect Union,' and the Prairie State," 254–56; Paul Finkelman, *An Imperfect Union: Slavery, Federalism, and Comity* (Chapel Hill: University of North Carolina Press, 1981), 97–100.

26. *Jarrot v. Jarrot, Illinois Reports*, 12; *Illinois State Register* (Springfield), 10 Dec 1847 (Wilson quotes); Barnes and Dumond, *Letters of Theodore Dwight Weld, Angelina Grimké Weld, and Sarah Grimké*, 2:1005 ("battle ground" quotes).

27. *Eells v. The People of the State of Illinois, Illinois Reports* (4 Scammon), 504 (quotes), 509–10, 511 (quotes); Finkelman, "Slavery, the 'More Perfect Union,' and the Prairie State," 264; Harris, *History of Negro Servitude in Illinois*, 114–15.

28. *Illinois State Register* (Springfield), 16 Feb 1844 (quotes); Arthur C. Cole, ed., *The Constitutional Debates of 1847*, vol. 14, CISHL (Springfield: Illinois State Historical Library, 1919), xxvi, 237 ("negro-stealing" quote); Stephen Middleton, ed., *The Black Laws in the Old Northwest: A Documentary History* (Westwood, Conn.: Greenwood, 1993), 295, 300 ("high misdemeanor" quote); Jerome B. Meites, "The 1847 Illinois Constitutional Convention and Persons of Color," *JISHS* 108 (Fall/Winter 2015): 277–86 (quotes, 282); Finkelman, *Imperfect Union*, 154. For speeches that illuminate the perspective of central and southern Illinois Democrats on these issues, see the *Illinois State Register* (Springfield), 7 March 1845, and *Sangamo Journal* (Springfield), 1 July 1847.

29. A[lexander] B[ryan] Johnson to Sidney Breese, 25 May 1848, box 1, folder 8, Sidney Breese Papers, ALPLM; Arthur Charles Cole, *The Era of the Civil War, 1848–1870* (Springfield: Illinois Centennial Commission, 1919; reprint, Urbana: University of Illinois Press, 1987), 67–68.

30. *Western Citizen* (Chicago), 8 April, 30 June ("arts" quote), and 14 July 1846 ("robber-rulers" quote); 13 July 1847; 1 Feb 1848.

31. Gabor Boritt, *Lincoln and the Economics of the American Dream* (Memphis: Memphis State University Press, 1978), 115; *Weekly North-Western Gazette* (Galena), 27 March (quote) and 21 Aug (quote) 1846; *Journal* (Chicago), 2 April 1845 (quotes); 28th Cong., 1st Sess., *CG-NU* (17 Jan 1844), *Appendix*, 236 (Hardin quote); *Illinois Journal* (Springfield), 6 Jan 1848.

32. For Illinois Whig opposition to the annexation of Texas and slavery's extension, see the *Telegraph* (Alton), 30 Dec 1843; 11 May, 22 June ("robbery" quote), 27 July, 17 Aug, 12 Oct, and 2 ("extension" quote) and 30 ("slave holding" quote) Nov 1844; 12 April 1845; *Journal* (Chicago), 2, 21, 25, and 27 Sept, 21 and 25 Oct, and 11 and 27 Nov 1844; 11 and 21 March and 30 Dec 1845; *North Western Gazette and Galena Advertiser* (Galena), 20 Sept 1844; *CW*, 1:337. For the Whigs' support of the acquisition of Oregon, see 28th Cong., 1st Sess., *CG-NU* (3 June 1844), *Appendix*, 599; 29th Cong., 1st Sess., *CG-NU* (3 Jan 1846), 136–37, (29 Jan 1846), *Appendix*, 151–54; *Illinois State Register* (Springfield), 23 May and 13 June 1845; Robert W. Johannsen, *Stephen A. Douglas* (New York: Oxford University Press, 1973; reprint, Urbana: University of Illinois Press, 1997), 148, 169–70. On the Illinois Whigs and expansion more generally, see Eric John Bradner, "The Attitude of Illinois to Western Expansion in the 1840s"

(PhD diss., Northwestern University, 1942), 40–51, 69–116, 123–35, 153–56, 171; and Norman E. Tutorow, *Texas Annexation and the Mexican War: A Political Study of the Old Northwest* (Palo Alto, Calif.: Chadwick House, 1978), 68–69, 95–98, 112–13, 117, 133–35, 153–55, 174–80, 196–97, 249–50, 262–63, 284–88.

33. 28th Cong., 2nd Sess., *CG-NU* (15 Jan 1845), *Appendix*, 276 (Hardin quotes); 29th Cong., 1st Sess., *CG-NU* (26 March 1846), 558–59; James Shields to Sidney Breese, 13 July 1844, box 1, folder 6, Sidney Breese Papers, ALPLM ("nationality" quote). In *Storm over Texas: The Annexation Controversy and the Road to Civil War* (Oxford: Oxford University Press, 2005), 146–81, Joel H. Silbey emphasizes the corrosive long-term consequences of the annexation of Texas for party politics.

34. *Western Citizen* (Chicago), 11 July 1848 (quotes); Harris, *History of Negro Servitude in Illinois*, 165–66. For the formation of the Free Soil Party, see John Mayfield, *Rehearsal for Republicanism: Free Soil and the Politics of Antislavery* (Port Washington, N.Y.: Kennikat, 1980), 3–125; Joseph G. Rayback, *Free Soil: The Election of 1848* (Lexington: University Press of Kentucky, 1970), 171–230; Frederick J. Blue, *The Free Soilers: Third Party Politics, 1848–54* (Urbana: University of Illinois Press, 1973), 1–80; Brooks, *Liberty Power*, 129–49.

35. *Western Citizen* (Chicago), 22 Aug ("Liberty" quote); 17 Oct 1848 (platform quotes); Harris, *History of Negro Servitude in Illinois*, 168–70; Moore and Moore, *His Brother's Blood*, 83–84, 87.

36. *Advocate* (Belleville), 2 Dec 1847; 11 May, 15 June, and 20 July 1848; *Illinois State Register* (Springfield), 5 Feb, 19 March, 8 Oct, and 17 and 24 Dec 1847; 21 Jan ("people," "cordial," and "original" quotes), 14 and 28 ("agitation" quote) April, 5 May, 9 June, 7 and 21 (Shields quotes) July, 8 Sept, 6 Oct, and 3 Nov 1848; A[lexander] B[ryan] Johnson to Sidney Breese, 23 and 29 June 1848, box 1, folder 8, Sidney Breese Papers, ALPLM; Johannsen, *Douglas*, 233. For the many Democratic county conventions that totally ignored slavery, see the *State Register*, 24 March, 7, 21, and 28 April, and 5 May 1848; and the *Democratic Press* (Peoria), 28 June 1848.

37. *Weekly Democrat* (Chicago), 22 Feb, 9 and 30 March, 13 and 20 (quote) April, 11, 18, and 25 May, 13 July, and 7 Sept 1847; 15, 22, and 29 Feb, 28 March, 4, 11, 18, and 25 April, 2 and 9 May, and 13 and 20 June 1848; *Illinois State Register* (Springfield), 17 March 1848; *IE*, 7; Stanley L. Jones, "John Wentworth and Anti-Slavery in Chicago to 1856," *Mid-America: An Historical Review* 36 (July 1954): 149–53.

38. *Weekly Democrat* (Chicago), 16 May, 20 June (quote), 15 Aug, 19 Sept, 10 Oct, and 7 Nov 1848; *Illinois State Register* (Springfield), 14 and 28 Jan, 18 Feb, 10 March, 7, 14, and 28 (convention quotes) April, and 21 July 1848 ("evils" quote); Carroll Francis Van Deventer, "The Free Soil Party in the Northwest in the Elections of 1848" (PhD diss., University of Illinois, 1968), 126–30. For the national sundering of northern Democrats on this issue, see Sean Wilentz, *The Rise of American Democracy: Jefferson to Lincoln* (New York: Norton, 2005), 594–601, 608–10, 614–31.

39. On Whig Provisoism, see the *Illinois Journal* (Springfield), 7 Oct and 25 Nov 1847; 13 Jan, 1 June, and 6 and 11 July 1848; *Journal* (Chicago), 29 Dec 1847; 3 April and 1 May 1848; John F. Henry to David Davis, 26 July 1848, box 1, A-11, David Davis

Family Papers; J. M. Hinkle to T. Lyle Dickey, 19 Aug 1848, box 1, folder 15, Wallace-Dickey Papers, ALPLM; Cole, *Era of the Civil War*, 60–61.

40. Appendix, table 1. James L. Huston argues that Democratic voters' hostility to "slavery's westward expansion" caused them to sit out the election. See "The Illinois Political Realignment of 1844–1860: Revisiting the Analysis," *Journal of the Civil War Era* 1 (Dec 2011): 508–20 (quote, 520).

41. The numbers above are all rough estimates because the available data and the political confusion produced by the rise of the Free Soilers makes a more precise calculation of defectors from Illinois's Whig and Democratic Parties very difficult. However, the calculations do account for the intense concentration of Free Soil votes in specific northern counties. Failing to recognize this important factor, previous historians have underestimated the number of new voters who supported Van Buren. For instance, voters in Boone, Bureau, Cook, DeKalb, DuPage, Kane, Kendall, La Salle, Lake, McHenry, Ogle, Putnam, Whiteside, Will, and Winnebago Counties cast 11,253 ballots for Van Buren, or 71.7 percent of his total vote. In 1844 those fifteen counties recorded 18,889 votes in the presidential election, including 2,259 for the Liberty Party candidate. However, voters in those counties cast 29,012 votes in the 1848 presidential election. This 53.6 percent increase closely parallels the counties' roughly 51 percent increase in population since 1844, thus demonstrating the presence of many new voters, whose support for the Free Soil Party can be deduced from voting records. Comparison of the respective 1848 Whig and Democratic presidential returns to the 1848 Whig congressional and Democratic gubernatorial returns indicate that Van Buren poached at least 5,200 Whig and Democratic votes in those counties, although 6,200 is a more realistic estimate because the comparison understates defectors. The subtraction of those 6,200 votes from Van Buren's total of 11,253, and the further subtraction of the 2,259 Liberty Party votes in 1844, which Van Buren almost certainly retained, suggests that approximately 2,800 new voters joined the Free Soil Party in those fifteen counties. *IE*, 118, 120–23, 125–26. For other analyses, see Thomas B. Alexander, "Harbinger of the Collapse of the Second Two-Party System: The Free Soil Party of 1848," in *A Crisis of Republicanism: American Politics in the Civil War Era*, ed. Lloyd E. Ambrosius (Lincoln: University of Nebraska Press, 1990), 17–54; Michael F. Holt, *The Rise and Fall of the American Whig Party: Jacksonian Politics and the Onset of the Civil War* (Oxford: Oxford University Press, 1999), 377–78; Rayback, *Free Soil*, 300.

42. Appendix, table 2.

43. *Weekly Democrat* (Chicago), 14 Nov 1848.

Chapter 5. Stephen A. Douglas and the Northern Democratic Origins of the Kansas-Nebraska Act, 1849–1854

1. Appendix, table 3; *Weekly Democrat* (Chicago), 9 Jan 1849; 16th Gen. Ass., 1st Sess., *House Journal* (9 Jan 1849), 52 ("constitutional" quote); *Illinois State Register* (Springfield), 1 Dec 1848.

2. David M. Potter, *The Impending Crisis, 1848–1861* (New York: Harper and Row, 1976), 18–23, 63–76; 30th Cong., 2nd Sess., *CG-NU* (13 Dec 1848), 1, 39; Leonard L.

Richards, *The Slave Power: The Free North and Southern Domination, 1780–1860* (Baton Rouge: Louisiana State University Press, 2000), 151–54. The computation of the proviso vote is my own.

3. Don E. Fehrenbacher, *Chicago Giant: A Biography of "Long John" Wentworth* (Madison: American History Research Center, 1957), 86–91; Robert W. Johannsen, *Stephen A. Douglas* (New York: Oxford University Press, 1973; reprint, Urbana: University of Illinois Press, 1997), 240–51; Mark J. Stegmaier, *Texas, New Mexico, and the Compromise of 1850: Boundary Dispute and Sectional Crisis* (Kent, Ohio: Kent State University Press, 1996), 39–44.

4. Fehrenbacher, *Chicago Giant*, 91–99; Johannsen, *Douglas*, 262–94; Potter, *Impending Crisis*, 90–108; Stegmaier, *Texas, New Mexico, and the Compromise of 1850*, 85–114, 135–200; Michael F. Holt, *The Rise and Fall of the American Whig Party: Jacksonian Politics and the Onset of the Civil War* (New York: Oxford University Press, 1999), 435–532.

5. Fehrenbacher, *Chicago Giant*, 99–103; Johannsen, *Douglas*, 294–98; Potter, *Impending Crisis*, 108–20; Stegmaier, *Texas, New Mexico, and the Compromise of 1850*, 201–20, 261–314; Holt, *Rise and Fall*, 532–52.

6. Stegmaier, *Texas, New Mexico, and the Compromise of 1850*, 85–114, 135–220, 261–322 (quote, 322), 329, 345; Holt, *Rise and Fall*, 435–36, 464; Don E. Fehrenbacher, *Sectional Crisis and Southern Constitutionalism* (Baton Rouge: Louisiana State University Press, 1995), 39–44; Thomas Brown, *Politics and Statesmanship: Essays on the American Whig Party* (New York: Columbia University Press, 1985), 204–11; Christopher Childers, *The Failure of Popular Sovereignty: Slavery, Manifest Destiny, and the Radicalization of Southern Politics* (Lawrence: University Press of Kansas, 2012), 166–99. For a contrasting interpretation that emphasizes the significance of party patronage and factional rivalries to passage of the compromise measures, see Holt, *Rise and Fall*, 383–552.

7. *Advocate* (Belleville), 23 May 1850; William Richardson to Chauncey L. Higbee, 18 May 1850, SC 1267, William Richardson Papers; James Conkling, Speech at Mechanicsburg, Sangamon County, Illinois, 4 July 1850, box 1, folder 4, page 22, Conkling Family Papers, ALPLM; *Weekly Democrat* (Chicago), 2 Feb 1850; *Illinois Daily Journal* (Springfield), 27 Dec 1849; 6 Feb, 15 April, and 2 May 1850; *Whig* (Quincy), 22 Jan, 19 Feb, 18 June, 30 July, 17 Sept, and 1 and 8 Oct 1850; Arthur Charles Cole, *The Era of the Civil War, 1848–1870* (Springfield: Illinois Centennial Commission, 1919; reprint, Urbana: University of Illinois Press, 1987), 69–70.

8. 31st Cong., 1st Sess., *CG-LOC* (7 March 1850), *Appendix*, 274 (Webster quote), *CG-NU* (13–14 March 1850), *Appendix*, 366, 371–73, (25 March 1850), *Appendix*, 411, (3 April 1850), *Appendix*, 423–24, (5 April 1850), 646–49, (29 Aug 1850), 1700–1701; William Bissell to Joseph Gillespie, 19 April 1850, Joseph Gillespie Papers, folder 1, SC 558, ALPLM; *Democratic Press* (Peoria), 9 Jan, 6 Feb, 6 March, and 8 May 1850; Cole, *Era of the Civil War*, 70; *Illinois Daily Journal* (Springfield), 6 Feb, 15 April ("California" quote), and 2 May 1850; *Weekly Democrat* (Chicago), 21 Sept 1850 (Wentworth quote); Fehrenbacher, *Chicago Giant*, 102.

9. *Weekly Democrat* (Chicago), 19 Jan, 2 and 23 ("abhorrence" quotes) Feb, 16 March, 6, 20, and 27 April, and 13 July 1850; Stanley L. Jones, "John Wentworth and Anti-Slavery in Chicago to 1856," *Mid-America: An Historical Review* 36 (July 1954): 154–55; *Western Citizen* (Chicago), 11 June 1850 (Joliet quotes); *Galena Advertiser*, clipped by the *City Advertiser* (Rock Island), 23 April 1850; 31st Cong., 1st Sess., *CG-NU* (3 June 1850), 1119 (Hale quotes); Cole, *Era of the Civil War*, 68; Fehrenbacher, *Sectional Crisis and Southern Constitutionalism*, 43; Potter, *Impending Crisis*, 112–13. The Utah bill was the only bill that measured northern sentiment on popular sovereignty because House leaders combined the New Mexico bill and the Texas boundary bill for strategic purposes.

10. Appendix, table 4. The House and Senate introduced different resolutions on the slavery issue, and only the Senate resolutions passed both houses. The House members approved the Senate resolutions in one vote, while they approved individual resolutions for the House version. Statistics in the text therefore represent a cobbling together of votes on resolutions that were worded differently, but were essentially the same. For the Unionist convictions that precipitated the resolutions, see the *Advocate* (Belleville), 28 Nov 1850; 2 Jan 1851.

11. Fehrenbacher, *Chicago Giant*, 117–23; *Rock Island Republican*, clipped by the *Advertiser* (Rock Island), 1 Sept 1852; *Advocate* (Belleville), 18 Aug 1852; Donald Bruce Johnson, comp., *National Party Platforms*, vol. 1, *1840–1956* (Urbana: University of Illinois Press, 1978), 17 (quotes), 20–21; Richard Yates to Simeon Francis, 9 Sept 1852, box 1, folder 3, Yates Family Papers, ALPLM; *Daily Democrat* (Chicago), 17 May 1852.

12. Johnson, *National Party Platforms*, 1:16 (quote), 20; *CW*, 2:152.

13. Johannsen, *Douglas*, 304–21, 341–43; 32nd Cong., 1st Sess., *CG-LOC* (22 July 1852), 1889; Abdus Samad, "The Free Banking Experience in Illinois" (PhD diss., University of Illinois at Chicago, 1991), 123, 176; *LSAD*, 188, 235 (quotes), 272–82; *Advertiser* (Rock Island), 1 Sept 1852 ("question" quote). For bipartisan support of a homestead law, see Cole, *Era of the Civil War*, 90–91; for bipartisan support of railroad land grants, see *CW*, 2:26–27, and Peter Delva Brown, "The Economic Views of Illinois Democrats, 1836–1861" (PhD diss., Boston University, 1970), 113–15; for bipartisan support of rivers and harbors improvements, see the *Advocate* (Belleville), 1 Sept 1852, and Theodore Calvin Pease and James G. Randall, eds., *The Diary of Orville Hickman Browning, 1850–1881*, vol. 20, *CISHL* (Springfield: Illinois State Historical Library, 1925), 68–69, 74. Michael F. Holt's work is especially important in explaining how economic changes eroded Jacksonian economic debate during this period. See Holt, *The Political Crisis of the 1850s* (New York: Wiley, 1978), 102–18; and "From Center to Periphery: The Market Revolution and Major-Party Conflict, 1835–1880," in *The Market Revolution in America: Social, Political, and Religious Expressions, 1800–1880*, ed. Melvyn Stokes and Stephen Conway (Charlottesville: University Press of Virginia, 1996), 242–50.

14. *Illinois State Register* (Springfield), 6 Nov 1851 ("mutual" quotes); *LSAD*, 223 ("valueless" quotes); Johannsen, *Douglas*, 306–17; Johannsen, *The Frontier, the Union, and Stephen A. Douglas* (Urbana: University of Illinois Press, 1989), 77–102.

15. W. Edwards to Benjamin Hinch, 19 Oct 1851, folder 2, SC 1763, Benjamin P. Hinch Papers, ALPLM; 33rd Cong., 1st Sess., *CG-NU* (13 June 1854), *Appendix*, 966; *Advertiser* (Rock Island), 31 Aug 1853.

16. Stephen L. Hansen, *The Making of the Third Party System: Voters and Parties in Illinois, 1850–1876* (Ann Arbor: UMI Research, 1980), 11–17, 205–6; Barbara Lawrence and Nedra Branz, eds., *The Flagg Correspondence: Selected Letters, 1816–1854* (Carbondale: Southern Illinois University Press, 1986), 131; Evarts B. Greene, ed., "Letters to Gustav Koerner, 1837–1863," *TISHS* (1907), 241–42 (politician's quote); David Davis to William P. Walker, 17 Oct 1852, box 2, A-20, David Davis Family Papers, ALPLM. For the voter turnout figures, see Appendix, table 5. For a breakdown of nonvoting by party and region, see James L. Huston, "The Illinois Political Realignment of 1844–1860: Revisiting the Analysis," *Journal of the Civil War Era* 1 (Dec 2011): 510–11, 520–23. It is difficult to ascertain purely from voting records if voters switched parties. In *The Origins of the Republican Party: 1852–1856* (New York: Oxford University Press, 1987), 482, William E. Gienapp's statistical estimates suggest that Illinois's Whigs, Democrats, and Free Soilers did not switch parties between 1848 and 1852. James Huston's estimates, broken down by region, suggest voters switched parties in the northern counties. Meanwhile, Hansen's calculations suggest considerable fluidity in voter loyalties. I have drawn heavily on Hansen because other documentary evidence appears to bear him out.

17. Bruce Levine, *The Spirit of 1848: German Immigrants, Labor Conflict, and the Coming of the Civil War* (Urbana: University of Illinois Press, 1992), 15–16, 57–64; James Manning Bergquist, "The Political Attitudes of the German Immigrant in Illinois, 1848–1860" (PhD diss., Northwestern University, 1966), 21–46; Gienapp, *Origins of the Republican Party*, 37–67; Bessie Louise Pierce, *A History of Chicago*, vol. 1, *The Beginning of a City, 1673–1848* (New York: Knopf, 1937), 179–86, 418; Pease and Randall, *Diary of Orville Hickman Browning*, 79–80; James L. D. Morrison to Lincoln, 13 Dec 1848, SC 914A, Letters to Abraham Lincoln, 1848–1861; F[rancis] Arenz to unknown correspondent, 15 Oct 1850; John B. Shaw to Richard Yates, 22 Aug 1850, box 1, folder 2, Yates Family Papers; O. H. Browning to John Courts Bagby, 12 Nov 1852, John Courts Bagby Papers, folder 1, SC 61; Lyman Trumbull to Sisters, 5 March 1848, box 1, folder 6, Benjamin Trumbull Family Papers, ALPLM.

18. For the temperance petitions, see Bills, Resolutions, and Related General Assembly Records, 1851, record series 600.001, folders 534–40, ISA. Also see B-66, B-322, BC-ALPLM; Pierce, *History of Chicago*, 2:199, 435–39.

19. E. Rust, ed., "A List of the Members Composing the Seventeenth General Assembly of the State of Illinois," *Illinois Organ*, 1851, B-309; Rust, ed., "A List of the Members Composing the Eighteenth General Assembly of the State of Illinois," B-175, BC-ALPLM; *IE*, 8–9, 128.

20. N. Dwight Harris, *The History of Negro Servitude in Illinois and of the Slavery Agitation in that State, 1719–1864* (Chicago: McClurg, 1904; reprint, New York: Haskell House, 1969), 177–85; *Western Citizen* (Chicago), 7 Aug and 4 Dec 1849; 1 and 15 Oct, and 24 Dec 1850 (quote); 20 July and 17 Aug 1852; *IE*, 130.

21. *IE*, 128, 130, 133; Coles, *Era of the Civil War*, 107–12; John Moses to Richard Yates, 28 March 1852; Martin Cassell to Yates, 24 April 1852; Yates to Simeon Francis, 9 Sept 1852; Alex B. Morcan to Yates, 29 Oct 1852, box 1, folder 3, Yates Family Papers, ALPLM; Gienapp, *Origins of the Republican Party*, 13–35.

22. Lawrence and Branz, *Flagg Correspondence*, 152 (quote); Cole, *Era of the Civil War*, 27–52; Johannsen, *Douglas*, 304–17; Fehrenbacher, *Chicago Giant*, 105–12.

23. William Cronon, *Nature's Metropolis: Chicago and Great West* (New York: Norton, 1991), 55–206, 310–33; James William Putnam, *The Illinois-Michigan Canal: A Study in Economic History* (Chicago: University of Chicago Press, 1918), 92–111; Jesse B. Thomas, *Report of Jesse B. Thomas, as a Member of the Executive Committee Appointed by the Chicago Harbor and River Convention, of the Statistics concerning the City of Chicago* (Chicago: Wilson, 1847), 12–19; Pierce, *History of Chicago*, 2:492; Cole, *Era of the Civil War*, 5–6, 75–77, 84–85.

24. Illinois's census data: 15th Gen. Ass., 1st Sess., *House Reports* (2 Jan 1847), 46–48; *Illinois State Register* (Springfield), 16 Oct 1855; 3 and 5 Jan 1856. For 1855, I corrected tabulation errors for the total state population and divided the regions as follows: southern Illinois's northern boundary included Madison, Bond, Fayette, Effingham, Jasper, and Crawford Counties; and northern Illinois's southern boundary included Mercer, Henry, Stark, Marshall, La Salle, Grundy, and Kankakee Counties. Chicago's census data: *Fourth Annual Review of the Commerce, Manufactures, and the Public and Private Improvements of Chicago, for the Year 1855; With a Full Statement of Her System of Railroads: And a General Synopsis of the Business of the City* (Chicago: Democratic Press, 1856), 22.

25. David Davis to William P. Walker, 17 Oct 1852, box 2, A-20, David Davis Family Papers, ALPLM; Cole, *Era of the Civil War*, 12–26; Levine, *Spirit of 1848*, 57–62. The 1845 and 1855 state censuses did not include nativity information. I calculated the 1850s nativity data from the table in Don E. Fehrenbacher, "Illinois Political Attitudes, 1854–1861" (PhD diss., University of Chicago, 1951), 7.

26. David E. Schob, *Hired Hands and Plowboys: Farm Labor in the Midwest, 1815–60* (Urbana: University of Illinois Press, 1975), 4; Lyman Trumbull to John Trumbull, 13 Oct 1851, box 1, folder 3, Lyman Trumbull Family Papers; David Davis to William P. Walker, 17 Oct 1852, box 2, A-20, David Davis Family Papers, ALPLM; Cole, *Era of the Civil War*, 7–8, 85–89; Stephen J. Buck, "Political and Economic Transformation in the Civil War Era: DuPage County, Illinois, 1830–1880" (PhD diss., Northern Illinois University, 1992), 103; Susan Sessions Rugh, *Our Common Country: Family Farming, Culture, and Community in the Nineteenth-Century Midwest* (Bloomington: Indiana University Press, 2001), 59.

27. James L. Huston, *The British Gentry, the Southern Planter, and the Northern Family Farmer: Agriculture and Sectional Antagonism in North America* (Baton Rouge: Louisiana State University Press, 2015), 77–81, 93–96; Cole, *Era of the Civil War*, 85; Schob, *Hired Hands and Plowboys*, 251, 257; Jeremy Atack and Peter Passell, *A New Economic View of American History from Colonial Times to 1940*, 2nd ed. (New York: Norton, 1994), 274–79; John Mack Faragher, *Sugar Creek: Life on the Illinois Prairie*

(New Haven, Conn.: Yale University Press, 1986), 184–87, 266; Buck, "Political and Economic Transformation," 102–10, 498; Allan G. Bogue, *From Prairie to Corn Belt: Farming on the Illinois and Iowa Prairies in the Nineteenth Century* (Chicago: University of Chicago Press, 1963; reprint, Ames: Iowa State University Press, 1994), 25–28, 58–66, 184–87.

28. John L. Andriot, ed. and comp., *Population Abstract of the United States*, vol. 1, *Tables* (McLean, Va.: Andriot, 1983), 182; Pierce, *History of Chicago*, 2:153–56, 160–61, 164–65, 186–89, 464, 500; Robin L. Einhorn, *Property Rules: Political Economy in Chicago, 1833–1872* (Chicago: University of Chicago Press, 1991), 112–14, 250–51; Hartmut Keil and John B. Jentz, eds., *German Workers in Chicago: A Documentary History of Working-Class Culture from 1850 to World War I* (Urbana: University of Illinois Press, 1988), 21–39 (quotes 25, 28, 29, 32, 36, and 37); Keil and Jentz, eds., *German Workers in Industrial Chicago, 1850–1910: A Comparative Perspective* (DeKalb: Northern Illinois University Press, 1983), 164–65. For a similar growth in inequality in Jacksonville, see Don Harrison Doyle, *The Social Order of a Frontier Community: Jacksonville, Illinois, 1825–70* (Urbana: University of Illinois Press, 1978; reprint, Urbana: Illini Books, 1983), 79–108, 128, 261–63.

29. Huston, *British Gentry, the Southern Planter, and the Northern Family Farmer*, 77; *Western Citizen* (Chicago), 28 March 1848; 9 Jan and 11 Dec 1849; 25 June 1850 (quote); 29 June 1852; "Land Limitation and Homestead Exemption," Bills, Resolutions, and Related General Assembly Records, 1851, record series 600.001, folders 541–542, ISA; Cole, *Era of the Civil War*, 89–91.

30. *Whig* (Quincy), 24 Oct 1853 (quotes); Cole, *Era of the Civil War*, 240–45.

31. Lyman Trumbull to John Trumbull, 13 Oct 1851, box 1, folder 3, Lyman Trumbull Family Papers; James Conkling, Speech at Hall of Sons of Temperance (p. 17), 5 Feb 1852, box 1, folder 5, Conkling Family Papers; J. C. Dickerson to Augustus French, 30 Sept 1851, box 1, folder 2, French-Wicker Family Papers; A. Russel to Mrs. James C. Murray, 30 Jan 1851, SC 1759, A. Russel Papers, ALPLM; William Bross, *Banking, Its History, Commercial Importance, and Social and Moral Influence* (Chicago: Langdon and Rounds, 1852), 19–20.

32. *New York Daily Times*, clipped by the *Tribune* (Chicago), 9 May 1853 (quote); *Alton Telegraph*, clipped by the *Tribune* (Chicago), 30 May 1853; Cole, *Era of the Civil War*, 9–12; James Conkling, Speech at Hall of Sons of Temperance (p. 11), 5 Feb. 1852, box 1, folder 5, Conkling Family Papers, ALPLM.

33. *LSAD*, 267–72 (quotes, 267). Douglas's motives have long been a source of contention among historians. Three motives have received the most emphasis: his desire to organize western territories in order to build a Pacific Railroad, his goal of invigorating the Democratic Party, and his principled support of popular sovereignty as territorial policy. For the argument that he sought to promote a Pacific Railroad, see Frank Heywood Hodder, "Genesis of the Kansas-Nebraska Act," *Proceedings of the State Historical Society of Wisconsin* (1912): 69–86; Hodder, "The Railroad Background of the Kansas-Nebraska Act," *MVHR* 12 (June 1925): 3–22; and Potter, *Impending Crisis*, 145–76. For interpretations that emphasize his desire to resuscitate the Democratic

Party, see Holt, *Political Crisis of the 1850s*, 139–49; Gienapp, *Origins of the Republican Party*, 69–87; Michael A. Morrison, *Slavery and the American West: The Eclipse of Manifest Destiny and the Coming of the Civil War* (Chapel Hill: The University of North Carolina Press, 1997), 126–56; and Holt, *Rise and Fall of the American Whig Party*, 804–7. For the argument that he was deeply committed to the principle of popular sovereignty, see Robert W. Johannsen, "The Kansas-Nebraska Act and Territorial Government in the United States," in *Territorial Kansas: Studies Commemorating the Centennial*, ed., Committee on Social Science Studies (Lawrence: University of Kansas Publications, 1954), 17–32; Johannsen, "Stephen A. Douglas, Popular Sovereignty and the Territories," *Historian* 22 (Aug 1960): 378–95; and Johannsen, *Douglas*, 401–34. Additionally, Harry Jaffa contended that Douglas boldly sought "simultaneously to open the floodgates of free-soil expansion and to avert civil war," while Allan Nevins brilliantly argued that Douglas intended the bill to solve a handful of political concerns simultaneously. See Harry V. Jaffa, *Crisis of the House Divided: An Interpretation of the Issues in the Lincoln-Douglas Debates* (New York: Doubleday, 1959), 41–180 (quote, 62); and Allan Nevins, *Ordeal of the Union*, vol. 2, *A House Dividing, 1852–1857* (New York: Scribner's, 1947), 78–159. The argument of this chapter incorporates many insights from prior scholarship, but emphasizes to a far greater degree Douglas's determination to end the nation's conflict over slavery and freedom permanently.

34. Johannsen, *Douglas*, 163–65, 220–21, 391, 395–400; *LSAD*, 270 (quotes).

35. Johannsen, *Douglas*, 401–26 (quotes, 415, 426); Robert R. Russel, "The Issues in the Congressional Struggle over the Kansas-Nebraska Bill, 1854," *JSH* 29 (May 1963): 192–210. For southern influence on the bill, also consult P. Orman Ray, *The Repeal of the Missouri Compromise: Its Origin and Authorship* (Cleveland: Clark, 1909); Ray, "The Genesis of the Kansas-Nebraska Act," *American Historical Association Annual Report* 1 (1914): 261–80; Roy F. Nichols, "The Kansas-Nebraska Act: A Century of Historiography," *MVHR* 43 (Sept 1956): 187–212; Nichols, *Blueprints for Leviathan: American Style* (New York: Atheneum, 1963), 80–121; William W. Freehling, *The Road to Disunion*, vol. 1, *Secessionists at Bay, 1776–1854* (New York: Oxford University Press, 1990), 536–60.

36. 33rd Cong., 1st sess., *CG-NU* (30 Jan 1854), 279 ("geographical" quote), 280 ("trust" quote), (3 March 1854), *Appendix*, 337–38 (quotes).

37. H. M. Flint, *Life of Stephen A. Douglas, To Which Are Added His Speeches and Reports* (Philadelphia: Potter, 1863), 28 ("civilized" quotes); 33rd Cong., 1st sess., *CG-NU* (30 Jan 1854), 280 ("gist" quote); *LSAD*, 285, 319–20 ("understand" quotes); J. L. O'Sullivan to Stephen A. Douglas, 10 Feb 1854, box 4, folder 5, Stephen A. Douglas Papers, UChicago SCRC. James Lander advances the intriguing hypothesis that Douglas's racial views were shaped by the controversial scientific theory of polygenesis, or multiple creations, but making a judgment on this point is difficult given the limited documentary evidence. Lander, *Lincoln and Darwin: Shared Visions of Race, Science, and Religion* (Carbondale: Southern Illinois University Press, 2010), 76–86, 97–127. For other interpretations of Douglas's conception of slavery's morality, see Potter, *Impending Crisis*, 329, 340–42; David Zarefsky, *Lincoln, Douglas, and*

Slavery: In the Crucible of Public Debate (Chicago: University of Chicago, 1990), 166–97; James L. Huston, "Democracy by Scripture versus Democracy by Process: A Reflection on Stephen A. Douglas and Popular Sovereignty," *CWH* 63 (Sept 1997): 189–200; and John Burt, *Lincoln's Tragic Pragmatism: Lincoln, Douglas, and Moral Conflict* (Cambridge, Mass.: Harvard University Press, 2013), 10–26, 367–97, 701.

38. 33rd Cong., 1st Sess., *CG-NU* (30 Jan 1854), 276 ("demarkation" quote), 281 ("betrayal" quote), (3 March 1854), *Appendix,* 338 ("Revolution" quotes); *LSAD,* 320–21 ("principle" quotes).

39. 33rd Cong., 1st Sess., *CG-NU* (30 Jan 1854), 282 ("blight" quote); Stephen A. Douglas, *Address of the Hon. Stephen A. Douglas, at the Annual Fair of the New-York State Agricultural Society,* held at Rochester, September, 1851 (Washington: Towers, 1852), 8 ("lever" quote), 24 ("interest" quote).

40. 33rd Cong., 1st Sess., *CG-NU* (30 Jan 1854), 279 ("idea" and "continue" quotes); *LSAD,* 289 ("candid" quotes), 320 ("temporal" quotes); Ray, *Repeal of the Missouri Compromise,* 195–219; Freehling, *Road to Disunion,* 1:550–53; Morrison, *Slavery and the American West,* 150–51. For a contrasting explanation about how northern Democratic attitudes toward slavery and popular sovereignty influenced Douglas in 1854, see John Ashworth, *Slavery, Capitalism, and Politics in the Antebellum Republic,* vol. 2, *The Coming of the Civil War, 1850–1861* (New York: Cambridge University Press, 2007), 416–36.

41. *LSAD,* 300 ("storm" quote), 322; 30th Cong., 1st Sess., *CG-NU* (20 April 1848), *Appendix,* 506 ("abolitionism" quote); 33rd Cong., 1st Sess. (30 Jan 1854), 279 ("tornado" quotes), (3 March 1854), *Appendix,* 332 ("believe" quotes), 338 ("popular" quotes); S. W. Johnston to Douglas, 24 March 1854; D. P. Rhodes to Douglas, 27 March 1854; Horatio Seymour Jr. to Douglas, 14 April 1854, box 4, folder 6, Stephen A. Douglas Papers, UChicago SCRC.

42. *LSAD,* 283–84 ("united" quotes), 289–90, 300 ("impart" quote), 330; John M. Palmer, *Recollections of John M. Palmer: The Story of an Earnest Life* (Cincinnati, Ohio: Clarke, 1901), 69; 33rd Cong., 1st Sess., *CG-NU* (3 March 1854), *Appendix,* 338 ("arbitrament" quote).

43. Cole, *Era of the Civil War,* 119–24; Johannsen, *Douglas,* 447–56; Pierce, *History of Chicago,* 2:206–9; *LSAD,* 308 (quote); *Weekly Herald* (Quincy), 27 March 1854; *Weekly Advocate* (Salem), 18 May 1854; *Free West* (Chicago), 30 March 1854; *Tribune* (Chicago), 6, 9, 13, and 25 Feb, 1, 2, 3, 9, and 25 March, and 8 June 1854; *Whig* (Quincy), 27 Feb 1854.

44. Appendix, table 6; *CW,* 2:322.

45. Nichols, *Blueprints for Leviathan,* 107–19; Fehrenbacher, *Sectional Crisis and Southern Constitutionalism,* 49; Potter, *Impending Crisis,* 167.

46. Southern Whigs also were located at the intersection of slavery and freedom, as their votes for compromise in 1850 demonstrated. However, their party was in its death throes after the 1852 election, and they had far less political power than northern Democrats. Nevertheless, their critical role enabling passage of the Nebraska bill underscored the responsibility of disunion's enemies for plunging the nation into sectional strife.

47. *LSAD*, 300 (quote).

48. This interpretation of the Kansas-Nebraska Act contradicts that of Michael F. Holt and William E. Gienapp, who deemphasize the act's significance both to the collapse of the Whig Party and the emergence of the Republican and Know Nothing Parties. For historiography on this and related points, see herewith chapter 6, n4.

Chapter 6. The Collapse of the Douglas Democracy, 1854–1860

1. Jeff L. Dugger to Richard Yates, 22 Jan 1854; J. J. Cassell to Yates, 20 Feb 1854 ("largest" quote), box 1, folder 5, Yates Family Papers, ALPLM; Victor B. Howard, "The Illinois Republican Party: Part I, A Party Organizer for the Republicans in 1854," *JISHS* 64 (Summer 1971): 128–31, 143–45; Arthur Charles Cole, *The Era of the Civil War, 1848–1870* (Springfield: Illinois Centennial Commission, 1919; reprint, Urbana: University of Illinois Press), 122–33; Robert W. Johannsen, *Stephen A. Douglas* (New York: Oxford University Press, 1973; reprint, Urbana: University of Illinois Press, 1997), 447–61 (Shields quote, 461); Bessie Louise Pierce, *A History of Chicago*, vol. 2, *From Town to City, 1848–1871* (New York: Knopf, 1940), 201–11.

2. 33rd Cong., 1st Sess., *CG-NU* (28 March 1854), *Appendix*, 448; Theodore Calvin Pease and James G. Randall, eds., *The Diary of Orville Hickman Browning, 1850–1881*, vol. 20, *CISHL* (Springfield: Illinois State Historical Library, 1925), 129–33; Paul Selby to Richard Yates, 8 April 1854 ("independence" quote); B. B. Hamilton to Yates, 17 April 1854 ("recreant" quote), box 1, folder 5, Yates Family Papers, ALPLM; Howard, "Illinois Republican Party: Part I," 125–44; *Weekly Whig* (Quincy), 6 and 13 Nov 1854; Bruce Levine, *The Spirit of 1848: German Immigrants, Labor Conflict, and the Coming of the Civil War* (Urbana: University of Illinois Press, 1992), 207; *Daily Illinois State Register* (Springfield), 7 July (McClernand quotes), 3, 7, 9, 10, 12, 14, and 31 Aug, and 16 Sept 1854.

3. "Maine Law State Temperance Convention," 7 Dec 1853, B-322, BC-ALPLM; Cole, *Era of the Civil War*, 205–9; David A. Smith to John Palmer, 18 Sept 1854 ("exterminating" quote), box 1, folder 5, John McAuley Palmer Papers II, ALPLM; John T. Flanagan, ed., "Letters by John Mason Peck," *JISHS* 47 (Autumn 1954): 297 ("skeered" quote).

4. Tyler Anbinder, *Nativism and Slavery: The Northern Know Nothings and the Politics of the 1850s* (New York: Oxford University Press, 1992), 3–22, 43; Cole, *Era of the Civil War*, 136–38; Thomas M. Keefe, "Chicago's Flirtation with Political Nativism, 1854–1856," *Records of the American Catholic Historical Society of Philadelphia* 82 (Sept 1971): 135 ("standard" quote), 141 ("majority" quotes). Scholars have sharply debated nativism's role in shaping northern politics in the 1850s. Michael F. Holt and William E. Gienapp have argued that economic change, the temperance issue, and nativist politics in the early 1850s at the local and state level eroded the loyalties of Whig and Democratic voters, who flocked into the Know Nothing order after passage of the Kansas-Nebraska Act and later shaped the Republican Party's political appeal. By their logic, nativism was as important as slavery in precipitating the emergence and development of the Republican Party. Consequently, they deemphasize the significance of the Kansas-Nebraska Act in precipitating the political crisis of the 1850s. See

Holt, "The Politics of Impatience: The Origins of Know Nothingism," *JAH* 60 (Sept 1973): 309–31; Holt, *The Political Crisis of the 1850s* (New York: Wiley, 1978), 101–81; Holt, *The Rise and Fall of the American Whig Party: Jacksonian Politics and the Onset of the Civil War* (New York: Oxford University Press, 1999), 765–878, 953–58; Gienapp, *The Origins of the Republican Party: 1852–1856* (New York: Oxford University Press, 1987), 37–166, 443–46. For challenges to their conclusions, see Anbinder, *Nativism and Slavery*, 43–101, 162–219; James L. Huston, *Calculating the Value of the Union: Slavery, Property Rights, and the Economic Origins of the Civil War* (Chapel Hill: University of North Carolina Press, 2003), 153–286; Huston, "The Illinois Political Realignment of 1844–1860: Revisiting the Analysis," *Journal of the Civil War Era* 1 (Dec 2011), 506–35; Huston, *The British Gentry, the Southern Planter, and the Northern Family Farmer: Agriculture and Sectional Antagonism in North America* (Baton Rouge: Louisiana State University Press, 2015), 219–39.

5. *Speech of Senator Douglas, at the Democratic Celebration of the Anniversary of American Freedom, in Independence Square, Philadelphia,* 4 July 1854 (n.p.), 5 ("great northern" quotes); *LSAD,* 330 ("great abolition" quote); *Daily Illinois State Register* (Springfield), 10 and 12 July, 4 ("fusion" quote), 25, and 29 Sept, and 2 and 9 ("parties" quote) Oct 1854; *Weekly Democratic Press* (Peoria), 21 June, 12 July, and 6 and 27 Sept 1854; *City Times* (Cairo), 11 Oct 1854.

6. *Speech of Douglas at Philadelphia,* 4 July 1854, 6 ("alliance" and "civil" quotes); *Daily Illinois State Register* (Springfield), 1 Aug 1854; *LSAD,* 330 ("boldly" quotes).

7. *Weekly Herald* (Quincy), 23 Oct 1854; *Daily Illinois State Register* (Springfield), 18 (Shields quote) and 21 (quote) Oct 1854; *Weekly Democratic Press* (Peoria), 11 Oct and 1 Nov 1854; *CW,* 2:276; Elder Benjamin Bradbury to Stephen A. Douglas, 12 Dec 1854, box 4, folder 10, Stephen A. Douglas Papers, UChicago SCRC; *Speech of Douglas at Philadelphia,* 4 July 1854, 7 (quote).

8. *LSAD,* 318 ("only wrong" quote), 320 ("right and capacity" quotes); *Daily Illinois State Register* (Springfield), 6, 11, 16, 18, 27, and 31 ("nothing" quotes) Jan, and 26 July 1854 ("recognizes" quotes); *City Times* (Cairo), 31 May, 21 June, 12 July, and 11 and 25 Oct 1854; *Weekly Democratic Press* (Peoria), 31 May, 9 Aug, 6 Sept, and 4 Oct 1854.

9. *Eastern Illinoisan,* clipped in the *Daily Illinois State Register* (Springfield), 17 Feb 1854; Don E. Fehrenbacher, *Sectional Crisis and Southern Constitutionalism* (Baton Rouge: Louisiana State University Press, 1995), 42–43; *Daily Illinois State Register* (Springfield), 18 Jan 1854 (quotes); *Weekly Democratic Press* (Peoria), 30 Aug 1854; Sidney Breese to unknown correspondent, 20 March 1854, box 1, folder 10, Sidney Breese Papers, ALPLM; Elder Benjamin Bradbury to Stephen A. Douglas, 12 Dec 1854, box 4, folder 10, Stephen A. Douglas Papers, UChicago SCRC.

10. *LSAD,* 320.

11. *Speech of Douglas at Philadelphia,* 4 July 1854, 2 (quotes); Martin H. Quitt, *Stephen A. Douglas and Antebellum Democracy* (New York: Cambridge University Press, 2012), 132.

12. *Speech of Douglas at Philadelphia,* 4 July 1854, 2 ("recognise" quotes), 3 ("equal footing" quote), 4 ("new State" quotes); *Weekly Democratic Press* (Peoria), 21 June 1854

(New York quotes); *LSAD*, 329 ("carry" quote), 330 ("gain" quote). Quitt, *Stephen A. Douglas and Antebellum Democracy*, 107–33, cogently analyzes Douglas's interpretation of the equal footing clause from 1845 to 1860, although he does not take note of Douglas's Philadelphia speech.

13. David M. Potter, *The Impending Crisis, 1848–1861* (New York: Harper and Row, 1976), 175; Huston, *Calculating the Value of the Union*, 207; 19th Gen. Ass., 1st Sess., *House Journal* (6 and 7 Feb 1855), 283–84, 306–9; Cole, *Era of the Civil War*, 209. Both nativism and slavery influenced the election results in 1854, but scholars have debated which played a greater role. For the pertinent historiography, consult n4.

14. The scale of anti-Nebraska Democratic defections in the congressional contests was indicated by the vote given to the Democratic candidate for state treasurer, who received 41.6 percent more votes than the party's Districts 1 and 2 congressional candidates in northern Illinois, and 46.6 percent more votes than the party's District 8 candidate. See Appendix, table 7. For lower estimates of Democratic defections, see Gienapp, cited in n15.

15. *IE*, 9; Huston, "Illinois Political Realignment," 510–11, 521–25; Stephen L. Hansen, *The Making of the Third Party System: Voters and Parties in Illinois, 1850–1876* (Ann Arbor: UMI Research Press, 1980), 42–52; Gienapp, *Origins of the Republican Party*, 125–26, 502–3; James Manning Bergquist, "The Political Attitudes of the German Immigrant in Illinois, 1848–1860" (PhD diss., Northwestern University, 1966), 158–62; Cole, *Era of the Civil War*, 133.

16. Elder Benjamin Bradbury to Stephen A. Douglas, 12 Dec 1854, box 4, folder 10, Stephen A. Douglas Papers, UChicago SCRC; *Speech of Senator Douglas at a Public Dinner Given Him by His Personal and Political Friends at Chicago, 9 Nov 1854*, 16 ("incongruous" quote); 19th Gen. Ass., 1st Sess., *Senate Journal* (8 and 13 Feb 1855), 239, 330–31; *House Journal* (6 and 7 Feb 1855), 283–84, 306–9; *LSAD*, 331 ("Nebraska" quotes), 334 ("Democratic" quotes).

17. *LSAD*, 340–41 (Boston quotes), 344; *Illinois State Register* (Springfield), 17 Oct 1855 (platform quote); Robert E. May, "Squatter Sovereignty as the Freeport Doctrine: A Note on the Territorial Controversy in the U.S. House of Representatives in the Winter of 1855–1856," *JSH* 53 (May 1987): 304–6; 33rd Cong., 1st Sess., *CG-NU* (30 Jan 1854), 276–77; Quitt, *Stephen A. Douglas and Antebellum Democracy*, 111, 114. In July 1854 Douglas began edging toward the position that Congress could not prohibit territorial slavery. While publicly acknowledging that Congress could have applied "the Wilmot proviso to Nebraska and Kansas," he strongly implied that such prohibition was "subversive of constitutional right." *Speech of Douglas at Philadelphia*, 4 July 1854, 3–4.

18. John Craig Hammond, *Slavery, Freedom, and Expansion in the Early American West* (Charlottesville: University of Virginia Press, 2007), 162–64; Johannsen, *Douglas*, 482–84; *LSAD*, 342–44 (quotes); Robert E. May, "A 'Southern Strategy' for the 1850s: Northern Democrats, the Tropics, and the Expansion of the National Domain," *Louisiana Studies* 14 (Winter 1975): 333–59; James N. Shine to Douglas, 11 Feb 1856, box 4, folder 16; E. Floyd Lawson to Douglas, 3 March 1856, box 4, folder

20; Horatio Boxley to Douglas, 12 May 1856, box 5, folder 6; William R. Vaughan to Douglas, 22 May 1856, box 5, folder 7, Stephen A. Douglas Papers, UChicago SCRC.

19. Johannsen, *Douglas*, 289, 405–6, 425–27.

20. James A. Rawley, *Race and Politics: 'Bleeding Kansas' and the Coming of the Civil War* (Philadelphia: Lippincott, 1969; reprint, Lincoln: University of Nebraska Press, 1979), 85–99, 129–34, 158–60; Johannsen, *Douglas*, 471–75; Nicole Etcheson, *Bleeding Kansas: Contested Liberty in the Civil War Era* (Lawrence: University Press of Kansas, 2004), 55–137.

21. Johannsen, *Douglas*, 488–505, 524–33; 34th Cong., 1st Sess., *CG-NU* (20 March 1856), *Appendix*, 285 ("undisguised" quote), 286 (other quotes), 287–88; (4 April 1856), *Appendix*, 359–62.

22. Johannsen, *Douglas*, 530–32; Robert E. May, *The Southern Dream of a Caribbean Empire, 1854–1861* (Baton Rouge: Louisiana State University Press, 1973), 77–110; May, *Slavery, Race, and Conquest in the Tropics: Lincoln, Douglas, and the Future of Latin America* (New York: Cambridge University Press, 2013), 117–25; Tom Chaffin, "'Sons of Washington': Narciso Lopez, Filibustering, and U.S. Nationalism, 1848–1851" *JER* (Spring 1995): 86–108; 34th Cong., 1st Sess., *CG-NU* (1 May 1856), 1071–72.

23. Joseph Gillespie to Lyman Trumbull, 3 Jan 1856; Ebenezer Peck to Trumbull, 24 Feb 1856, box 1, folder 5, Lyman Trumbull Family Papers, ALPLM; Samuel Mills to Stephen A. Douglas, 22 Feb 1856, box 4, folder 18, Stephen A. Douglas Papers, UChicago SCRC.

24. Lyman Trumbull to Abraham Lincoln, 5 July 1856, box 1, folder 7, Lyman Trumbull Family Papers, ALPLM; George Thomas Palmer, ed., "A Collection of Letters from Lyman Trumbull to John M. Palmer, 1854–1858," *JISHS* 16 (April–July 1923): 27 ("opening" quote); George Triezenberg, "Chicago Daily Democratic Press and Slavery" (MA thesis, Northwestern University, 1949), 45–47, 62; *Whig* (Quincy), 7 June 1856 (quote).

25. Johannsen, *Douglas*, 505–20; Allan Nevins, *Ordeal of the Union*, vol. 2, *A House Dividing, 1852–1857* (New York: Scribner's, 1947), 452–60; *Official Proceedings of the National Democratic Convention, Held in Cincinnati* (Cincinnati, Ohio: Enquirer, 1856), 26 (quotes), 39–45.

26. *Daily Illinois State Register* (Springfield), 1, 2, and 3 ("constitution" quotes) May, 17 Sept, and 26, 27, and 28 Aug 1856; *Weekly Herald* (Quincy), 7 April 1856 (quotes); *City Times* (Cairo), 3 (quotes) and 24 Sept 1856; *Weekly Democratic Press* (Peoria), 13 and 27 Aug, 10 Sept, and 8 Oct 1856. For the freesoil articles, see *New York Journal of Commerce*, clipped in the *Daily Illinois State Register* (Springfield), 20 Aug 1856, and the *Washington Union*, *Boston Post*, and *Illinois State Register*, clipped in the *Weekly Democratic Press* (Peoria), 3 Sept and 8 Oct 1856.

27. Potter, *Impending Crisis*, 264; Gienapp, *Origins of the Republican Party*, 414; Huston, "Illinois Political Realignment," 523–28; *IE*, 134–39.

28. Palmer, "Collection of Letters," 33–34.

29. Potter, *Impending Crisis*, 267–72, 287 (quote); Don E. Fehrenbacher, *The Dred Scott Case: Its Significance in American Law and Politics* (New York: Oxford University Press, 1978), 2, 335–88.

30. Fehrenbacher, *Dred Scott Case*, 379.

31. *CW*, 2:464; *Kansas, Utah, and the Dred Scott Decision: Remarks of the Hon. S. A. Douglas*, delivered in the State House at Springfield, 12 June 1857 (n.p.), ALPLM, 3.

32. Douglas, *Kansas, Utah, and the Dred Scott Decision*, 2–6.

33. Ibid.; Murray McConnel to Stephen A. Douglas, 20 July 1857, box 8, folder 8, Stephen A. Douglas Papers, UChicago SCRC.

34. *Daily Times* (Chicago), 21 Aug, 8 and 24 Sept, and 4 and 8 Oct 1857; F. G. Adams, ed., "Governor Walker's Administration," *Transactions of the Kansas State Historical Society* 5 (1896), 290, 329, 339; Johannsen, *Douglas*, 560–66.

35. *Daily Times* (Chicago), 10, 11 (quotes), and 27 Oct, and 6 and 15 Nov 1857.

36. Allan Nevins, *The Emergence of Lincoln*, vol. 1, *Douglas, Buchanan, and Party Chaos, 1857–1859* (New York: Scribner's, 1950), 144–55, 161–62; Potter, *Impending Crisis*, 297–300; Etcheson, *Bleeding Kansas*, 139–47.

37. Nevins, *Emergence of Lincoln*, 1:229–34, 264–70; Potter, *Impending Crisis*, 300–318; Etcheson, *Bleeding Kansas*, 151–67.

38. Douglas, *Kansas, Utah, and the Dred Scott Decision*, 1 (quotes); Johannsen, *Douglas*, 567; Fehrenbacher, *Dred Scott Case*, 461; LSAD, 404 (Sheahan quote).

39. Roy Franklin Nichols, *The Disruption of American Democracy* (New York: Macmillan, 1948), 150–76; Johannsen, *Douglas*, 587–613; Kenneth M. Stampp, *America in 1857: A Nation on the Brink* (New York: Oxford University Press, 1990), 312–15; Nevins, *Emergence of Lincoln*, 1:271; Etcheson, *Bleeding Kansas*, 168–85. In *Northern Men with Southern Loyalties: The Democratic Party and the Sectional Crisis* (Ithaca, N.Y.: Cornell University Press, 2014), 176–203, Michael Todd Landis vigorously but unpersuasively portrays the struggle over Lecompton as a victory for the Buchanan administration.

40. Fehrenbacher, *Dred Scott Case*, 466.

41. Thomas Langrell Harris to John McClernand, 16 Feb 1858, box 1, folder 12, John A. McClernand Papers, ALPLM; Cole, *Era of the Civil War*, 158–62; 35th Cong., 1st Sess., *CG-NU* (15 June 1858), 3055; LSAD, 418 (Douglas quote).

42. Paul M. Angle, ed., *Created Equal? The Complete Lincoln-Douglas Debates of 1858* (Chicago: University of Chicago Press, 1958), 58–59 (quote); *CW*, 3:43, 51–52, 132, 141–42, 208–10, 269–70; Don E. Fehrenbacher, *Prelude to Greatness: Lincoln in the 1850s* (Stanford, Calif.: Stanford University Press, 1962), 128; Fehrenbacher, *Dred Scott Decision*, 485–513; *Speech of Hon. Samuel S. Hayes, at the Democratic Meeting at Metropolitan Hall*, 18 Oct 1858 (n.p.), 3–5. Although his statement on squatter sovereignty represented an aggressive variant of his 1857 doctrine that territorial legislatures had no obligation to pass positive laws for slavery's benefit, it did not represent a significantly greater break with the Dred Scott decision than his prior position.

43. *CW*, 3:10 ("must" quote), 36 ("knock" quote), 113 ("all men" quote), 221–26, 238 ("only a question" quotes), 275 ("right" quote), 322 ("forward" quote); *Speech of Senator Douglas*, delivered at Bloomington, Illinois, 16 July 1858 (n.p.), 13–14.

44. *CW*, 3:54–55 ("bold" and "more territory" quotes), 114–15 ("Mexico" and "expand" quotes); Angle, *Created Equal?*, 19 ("varieties" quotes); *Illinois State Register* (Springfield), 14 July 1853.

45. Fehrenbacher, *Prelude to Greatness*, 118–20; Fehrenbacher, *Dred Scott Case*, 501–3; Allen C. Guelzo, *Lincoln and Douglas: The Debates That Defined America* (New York: Simon and Schuster, 2008), 282–87. I aggregated the votes from the Senate and House races before calculating percentages.

46. Johannsen, *Douglas*, 682–85; May, *Slavery, Race, and Conquest in the Tropics*, 160–65; *Daily Appeal* (Memphis), 30 Nov 1858 (St. Louis and Memphis quotes); *Speeches of Senator S. A. Douglas, on the Occasion of his Public Receptions by the Citizens of New Orleans, Philadelphia, and Baltimore* (Washington, D.C.: Towers, 1850), 6 ("virtue" quote), 9 ("same is true" quote), 10 ("globe" quote), 14 ("tenacity" quote). Douglas also retreated from his assertion that territorial settlers could discourage slavery with "unfriendly laws." Instead, he returned to his earlier language, stating that settlers could discourage slavery by refusing to pass positive laws to protect it. Fehrenbacher, *Dred Scott Case*, 504. This position could be considered tacitly antislavery because abolitionists had long maintained that slavery could only exist by virtue of "positive law," but Douglas had contempt for abolitionists and in fact embedded his argument in the proslavery context of southern expansion.

47. Johannsen, *Douglas*, 685–97; Fehrenbacher, *Dred Scott Case*, 506–13; 35th Cong., 2nd Sess., *CG-NU* (23 Feb 1859), 1241–74.

48. Harry Jaffa and Robert W. Johannsen, eds., *In the Name of the People: Speeches and Writings of Lincoln and Douglas in the Ohio Campaign of 1859* (Columbus: Ohio State University Press, 1959), 50–106 (quote, 65).

49. Jaffa and Johannsen, *In the Name of the People*, 104 ("distinctly" quote), 105 ("States" quote), 173–99; Fehrenbacher, *Dred Scott Case*, 373–84, 514–24; Johannsen, *Douglas*, 697–714. My interpretation of Douglas's response to Taney emphasizes a point of disagreement between the two men that I think is important. However, both Taney and Douglas reasoned through the constitutional issues poorly, making a brief summary of their disagreement almost impossible. Douglas in many respects talked past Taney, who for his part never really explained why the Missouri Compromise was unconstitutional. To some degree, my interpretation imposes a logic on their not-so-precise arguments. For an interpretation that emphasizes the convergence between Douglas and Taney, and hence is more sympathetic to Douglas's legal reasoning, see Austin Allen, *Origins of the* Dred Scott *Case: Jacksonian Jurisprudence and the Supreme Court, 1837–1857* (Athens: University of Georgia Press, 2006), 212–20.

50. *Daily Illinois State Register* (Springfield), 5 Jan 1860 (convention quotes); *LSAD*, 481; 36th Cong., 1st Sess., *CG-LOC* (23 Jan 1860), 554–55, (29 Feb 1860), 916; Johannsen, *Douglas*, 721–40.

51. Nichols, *Disruption of American Democracy*, 281–84; Johannsen, *Douglas*, 727–32, 740–45; Potter, *Impending Crisis*, 401–4; Fehrenbacher, *Dred Scott Case*, 529–32 (quote, 531).

52. Nichols, *Disruption of American Democracy*, 288–314; Allan Nevins, *Emergence of Lincoln*, vol. 2, *Prologue to Civil War, 1859–1861* (New York: Scribner's, 1950), 203–28, 262–68; Johannsen, *Douglas*, 745–67; Potter, *Impending Crisis*, 405–12; Fehrenbacher, *Dred Scott Case*, 533–37.

53. Nichols, *Disruption of American Democracy*, 314–22; Nevins, *Emergence of Lincoln*, 2:268–72; Johannsen, *Douglas*, 767–73; Potter, *Impending Crisis*, 412–14; Fehrenbacher, *Dred Scott Case*, 537–38; *LSAD*, 493 (quote).

54. 36th Cong., 1st Sess., *CG-NU* (15 and 16 May 1860), *Appendix*, 311 ("good faith" quotes), 314 (New Mexico and Mexico quotes), 316 ("differ" quotes).

55. Kirk H. Porter and Donald Bruce Johnson, comp., *National Party Platforms, 1840–1856* (Urbana: University of Illinois Press, 1956), 31 (quote); Fehrenbacher, *Dred Scott Case*, 537–38.

56. *Mercury* (Shawneetown), 7 June 1860; *Times and Herald* (Chicago), 22 Sept 1860 (Ficklin quote) and *Missouri Republican* (St. Louis), late July 1860 (Morrison quotes), Lyman Trumbull Scrapbook, box 6, BV 1, Lyman Trumbull Family Papers, ALPLM.

57. *Daily Illinois State Register* (Springfield), 4 ("hypocrisy" quotes), 10 ("unfounded" quotes), and 28 ("republican party" and emancipation quotes) Sept 1860.

58. Eric Foner, *Free Soil, Free Labor, Free Men: The Ideology of the Republican Party Before the Civil War* (New York: Oxford University Press, 1970), 11–39; O. D. Critizer to McClernand, 31 May 1860, box 1, folder 14, John A. McClernand Papers, ALPLM.

59. Charles Lanphier to John McClernand, 6 Jan 1860; Orlando Bell Ficklin to McClernand, Stephen Douglas, and James C. Robinson, 19 March 1860, box 1, folder 13, John A. McClernand Papers; James O'Donnell to Stephen A. Douglas, 8 May 1860, folder 5, SC 2120, Stephen Arnold Douglas Papers, ALPLM.

Chapter 7. Abraham Lincoln and the Triumph of an Antislavery Nationalism, 1854–1860

1. *CW*, 2:289, 4:67 (quotes).

2. 33rd Cong., 1st Sess., *CG-NU* (28 March 1854), *Appendix*, 448 (Yates quotes); *CW*, 2:262 (Lincoln quotes); *Alton Daily Courier, Extra*, 30 Oct 1854, box 6, BV 1, Lyman Trumbull Scrapbook, Lyman Trumbull Family Papers ("time" quotes), ALPLM; *Weekly Whig* (Quincy), 7 Aug, 30 Oct ("*outlets*" quote), and 6 Nov ("*intended*" quote) 1854.

3. *Free West* (Chicago), 21 Sept 1854 (Republican Party quotes); 33rd Cong., 1st Sess., *CG-NU* (28 March 1854), *Appendix*, 447–48 (Yates quotes); Richard H. Sewell, *Ballots for Freedom: Antislavery Politics in the United States, 1837–1860* (New York: Oxford University Press, 1976), 259–60.

4. *Weekly Whig* (Quincy), 11 Sept 1854 (Palmer quote); *Free West* (Chicago), 21 Sept 1854; *Daily Tribune* (Chicago), 28 June 1854; William Butler to Richard Yates, 10 Aug 1854, box 35 1/2, folder 1, Yates Family Papers; David Davis to Julius Rockwell, 15 July 1854, box 2, A-23, David Davis Family Papers, ALPLM; Victor B. Howard, "The Illinois Republican Party: Part I, A Party Organizer for the Republicans in 1854," *JISHS* 64 (Summer 1971): 134–35.

5. E. J. Palmer to John Palmer, 22 June 1854; Benjamin Baldwin to Palmer, 14 Sept 1854 (quote), box 1, folder 5, John McAuley Palmer Papers II, ALPLM; *Free West* (Chicago), 21 Sept 1854; William E. Gienapp, *The Origins of the Republican Party:*

1852–1856 (New York: Oxford University Press, 1987), 122–25; Stephen L. Hansen, *The Making of the Third Party System: Voters and Parties in Illinois, 1850–1876* (Ann Arbor: UMI Research, 1980), 51–56.

6. James Manning Bergquist, "The Political Attitudes of the German Immigrant in Illinois, 1848–1860" (PhD diss., Northwestern University, 1966), 128–62; *Free West* (Chicago), 20 July 1854; *Daily Tribune* (Chicago), 19 and 30 Jan and 20 March (German quote) 1854; 10 June 1854.

7. Howard, "Illinois Republican Party: Part I," 124–60; Paul Selby, "Genesis of the Republican Party in Illinois," *TISHS* (1906): 270–83; Selby, "Republican State Convention, Springfield, Ill., October 4–5, 1854," *MCHST* 3 (1900): 43–47; *CW*, 2:288; Gienapp, *Origins of the Republican Party*, 122–27; Arthur Charles Cole, *The Era of the Civil War, 1848–1870* (Springfield: Illinois Centennial Commission, 1919; reprint, Urbana: University of Illinois Press, 1987), 127–31; Sewell, *Ballots for Freedom*, 261.

8. *Oquawka Plaindealer*, clipped in the *Weekly Whig* (Quincy), 11 Sept 1854; *Free West* (Chicago) 21 Sept 1854 (Whig quotes); *Daily Tribune* (Chicago), 2, 13, and 16 Sept 1854; *Journal* (Freeport), 12 Oct 1854 (Republican quotes); *Advocate* (Belleville), 5 April and 24 May 1854. For a more detailed explanation of how nationalist antislavery arguments united the various constituencies of the Republican Party between 1854 and 1856, see Graham A. Peck, "How Moderate Were the Moderates? Reconsidering the Origins of the Republican Party in Illinois," *JIH* 17 (Autumn 2014): 158–82.

9. Ralph J. Roske, *His Own Counsel: The Life and Times of Lyman Trumbull* (Reno: University of Nevada Press, 1979), 19–23; *Weekly Whig* (Quincy), 23 and 30 (Trumbull quotes) Oct 1854; Howard, "Illinois Republican Party: Part I," 127–60; Ichabod Codding, *Codding's Reply to Douglas: Substantially Codding's Speech in Reply to Douglas at Joliet and Geneva, in the Fall of '54, on the Kansas-Nebraska Bill, and Slavery Extension*, 11 and 21 Sept 1854, (n.p.), 7 ("sanctity" quotes), 8 ("*all that*" quotes), 11 ("nationalized" quote), 15 ("principles" quote).

10. *CW*, 2:248 ("National" quote), 250 ("liberty" quote), 266 ("despotism" and "negro" quotes), 276 ("moral right" and "repurify" quotes); Don E. Fehrenbacher, *Prelude to Greatness: Lincoln in the 1850s* (Stanford, Calif.: Stanford University Press, 1962), 23–24.

11. *IE*, 10, 134–35; *CW*, 2:296–98; Lyman Trumbull to John Trumbull, 4 Dec 1854, box 1, folder 3, Lyman Trumbull Family Papers, ALPLM (quote); David Herbert Donald, *Lincoln* (New York: Simon and Schuster, 1995), 179–80.

12. Gienapp, *Origins of the Republican Party*, 124–26, 502–3; Hansen, *Making of the Third Party System*, 41–51; George Thomas Palmer, ed., "A Collection of Letters From Lyman Trumbull to John M. Palmer, 1854–1858," *JISHS* 16 (April–July 1923): 20–24.

13. Appendix, table 8.

14. *CW*, 2:304–7 (quote, 307); 19th Gen. Ass., 1st Sess., *House Journal* (6 Feb 1855), 283–84.

15. Cole, *Era of the Civil War*, 208–10; Committee of the Stephenson County branch of the Maine Law Alliance, "Address to the Friends of the Maine Law," 1855, B-64, BC-ALPLM (quotes); Bergquist, "Political Attitudes of the German Immigrant," 168,

179; Gienapp, *Origins of the Republican Party*, 488, 520; Hansen, *Making of the Third Party System*, 62–66.

16. Thomas M. Keefe, "Chicago's Flirtation with Political Nativism, 1854–1856," *Records of the American Catholic Historical Society of Philadelphia* 82 (Sept 1971): 136–50; John P. Senning, "The Know-Nothing Movement in Illinois, 1854–1856," *JISHS* 7 (April 1914): 18–21, 29 (nativist platform quote); *Free West* (Chicago), 11 Jan, 26 April, 17 May, and 21 June 1855; *Weekly Whig* (Quincy), 30 June 1855; *Daily Tribune* (Chicago), 18 and 22 May, 12 June, and 13 July 1855; Gienapp, *Origins of the Republican Party*, 179–87; Tyler Anbinder, *Nativism and Slavery: The Northern Know Nothings and the Politics of the 1850s* (New York: Oxford University Press, 1992), 165–72. Michael F. Holt emphasizes the Know Nothings' impressive strength in 1855. However, the party's success in the North primarily reflected nativism's popularity at the local and state levels. Consequently, the American Party's national convention—which raised the issue of slavery—posed a greater danger to the fledgling organization than he acknowledges. See Holt, *The Political Crisis of the 1850s* (New York: Wiley, 1978), 157–81.

17. Victor B. Howard, "The Illinois Republican Party: Part II, The Party Becomes Conservative," *JISHS* 64 (Autumn 1971): 285–95; Palmer, "Collection of Letters from Lyman Trumbull to John M. Palmer," 22 ("proper" quote); Lyman Trumbull to Owen Lovejoy, 20 August 1855, box 1, folder 4, Lyman Trumbull Family Papers, ALPLM; Theodore Calvin Pease and James G. Randall, eds., *The Diary of Orville Hickman Browning, 1850–1881*, vol. 20, CISHL (Springfield: Illinois State Historical Library, 1925), 139; *Illinois Daily Journal* (Springfield), 10 Aug 1855; CW, 2:316–17.

18. Cole, *Era of the Civil War*, 148; B. B. Hamilton to Richard Yates, 13 Aug 1855, box 1, folder 6, Yates Family Papers ("practical" quote); George T. Brown to Lyman Trumbull, 14 Dec 1855, box 1, folder 4 ("Kansas" quotes); Joseph Gillespie to Trumbull, 6 Jan 1856, box 1, folder 5 ("horrible" quotes), Lyman Trumbull Family Papers, ALPLM; Don E. Fehrenbacher, *Chicago Giant: A Biography of "Long John" Wentworth* (Madison: American History Research Center, 1957), 136–38; George Triezenberg, "Chicago Daily Democratic Press and Slavery" (MA thesis, Northwestern University, 1949), 48–60; *Speech of S. S. Hayes, Esq., at a Democratic Meeting in Chicago*, 18 Oct 1855, 7 ("stupendous" quote); "To his Excellency, Joel A. Matteson, Governor of the State of Illinois," 1856, B-112, BC-ALPLM ("armed" quote).

19. CW, 2:316–17; Palmer, "Collection of Letters from Lyman Trumbull to John M. Palmer," 26–30; John H. Krenkel, ed., *Richard Yates: Civil War Governor* (Danville, Ill.: Interstate, 1966), 115–16 (Washburne quote); Lyman Trumbull to Owen Lovejoy, 20 August 1855, box 1, folder 4; Joseph Gillespie to Trumbull, 3 Jan 1856 (quote); T. Southern to Trumbull, 7 Jan 1856; Ebenezer Peck to Trumbull, 17 Jan and 24 Feb (quotes) 1856, box 1, folder 5, Lyman Trumbull Family Papers, ALPLM; Howard, "The Illinois Republican Party, Part II," 293–97.

20. Paul Selby, "The Editorial Convention, February 22, 1856," *MCHST* 3 (1900): 34 ("policy" quote); *Daily Illinois State Journal* (Springfield), 27 Feb 1856 (Decatur resolutions); Ezra M. Prince, ed., "Official Record of Convention," *MCHST* 3 (1900): 160–61 (Bloomington resolutions); CW, 2:341; Gienapp, *Origins of the Republican*

Party, 286–95; Mildred C. Stoler, "The Democratic Element in the New Republican Party in Illinois, 1856–1860," *Papers in Illinois History and Transactions for the Year 1942* (Springfield: Illinois State Historical Society, 1944): 38–47.

21. J. O. Cunningham, "The Bloomington Convention of 1856 and Those Who Participated in It," *TISHS* 10 (1905): 105; Pease and Randall, *Diary of Orville Hickman Browning*, 253; *Weekly Whig* (Quincy), 28 June ("extinction" quote) and 5 July ("propagandists" quote) 1856; *Daily State Journal* (Springfield), 29 Sept and 2 (*"abstraction"* quote), 22 (*"free"* quote), and 29 ("natural condition" quote) Oct 1856; Gienapp, *Origins of the Republican Party*, 295–303.

22. *CW*, 2:364–65.

23. Gienapp, *Origins of the Republican Party*, 259–64, 287–88, 292–95, 329–46; Anbinder, *Nativism and Slavery*, 206–9; Bergquist, "Political Attitudes of the German Immigrant," 194–213; Norman P. Judd to Trumbull, 23 March 1856, box 1, folder 6, Lyman Trumbull Family Papers, ALPLM; Palmer, "Collection of Letters from Lyman Trumbull to John M. Palmer," 30 (quotes); Keefe, "Chicago's Flirtation with Political Nativism," 149–51.

24. *IE*, 135–39; Gienapp, *Origins of the Republican Party*, 417–18, 425–29, 435–37, 527, 531, 537; Hansen, *Making of the Third Party System*, 99; *CW*, 2:385; Palmer, "Collection of Letters from Lyman Trumbull to John M. Palmer," 33 (quotes).

25. *Kansas, Utah, and the Dred Scott Decision: Remarks of the Hon. S. A. Douglas*, delivered in the State House at Springfield, 12 June 1857 (n.p.), 4–5; *CW*, 2:385 ("central" quotes), 405 ("odium" quote).

26. *CW*, 2:318, 404, 406 ("maxim" and "perfectly" quotes), 409 ("negro" quotes).

27. Fehrenbacher, *Prelude to Greatness*, 48–69; *CW*, 2:449 ("think slavery" quotes), 451 ("the people" quotes). In early 1858, Indiana Republicans illustrated the potential danger that popular sovereignty posed to the Republican Party's antislavery extension policy. In an effort to recruit nativists and Democrats, Republicans incorporated popular sovereignty into the 1858 state platform. Gregory Peek, "'The True and Ever Living Principle of States' Rights and Popular Sovereignty': Douglas Democrats and Indiana Republicans Allied, 1857–1859," *Indiana Magazine of History* 111 (Dec 2015): 394–402.

28. Fehrenbacher, *Prelude to Greatness*, 70–95; *CW*, 2:461–62 (quotes).

29. John L. Scripps to Abraham Lincoln, 22 June 1858, Abraham Lincoln Papers, series 1, LOC, http://memory.loc.gov/cgi-bin/query/P?mal:10:./temp/~ammem _iRfF:: (accessed August 11, 2010); Fehrenbacher, *Prelude to Greatness*, 123 (Ray quotes); *CW*, 2:512–15 (quotes, 513), 522.

30. *CW*, 2:521, 525–26, 538–41, 548–53, and 3:20–29, 38, 45–49, 73–76, 146–58, 183–86; Richard J. Carwardine, *Lincoln* (Harlow: Pearson Education, 2003), 77, 89n51.

31. *CW*, 3:220, 234, 254 ("moral" quote), 257 ("real" quote), 276 ("the course" quote), 280–81, 300–305, 308 ("proposed" quote), 313 ("provision" and "peaceful" quotes), 314–16.

32. *CW*, 2:464 ("care not" quote), 465 (*"educate"* quotes), 500–501, and 3:231 ("laws" quotes), 233 ("preparing" quotes), 250–51, 277–78, 312–16 (*"cotton gin"* quote, 316).

33. Fehrenbacher, *Prelude to Greatness*, 112–20; Allen C. Guelzo, *Lincoln and Douglas: The Debates That Defined America* (New York: Simon and Schuster, 2008), 282–87.

34. *CW*, 3:340, 342 ("blow up" quote), 345 ("struggle" quote), 365–66.

35. *CW*, 3:366–70 ("upon every" quotes, 366), 378–81 ("preventing" quote, 379), 384, 386, 389 ("ultra" quote), 391 ("explosive" quote), 394–95, 432–35.

36. Harry Jaffa and Robert W. Johannsen, eds., *In the Name of the People: Speeches and Writings of Lincoln and Douglas in the Ohio Campaign of 1859* (Columbus: Ohio State University Press, 1959), 58–125; *CW*, 3:77, 404 ("original" quotes), 412–17, 464–66 ("fathers" quote, 466).

37. *CW*, 3:437, 454–59, 462 ("inspiration" and "order" quotes), 466–69, 478 ("*mudsill*" quote), 479 ("just" quote).

38. Donald, *Lincoln*, 237–41; Carwardine, *Lincoln*, 97.

39. *CW*, 3:522–50; Harry V. Jaffa, *Crisis of the House Divided: An Interpretation of the Issues in the Lincoln-Douglas Debates* (Chicago: University of Chicago Press, 1959; reprint, 1982), 310–29; George B. Forgie, *Patricide in the House Divided: A Psychological Interpretation of Lincoln and His Age* (New York: Norton, 1979), 124–42; David Zarefsky, *Lincoln, Douglas, and Slavery: In the Crucible of Public Debate* (Chicago: University of Chicago Press, 1990), 141–54, 213–14; Harold Holzer, *Lincoln at Cooper Union: The Speech That Made Abraham Lincoln President* (New York: Simon and Schuster, 2004), 128–29, 134–36, 144, 233.

40. Staughton Lynd, "The Abolitionist Critique of the United States Constitution," in *The Antislavery Vanguard: New Essays on the Abolitionists*, ed. Martin Duberman (Princeton, N.J.: Princeton University Press, 1965), 209–39; William W. Freehling, "The Founding Fathers and Slavery," *American Historical Review* 77 (Feb 1972): 81–93; William M. Wiecek, "'The Blessings of Liberty': Slavery in the American Constitutional Order," in *Slavery and Its Consequences: The Constitution, Equality, and Race*, ed. Robert A. Goldwin and Art Kaufman (Washington: American Enterprise Institute, 1988), 23–44; Leonard L. Richards, *The Slave Power: The Free North and Southern Domination, 1780–1860* (Baton Rouge: Louisiana State University Press, 2000), 28–51; Don E. Fehrenbacher, *The Slaveholding Republic: An Account of the United States Government's Relations to Slavery*, completed and edited Ward M. McAfee (New York: Oxford University Press, 2001), ix–xiii, 15–47; James Oakes, *The Scorpion's Sting: Antislavery and the Coming of the Civil War* (New York: Norton, 2014), 13–103.

41. *CW*, 3:537 ("old policy" quotes), 538 ("prominence" quotes), 547 ("crime" quote).

42. *CW*, 3:547 ("*peace*" quotes), 550 ("thinking" and "END" quotes).

43. Fehrenbacher, *Prelude to Greatness*, 143–59; Donald, *Lincoln*, 240–50; Eric Foner, *Free Soil, Free Labor, Free Men: The Ideology of the Republican Party Before the Civil War* (New York: Oxford University Press, 1970), 205–18; Carwardine, *Lincoln*, 90–109; *CW*, 3:453 (quotes).

44. William E. Gienapp, "Who Voted for Lincoln," in *Abraham Lincoln and the American Political Tradition*, ed. John L. Thomas (Amherst: University of Massachusetts Press, 1986), 67–68, 76–77, 80–81; John M. Rozett, "Racism and Republican Emergence in Illinois, 1848–1860: A Re-Evaluation of Republican Negrophobia" *CWH* 22 (June 1976): 113–14; Bergquist, "Political Attitudes of the German Immigrant," 317–21.

45. For stimulating treatments of Lincoln's nationalism, see Jaffa, *Crisis of the House Divided*, 330–33; Mark E. Neely Jr., "Abraham Lincoln's Nationalism Reconsidered," *Lincoln Herald* 76 (Spring 1974): 12–28; Otto H. Olsen, "Abraham Lincoln as Revolutionary," *CWH* 24 (Sept 1978): 213–24; Stewart Winger, *Lincoln, Religion, and Romantic Cultural Politics* (DeKalb: Northern Illinois University Press, 2003), 134–46, 199–208; Joseph R. Fornieri, *Abraham Lincoln's Political Faith* (DeKalb: Northern Illinois University Press, 2003); Dorothy Ross, "Lincoln and the Ethics of Emancipation: Universalism, Nationalism, Exceptionalism," *JAH* 96 (Sept 2009): 379–99.

46. Anbinder, *Nativism and Slavery*, 246–70; Bruce Levine, "Conservatism, Nativism, and Slavery: Thomas R. Whitney and the Origins of the Know-Nothing Party," *JAH* 88 (Sept 2001): 455–88; Mark Voss-Hubbard, *Beyond Party: Cultures of Antipartisanship in Northern Politics before the Civil War* (Baltimore, Md.: Johns Hopkins University Press, 2002), 178–216.

47. Susan-Mary Grant, "'The Charter of Its Birthright': The Civil War and American Nationalism," in *Legacy of Disunion: The Enduring Significance of the American Civil War* (Baton Rouge: Louisiana State University Press, 2003), ed. Susan-Mary Grant and Peter J. Parish, 193–95; Robert E. Bonner, *Mastering America: Southern Slaveholders and the Crisis of American Nationhood* (Cambridge: Cambridge University Press, 2009).

Conclusion

1. John Francis Snyder, *Adam W. Snyder and His Period in Illinois History, 1817–1842* (Virginia: Needham, 1906; reprint, Ann Arbor: University Microfilms, 1968), 1–63; Adam Snyder to Jesse B. Thomas, 23 Dec 1837, box 29, folder 4; Snyder to Hiram Snyder, 21 April 1838, box 29, folder 5, John Francis Snyder Papers, ALPLM.

2. Clyde N. Wilson, ed., *The Papers of John C. Calhoun*, vol. 13 (Columbia: University of South Carolina Press, 1980), 395 ("positive good" and civilization quotes); Wilson, ed., *The Papers of John C. Calhoun*, vol. 14 (Columbia: University of South Carolina Press, 1981), 31–32, 82–84 ("first duty" and race relations quotes); Adam Snyder to Hiram Snyder, 21 April 1838, box 29, folder 5, John Francis Snyder Papers, ALPLM.

3. Samuel Mills to Stephen A. Douglas, 22 Feb 1856, box 4, folder 18, Stephen A. Douglas Papers, UChicago SCRC.

4. Thomas C. Minter to Douglas, 4 March 1852, box 3, folder 3; James N. Shine to Douglas, 11 Feb 1856, box 4, folder 16; E. Floyd Lawson to Douglas, 3 March 1856, box 4, folder 20; Horatio Boxley to Douglas, 12 May 1856, box 5, folder 6; William R. Vaughan to Douglas, 22 May 1856, box 5, folder 7, Stephen A. Douglas Papers, UChicago SCRC.

5. Don E. Fehrenbacher, *The Slaveholding Republic: An Account of the United States Government's Relation to Slavery*, completed and edited by Ward M. McAfee (New York: Oxford University Press, 2001), 15–47; Jan Lewis, "The Three-Fifths Clause and the Origins of Sectionalism," in *Congress and the Emergence of Sectionalism: From the Missouri Compromise to the Age of Jackson* (Athens: Ohio University Press, 2008),

19–46; Richard Beeman, *Plain, Honest Men: The Making of the American Constitution* (New York: Random House, 2009), 200–225, 308–36; David Waldstreicher, *Slavery's Constitution: From Revolution to Ratification* (New York: Hill and Wang, 2009), 71–151; George William Van Cleve, *A Slaveholders' Union: Slavery, Politics, and the Constitution in the Early American Republic* (Chicago: University of Chicago Press, 2010); Thomas D. Morris, *Free Men All: The Personal Liberty Laws of the North, 1780–1861* (Baltimore, Md.: Johns Hopkins University Press, 1974); Matthew Mason, *Slavery and Politics in the Early American Republic* (Chapel Hill: University of North Carolina Press, 2006); John Craig Hammond, *Slavery, Freedom and Expansion in the Early American West* (Charlottesville: University of Virginia Press, 2007).

6. James L. Huston, *Calculating the Value of the Union: Slavery, Property Rights, and the Economic Origins of the Civil War* (Chapel Hill: University of North Carolina Press, 2003), 24–66; Adam Rothman, *Slave Country: American Expansion and the Origins of the Deep South* (Cambridge, Mass.: Harvard University Press, 2005); Gavin Wright, *Slavery and American Economic Development* (Baton Rouge: Louisiana State University Press, 2006), 14–122; Brian Schoen, *The Fragile Fabric of Union: Cotton, Federal Politics, and the Global Origins of the Civil War* (Baltimore, Md.: Johns Hopkins University Press, 2009); James L. Huston, *The British Gentry, the Southern Planter, and the Northern Family Farmer: Agriculture and Sectional Antagonism in North America* (Baton Rouge: Louisiana State University Press, 2015), 208–39.

7. Wayne C. Temple, "A Case of Abraham Lincoln's True Humanitarianism," *For the Record* 23 (Winter 2009): 1–2; Edward Bartlett Rugemer, *The Problem of Emancipation: The Caribbean Roots of the American Civil War* (Baton Rouge: Louisiana State University Press, 2008), 145–79, 222–57; Stanley Harrold, *Border War: Fighting over Slavery before the Civil War* (Chapel Hill: University of North Carolina Press, 2010), 94–115, 138–58; John L. Brooke, "Party, Nation, and Cultural Rupture: The Crisis of the American Civil War," in *Practicing Democracy: Popular Politics in the United States from the Constitution to the Civil War* (Charlottesville: University of Virginia Press, 2015), 72–95.

8. Mark A. Noll, *The Civil War as a Theological Crisis* (Chapel Hill: University of North Carolina Press, 2006); Noll, *America's God: From Jonathan Edwards to Abraham Lincoln* (New York: Oxford University Press, 2002), 367–421; Richard J. Carwardine, *Evangelicals and Politics in Antebellum America* (New Haven, Conn.: Yale University Press, 1993).

9. 30th Cong., 1st Sess., *CG-NU* (20 April 1848), *Appendix*, 507.

10. For a valuable account of how the tension between northern antislavery sentiment and proslavery southern politics similarly vexed northern Jeffersonian Republicans during the nation's first thirty years, consult Padraig Riley, *Slavery and the Democratic Conscience: Political Life in Jeffersonian America* (Philadelphia: University of Pennsylvania Press, 2016).

11. Robert W. Johannsen, *Stephen A. Douglas* (New York: Oxford University Press, 1973; reprint, Urbana: University of Illinois Press, 1997), 140–45; Richard C. Bain, *Convention Decisions and Voting Records* (Washington, D.C.: Brookings Institution,

1960), Appendix D, 327; Charles Sellers, *James K. Polk, Continentalist, 1843–1846* (Princeton, N.J.: Princeton University Press, 1966), 49–89.

12. Hammond, *Slavery, Freedom and Expansion in the Early American West,* 24–27, 37–40, 108–12, 154–61; Fehrenbacher, *Slaveholding Republic,* 253–71; Fehrenbacher, *Sectional Crisis and Southern Constitutionalism* (Baton Rouge: Louisiana State University Press, 1995), 33–39; David M. Potter, *The Impending Crisis, 1848–1861* (New York: Harper and Row, 1976), 51–82.

13. James L. Huston, "Putting African-Americans in the Center of National Political Discourse: The Strange Fate of Popular Sovereignty," in *Politics and Culture of the Civil War Era: Essays in Honor of Robert W. Johannsen,* ed. Daniel McDonough and Kenneth W. Noe (Selinsgrove, Penn.: Susquehanna University Press, 2006), 96–128; George B. Forgie, *Patricide in the House Divided: A Psychological Interpretation of Lincoln and His Age* (New York: Norton, 1979), 123–58.

14. On the importance of the Declaration of Independence to Republican Party politics, also see Jeremy J. Tewell, *A Self-Evident Lie: Southern Slavery and the Threat to American Freedom* (Kent, Ohio: Kent State University Press, 2013).

15. Rita McKenna Carey, *The First Campaigner: Stephen A. Douglas* (New York: Vantage, 1964), 94 (quote).

16. *CW,* 8:333.

Index

Page numbers in italic refer to maps and tables.

GRAHAM A. PECK is a professor of History at Saint Xavier University in Chicago. He is the writer, director, and producer of *Stephen A. Douglas and the Fate of American Democracy*, an award-winning documentary that aired on Chicago's premier PBS station. His film, podcasts, and publications are available at civilwarprof.com.

The University of Illinois Press
is a founding member of the
Association of American University Presses.

_____

Composed in 10.5/13 Minion Pro
by Kirsten Dennison
at the University of Illinois Press
Cover designed by Dustin J. Hubbart
Cover illustration: Print of 1860 campaign banner with American flag
(Philadelphia?: H. C. Howard, 1860: Library of Congress).
Manufactured by Sheridan Books, Inc.

University of Illinois Press
1325 South Oak Street
Champaign, IL 61820-6903
www.press.uillinois.edu